ALSO BY BEATE AND SERGE KLARSFELD

BEATE KLARSFELD

Wherever They May Be!

SERGE KLARSFELD

French Children of the Holocaust: A Memorial
The Children of Izieu: A Human Tragedy
Remembering Gregory: Letters from the House of Izieu

HUNTING THE TRUTH

HUNTING THE TRUTH

MEMOIRS OF
BEATE AND SERGE KLARSFELD

Translated from the French by Sam Taylor

FARRAR, STRAUS AND GIROUX | NEW YORK

Farrar, Straus and Giroux
175 Varick Street, New York 10014

Library of Congress Cataloging-in-Publication Data
Names: Klarsfeld, Beate, 1939– author. | Klarsfeld, Serge,
    1935– author. | Taylor, Sam, 1970– translator.
Title: Hunting the truth : memoirs of Beate and Serge Klarsfeld /
    Beate and Serge Klarsfeld ; translated from the French by
    Sam Taylor.
Other titles: Mémoires. English
Description: First American edition. | New York : Farrar, Straus
    and Giroux, 2018. | Includes index. | "Originally published in
    2015 by Fayard/Flammarion, France, as Mémoires."
Identifiers: LCCN 2017035981 | ISBN 9780374279820
    (hardcover)
Subjects: LCSH: Klarsfeld, Beate, 1939– | Klarsfeld, Serge, 1935– |
    Holocaust, Jewish (1939–1945)—Personal narratives.
Classification: LCC DS135.F8 K396 2018 | DDC 940.53/18092
    [B] —dc23
LC record available at https://lccn.loc.gov/2017035981

Designed by Richard Oriolo

www.fsgbooks.com
www.twitter.com/fsgbooks • www.facebook.com/fsgbooks

1   3   5   7   9   10   8   6   4   2

Abbreviations Used in the Text

AA	*Auswärtiges Amt* (Foreign Office)
ADF	Party for Democratic Action and Progress
AFP	Agence France-Presse (the third-biggest news agency in the world)
APO	Außerparlamentarische Opposition (political protest movement)
BND	Bundesnachrichtendienst (West German intelligence service)
CDJC	Center of Contemporary Jewish Documentation
CDU	Christian Democratic Union
CRIF	Representative Council of Israelites in France
DVU	Deutsche Volksunion
DPA	German press agency
EEC	European Economic Community
FDP	Free Democratic Party
FFDJF	Association of Sons and Daughters of Jews Deported from France
FMS	*Fondation Pour la Mémoire de la Shoah* (Holocaust Remembrance Foundation)
FSJU	United Jewish Welfare Fund
GPU	State Political Directorate
HICEM	Jewish emigration company
LICA	International League Against Racism and Anti-Semitism
MEJ	Jewish Student Movement
NPD	National Democratic Party (neo-Nazi party)
ORTF	France's national broadcasting agency
OSE	Children's Aid Society
RSHA	Reich Main Security Office
SA	*Sturmabteilung* (Nazi party storm troopers)
SD	*Sicherheitsdienst* (SS's intelligence service)
SDS	radical German student movement
Sipo	*Sicherheitspolizei* (security police)
Sipo-SD	umbrella organization combining the Gestapo (secret state police) and the Kripo (criminal police)
SNCF	French national railway company
SPD	Social Democratic Party of Germany
UGIF	General Union of Israelites in France
VVN	association for victims of Nazism

BEATE

A German Childhood

THREE WEEKS AFTER my birth, Hitler entered Prague. In Berlin, my father calmly put away the pencils he used in his job at an insurance company. He kissed my mother, Hélène, and his only daughter, Beate-Auguste, then left the Hohenzollerndamm—the residential district that still contained a few working-class houses, including ours—and set off on a long journey. After joining up with his regiment, Infantryman Kurt Künzel spent the summer of 1939 on maneuvers, and the following summer he was somewhere in Belgium.

I have a photograph of him smiling as he stands guard outside a military headquarters. In the summer of 1941, his regiment moved east toward Russia. That winter, he was lucky enough to catch double pneumonia, meaning that he was sent back to Germany, where he became an army accountant. After the liberation in 1945, he rejoined his family in the village of Sandau, where my mother and I had reluctantly taken refuge with relatives. Here, in a barn, surrounded by terrified women, children, and old people, we witnessed the arrival of the Mongols. Polish laborers invaded our cousin's house and took our belongings. This was poetic justice, as in 1943 we spent several months living a life of ease with my godfather, a high-ranking Nazi in Lodz.

For those who believe that childhood impressions are a critical factor in decisions made later in life, I should point out that the Soviet Mongols never hurt or sexually abused us.

IN LATE 1945, we returned to Berlin, where the three of us and a kitchen worker shared a room for the next eight years. The apartment belonged to an opera singer who could now only find work singing at funerals and who was forced by the Allies—like many other German property owners—to sublet his home to refugees. This was a strange period for me as a little girl. There might seem something enjoyable about such a nomadic, unpredictable existence, but my parents' anxiety and sadness, added to the general atmosphere of confusion and bitterness, had a negative effect on my morale. My parents found it very difficult to live among strangers.

I grew older—seven, eight, nine years old—but my family's situation did not improve. Some of my friends' families were living in their own apartments by now, with a kitchen and bathroom just for them, but we remained at the mercy of our landlords' whims. Being a child, however, I found it easier to adapt to this reality than an adult or a teenager would. Without realizing it, I became hardened. Not in a bad way. I simply mean that I didn't whine or curse my misfortune or envy those who were luckier than me. I see this part of my life as formative for my character: it taught me to deal with adversity. Besides, I knew there were people worse off than me. Some of the girls I went to school with had lost their fathers during the war, while others waited endlessly for them to return from Soviet POW camps.

At the local school, I was a quiet and conscientious student. There weren't enough places, so half the students attended in the morning, the others in the afternoon. And in winter, there wasn't enough coal to heat the building, so we were completely free. My mother worked as a housecleaner, while my father salvaged bricks from the city's ruins for its reconstruction, before being employed at the courtroom in Spandau. It was in those ruins that I spent whole days with my friends, playing hide-and-seek, climbing up to the roofs of damaged houses, and—best of all—searching for buried treasure.

The school was located in an imposing building, a five-minute walk from where we lived, its white façade riddled with bullet holes. I loved going to school. Our teachers were kind and attentive, we were given chocolate and warm milk every day, and I also got to see my best friend there. Her name was Margit Mücke.

In the mornings, I would leave for school with my lunch in a mess tin. I don't remember ever going hungry. On the other hand, I do remember eating an awful lot of potatoes, rarely accompanied by any meat. Our meals became slightly more varied when my mother started bringing back gifts from the houses where she worked. There was a sort of lard, which we used instead of butter and which my mother would keep cool by storing it in the space between the double-glazed windows. But the outer pane was broken, and birds sometimes flew in. I would watch, rapt, from the other end of the room as they pecked at the lard.

Occasionally, for a treat, my father would buy me an ice cream; that was the only way my parents had of spoiling me. I remember women taking the train to the countryside and returning with bags over their shoulders containing eggs and vegetables. I remember the wooden soles on my shoes. I remember the fabric that my mother would receive in exchange for coupons that were much like ration cards and that she would use to make our clothes. I remember how the women of Berlin were able to transform a too-small coat into a dress, how they made "getting by" into an art form.

We avoided speaking about Hitler. Prior to 1945, I used to recite little poems for the Führer at my kindergarten. I lived in the ruins, but I didn't know why Berlin had been destroyed and divided into four occupied sectors. The world where I grew up was never explained to me beyond the simple formulation: "We lost a war, now we must work." My father was not very talkative, and my mother didn't say much, either, except when she was scolding my father, which was pretty often.

When I reached the age of ingratitude, at about fourteen, my parents grew closer again, and I became the object of their disapproval. They had neither learned nor forgotten anything from the epochal events they had sleep-walked through. They weren't Nazis, but they had voted for Hitler like everyone else, and they did not feel any responsibility for what had occurred under Nazism. When my mother and her neighbors chatted, they always ended up whining about the injustice of what had happened to them, waxing nostalgic over beloved objects they had lost amid the turmoil. There was never a word of pity or compassion for the people of other countries—least of all the Russians, whom they criticized bitterly.

Berlin echoed with the roar of airplanes bringing us supplies because it was the time of the blockade. I never asked questions, whether of others or myself. I merely walked along the path that had been prepared for me: in 1954, I was confirmed at the Evangelical Lutheran church in Hohenzollern-platz, but I had already lost my faith; even today, I do not believe in God. Back then, however, Providence finally came to our rescue. We moved to a bigger apartment, and at last I had my own bedroom.

It is difficult to describe the joy I felt. For the first time in my life, I was going to live in a normal home with my parents. Number 9 Ahrweilerstrasse was a rather plain-looking building, but to my eyes it was wonderful—a home, belonging just to us, and it was located in my beloved Wilmersdorf neighborhood. The apartment's windows looked out at both the courtyard and a quiet, tree-lined street filled with houses similar to ours.

It had a kitchen and a bathroom, hot water, and central heating; my room, like my parents', had a sofa bed, which we unfolded every night before going to sleep. It felt so luxurious to have radiators that actually heated the apartment—before this, the places we lived in had been freezing cold in winter. I remember the tiny stove we would huddle around—and we owed this dramatic improvement in our existence to Aunt Ella, who was infinitely more resourceful than my parents. I spent seven years in that apartment, remaining there until I left Berlin in 1960.

Very close to where we lived was Rüdesheimer Platz, a square where the people of the neighborhood would come with their children during the summer months to have picnics, play games, and chat with one another. I used to go for walks there with my new friend—a basset hound belonging to a Jewish woman for whom my mother worked as a cleaner. She would let me look after him when I got home from school or after I had done my homework. She lived next door at number 7 Ahrweilerstrasse and was now the only Jew in that neighborhood. Before 1933, I was told, there used to be so many of them.

At sixteen, I left the high school and enrolled in Höhere Wirtschafts-schule in Schöneberg, a technical college that I hoped to use as a springboard into working life. I had been so bored in high school. I wanted to learn a trade so I could free myself from my parents. Because life as a teen-ager was no fun at all. My father drank and always seemed to be sick, which only aggravated my mother's irritability. (He would die of cancer in 1966, at the age of fifty-eight.) Their daily arguments made the atmosphere tense and unbearable. Day after day, I felt like I was suffocating.

I didn't know myself and I didn't try to know myself. But simply from waiting—for what?—and seeing nothing happen, I must have felt some kind of dissatisfaction. I expressed it through a total lack of enthusiasm for the future that my mother was planning for me: a savings account, the prepa-ration of my trousseau, and a suitable marriage like my cousin Christa's. The family called me ungrateful, but in all probability I saved myself. I held firm, and never again did I follow that "straight path" that led, from what I could see, to anything but happiness.

As soon as I turned twenty-one—on February 13, 1960—I had only one idea in mind: to leave this city, despite the deep if inexplicable attachment I felt for it. I often traveled into East Berlin, particularly on Sundays, and for me the city did not end at the Brandenburg Gate; it continued on through Unter den Linden, which belonged to me just as much as the Tiergarten did. Politics and history did not enter my mind, only an indefinable feeling that, in spite of appearances to the contrary, Berlin was one city, not two.

In fact, I preferred the eastern zone. It was so dark and poor, but I was drawn by its unknown past. In the course of those dreamy wanderings, I belatedly forged the surprising certainty that my country was united. I was solitary, but my roots clung deeply to German soil.

ENCOUNTER AT A METRO STATION

A T 7:00 A.M. on March 7, 1960, I saw Paris for the first time; the sky was gray, so was the Gare du Nord, and so was my mood. My mother had warned me of the terrible things that would happen to me. For her, I was beyond saving. My father had turned his back on me, too; in his eyes, Paris was the whorehouse of Europe, and he already imagined me working on the street. I knew only a few words of French, and I immediately joined the Alliance Française. Three days later, I was an au pair. And I would remain an au pair for more than a year.

My employers lived on Rue du Belvédère in Boulogne. I slept in a filthy little attic room, where I would tremble with fear because of the spiders. I went to the school twice a day to drop off and pick up the family's child. For seven hours a day, I cleaned, ironed, cooked. Naturally hardworking and in love with cleanliness, I had not yet learned to slack off, so when the time came to study French in the evenings, I was too exhausted to remember anything.

Thankfully, one day, I was fired. It was a Sunday, and as my employers were not around, I summoned the nerve to invite a couple of friends to the house. The father returned to find us watching television. *His* television: "You could have broken it—and you wouldn't have paid for it to be repaired, would you? You can find yourself another job . . ."

Which I did, this time on Rue Darcel, near the Bois de Boulogne, with the Fallaud family. The man of the house attempted to seduce me, while Mrs. Fallaud took no interest in her family and just chatted endlessly on the phone with her friends. I was given almost sole responsibility for the two children, a four-year-old girl and a six-year-old boy. And I learned to make pasta. Always pasta. Two months after my arrival, I finally dared to start speaking French when I went grocery shopping. At the Alliance I had met only foreigners, but in the Latin Quarter I was too frightened to reply to the people who approached me.

I barely knew Paris, but already I was under its spell. It was so different from the newly constructed monotony of West Berlin. I loved walking around the old streets of the Marais, or the ones that went from the Seine to Boulevard Saint-Germain, gazing up at the buildings' unique, harmonious façades. Here, people seemed to have a lust for life, and everyone was different. Walking on the Champs-Élysées was like going to the theater. I felt, and still feel, a thrill at the idea that I was destined to be connected to this city; in Paris, I thought, I would bloom.

One day in May, I was waiting to catch the 1:15 p.m. metro, as usual, at the Porte de Saint-Cloud station, when I felt someone staring at me. I looked up. A dark-haired young man in a Prince of Wales suit, holding a briefcase, asked me, "Are you English?"

It was a ruse, of course; he would admit to me later that a German girl always says no when asked this question. After that, it is hard to remain silent. At Sèvres-Babylone, he got off to walk to Sciences Po, with my phone number in his pocket. Three days later, he called me. I was so happy. We went to see *Never on Sunday* at a movie theater on Rue du Colisée.

Serge completed his degree and was soon almost as poor as me. I immediately liked his seriousness, as well as his more whimsical side. On a bench in the Bois de Boulogne, I found out that he was Jewish, that he had lost his father in Auschwitz. I was surprised, and moved, but my instinctive reaction was to hold myself back. In Berlin, I had rarely heard a good word about Jews. What had I done to deserve such a complication? But the look in Serge's eyes was so warm; I had difficulty resisting him.

He told me about his father, and I sensed that his example lived on inside the son: how he had volunteered for the Foreign Legion in 1939, had been one of the few survivors in his regiment of the Battle of the Somme, had escaped from captivity, had been arrested in Nice in September 1943. How he had died in the gas chambers of Auschwitz.

I SPENT MY summer vacation on the Basque Coast with my new family, who lived in Asnières, in an ugly suburban house set in a yard without a single blade of grass. Serge and I wrote to each other regularly, and he often corrected my mistakes in French. At times I would grow irritated by his pedantic tone, and I would call him "professor." He became annoyed in turn and told me, "You should enrich your mind. You should read, you should draw on what the great men of the past have left for us. Dostoyevsky, Tolstoy, Stendhal . . . they didn't write for money; they wrote for themselves, and also for you, so that you can become aware of what you are." Sometimes I would complain, "I envy you. Your job isn't as mundane as mine. You don't know how lucky you are: you know where you're going in life, but what will happen to me? I need a lot of courage, and you're not there anymore to help me find it."

We saw each other again that fall on the Pont des Arts, and we didn't stop seeing each other. Serge brought Paris to life for me. He knew it so well. We talked constantly. I had been silent for too long; being with him was like a deliverance. He also brought history, art, the world of living ideas into my life. Suddenly, I needed more time than before: until then, I had been sleeping ten hours every night; now, like him, I learned to get by on six.

When he realized how ignorant I was of my own country's history, Serge—who had studied history at the Sorbonne—began teaching it to me. That was how I discovered the terrifying reality of Nazism. I did not feel even remotely responsible as an individual, but, as a part of the German people, that was another matter. Was I tempted to stop being German? Serge himself never considered that. Not for a second: that would have been too easy. That was how I came to understand that it was not only difficult but thrilling to be German after Nazism. One day, Serge told me how learning about the brief lives of Hans and Sophie Scholl had prevented him from hating Germans. I felt like a member of the Scholl family.

Hans and Sophie Scholl, their fellow student Christoph Probst, their professor Kurt Huber, and a few others in the White Rose organization were responsible for writing and distributing leaflets in Munich, in February 1943, attacking Nazism for its crimes. Their words went unheeded. They were arrested and executed, accepting their fate with courage. I read what Thomas Mann told Germans on the BBC radio on June 27, 1943: "Now their eyes are open and they put their young necks on the chopping block, a testament to their faith and to the honor of Germany . . . They do that after declaring to the judge in the Nazi courtroom: 'Soon, you will be where I am now,' after saying, when confronted with death: 'A new faith is born—faith in honor and freedom.' Courageous, magnificent young people! You will not die in vain! You will not be forgotten!"

On the fringes of ideologies, parties, and groups, they were driven to act, to give their lives, by their conscience as Catholics and Germans. Though it seemed futile in 1943, the impact of their acts had continued to grow over time, until it reached Serge, until it reached me. I saw myself in them.

IN NOVEMBER 1960, Serge started his two-year military service in Montlhéry, and we were separated once again. We wrote to each other every day. In my rudimentary French, I told him:

> Your letters make my feelings for you even stronger. I don't know
> myself anymore. I read and reread your letters, learn your phrases
> about love by heart and no longer hesitate to believe it. To start
> with, I still doubted a little in the truth of those words because I
> feared disappointment. But in the nights when you loved me, I felt
> reassured. I felt your love for me and I respond with all my heart.
> I am writing to you for the first time aware that I love you.

Every night, or just about, Serge would call me in Asnières. My boss, Mrs. Pontard—a math teacher whose daughter, Monique, was still unmarried—repeated to me, "Beate, he won't marry you. It's not serious. The French don't marry foreigners." I didn't care! Meanwhile, Serge wrote to me from Mourmelon, where he was on maneuvers:

> You must poeticize your life, Beate, re-create it, live it consciously, by living simply . . . by making it your own. Homer turned a small Greek expedition in Troy into the *Iliad*, and we all have that power— if not in art, then at least in life. A bit of courage, cheerfulness, energy, connection to humanity. A lot of poetry to transform how we live and raise it to the level of a transcendent experience.
>
> Sweetheart, you're probably falling asleep or smiling at this advice, but this is the best I have to offer you for your birthday, the most sincere and lasting present I could give you. This is not "the professor" writing to you, but your Serge, who loves you.

And I replied clumsily:

> My darling,
> It is a quarter to nine and I am starting every morning to watch the mailbox. And if I see letters, I rush to the door and pick them up, open them, read them and read them again very carefully.
> Don't complain about your life in the barracks—another four weeks and you will be in Paris again. You think I find it interesting to pick up other people's mess? I know why I do this work, but I find it sad like a gray sky or a day without you.
> At school we did exercises and I made a ton of mistakes, but foolish mistakes, because I didn't concentrate.
> You ask me what I think of you. I love you too much to be neutral.
> To come back to your letter of yesterday, I wonder what ideas you are preoccupied with. Do you intend to write the story of your life in a tribute for you alone or for posterity so you are not forgotten in a hundred and fifty years?
> Do you really want to be famous, to make your mark or to leave just a trace of memory? You must first think of doing something wonderful, things that help others. If you manage to do this, you will inevitably become very well known.
> I understand that you want to use everything, what you have

seen, your travels, what you have learned, etc. But you will be able to do that in a job like politics. I believe, my darling, that your dreams are too grandiose. I regret that I cannot say these things in a good French, to be better understood.

IN JUNE 1961, I met Tania, Serge's sister, at the Deux Magots, and afterward they took me home to see their mother, Raïssa, a moment I had been simultaneously longing for and dreading.

Raïssa took my hand. There was something naturally distinguished about her. She was also deeply generous, with a surprisingly youthful spirit. I helped her to make tea. We quickly got along. She told me about her memories of Germany and how she arrived in Paris at the age of sixteen; how she was one of the few women at that time to take a science degree at the Sorbonne, and how afterward she married a charming Romanian. Then, finally, in her sweet Russian accent, she talked about the war. And as she told me about the night her husband was arrested, I understood the suffering that separated the Jews from the Germans.

That night, I became part of the little Klarsfeld family, where everyone cared more about one another than about themselves, where the mother had sacrificed herself for her children, who remained intimately connected with her without losing an iota of their freedom.

IN THE SUMMER OF 1962, Serge, who was still doing his military service, encouraged me to visit Romania without him. In Bucharest, I went to see his aunt Lida. She lived surrounded by cats. I loved cats, and perhaps that worked in my favor with Lida, who was extremely affectionate and generous with me. In fact, Raïssa had planned this visit: she wanted her sister to meet me, in spite of the Iron Curtain that then separated East from West. Raïssa wanted an impartial opinion about me, not in order to reinforce a feeling she already had but to extend the family circle and to help her decide if she could entrust her son to me.

In March 1963, Serge's sister Tania became engaged to her boyfriend, Alik. In the middle of the reception, Serge stood up and announced, "While we are celebrating Tania and Alik's engagement, Beate and I would also like to announce ours!"

We were married on November 7, 1963, at the town hall in the six-teenth arrondissement of Paris. Serge confessed to me later that he'd had a terrible toothache that day and had not even registered for a minute the reality of our wedding.

In July 1964, after finishing first in the qualifying exams, Serge was given a job as an administrator at France's national broadcasting agency. Meanwhile, I became a bilingual secretary at the newly formed Franco-German Youth Office, whose mission to strengthen relations between our two countries was something I was passionate about.

And so, happy on a personal and family level, each of us starting a career that genuinely interested us, we had built the foundations for an orderly, stable life similar to so many other young couples . . .

SERGE

Hunted by the Gestapo

SEPTEMBER 30, 1943. I am eight years old. We live in Nice, in southern France, in a 1920s house at number 15 Rue d'Italie. At the end of the street is the basilica, which looks out on the city's main road, Avenue de la Victoire. At the other end of that road, perpendicular to Rue d'Italie, is Avenue Durante, which leads to the train station. On the left-hand sidewalk, fewer than a hundred yards from the junction, is the Hôtel Excelsior. For the last three weeks, this hotel has been the headquarters of the Gestapo, the secret state police. The Germans, who have just occupied Nice after taking over from the Italians, are raiding the houses of Jews and sending them to Drancy. We quickly learned to avoid going anywhere near Avenue Durante.

It is midnight and I am sleeping peacefully in our sparsely furnished three-room apartment. As are my sister, my mother, and my father. Suddenly, searchlights illuminate the windows, and we hear orders shouted in

German. We jump out of bed, and my sister and I run over to the hiding place that my father made for us. It is set in a deep cupboard, about five feet wide. A thin partition conceals us from view. It opens from the inside with a simple latch at the bottom.

ON SEPTEMBER 8, 1943, less than a month before this, the Germans entered Nice. They now occupied all eight départements in southeastern France, which had been under the control of their Italian allies since November 11, 1942, when the Third Reich invaded what had previously been the French-administered *zone libre*, or "free zone."

That ten-month respite, between November 1942 and September 1943, was a happy period for many Jewish families who would later suffer so badly under the Nazis. Our family, like most of those around us, was still intact: Papa, Mama, and the children. Newspaper articles often illustrate my childhood with a photograph showing the four of us—Arno, Georgette, Serge, and Raïssa—walking along the Promenade des Anglais, together for the last time. Our safety seemed assured by the carabinieri and the bersaglieri, and thousands of Jews were fleeing the German-occupied zone and taking refuge in the Italian zone.

I have retained from this period a profound gratitude toward the Italians, and ever since my childhood I have regarded Italy as a second home. As a teenager, I hitchhiked all over the country, and I have constantly gone back there as an adult. I have also passed on this passion to our children: our son, Arno, lived with Carla; and our daughter, Lida, married Carlo.

The Italian occupation was a blessing for Jewish families like ours. No more murderous raids by the Vichy police; no more identity papers stamped with "Jew"; no more arrests of Jews simply for being Jews. The Italians protected not only Italian Jews but French Jews and foreign Jews, too.

For us, the German takeover was a catastrophe. Italian soldiers tried to smuggle Jews to safety, but the occupation was so sudden that most of those attempts were doomed to failure.

Terror spread like wildfire among the twenty-five thousand Jews in Nice. Barricades were erected in the streets, at various intersections, and on the roads leading out of town, while any traveler taking a bus or train had to go through rigorous identity checks. Security was so tight that it was even riskier to try to escape than it was to stay.

Recognizing the danger we were in, my father decided to create the hiding place. He attached a rod in front of it and hung clothes from the rod to hide the entrance. Our situation was still precarious, though. All it would have taken was a hand pressing on the partition or a rifle butt banged against the thin wooden wall, and the subterfuge would have been exposed—and us along with it.

MY SISTER IS ELEVEN, three years older than me. We argue all the time. When the moment comes for us to enter the cupboard, however, we are perfectly quiet and obedient. We squeeze in there along with our mother, all three of us dressed in the clothes we wore the previous day, which we grabbed when we leaped out of bed. Seized by a sudden fear, Raïssa goes back out to make the beds. She must eliminate any trace of our presence in the apartment. Seconds later, she returns to the hiding place and shuts the door.

We know the scenario by heart. If the Gestapo raids our apartment, my father will give himself up, telling the Germans that the apartment is being disinfected, so he sent his family to the countryside. If he were to hide, too, the risk is that the soldiers would sound every wall and every cupboard with their rifle butts, and the game would be up for all of us.

Our father has made clear to us the danger we are in. We are perfectly aware that this refuge constitutes our only hope. A few days before, he explained to us that, if the Germans do arrest him, he would be more likely to survive than we would: "I'm strong. I would survive. The same is not true for you."

IN NICE, ALOIS BRUNNER, the new Nazi head of the Drancy camp near Paris, ordered one of the most brutal raids on Jews ever seen in Western Europe. Papers were checked in the street, attics and cellars were searched, and men were forced to undress to see if they had been circumcised. Hundreds of people were arrested in the course of a few days.

ON THE NIGHT of September 30, 1943, the Gestapo raids our building. They proceed methodically, moving up floor by floor, knocking on every door but only entering apartments occupied by Jews. Presumably those

Jewish families, like ours, who did not report their arrival in Nice to the authorities, have been denounced. The blame for this does not lie with the local authorities, however: the prefect Jean Chaigneau destroyed the file listing all the city's Jews in order to prevent the Nazis from having that information. Arrested and deported in 1944, Chaigneau survived.

The hiding place shares a wall with the neighboring apartment, home to the Goetz family, who claim to be Alsatian but are in fact Polish Jews. We hear the Germans enter, and Yvonne, their daughter, cries out in pain after being hit in the face with a rifle butt for daring to ask to see their papers. Little Marguerite, my sister's friend, weeps as the soldiers twist her arm in order to make her give them the address of her older brother, Lucien. She screams, "I don't know! I don't know!" They threaten and hurt each member of the family, one after another, and finally succeed in making them talk. Lucien is arrested a few hours later.

We hear their father yell, "Help! French police, help us! We're French! Save us! Save us!"

UNLIKE THAT OF so many of my friends, of so many children of deported Jews, our home was not raided by the French police but by members of the Gestapo. As a child, I knew nothing about the arrests made by the French police on the orders of the collaboration government, and I would not learn the truth for a long time afterward. Unlike other Jewish children in France, I never feared the French police. In Nice, in particular, they did not take part in the German-led operations. True, we were in Nice on August 26, 1942, when the big raid on "stateless" Jews (former Germans, Austrians, Poles, Russians, and Czechs who had entered France after 1935) took place, but Romanians were not targeted in that raid.

If we had stayed in Paris instead of fleeing when the Germans invaded, we would have been arrested in 1942, along with more than fifteen hundred other Romanian Jews, when the Gestapo was informed that the Romanian government had abandoned its sovereignty over its emigrant Jews living abroad. They were arrested by French police at dawn on September 24, and at 8:55 a.m. on September 25, they were deported. On the morning of September 27, three-quarters of the deportees from that convoy were gassed in Birkenau. Less than seventy-two hours had passed between their rude awakening in Paris by those "guardians of the peace" and their murder by the SS at the other end of Europe.

Yes, I was lucky not to have suffered as so many other Jews did from what the current French president, François Hollande, finally acknowledged as "this crime . . . committed in France, by France."

The night of that raid has stayed with me all of my life—as it has for all the Jewish children who experienced that terror and lost loved ones—as an experience that forged my identity as a Jew. I did not inherit that identity through religion or culture: my Jewish identity is defined by the Holocaust and an unswerving attachment to the Jewish state of Israel. It is my past as a Jew, and it is the future of the Jewish people.

SUDDENLY, THEY ARE banging on our door. My father opens it. A voice with a strong German accent demands in French, "Where are your wife and children?" My father tells them his prepared story.

My sister has bronchitis. To stop herself from coughing, she stuffs a handkerchief in her mouth like a gag.

The Germans enter and start searching the apartment. One of them opens the cupboard door. Seventy years later, I can still hear the sound of the clothes sliding along the rod. They do not inspect the partition that conceals us. Instead, they close the cupboard door. The voice orders: "Get dressed and follow us!"

Our father is about to leave when, at the last moment, he changes his mind. How can he pretend we are absent if he leaves without taking his keys? He is not supposed to know that he will never return. If he leaves without locking the door, the Germans might realize that we are in the apartment. My father walks to the cupboard, leans inside, and whispers, "My keys." My mother, on all fours, opens the door a crack and hands the keys to my father. He kisses her hand one last time before taking the keys and leaving.

Eventually, the building falls silent. We remain in the cupboard for hours, paralyzed with fear. We don't know if a German has stayed behind on the landing. In the early hours of the morning, my mother goes out onto the landing when she hears a neighbor walking downstairs. She asks him to check that the Germans have left. After that, we come out of our hiding place, get dressed, and leave the building.

. . .

FOR THE NEXT few weeks, we move around Nice and its suburbs, evading the clutches of death. We stay in furnished apartments and guesthouses because hotels full of Jews are the Gestapo's favorite hunting grounds. Out on the street, my mother walks along one sidewalk while my sister and I take the other. In the trolleybus, she stands at the back while we stand at the front. We know what to do if she is arrested: which friends we should stay with, whom to write to; we have money, just in case. We often go to the basilica. There is a feeling of peace and safety there. We pray for our father, Arno.

THE GESTAPO TOOK our father to the Hôtel Excelsior, which had become an annex of the Drancy camp. As soon as there were more than fifty Jews in the hotel, Brunner would send them away. On October 2, our mother bravely went to the train station to see her husband off. With a glance, he told her to move away, because the Germans would arrest anyone who watched the train too intently. They had honeymooned in Nice in February 1929; now, in Nice, fourteen years and eight months later, they were separated for the last time.

It was in Nice that I lost my father; in Nice, too, I lost my mother. It was April 20, 1981. She wanted to visit our old apartment building again. She was suffering with heart problems. My sister went with her and took a photograph of her outside the door of 15 Rue d'Italie. Then they went back to the Negresco Hotel. Soon after, my mother died of a heart attack. That was how she had wanted to die: while living her life, not lying in a hospital bed.

AFTER THOSE EXHAUSTING weeks spent traveling around Nice, my mother decided we should return to our apartment. She'd had enough of being hunted in other people's homes. Instead, she showed us what we should do if there was another raid: we, the children, would go into the hiding place, and she would open the door to the Germans. Every night, we put our clothes in the hiding place with the documents we needed for our escape, and then the three of us went to bed together—our mother between me and my sister—where she would stay up, on the alert, reading detective novels almost all night long. I would read them with her until I fell asleep, and that was how I acquired my love for detective stories, which still have the ability to calm me if I am feeling anxious.

We went back to the local girls' school, where I managed to take classes, until the Gestapo arrested a Jewish girl there, and our mother decided we shouldn't return. When we walked back to our apartment in the evening, we never knew if we would find our mother waiting for us. The sky could fall in on a Jew at any moment. It was not until February 1944 that we were able to leave Nice.

WHEN CONVOY 61 arrived in Auschwitz on October 28, 1943, my father, Arno Klarsfeld, punched a *Kapo* who had hit him. That instant of defiance cost him his life. For punishment, he was sent to work in a coal mine in Fürstengrube. The average survival time there was less than six weeks. My father survived for nine months before dying at the age of thirty-nine. Why, for once in his life, couldn't he have deferred to authority? I will never know, but I do feel certain that, if he hadn't retaliated that day when the *Kapo* struck him, he might well have gotten out alive.

Arno, My Father

M Y FATHER WAS a tall, strong man, with an independent spirit. A selfish man, too, no doubt, but, above all, independent. He had a magnetic personality and looked like the actor Victor Mature, who played Samson in the movies.

Born in 1905 in Braila, a port on the Danube, my father lived his life as if he knew he would die young. He enjoyed the present without worrying about the future. He began traveling at a young age; I believe he even spent a year on a German freighter. Why was he named Arno? Because his parents had gone on vacation to Florence and loved it so much that they decided, if their next child was a girl, to call her Florence and, if it was a boy, to name him after the city's famous river.

Wolf, Arno's grandfather, was from Stryj in Poland and was born in 1840. A diamond merchant, he moved to Bucharest with his wife and died there in 1912. His son—my grandfather Salomon—was born in 1862. He married Sophie Abramoff and moved to Braila, where he became an important shipowner, with a fleet of a hundred boats and an export business that operated as far abroad as China.

Braila was a cosmopolitan city, and Arno—the youngest of six children—spoke seven languages. The list of places where those six siblings died gives a snapshot of the Jewish diaspora in the twentieth century: Rachel died in Quito in 1970, Myriam in Bucharest in 1940, Moreno in Paris in 1985, Ernestine in São Paulo in 1982, Édouard in Paris in 1977, and Arno in Auschwitz in 1944.

In the nineteenth century, the Jews of the Austro-Hungarian Empire had to give up their Hebraic family names in favor of ones that were more Germanic sounding: a pale field made the name "Klarsfeld," just as a golden mountain created "Goldenberg" or a silver stone "Silberstein."

My generation of the family was poorer than my grandfather's. His fortune was lost in 1930; his son Moreno built another fortune as a shipowner and a salesman for a large cereal-exporting firm but lost it in 1948 when the Communist government arrested him and sent him to a labor camp. My grandfather's grandchildren became a materials engineer in Saint-Gobain, an impresario, hoteliers in Brazil, a physicist in Orsay, a Russian professor (my sister), a lawyer (me), a businessman in Guatemala, and an agri-food producer in Ecuador.

About sixty miles from Braila, on the other side of the Prut River in Bessarabia, is the small town of Cahul. This was where my mother was born in 1904. Arno and Raïssa met at a dance in the Latin Quarter of Paris. My mother had arrived with a boyfriend, my father with a girlfriend; they left together. Raïssa came from a wealthy family of pharmacists and, when she met my father, she was studying pharmaceutical science in Paris.

She was twenty-four, and so was he. It was love at first sight. Raïssa asked her mother's second husband for his opinion of the match; after researching the Klarsfeld family and discovering its wealth (all of which would be lost one year later in the financial crisis following the Wall Street crash), he sent her a telegram urging "Marry him!" The wedding took place in February 1929, just one month after their first meeting.

My sister was born in Paris, on November 2, 1931. In tribute to Clemenceau, my father named her Georgette, which she grew to hate. She chose the name "Tania." During the war, however, "Georgette" was perfect, as it sounded so French.

The first year of my life was spent in Cahul, which is now part of Moldavia, where my mother had moved back in with her parents. I don't know if my father came to visit us; back then, my parents were always fighting. But they always made up afterward, because my mother made excuses for my father's infidelities. "Women were always chasing him," she said, and it was true; my father's contemporaries have told me the same thing. In the 1960s, one of the oldest waiters at La Coupole confided, "When your father walked in the door, the women only had eyes for him."

Raïssa always forgave Arno his flings, and she told us that the year before his arrest had been the happiest of their marriage. "He saved our lives and sacrificed himself for us," she often said.

IN 1937, THE four of us were living in Paris, in a two-room apartment that my parents rented on Avenue de Versailles, in Porte de Saint-Cloud. In a photograph dated April 29, 1938, my sister and I are standing on that wide sidewalk, where I still like to go even now when I need to feel refreshed, opposite that ancient market where, on Sundays after the Liberation, I would queue for hours to buy potatoes. On April 29, 2013, my sister and I were photographed in the exact same place where the original picture had been taken seventy-five years earlier—alone, and then with my grandchildren, who also live in Porte de Saint-Cloud. Since 1972, we have lived above the bus station, and I learned only a few years ago that it was from this station that the fifty buses requisitioned by the police prefecture left for the notorious Vél' d'Hiv raid. My sister, my daughter and her family, my nephew and his family, all live in Porte de Saint-Cloud, which has become my village, my home.

Whenever my parents suffered financial difficulties, my mother did not hesitate to ask her parents for help. And even though they disapproved of their son-in-law's spending, they always ended up saying yes. My parents lived a carefree life. For them, Paris was a passion: they often went out at night to meet with friends in cafés and bars.

Arno and Raïssa belonged to a cosmopolitan, secular Judaism that had drifted away from God. My parents were not religious. My mother respected certain traditions—fasting on Yom Kippur, for example—but I never saw her celebrate Shabbat.

And yet, almost all of their friends were Jews, even if they were just as casual about religious traditions as were my parents. And after the war, my mother's friends were not very devout, either. The fact of being born Jewish had brought them terrible misfortune, giving them nothing in return. With the exception of those who fought in the Resistance, the Jewish victims were not heroic. During the Inquisition, the executed Jews were heroes of the faith; they had been offered the chance to live if they converted and had refused. The Nazis did not give anyone the chance to convert. All it took to be sentenced to death was three Jewish grandparents—or two, if the person's spouse was Jewish. Some of those who perished did not even consider themselves Jews anymore; and many of those who did feel Jewish would certainly have agreed to deny their faith in order to escape death.

I have often wondered, beyond what happened during the Holocaust, what it means to be Jewish. As a child, I learned that it meant concealing part of my identity, that there was something that singled me out, but my parents could not explain to me what it was to be a Jew. Had it not been for the war against the Jews that raged in the middle of the wider war, I would probably never have considered myself a Jew, except in terms of birth.

I have a superficial knowledge of Jewish history, but I do not speak Yiddish or Hebrew; I spent a few months studying the latter at the Maimonides School, but I have forgotten it all in the intervening years. And I am not a believer. And yet, I am a Jew. I wish to be a Jew, even if I do not want to pass on my Judaism, since I married a non-Jew. This is, first of all, a choice based on love; but it is also a choice that goes beyond love. If I had married a Jew, my children would be Jewish. But according to Jewish law, they are not, because Judaism is transmitted by the mother. Not that it matters, really, since Arno, my son, feels Jewish, in spite of the fact that he isn't in the eyes of Orthodox Jews.

On February 14, 2001, I was decreed an Israeli citizen by the minister of the interior in recognition of my services to the Jewish people. Around that time, Arno chose to be Israeli—which was possible because his father was Israeli—and performed his military service in Israel, but his religion posed an administrative problem. Arno could not be considered a Jew because his mother was not Jewish, so he won the right to leave that box on the form unchecked, in spite of the bureaucrats who insisted he should mark down a religion. For the state of Israel, my son Arno is a "freethinker," even though he considers himself Jewish. As for my daughter, she is a determined atheist who married a Catholic, and her children have been blessed in Rome by two popes.

IN SEPTEMBER 1939, my father volunteered for the French army "for the duration of the war," along with his nephew Willy and thousands of other foreign Jews. He was assigned to the Twenty-Second Marching Regiment of the Foreign Legion.

He was given the rank of corporal in February 1940. On May 21, the Twenty-Second Regiment fought in the Battle of the Somme. Arno took part in fighting at Villers-Carbonnel, Misery, and Marchélepot. On June 5 and 6, his regiment heroically resisted Rommel's tanks for forty-eight hours before running out of ammunition and being decimated.

Arno's nephew, Willy Goldstein, was killed fighting beside him. In 1999, standing in front of the monument for Jewish volunteers at the cemetery in Bagneux, General Brothier declared, "It would take too long to make a list of all those foreigners who gave their lives around me; but, as I have said before and as I will never tire of saying, the first name on this long list is that of a young Jew, aged twenty-five, who fell heroically at the Somme, battling against Rommel's tanks. His name was Goldstein and, as long as I have the breath of life in my body, there will be a place for Goldstein in my heart." On May 28, 1943, Philippe Pétain posthumously awarded Wilhelm Goldstein the Médaille Militaire, even though he must have known he was Jewish, a member of that race whose newborn babies were being arrested by Pétain's police and delivered to the SS. This is just one of the paradoxes of Vichy, for whom Jews that died in combat were heroes, while Jewish infants were potentially dangerous elements that had to be eliminated.

Another irony of fate: while the Germans were putting to death so many Jews who had never threatened their security, they respected the Geneva Convention and spared the thousands of Jewish POWs from the French army, many of whom had fought against and killed German soldiers.

Yet another irony of fate: the volunteer marching regiments were trained in the camp at Barcarès, in the Pyrénées-Orientales, from 1939 to 1940, while in that same département, in Saint-Cyprien and in Argelès, thousands of stateless Austrian and German Jews, refugees from the Third Reich, were considered enemies and treated in a degrading, inhuman way by the authorities of the Third Republic.

And one final irony of fate: the volunteer Jews left in May 1940 from Rivesaltes station, in the Pyrénées-Orientales, to spill their blood and the enemy's on every front. Could they have suspected that, two years later, in August and September of 1942, thousands of other foreign Jews—men, women, and children—would be deported from that same station to Drancy and Auschwitz and that these Jews would be delivered to the Nazis by a French marshal?

AFTER BEING CAPTURED, Arno was sent to Cambrai, where he managed to escape. He was caught again in Villers-Cotterêts and sent to Front-stalag 131 in Cherbourg, where his presence was recorded under the name of Klarstel. Transferred to Verneuil, he escaped again in March 1941 and joined us in the free zone in Creuse.

If my father had not escaped that second time, he would have survived the war; but what would have happened to us? When we were in Creuse in 1941, an Austrian Jewish woman, Rosalie Glaser, tried to convince my mother that the Nazis were set on destroying the Jewish race. My mother, who had lived in Germany for a long time in the 1920s, refused to believe it. She thought she knew the Germans.

WE ARRIVED IN Creuse toward the end of a turbulent year. On September 2, 1939, I was among the "first casualties" of the war, sent to the Hospital Henri Dunant because my parents had reacted so vocally when they heard the declaration of war on the radio that I became frightened. I tripped and broke the bone of my right eye socket. I still have the scar.

The exodus in 1940 is one of my earliest memories: an interminable line outside the Gare d'Austerlitz; Jewish families storming the train the day before the Germans arrived in Paris; the train being bombed by planes and attacked by machine guns; the arrival in Capbreton, where the Germans caught us soon afterward. The first ones we saw were on motorcycles with sidecars; I was less scared of them than of the ocean. Rightly, perhaps, as several German soldiers went swimming there and were drowned in the Atlantic.

From occupied Capbreton, we went to Moissac, in the free zone, where lots of Jews had gathered. In Moissac, my mother, who was penniless, heard about a Jewish organization of Russian origin, the OSE (Children's

Aid Society), which helped children in need and had a center in Creuse, at the Masgelier château near Grand-Bourg, where she could send us while she found a place to live in Grand-Bourg. She followed this plan in the fall of 1940. The Masgelier château was a magnificent place, but the discipline was extremely strict, and my sister hated it. I remember having to work in the vegetable garden, which I suspect put me off gardening for life. The food was monotonous, too: chickpeas, chickpeas, and more chickpeas. Our mother walked over to see us every week. The children—about a hundred of us—were mostly German, Austrian, and Polish; they owe their lives to the OSE, which enabled some of them to emigrate to the United States in 1941, while the others were smuggled out later.

I ALMOST DIED in Masgelier. I had an undiagnosed appendicitis, and my fever rose to 106 degrees Fahrenheit. It was my good fortune that a Romanian doctor returned to the château that evening. His name was Élysée Cogan. After making the diagnosis, he took me in the middle of the night to the hospital in Guéret, where we were told that it was too late to operate. Thankfully, the surgeon opted to try to save me anyway. The operation was a success, and I spent three weeks in the hospital, hovering between life and death, with my mother at my bedside. The surgeon told her that, if I survived, it would be because she breastfed me for so long. I remember my very high bed—I was only five—and the painful daily changing of bandages, but most of all I remember my first illustrated history book, about Charlemagne and the Lombards. My vocation as a historian was born in that hospital, where I attempted to escape my boredom and suffering through the joys of reading.

IN THE SPRING of 1941, my father came to join us. You can see our happiness in a photograph that shows him in uniform, hugging my sister and me outside the Masgelier château, which we now left for Guéret.

My father had the nerve to write to Marshal Pétain; he did not receive a reply, so he wrote another letter seven weeks later. I still possess that second letter because it was returned to him, bearing the postmark "Sent by the Marshal." In this letter, dated May 26, 1941, my father complained that his first letter had not been answered: "In that letter, I provided you with a complete account of my personal situation and did not conceal from you the great need I had to find work as quickly as possible; two weeks later, I was visited by a brigadier from the gendarmerie, who asked me for information that I willingly supplied. As I have not received anything since then, I now wonder whether it was even in connection with my letter that he came."

The response arrived on June 9. Arno was invited to present himself at the regional employment office, where he was hired by an office of the Commission Against Unemployment. Three months later, my parents decided to leave Guéret for Nice, where my mother had lived several times before with her parents, and where she and Arno had spent their honeymoon. What a change this was for us as children: the sea, the sun, the lively city, with so many new and old friends. A large number of Jews had taken refuge in Nice, and my parents' social life was once again as full as it had been in Paris.

Arno joined the Resistance in 1942. I do not know a great deal about his activities because his death robbed me of the chance to hear about them first-hand, but I do know from Pierre Merli, who would later become the mayor of Antibes, that they had worked together for an organization that helped repatriated POWs. It was probably here that he met one of the first Resistance fighters, Antoine Mauduit, who had created the network known as the Chain, which helped French officers escape from the stalags. The network's headquarters, Montmaur château, was located near Gap, in the Hautes-Alpes.

We went to live nearby for a few weeks before returning to our apartment in Nice. In the basement of the chalet where we lived, not far from the château, the Resistance printed fake ID papers at night. Our mother was not aware of our family's role as cover for this clandestine activity, and when she found out, she was mad at Arno for endangering their children. She demanded that we leave immediately. It was so cold that winter that the sheets were frozen, and one of the best memories I retain of my father is of those nights when he would persuade us to get in bed, using a variety of grimaces, mimicry, and jokes. He was always cheerful, and he loved to eat. I remember one occasion when, after we had received our sugar ration, he swallowed what he thought was a big spoonful of cocoa powder but which was actually cinnamon. He spat it out immediately, and we burst out laughing.

AFTER MY FATHER'S arrest in Nice, I felt certain that he would come back. He had promised us he would. After all, he had escaped from two POW camps already. So I suffered less than other children who suddenly learn that their father is dead. Mine died little by little; but this time he did not return. Later, in May and June 1945, at the Hôtel Lutetia in Paris, where we had gone with his photograph to look for him, our hope gradually faded. In August, I was at a summer camp when my mother wrote to me that a Greek deportee had identified my father, whom he had known in August 1944 at the infirmary, where he was terribly thin but still capable of boosting the morale of his fellow patients. At that moment, I realized I would never see my father again. I fled the summer camp and went back to Paris, where I wept in my mother's arms.

Several times in my life, I have dreamed that my father came back to us.

FROM THE CAMP in Drancy, my father managed to send us a letter, which sadly we did not keep. In the letter, he told me: "You are the head of the family now." In Drancy, he shared a barracks with Raymond-Raoul Lambert, the head of the UGIF (General Union of Israelites in France), who was arrested by the Gestapo for protesting to the prominent Vichy leader Pierre Laval, and who refused to send his wife and four children to safety in Switzerland because he wanted his family to share in the fate of the Jews he represented. All six of them were deported on November 20, 1943.

AT 5:30 A.M. on October 28, one thousand people were woken for their departure in a convoy of twenty groups. SS captain Brunner, who had been in charge of the Drancy camp since June 1943, was a cunning man and a fanatical anti-Semite. He wanted the departures to take place in an orderly fashion so that they would cause him as few problems as possible. He had managed to convince many of the inmates that they would be taken to a camp where conditions were the same as in Drancy, which had been improved since Brunner's arrival. Back then, the camp was run by the police prefecture. Now the French gendarmes guarded the outside of the camp, while a few Germans supervised a reign of terror inside. But the camp was actually managed by Jews. They were mostly from the eastern part of France and spoke good German. They and their families had been exempted from deportation, as long as they served Brunner's needs. There was even a Jewish security detail at Drancy. This is the only example of forced Jewish collaboration in France during the entire occupation.

At 3:00 p.m. on October 27, the train of twenty-three freight cars and three passenger cars had been handed over to the Reich Main Security Office by the German transport minister. This was not a French train; it was German, driven to the German border on French railroad tracks by a Frenchman, probably with a German beside him.

Of the 1,000 people who made up this convoy—125 of them children, some just babies—only 50 people survived. Among them was one of my father's friends, Samuel Stern. He testified about what happened when they arrived in Auschwitz, where 284 men and 103 women were selected for labor, and 613 others were immediately sent to be gassed: "Arno Klarsfeld was punched by the block's Polish *Kapo* when he arrived. He retaliated— something that had not happened before—because he was physically big enough to do so. This produced a certain respect for our group of French prisoners. But it must have been duly noted . . . Later he had to leave for the Fürstengrube [subcamp] . . . I was told that he was taken there, worked nine months to the point of exhaustion, and was liquidated."

WHEN I FIRST visited Auschwitz, in February 1965, I wanted to discover my father's identification number. I was able to work it out logically. The 284 men assigned to forced labor were given the numbers 159546 to 159829. There are four unidentified numbers on a list from the Fürstengrube Kommando: 159565, 159630, 159647, and 159683. Among those whose identity is known, number 159682 was Klajn, and 159684 was Lempert; alphabetically, my father's number must have been between these two numbers, and it is absolutely certain that he was sent to Fürstengrube; therefore, his number was 159683. On the infirmary registry, where only the patients' numbers were recorded, I found 159683 with the note "Fürstengrube" next to a cross and the letter *v* (*verstorben*, "deceased"). In all likelihood, the cross indicated that he had been selected for the gas chambers. This likelihood was admitted by the director of the Auschwitz state museum, Kazimierz Smolen, who confirmed it to me in writing on February 20, 1965.

It was of the utmost importance to me to find out that identification number. I had to commit it to memory, as if my father were sending me a message: the Nazis wanted to dehumanize the deportees whose lives they spared for a short time in order to exploit their capacity for work. Replacing their names with numbers facilitated their task. It was also typical of the contempt they had always shown to Jews. Even before the war, the German government had designated all Jews as either "Israel" or "Sarah." Upon the Jews' arrival at the concentration camps, the Nazis immediately destroyed their personal papers before gassing and burning the vast majority. Those people were transformed into ashes; the others were transformed into numbers. They lost their identity, and the identification number that replaced it was not printed on paper but tattooed into their flesh. How my father must have hated that identification number! How he must have hated being only a number before vanishing into scattered ashes. But we Jews oppose the Nazis' determination to destroy and annihilate the Jewish people with our own determination to remember, with our precise and intransigent Jewish memory.

Raïssa and Her Children

WHILE I WAS conducting research in 1965 in the Center of Contemporary Jewish Documentation at the Memorial to the Unknown Jewish Martyr, now known as the Mémorial de la Shoah, I came across a Gestapo list that featured our names: "Klarsfeld, Raïssa and her children." It concerned a request for repatriation to Romania that my mother had made in late 1943 following receipt of a letter from the Romanian embassy informing us that the Germans had agreed to this measure; the repatriation was supposed to take place in February 1944, from Lyon. Later, through another document, I learned that it was Klaus Barbie who had been in charge of this railroad repatriation of seventy-eight people. I never discovered whether the Romanian Jews on that list did indeed go back to their homeland; what I do know is that my mother had given the Germans our names but, prudently, not our address, and that she had later given up on this plan, which she considered too dangerous. On yet another Gestapo document, our address is listed as *unbekannt* (unknown).

In February 1944, the authorities decided to evacuate women and children from Nice; certain départements were chosen to welcome them. But the rumor among the Jews in Nice was that the Haute-Loire was the least dangerous destination because the German major headquartered at Puy-en-Velay was not interested in the Jews. This information turned out to be accurate: there was no Gestapo branch in the Haute-Loire and Major Julius Schmäling— a schoolteacher in civilian life—did not order a single raid in the département during the twenty months of German occupation. He was a member of the Nazi Party; but men who were officially Nazis could prove themselves humane and indifferent to anti-Semitic ideology, while others who did not belong to the party perpetrated the most heinous crimes.

Our mother decided we should go to Puy. During this period, the fate of the Jews was also a question of luck, and this time, luck was on our side. In Puy, we were advised to move to Saint-Julien-Chapteuil, a village where the Germans hardly ever went.

On March 24, 1944, newly arrived in Saint-Julien-Chapteuil, we found lodgings on the second floor of a house belonging to Mrs. Adhémard, who ran a bar on the ground floor, where she also sold the few newspapers that were published back then. Our apartment was quite large. Raïssa had her own room, and my sister and I shared another. The main room, overlooking the courtyard, combined kitchen and dining room. There was no running water or heat in the bedrooms, and the toilets were at the far end of the courtyard. To fetch water, we had to carry jugs to the pump, about a hundred yards farther up the village's only street.

We were officially refugees, like the other ten or so Jews who lived in this village. At the mayor's office, they did not ask us for our religion. We simply had to declare to the prefecture that we were not Jews. No one asked us to prove it. We were supposed to be members of the Orthodox Church. Soon after our arrival, our mother enrolled us in the local schools—a girls' school for Georgette and a boys' school for me, both of them Catholic.

Saint-Julien is a hilltop village set in a bucolic landscape studded with rocky outcrops. From the church square, we could look down over the village rooftops at a panoramic view of the surrounding countryside. How I loved that church, where, at eight years old, I briefly believed in God and prayed ardently for my father's return.

I dreamed of being an altar boy and wearing the same ceremonial robes as my school friends. I loved the history contained in the Bible. At catechism, I was the only one who listened carefully and remembered everything. One day, the bishop came to inspect the school and question the students. I was the first to respond to all his questions:

"Tell me, who is that gifted child?"

"A little refugee boy, Monseigneur."

"Is he a choirboy?"

"No, Monseigneur, we're not allowed to take him because he's not Catholic!"

"What? Then you must baptize him!"

The next day, three monks from my school turned up at our house amid great pomp. "Monseigneur singled out your son for praise. He would like him to be baptized so that he can serve Mass. And who knows, perhaps he could enter the seminary one day and become a priest, and then a bishop, even a cardinal." They tried to persuade my mother to convert me. Raïssa was disturbed by this because she desperately wanted us to remain Jewish and regarded conversion as an act of cowardice. "My brothers," she told them, "we are Orthodox Christians. I have nothing against Serge becoming Catholic, but it is a very important decision and I cannot make it alone, while my husband is a prisoner of the Germans. So we will wait until he returns and then decide."

They seemed persuaded by this argument.

We were happy in Saint-Julien-Chapteuil. People told us about the local peasants who could sell us food or exchange it for clothes or, best of all, wine, which was rationed but very popular in the village, where almost every other house was a bar. Sometimes we would accompany my mother to the farms, where we would find milk, butter, lard, cured ham, and eggs. From time to time, they would even kill a chicken for us. This was like a wonderland in comparison with the restrictions in Nice, where fresh food was a rarity and incredibly expensive on the black market. It was in Saint-Julien-Chapteuil that I saw the harvests, the yoked cattle, the glories of nature, and the kindness of people, a way of life that has now disappeared, even from that lost corner of France, and that has left me with a powerful feeling of nostalgia.

While we lived there, I was impressed by my mother's evenhandedness toward the Germans. She was horrified to hear about the destruction of German cities where she had lived or visited. But she drew a clear distinction between the guilty Germans and the others. Everyone in the village spoke badly of the Germans—of all Germans—except for my mother. This very personal viewpoint, so different from that of those around us, certainly had a profound influence on me at an age when, consciously or subconsciously, clear principles about how to live were being made.

AFTER THE WAR, my sister often went back to Saint-Julien, and I went three times, one of them memorable, as a profound change in Beate's and my life took place during that stay in "my" village. We had gone there to meet up with our family, and we were staying once again with Mrs. Adhémard, in the same house I had lived in twenty-four years earlier. Beate and I were working together on her third article for *Combat* about Chancellor Kurt Georg Kiesinger, an article that was published on July 21, 1967, and which, by August 30, had led to Beate's dismissal from her job at the Franco-German Youth Office. The most notable line in the article stated: "Mr. Kiesinger's first steps were modest and quiet, because this man, who was able to forge an equally good reputation among Brownshirts and among Christian Democrats, was well aware of what was at stake during the first weeks of his rise."

ON AUGUST 18, 1944, the Haute-Loire was liberated by the Resistance, and the celebrations began in Saint-Julien-Chapteuil. We left the village on September 24, in order to be in Paris for the start of classes on October 1. The journey seemed to last forever, and when we reached Porte de Saint-Cloud, we found our apartment occupied; it had been looted in 1941 and assigned to other tenants. This marked the beginning of another nomadic period for our family, which lasted about eighteen months, the time it took for the legal system to restore our rights as tenants. When we finally got our apartment back, it had been stripped bare. Even the wallpaper had been ripped off the walls, so that we would not be able to profit from the previous tenants' investment.

In the meantime, we stayed at a variety of addresses. I remember in particular spending the coldest months of winter in an unheated room in a run-down hotel named Chez Ernest. Georgette would spend hours every night studying in spite of the cold, a blanket covering her back and mittens on her hands. We had no money, as my mother had not yet found work, and her family, who had survived in Bucharest, did not know how to help her: Europe was broken up by military, political, and financial barriers, impossible for a civilian to cross without connections in high places.

I went to several schools without any real idea of what I wanted to do with my life—I was waiting for my father to come home, and life got even worse when I realized he never would. Then my mother started working for the OSE in a free clinic that treated survivors. Sometimes I would go with her. I listened to people's stories, and I realized what kind of hell had swallowed up my father; it was then that I truly understood that we owed our lives to his courage and his sacrifice. I managed to stay close to him by imagining what must have gone through his mind in those final, weakened moments. There was nothing morbid about this; it was simply that I felt a need to continue a dialogue with him and to remain faithful to him. An orphan, who lost both his parents when he was too young to remember them, once wrote to me that the only means he had found to create a kind of contact with his mother and father was to hold his breath for as long as he could, almost to the point of asphyxia, in order to imagine he was with them while they were being gassed.

In the fall of 1945, my mother enrolled me as a boarder at the Maimonides School in Boulogne. Having been almost Christian in the spring of 1944, I was now a model little Jew. In truth, I had not believed in God since He had refused to give me back my father, but there was nothing on the surface to distinguish me from the other children in berets and kippas who surrounded the school's headmaster, the renowned Marcus Cohn. In the photograph I have of that year, I am closer to him than any other student. This was because I excelled in Jewish history. I was bored stiff in synagogue, though, and found it difficult to learn Hebrew.

I do not remember much of 1946, until the moment, that fall, when my mother succeeded in obtaining the necessary visas for us to return to Romania. Prudently, she did not give up our apartment, as Romania's fate still hung in the balance, and there was a chance that it might fall into the hands of the Communists. We took the first Orient Express train from Paris to Bucharest on November 9, 1946, and, after three days of travel, arrived in the promised land. Here, we once again lived a life of ease and plenty. In Romania, there was no restriction on what you could buy if you had the money, and the pastries were delicious. My grandparents owned a large apartment in the very center of Bucharest, with windows overlooking the city's equivalent of the Champs-Élysées, and my paternal uncles and aunts all lived in mansions. Georgette and I were enrolled in the French high school, and finally my mother was able to relax a bit after so many years of hardship.

It turned out to be a brief respite: the legislative elections were due to take place in January 1947, and the Communist Party was expected to win. Its campaigners went door to door, intimidating people into voting for them. My mother was outraged: "After the Gestapo, I'm not going to put up with the GPU [State Political Directorate]. If the Communists win, we'll go back to Paris." My grandparents tried to dissuade her. Besides, how would she leave Romania? My mother and I both had Romanian nationality, and we would need an exit visa, which only the Soviet military could provide.

When the Communist Party won the elections, my mother immediately went to see General Borissov, a Russian military leader in Bucharest, who received us without ceremony. He was an elderly man, dressed in simple clothes. My mother, who was Russian, explained our situation to him: that her daughter was French and that she wished both her children to go to school in France. The general signed our exit visa, to my mother's immense gratitude.

Thanks to my mother's bravery and that visa, we were the first people to leave that country after the election, before it sank into tyranny. Some of my relatives went to prison, while others suffered endless bureaucratic hassles and were banished from society; all had their belongings confiscated. My grandparents died in 1950, but my uncles, aunts, and cousins did eventually manage to escape Romania after the payment of a ransom. Only Lida, my mother's beloved sister, remained in Bucharest. Ten years later, I was given the happy task of getting back in touch with her. That was one of my favorite roles, in fact: being able to bring a family back together despite the Cold War.

Return to Paris

B ACK FROM BUCHAREST and once again in Paris in January 1947, my mother did not get her old job back, and I did not return to the Maimonides School; instead, I became a pupil at the Lycée Claude-Bernard. The years that followed were very tough for my mother, who worked a variety of jobs with periods of unemployment in between. She sold children's clothes and perfume and taught Russian in two different high schools, not to mention the work she did with a sewing machine and a job copying addresses onto labels for a mail-order company, an activity that all three of us would sometimes spend the entire night doing.

Although she was a war widow, the French government did not view her that way. The bureaucrats refused to admit that my father had been arrested by the Nazis for his Resistance work—and they were probably right, since it is more likely he was taken away as part of an anti-Jewish raid—but an article of law specified that the French wife of a foreigner who had volunteered for the French army and died as a deportee was entitled to receive a civilian war victim's pension. As the vast majority of these widows of foreigners were themselves foreigners during the war, it seemed clear that the legislator's intention was to assign this pension to widows who later became French, but that was not sufficiently evident in the letter of the law. I became determined to obtain this pension for my mother: an arduous task that demanded great patience. In the end, I managed to convince the National Assembly of my cause. On March 4, 1965, the court gave my mother the long-awaited pension, a judgment confirmed in 1968 by the Council of State—a government legal advisory body—which rejected the ministry's appeal:

> Given that the evidence in the dossier indicates that Klarsfeld, after his escape and demobilization, returned to Nice where he served in the armed Resistance movement Combat, helping them to rescue patriots from the Germans, to distribute leaflets and to falsify identity papers, that he was arrested by the Gestapo on September 30, 1943; Given that Mr. Klarsfeld, having provided direct and personal support to members of the Resistance from his demobilization until his arrest, in other words for a period of two and a half years, must be considered a member of the Resistance [. . .]; Given that, as such, his widow is also entitled to a pension, and given the particularly noteworthy situation of these two persons of foreign origin who demonstrated their attachment to France, where they lived from 1923 onward, and particularly the praiseworthy conduct of the husband who spontaneously volunteered to serve his adopted country to the point of sacrificing his life; [. . .] It is hereby ruled and stated that the petitioner shall be eligible for a widow's pension [. . .] to begin the day after the presumed death of her husband.

I was not a lawyer and was not thinking of becoming one, but—as a son—this was my first legal victory. I had defended my mother's cause in court, and it was a cause worth defending.

RAÏSSA WAS BORN in Russian Bessarabia on March 12, 1904. Her father, Ghers Naoumovitch Strimban, belonged to an old family whose members could apparently be traced back to the Khazars' conversion to Judaism in the tenth century. He was a pharmacist, who died of a heart attack before he was forty. His widow, my grandmother Perl, was also Russian, from a wealthy family of tobacco planters, the Herzensteins.

At the time of Raïssa's birth, there was a terrifying wave of pogroms in Bessarabia, and her uncles were actively involved in organizing the defense of the Jewish community there. The house where they lived was huge and full of animals, children, and servants. She had two sisters and a brother. Nina studied medicine in Saint Petersburg but abandoned her studies to marry a bank manager who continued his career under the Communists. Lida, the dentist, took her degree in Warsaw. Leonid went to university in Prague but made the unwise decision to return to Russia to assist the new regime; accused of being a Trotskyite, he spent years in a gulag before finally being freed.

Raïssa's family was Jewish, but culturally she was very much a Russian. She adored the Russian language and spoke it perfectly, and she also spoke German, Yiddish, Romanian, and French with a charming Russian accent.

Photographs from that period, taken in Berlin, Nice, and Bucharest, show a beautiful young woman, always fashionably dressed. Her mother had re-married, to a Russian Jewish gentleman, and together they traveled widely around Europe during the interwar period. Confident as she was in the brightness of the future and her parents' wealth, Raïssa abandoned her studies as soon as she got married. That confidence was misplaced. The family's belongings in Bessarabia were confiscated when that region was an-nexed by the new Soviet Union. Both totalitarian regimes proved themselves efficient: the Nazis took Raïssa's husband, while the Communists took the belongings of both families.

I LOVED MY mother so much that I never left her for more than a few weeks; neither did my sister, although the two of them often argued. My sister was better than me academically, but I was my mother's favorite. Raïssa thought her daughter muddleheaded and flighty. Our mother spoke to us in Russian; my sister responded in Russian, and I responded in French.

When it came to marriage, my sister followed my mother's advice. My mother had made the acquaintance of a Jewish Bessarabian couple of her age, whose son, Alexandre, was an engineer. My sister liked him, and the next year, when the Davidovici family managed to leave Romania for Paris, they became engaged.

My sister's wedding took place on May 12, 1963, and mine on November 7 of that same year. Georgette and Alik later divorced after having a son, whom his mother named Maldoror for literary reasons. *Les Chants de Maldoror* (*The Songs of Maldoror*) is a poetic novel that inspired many twentieth-century artists.

MY SIXTH-GRADE YEAR at the Lycée Claude-Bernard in 1947 was a disaster. I was terrified of my homeroom teacher, Mr. Laboesse, who taught French and Latin and had a large scar on his chin left by a German lance in 1914. He seemed to enjoy the fear he inspired in me, although I had done nothing to deserve it. I had lost my father, and I had chosen to study Latin. Admittedly my grammar was awful, but that hardly seems an adequate reason to terrorize an eleven-year-old. I never forgave him. My fear was so great that I didn't go to school at all for two weeks, forging absence notes and roaming about Paris from eight in the morning until six in the evening before I could finally go home.

When the academic year ended, the lycée strongly advised my mother to move me to a different school. My mother enrolled me as a boarder at the *collège* in Châteaudun, which proved to be even worse. I was very isolated there; we were badly fed; the boarders, peasants' sons, brought their own food with them every week, and they had no inclination to share it. The school monitors were incredibly mean and used to beat us. My mother did not believe me when I told her this because she had chosen this school on the advice of a friend of hers whose son, a few years older than me, loved being there. What she didn't know was that he played cards for money, and often won, which made his life a lot easier.

I was miserable, dirty, unkempt, sick: when she came to visit me, my sister did not recognize me and thought I was some little beggar. She wept when she realized the truth. My mother decided to bring me back to Paris. I learned nothing at Châteaudun, and one of the few happy memories I cherish from that time is of renting a small boat and drifting off on the Loir; finally alone, I could stare up at the sky through the leaves of the trees and daydream, in communion with nature, which enveloped me like my mother's arms.

It was also while I was at Châteaudun that I first found out—in May 1948, in the pages of a local newspaper—about the birth of the Jewish state. I immediately realized the importance of this event. I also read in the paper that the Israeli army was fighting against several Arab armies and that the existence of the Jewish state depended on the outcome of this war. The only information I could get about Israel came through the newspaper, and I remember crawling past the concierge's office so I could run off to the newsagent's. I did not have any money to buy newspapers, so I just read the headlines, and I kept all my joys and anxieties to myself, having not a single friend with whom I could share them.

The years that followed blurred into one. My teachers taught me, but they did not succeed in awakening my personality and critical mind. I was passive, shut down in class. We never talked about ordinary life or recent events; our schoolbooks and teachers seemed to inhabit an unreal world, midway between the eighteenth and nineteenth centuries. Nevertheless, I remain genuinely grateful to my literature teachers—Mr. Guyon, Mr. Bellay, Mr. Carnoy, Mr. Michel—who helped to shape the sensitive adolescent that I was into a sensitive young man immersed in classical culture. My grammar was terrible, but I loved ancient history and did not want to give up Greek in favor of German or Italian. I feel certain that studying the classics had a profound effect on the choices I made later in life. My heroes were not David or the Maccabees; they were the heroes of Rome and Athens. Later, I would defend the Jewish cause with arms forged in a culture antagonistic to Jews. Who knows? Perhaps, deep down, I more closely resemble those I am fighting against than those I am defending.

I felt very isolated during this period. I did not have any friends, only classmates. I read books; I watched movies, especially American movies; my favorite directors were John Ford, Raoul Walsh, Howard Hawks, and Charlie Chaplin, my favorite actors Errol Flynn, Stewart Granger, and Humphrey Bogart; and I was a cycling fanatic, with my favorite rider being the Italian "champion of champions," Fausto Coppi, who one day took me with him from his hotel, where I was waiting outside the entrance, to the cycling stadium, the Vélodrome d'Hiver, where he got me in without having to pay.

I slowly started to become more aware of life around me during my junior year, in 1953. My history teacher, Louis Poirier—better known under his nom de plume, Julien Gracq, and who had just refused the Prix Goncourt—described me as "a very good student, hardworking, and alert."

During this time, I remained faithful to my father's memory. I went to the cemetery in Bagneux to see the unveiling of the proud monument to the foreign Jewish volunteers, and I watched as the first stone was laid at the Memorial of the Unknown Jewish Martyr.

That same year, I went to live on a kibbutz in Israel. As I was organizing this journey, a Jewish girl who was also going to Israel convinced me to accompany her to the ceremony in honor of the victims of the Vélodrome d'Hiver raid. It was then—and only then—that I discovered, not through the various orations but through the remarks of people whose families were destroyed by that raid, that the policemen responsible for the operation were all French.

When we arrived in Israel, it was thrilling to see a real-life policeman who was a Jew. How could a Jew be a policeman when the Jews had been hunted by the police? For young Jews like me, this was simply extraordinary. At the kibbutz, a representative of the Jewish Agency for Israel began teaching us Hebrew and tried to persuade us to remain in Israel; but he did so in a clumsy and arrogant way. He reproached us for being "too French" and made us feel guilty, telling us that our place was here, in Israel. Several of us, who felt French more than anything else, took this badly: we climbed through the window of the kibbutz's administration office, picked up our passports, and set off to discover Israel for ourselves. With my friend Daniel Marchac—who would later become an internationally renowned surgeon specializing in facial repair—I hitchhiked to Sodom to see the Dead Sea and then to Eilat, by the Red Sea. I also visited my aunt Rachel in Haifa, where she was living after escaping from Romania and before joining her son in Quito, Ecuador.

In 1954, I applied for a Zellidja travel grant, and my project "Ulysses, Son of Ulysses" was one of those chosen: I had to write a report, as well as keep a travel journal and an account book. I was given a very small grant and a diploma explaining that, in order to forge my character, I was traveling without money but with a project I had committed to completing. I failed my baccalaureate exams in July, after panicking and misunderstanding a question, but in spite of that I hitchhiked down to Marseille and then took a Greek ship to Athens, Delphi, and the Peloponnese. I was ecstatic to discover in real life all those wonders from my schoolbooks. There were barely any tourists at that time. After that, I explored Istanbul and hitchhiked through Greece, stopping off at Corfu and Brindisi. I slept on the ground in my sleeping bag, under the stars, and lived on sandwiches and fruit. In Italy, I discovered Capri, Naples, Rome, and Florence. It was sublime.

I failed my exams again in September. The headmaster wrote: "A brilliant student, whose failure came as a profound surprise." And yet I wasn't bad at philosophy. My teacher's name was Maurice Gaït. During one of his classes, he mentioned the concentration camps and claimed that the number of deaths had been exaggerated. Outraged, I stood up and stormed out of the classroom. The school supervisor saw me crying and asked me what was happening; I told him the truth. He then informed me that Maurice Gaït had been the commissioner for youth in the Vichy government, that he had been condemned at the Liberation, and that this was the first year he had been able to teach again. After that, I remained very distant from my teacher, who, at the year's end, wrote on my report: "Lively mind. Consistently good and often very good results." Maurice Gaït later quit teaching and became the editor of the far-right weekly newspaper *Rivarol*.

During the Easter holidays in 1955, I went to London, where I rented a room in Hampstead, above a pub. One night, I was woken by screams from below. Ruth Ellis, a model, had killed her lover with a revolver as he was coming out of the pub. In France, she would have served a very short prison sentence for this crime of passion, but her actual fate was much harsher: she was the last woman to be hanged in England.

Back in Paris, I began going to the Stade Géo André with two friends, Weiss and Perec. Three young Jews who had lost a father or a mother and who only ever talked about sports and movies. Perec's first name was Georges, and he would go on to become a very famous writer, whose work was strongly marked by the Holocaust. During this period, I read Inge Scholl's book about the White Rose movement led by Hans and Sophie Scholl. Theirs was a rebellion doomed to failure, but it proved to be a fertile failure: their deaths helped forge the existence of another Germany and, long after they were executed, Jews like me—victims of other Germans—would hear their call and learn to overcome natural prejudices.

A German Girl Named Beate

L ACKING ANY AMBITION—except a desire to be happy—and being by nature impulsive, I decided to become a literature or history teacher. Such an important decision would have been better made with a father to advise me. But perhaps he did influence me, in spite of everything: he died a slave, and ordering others or obeying others has always repulsed me. I am fine directing a collective action carried out by equals who agree to follow my suggestions, and I am fine taking orders that I accept of my own volition, but I have always preferred to remain free, not only in my head, but in my work, too. I am not the type of man who will be happy as an employee.

Anyway, I found myself in the first year of an intensive preparatory degree at the prestigious Lycée Henri-IV. To follow the best students, one must work hard; I did my best, and I passed my favorite subjects, but my Latin result was awful. Even so, I was accepted for my second year. The grading was so rigorous that the teachers' comments on my essays took up more space than my own writing. I worked hard and realized that I was becoming less superficial and more intelligent.

I passed my exams, receiving the best grades of all in history and literature. Having received another Zellidja travel grant in 1956, I decided to head east. I hitchhiked to Istanbul, stopping off in Venice, which I adored, then I took the train to Belgrade and Skopje, where a policeman threw me off a train for flirting with a Yugoslavian girl.

I went as far as Tehran and tried to reach Afghanistan but had to give up because flooding had destroyed so many bridges. In Thessaloníki, on my way back to France, I was seduced by a beautiful young woman named Helga, who consoled me for my romantic disappointment: a blonde girl with a ponytail, Djinn, a schoolgirl at the Lycée Jules-Ferry, had rejected me the previous year.

In the fall, I began a history degree at the Sorbonne. The following February, I visited my sister in Moscow, where she lived in a diplomatic ghetto, teaching Russian to French diplomats. Our quality of life there was good: with her modest wages, my sister was able to eat in the best restaurants. It was difficult to work out the true nature of the regime in that country, where on the surface everything seemed so orderly and, in social terms, similar to France in 1957. My knowledge of Russian came in handy, but even more useful for understanding that this was not the best form of governance was my experience of Romania in 1946.

IN 1958, I fell in love with the first young woman I met in the Descartes amphitheater in the Sorbonne. Mireille was born on November 2, the same day as my sister. She was from a Protestant family in Alsace. There was every reason for me to fall for her: she was beautiful and brilliant, with an intelligence founded not only on culture but on introspection. At Easter, I sailed on a small Dutch freighter to Casablanca, where I received a letter from Mireille telling me that she loved me. So I jumped on a boat that left the next day and never saw anything more of Morocco than the post office in Casablanca. We talked about marriage, but the relationship ended a few months later. She wrote to me: "We are too different. I know different personalities can complete one another, and I wanted to believe that for a long time. But I suffered too much from those differences to be able to delude myself any longer. Serge, when we do not have the same basic reactions to anything—not even the smallest things—we cannot be happy together. And that is what happened to us: we clashed constantly in spite of the love we felt for each other, and I probably suffered the most." Mireille was undoubtedly right. She was reasonable and clearheaded, and I was not.

I was not inconsolable; I met a Finnish girl and then a Dutch girl; I passed my degree and entered Sciences Po as a second-year student to study international relations. I felt at ease there: the work was within my capabilities, and I played on the soccer team. I was also studying history at the Sorbonne with the famous historian Pierre Renouvin.

In the summer of 1959, I went to Israel again, as one of my professors, Georges Balandier, had gotten me a grant so I could study the trade union confederation Histadrut. I returned from Israel on a Turkish boat that took me to Istanbul, where I went to see the Romanian consul. I convinced him to give me a visa allowing me to go to Bucharest to visit my aunt Lida because I feared I might never see her again: I was due to do my military service in the middle of the Algerian War.

At passport control on the Romanian border, the police told me that I was considered a deserter—my passport bore the words "born in Bucharest," even if I had been naturalized as French in 1950—and that, when I reached the capital, I would have to report to the police station. There, they examined my case and decided to leave me in peace. Aunt Lida had no idea I was coming, but as soon as I called out her name, standing outside her building, she immediately guessed who it was. It was so wonderful to see each other after twelve years of separation. I spent a few days with her and got back in touch with my father's family: my cousin Sylvio and his wife, Gaby, who had a two-year-old boy named André; they did not believe that I was who I claimed to be at first, so used were they to living in a climate of suspicion, but I was able to convince them in the end. My cousin Sophie accompanied me on the train to the Hungarian border. She dreamed of freedom; it would take her more than ten years to escape.

IN 1960, I passed both diplomas—at the Sorbonne and Sciences Po—but I remained careless and lacking in foresight. Instead of preparing seriously for the École nationale d'administration (National School of Administration), I chose to do my military service, when I could have gotten out of it.

Not only that, but I was not of much interest to the army, as my father's death spared me deployment to the war in Algeria. But I was stubborn, and I obeyed my instincts.

At the same time, however, I had met a young German woman and was beginning to feel a deep attachment to her. For all my travels, it was at Porte de Saint-Cloud, on the platform of the metro station, that I saw her for the first time. She was wearing a blue dress cinched at the waist; from behind, I could tell she had a nice figure, and when she turned around, I discovered that I liked her bright, spirited face, too. I was on my way to a meeting, and I was wearing my best three-piece suit, a Prince of Wales check. I was going to Sciences Po, at the metro station Sèvres-Babylone; she was holding a blue Alliance Française book, which suggested she would get off at Notre-Dame-des-Champs.

That meant she would have to change trains at Michel-Ange–Molitor and at Sèvres-Babylone. Standing near her in the carriage, I kept looking at her; at the first station, we climbed the stairs side by side, and it was on the platform at Molitor that I finally dared speak to her: "Are you English?" She replied, "No, I'm German." At Sèvres-Babylone, she gave me the telephone number for the family in Boulogne where she worked as an au pair. The day we met was May 11, 1960: the very day that Adolf Eichmann was kidnapped by the Israelis in Buenos Aires. Could that have been a sign of our destiny?

For me, energy was an essential quality in a woman. My mother and sister were both energetic, and so were Stendhal's heroines. I sensed that Beate had the energy of Mathilde de la Mole and the tenderness of Madame de Rênal. My mother sensed it, too; she liked Beate instantly and entrusted her son to a woman who she knew could love him all his life and, when it ended, have the courage to close his eyes.

Of the two of us, Beate is the more reliable, the more steadfast. She does everything, big or small, conscientiously, intelligently, and coolly. She is an excellent housewife; she always writes "hausfrau" in the box for occupation when filling out forms. She is capable of adapting to any situation and is always cheerful and smiling. In this, she resembles Marlene Dietrich, another Berliner, who became Beate's friend toward the end of her life and whom we consider to be one of the most iconic women of her century. Her first contact with Marlene came in the form of a postcard to Beate: "Dearest Madame, I am writing to tell you that I admire you and love you deeply, and I am sure you know why. As I have become an atheist, I cannot say: 'God bless you!' "

Beate was the woman of my dreams, capable of lifting me up above myself despite my flaws. I didn't know this yet, but I sensed it. From the start of our relationship, I respected her character. She was not East German or West German but simply German. When she was confronted with the image of Nazi Germany, she accepted it; but I could already feel the resolve accumulating within her to react against that image, not through denial, but through positive action. First she had to learn from her country's history how it had reached this point, this division of Germany and its capital. I gave her books and articles that enabled her to educate herself. She wanted to understand; she wanted to act, too.

The two of us rented a ground-floor studio apartment on Avenue de la Bourdonnais. We didn't stay there long. On an impulse, I bought an adorable kitten at a pet store. In my mother's family, everyone owned a cat; now it was our turn. That evening, we brought it to show my mother, who loved it so much she refused to let it go. As we refused to abandon it, we came up with a compromise. My sister, who lived with our mother, had seen our apartment, which she liked a great deal. So she moved into it, while Beate and I took her room in my mother's small apartment. My mother's open-mindedness can be gauged by the fact that she didn't bat an eyelid over us living together when we were not married or even engaged, and this at a time when such behavior was often judged harshly.

We married on November 7, 1963, at the town hall in the sixteenth arrondissement. The mayor, who married us, asked us to be an exemplary couple, as we were Franco-German. While we were on our honeymoon in Munich, I learned that I had finished first in the competitive exam for management assistants.

Not long before our wedding, one of my friends had tried to dissuade me from marrying Beate. A few days later, she and I had lunch in a little Russian restaurant, where a fortune-teller approached us and offered to read my palm. I had never done that before; I hesitated, but ended up agreeing. She looked at the lines in my hand, then took me aside and said, "You've been advised not to marry this woman. You *must* marry her." And I remember vividly what she said next: "She is the *only* woman in the world you can be happy with."

Today, after fifty-four years of marital bliss, I can confidently state that what the fortune-teller said to me was true: no other woman could have given me what Beate has brought into our private life and our public life. Together we are united, strong, and happy; without each other, we probably wouldn't have achieved very much. She owes me a lot, and I owe her even more . . .

1965, at Auschwitz-Birkenau:
The Decisive Moment

I HAD NO IDEA when I left home that morning that I was going to quit my job at the ORTF, France's national broadcasting agency. This impulsive act upset my wife and mother but would turn out to be one of the luckiest moments of my life.

Mr. François, the agency's assistant director, spent at least an hour trying to convince me not to resign. I held firm. When I went back to the house, Beate and Raïssa reproached me for my decision. At that moment, I regretted it, but France was going through a period of full employment, and I felt sure it wouldn't take me long to find another, equivalent job that I would find less frustrating. I didn't even register as unemployed. A few months later, I was appointed an executive assistant in a multinational cereal corporation: Continental Grain.

. . .

THE YEAR BEFORE, our son was born: Arno David Emmanuel came into the world on August 27, 1965. A short time before my son's birth, I became aware of a feeling of loss that was growing inside me, connected to the death of my father. Since I was about to have my first contact with my child, it seemed only right that I should reestablish contact with my father. So I began methodically retracing the final stage of his life: what had happened to him from the moment he left us until his death. Passing through Romania, where I got the transit visa from the Soviet Union, I arrived in Katowice, which was freezing cold, and from there, I went to Auschwitz II–Birkenau.

In the main camp, Auschwitz I, there were lots of visitors, all of them from Poland or other Soviet satellite countries. At Birkenau, the final destination for the Jewish people, I was alone, completely alone. At that moment, I felt certain that my life should have ended there, that the immense suffering of the slaughtered Jewish people had not been assuaged by the passage of time. It seemed that I could hear my people screaming, a scream as great as the crime that had provoked it, a scream that was impossible to interrupt, that would go on forever. I could not block my ears or my heart: if the child who had survived the genocide by a miracle, and by his father's sacrifice, remained deaf to that scream—which was also a call for him to assume his responsibilities as a Jew—wouldn't my life be an act of betrayal? I was a Jew who had survived the Holocaust, and I was a Jew who had seen the creation of an independent Jewish state, a Jew belonging to an exceptional generation assuming exceptional responsibilities. It felt like a revelation.

IN LATE 1966, my mother, my wife, my sister and her husband, our children, Arno and Maldoror, our two cats, Minette and Nikita, and our cocker spaniel, Petia, moved to a different part of the sixteenth arrondissement, Passy, where the metro emerges from underground.

Almost simultaneously, two events propelled Beate and me from a normal existence into a situation of total mobilization, as if each of us had accumulated an abundance of energy that simply had to be discharged into the world. For me, the catalyst was the Six-Day War in June 1967; for Beate, it was her dismissal from the Franco-German Youth Office, where she had worked since 1964.

The very morning the Six-Day War broke out, on Monday, June 5, I made plans to go to Israel with my friend and colleague Josy Fainas; in the office, we bought our Air France tickets to Tel Aviv. The office management did not discourage our leaving, but they were shocked, even though they, too, were Jewish. For the company directors, the firm was its employees' ultimate homeland.

We took off that afternoon. The plane was diverted to Athens because of an air battle taking place in the region. The next day, an El Al airplane transported volunteers stuck in Athens to Tel Aviv. Thanks to my ORTF card, which I had kept, I was accepted as a press war correspondent. With the Egyptian air force having been destroyed at the beginning of the conflict, Israel had no further need for volunteer soldiers. So I was able to witness, from the Wailing Wall, the first exhilarating hours of the liberation of Jewish Jerusalem, which had been in foreign hands since its conquest by Pompey in 63 B.C. and its destruction in A.D. 70 by Titus. I accompanied the units sent to conquer the Golan Heights, staying with them until they reached Quneitra in Syria.

On June 11, 1967, I went to Bucharest to see my aunt and tell the Romanian Jews—in absolute secrecy, because the Soviet government was extremely unhappy about it—what had happened in Israel. On Monday morning, I was back in the office, once again devoted to making a profit for my multinational company.

BEATE

Typist and Activist

I WAS EXTREMELY enthusiastic about my work for the Franco-German Youth Office; I even planned to write a guide and manifesto for young German au pair girls in Paris. And that is exactly what I did. The book ended up having a huge impact in Germany, due to the timing of its publication: it came out just after one of those young German girls was murdered in the upscale Parisian suburb of Neuilly.

That book also marked, for me, the beginning of a period of friction with two Youth Office executives: its general secretary, then in Bonn, François Altmayer, and the head of the French section, Robert Clément. Even though the Youth Office had given its blessing to the book's publication, even though it had actually followed the ideas I set forth in the manifesto, it was unpleasant for eminent men to have to admit that the ideas of a young female secretary could be of any importance.

In public appearances and conferences on Franco-German relations, I was invited as a specialist and placed by the organizers next to the Youth Office's directors, who coldly ignored me. Whenever I spoke, they made it plain that "Mrs. Klarsfeld is speaking only for herself," even though the audience was well aware that what I was saying was in no way at odds with the Youth Office's policies. I was helping to raise public awareness about the situation of au pair girls, and I was helping those girls by giving them practical advice on specific aspects of their daily and cultural life. I also wrote on their behalf in the "manifesto" part of the book:

> The French and the Germans still have a false image of each other: young French people see young Germans as hardworking, serious, sociable, polite, disciplined, courageous, and intelligent, but also bellicose, militaristic, authoritarian, arrogant, withdrawn, humorless, lacking a critical sense, false, and nationalistic. Meanwhile, young Germans regard young French people as kind, charming, happy, open, and intelligent, but also lazy, unpleasant, superficial, frivolous, and careless. These enduring clichés can be altered by sustained contact with the other nationality, however. From a German standpoint, in order for young people to acquire a genuine sympathy for France during their travels, they need to spend a prolonged period of time there, to gain a fluent understanding of the French language, to forge long-lasting personal relationships, and to enjoy a broad range of social contacts.
>
> Au pair girls are the only ones to meet all these conditions. They are able to engage in a specific form of travel that corresponds to what the Franco-German friendship requires of young people. Generally, returning to Germany more open-minded and with their character enhanced, they are worthy of the best help we can offer them.

But a secretary had no say in the matter—that is what I discovered, to my displeasure.

AN INCIDENT WITH VOGGENREITER, my book's German publisher, further cooled my relations with the Youth Office while also revealing the German section's subjection to the Bonn government, even though in theory the Youth Office was an independent binational organization.

In a chapter entitled "Germany in Paris," I gave the names and addresses of cultural associations, including Franco-German Exchanges, which organized conferences on German history at the Sorbonne. Now, this was a French charity with friendly links to the German Democratic Republic (GDR). My German publisher, who was hoping to sell a number of copies directly to the education ministries of the different administrative regions in the Federal Republic of Germany, was obliged to withdraw all the books from sale and to remove the page containing these addresses. The youth minister, who was planning to distribute the guide to German girls about to leave for France, pulled out at the last moment.

I was given a severe dressing-down: "Don't you understand? You mentioned an association with links to East Germany! It's unbelievable . . ." We could not understand each other: for them, Germany belonged to the Federal Republic; for me, it belonged to the entire German people.

SPRING 1966. I used to take little Arno for walks from Porte de Saint-Cloud to the Jardin des Poètes. We had decided that our son would be Jewish, that he would be circumcised by a rabbi and be named after Serge's father. The Youth Office had granted me one year's unpaid leave. I changed diapers and doted on my baby. Each smile that lit up his face was a precious moment of happiness.

Whenever I could, I would go to the mayor's office in the fifth arrondissement. There, in a room hidden amid a labyrinth of corridors, I found Marguerite Durand's feminist library. I was researching a subject close to my heart—the German woman as seen by the French—on which I hoped to write a book. Each weekend, I would stroll along the Seine with Serge and Arno, and I would pick up books from the secondhand stalls there, written by French travelers, prisoners of war, or journalists about the romantic, domestic, professional, and social lives of German women in the twentieth century. I learned a great deal about my fellow citizens and their observers. Around this time, a magazine, *La Femme du XXe siècle* (*The 20th Century Woman*), asked me to write an article on the postwar German woman.

I have come to wonder what drove me—and so many other German women—to leave our homeland. Of course, there were some obvious reasons, to do something specific in France or elsewhere: the in-depth study of a language and civilization. But, in my opinion, there is something more profound and often unconscious beneath this urge: the desire for liberation.

Under Wilhelm II, our ancestors' world could be summarized by the three *Ks* (*Kinder, Kirche, Küche*—"children," "church," "kitchen"). For a decade or so, under the Weimar Republic, our grandmothers were finally able to breathe and hope. Then Hitler sent them back to the children—and to the factory when the needs of the war machine became great enough.

Once again, it took the trauma of losing a world war to give the German woman a second chance. Our mothers worked; they actively contributed to rebuilding the cities from ruins. In return for which, German society largely opened its arms to them, enabling them to become laborers, engineers, doctors, farmers, teachers, or business leaders, without forgetting to ask them, too, to produce the men of tomorrow. Women actively contributed to the reconstruction of a new Germany. Sadly, this country was not new in any meaningful sense, because, as before, women still played practically no political role. What I mean by political is participation in the real task of shaping our nation's destiny. How many women have done that in the history of Germany? Once again, German public opinion is veering dangerously toward the idea of a domesticated woman, devoted exclusively to the well-being of her husband and her natural reproductive function.

I joined the Social Democrats in 1964. After my book was published, Willy Brandt, the mayor of West Berlin, received me in his office, where he told me about his stay in Paris, in his early twenties, in 1937, after he had fled Nazi Germany. I know many Germans consider him a traitor, but I admire him for not having followed the injunction: *Recht oder Unrecht, mein Vaterland* (My country, right or wrong).

I SAW WILLY BRANDT again two years later, at a reception given in the summer of 1966 by the German embassy in Paris; he looked crestfallen by his second electoral defeat. The comments about him in the German press had been scathing. He was labeled a "drunkard," and his political career was deemed over. I told him again how much confidence I had in him: "There is a whole younger generation in Germany that admires you for your stand against the Nazis. We need a German like you as our chancellor. Don't lose heart; I have confidence in you."

Impulsively, I took his hand. He smiled at me warmly. The look in his eyes reflected his honesty, and the creases around them the incessant struggles he'd faced, swimming against the tide of German opinion. For me, his voice was that of the German people, and his face was the true face of Germany.

WHEN I RETURNED to the Youth Office in October 1966, my position as a researcher had been axed—for "budgetary reasons." I found myself stuck behind a typewriter, or sometimes working the switchboard, and once again I was frustrated.

In December, our entire family rented an immense apartment on Rue de l'Alboni—overlooking the Seine, almost opposite the Eiffel Tower and with the metro roaring just under our windows. Serge and I paid two-fifths of the rent, Serge's sister Tania and her husband, Alik, the same, and Serge's mother, Raïssa, one-fifth.

Food was my responsibility. Two or three times a week, I would go to Les Halles to stock up. We were able to hire a cleaning lady and two au pairs— one for the morning, the other for the afternoon—to look after the children. For my sister-in-law and for me, this meant a considerable increase in our freedom. We lived communally. It was a fascinating experience, like a little kibbutz in the middle of Paris.

DURING THIS TIME, Kurt Georg Kiesinger, the minister president of Baden-Württemberg, was preparing to become chancellor of Germany. A few French newspapers discreetly mentioned his past as a Nazi propagandist. Shocked, I immediately scanned the German press. The only protests came from a great writer, Günter Grass, and a great philosopher, Karl Jaspers, who wrote: "What seemed impossible ten years ago is now happening almost without resistance. It was probably inevitable that former Nazis would occupy high-ranking political positions, simply because there are too few non-Nazis to look after the functions of the state. But that a former

National Socialist should now rule the entire Federal Republic implies that the fact of having been a Nazi no longer has any significance. No one objected when he was elected minister president of Baden-Württemberg, but chancellor? That is something else altogether."

I remembered Hans and Sophie Scholl's final leaflet: Who were they writing it for? For us, for all of us: "Once the war is over, the guilty must be severely punished in the interests of the future, so that no one will ever want to do something like this again . . . Do not forget the bastards who run this regime! Remember their names, so that not one of them may escape! So that they cannot, at the last moment, change sides and pretend that nothing ever happened."

As soon as Kiesinger was elected to the head of the West German government, there was a conspiracy of silence about his past in the newspapers. Particularly once the coalition of Christian Democrats and Social Democrats was sealed. Then Willy Brandt became the country's foreign minister.

We had to react, but how? I decided to follow the Scholls' example. The essential thing, in fighting against Nazism, is to recognize before acting that success is not a certainty. What matters most is to try, courageously, to follow your conscience, with your eyes wide open. My first act was a public statement.

I went to see two daily newspapers with my article. But they politely ushered me toward the offices of *Combat*. I had some difficulty finding the old building on Rue de Croissant, in Montmartre, that was home to the newspaper that preserved the spirit of the French Resistance.

The young editor I met, Michel Voirol, seemed surprised to meet a German who wished to protest against Kiesinger's nomination. My first op-ed appeared on the day of his official visit to Paris, on January 14, 1967.

> Mr. Kiesinger is a reassuring presence for Germans of a certain age. He has always walked in step with the German people. Like them, he went the wrong way for ten years, when he was a member of the Nazi Party . . . Willy Brandt is more frightening to Germans. How dare he always be right in the major decisions of his life, and to have indissolubly linked morality to politics. He is also reproached for his courage in leaving Nazi Germany when he was neither a

Communist nor a Jew, simply a free German. Many Germans do not like Brandt's courage and clear-sightedness; in fact, they cannot forgive him for possessing those qualities.

I was not motivated by hatred for Kiesinger nor by a morbid fascination with the past or even by despair. I believed that Germany had a bright future and that it lay with Willy Brandt. In a second article, published in March 1967, I wrote:

> As a German, I deplore the accession of Mr. Kiesinger to the position of chancellor. A former Nazi Party member at the head of our nation: this is equivalent to the public absolution of a certain era and a certain attitude. Hannah Arendt wrote about the "banality of evil" in relation to Eichmann, but for me, Mr. Kiesinger personifies the respectability of evil. Mr. Kiesinger was a member of the Nazi Party from 1933 until 1945, and his defense during the postwar trials could be summarized as: "I did not resign because remaining in power allowed me to limit the damage." Well, I may only have been born in 1939, but I know too much about the concentration camps and the ruins of Europe to thank Mr. Kiesinger for the way he limited the damage . . .
>
> Only Willy Brandt can give a new direction to Germany's political life . . . So any countries who fear Germany's ambitions should help Brandt to become chancellor. The countries of the East in particular should welcome him with all the consideration and respect due to a man who was—and remains—their ally in the battle against Nazism. They should regard him as their only valid contact and refuse all dialogue with Mr. Kiesinger. Last, they should help Brandt in his efforts to solve the German problem by bringing the two Germanys closer together within a socialist framework.

Each political stand I took increased the hostility toward me from my superiors and colleagues at the Franco-German Youth Office. No one mentioned those articles in my presence, but it was clear that they were trying to make my working conditions ever more unbearable.

WHILE THIS STORM was brewing at work, however, the joys of family life absorbed me at home. Everything was cheerful and happy between us. Arno was growing up, while Serge—after resigning from the ORTF—soon got another job at Continental Grain. When he told me he was going to Israel for the war, I did not try to dissuade him: I had been to Israel with him the previous year, and I knew how strong his attachment was to the Jewish cause.

Surrounded by such a family, I felt loved and secure. I would need those feelings in the ordeal that awaited me.

Fired by the Youth Office

O N AUGUST 30, 1967, the Youth Office fired me. I immediately phoned Serge. My throat was tight, my voice barely audible. Serge made me repeat what I'd said:

"The manager just gave me a letter from the Youth Office's general secretary informing me that they're opening disciplinary procedures against me."

"For turning up late?"

"No, for political reasons. Listen to what he wrote: 'Your article published in the newspaper *Combat* on July 21, 1967, constitutes a serious violation of the obligations attending Youth Office employees . . . It contravenes article three, paragraph two, of the Youth Office staff regulations, according to which all employees, in their declarations, activities, and publications, must abstain from any act incompatible with their duties and obligations toward the Youth Office or likely to cause moral or material damage to the Youth Office . . .'"

"Come to my office now," Serge said. "We'll talk about it here."

That letter devastated me. To be fired without any warning or compensation made me feel as if I had committed a shameful crime.

I walked quickly. I needed to calm down. It was only a few hundred yards from my office to the Continental Grain building. Serge's jaw was tense; I shared his rage, but my emotions do not show so clearly in my face.

Some of Serge's colleagues tried to calm us down, to talk us out of doing anything hasty. "You don't want to take this to court," one of them advised us. "It'll be complex and messy. You'll lose the case, and you'll be out of work." Others chimed in, too, but I didn't want to listen to them.

Serge took me to a nearby café where we sat face-to-face, in silence. Was it possible to just give up, to accept this humiliation? I tried to be strong. I had to confront this injustice. So I thought about the people who were on our side in this battle. Surely they couldn't accept the idea that, twenty years after the torture they underwent, a Nazi should regain power?

AS I SIT in that café, horrific images flash through my mind. The little boy in the Warsaw Ghetto, eyes tragic and terrified, his hands raised as a German soldier aims a gun at him. He looks like my son. He is my son. No, I can't keep quiet about this. Serge talks about his father and says, "How could I just let you be fired for telling the truth about a Nazi?"

He kisses my hand. I think about that photograph of a young couple lying in the ruins of the Warsaw Ghetto, surrounded by other Jews, who will, moments after the picture is taken, be massacred. The man and the woman huddle against one another, holding hands. They are not protecting each other—the time for protection is over—but their love survives. They are seconds from death, and yet you can see in their eyes and on their lips an indestructible emotion: the love they feel for one another.

This image fills my mind for only a second or two. This is the turning point of our lives. Our decision is made. We are going to fight, and this battle will be our priority. We have decided on all this without hesitation, almost without a word. We will fight not to clear our conscience but to win. And we know that, from this moment, the fight will be everything. Serge's career, our family, financial security . . . all of these matters will become secondary.

. . .

THE ÉLYSÉE PALACE was very close to Serge's office. I went there right away and asked to see the secretary-general, Bernard Tricot. I'm not sure how it happened—good luck? a mistake?—but I was shown directly to his office. Mr. Tricot was surprised to see me, but he heard me out anyway.

On September 13, he wrote to me: "I must inform you that I do not believe the office of the president of the Republic should intervene in this affair . . . It is not for us to interfere in a political process that has already begun." So the highest authority in France washed its hands of the situation. And yet I was French now and had been for four years.

I wrote to one of the most famous names of the French Resistance, Henri Frenay, who had founded the Combat movement. On September 21, I received his response. I opened the letter, heart pounding, expecting encouragement, moral support. My eyes blurred with bitter tears as I read what he had written to me. "Madame," he wrote, "after careful consideration of the matter, I have come to the conclusion that I cannot share your feeling, nor approve of your attitude, publicly expressed when you were a member of the Franco-German Youth Office. Nothing you have written publicly or told me in your letter suggests that the chancellor of the Federal Republic was ever an important member of the National Socialist Party, invested with serious responsibilities. Following your logic, then, all Germans who have ever had an NSDAP [National Socialist German Workers' Party] membership card in their pocket must be condemned. You know as well as I do that this would mean excluding from public life almost the entire male population of Germany aged forty or older . . . I understand your feelings in this matter, but I cannot share them in any way whatsoever."

If he had been German, I couldn't help thinking, would he have resisted Hitler?

Thankfully, Henri Frenay's reserve was opposed by the actions of Jean Pierre-Bloch, the president of LICA (International League Against Racism and Anti-Semitism), who wrote a vehement article in *Le Juvénal*.

We decided to fight the case in the French courts, rather than in the Franco-German Youth Office's arbitration committee, which was composed of two judges appointed by their respective governments. A committee of that kind would discreetly bury the affair, I knew, whereas if we were judged by the district court of the eighth arrondissement of Paris, there would be a chance of making the case public through the press.

OUR STRUGGLE HAD a serious impact on our daily lives. It was expensive. We stopped paying our taxes. We would be fined for this, but at least it allowed us to delay the moment when we would have to pay. We cut down on our food budget. We sold our old car. We dismissed our cleaning lady and kept only one au pair girl. The hours we devoted to politics bled into our family life. I had no trouble switching instantly from one to the other. I washed my family's dirty laundry with the same professional conscientiousness that I washed my nation's dirty laundry.

My mother-in-law feared what might happen to us; she understood that such a battle might drag us far from a normal existence. She reminded us of our responsibilities to Arno and expressed doubts about the effectiveness of our actions. We ignored her, focusing purely on our aims, and I put on a pair of mental blinkers so I would not see the peaceful shore as the wave swept me away. But, deep down, my mother-in-law approved of what we were doing. She took care of Arno while we were away and, when we needed money, it was she and my sister-in-law who helped us. As for my mother, widowed the year before, she was harshly critical of our campaign. She thought it was completely normal that I should lose my job for bad-mouthing the chancellor of Germany.

We realized the need to assemble a file on Kiesinger's Nazi activities. Serge, who had collected a few documents at the Center of Contemporary Jewish Documentation (CDJC) in Paris, pointed out to me that the first revelations about Kiesinger in the press clearly came from the Potsdam archives in East Germany. After further research, he decided to go and see Mr. Heyne, the director of the Franco-German Friendship in East Berlin. (At that time, there were no diplomatic ties between France and East Germany.)

Serge went to the building where Mr. Heyne worked—the building that used to house Goebbels's Propaganda Ministry, ironically, only about fifty yards from Hitler's former bunker—but he could not find the director. Serge went into the room where Goebbels used to hold meetings every morning—meetings which Kiesinger frequently attended—but it was in the Volkskammer, the People's Chamber, that he finally met Mr. Heyne. He was subsequently directed to the Ministry of the Interior, where he was eventually heard by a committee of seven or eight people. With the aid of an interpreter, he explained his plan to compile a dossier on Kiesinger's past. He did not hide the fact that he had volunteered for the Israeli army during the Six-Day War. Their response was favorable.

For four days, Serge consulted a thick file and took notes, eventually leaving East Berlin with a huge dossier of photocopies. During the course of his research, he noted down the name of the author of a book on Hitler's radio propaganda, Raimund Schnabel, but there was only one copy of this book in East Berlin. Its publisher, Europa-Verlag, was headquartered in Vienna. Simon Wiesenthal, the famous Nazi hunter, also lived in Vienna. Seeing this as a sign, Serge went there immediately. Wiesenthal spoke with him but unfortunately was unable to provide him with any documents. "I'm afraid that a politician like Kiesinger is not part of my field of inquiry. I am focused on the SS, the concentration camp executioners, and the men behind the Final Solution."

Ultimately, our documentation was supplemented by some papers found at the Wiener Library in London and thousands of microfiche bought for four hundred dollars from the archives of the U.S. German Foreign Ministry in Washington, D.C. The rapid examination of these documents allowed me to write—and have printed, at our own cost—a pamphlet entitled *The Truth About Kurt Georg Kiesinger*. It was ready just before Christmas.

Working methodically, poring over the microfiche every night, I was able to reconstruct the role played by Kiesinger in the Nazi Party. I also had a chance meeting in the summer of 1968 with the historian Joseph Billig at the CDJC. Billig was the author of a remarkable book, *L'Hitlérisme et le système concentrationnaire* (*Nazism and the Concentration Camp System*). He was one of the few historians to understand and describe the role played by certain German diplomats in the development of the Final Solution. Billig seemed reticent at first when I spoke to him about Kiesinger: "What did he do? That doesn't interest me. I doubt he did very much, anyway." All the same, he agreed to read the dossier. Soon afterward, he admitted he was convinced. And so we were able to write a more in-depth study: *Kiesinger, or Subtle Fascism* constituted my bill of indictment and definitively lifted the veil on Kiesinger's true face.

The Case Against Kiesinger

KIESINGER, A YOUNG lawyer, joined the Nazi Party on May 1, 1933. He was nearly thirty. His membership card, which he would keep until Hitler's fall, bore the number 2633930.

As a student, he belonged to Catholic organizations, but, from 1933 onward, he sought to join his Catholic activism to Hitler's policies. Apparently, his conscience as a Christian was able to accommodate the Nazi regime's anti-Semitism.

In August 1940, the foreign minister Joachim von Ribbentrop appointed Kiesinger to the political broadcasting department as an "auxiliary scientist." This thirty-six-year-old legal expert gradually became the assistant director of the political broadcasting department. Kiesinger's position in the AA (Auswärtiges Amt—the Foreign Office) also facilitated his delicate role as an intermediary between the perpetually warring ministries of Ribbentrop (AA) and Goebbels (Propaganda).

Kiesinger owed his job to Martin Luther, a Foreign Office undersecretary. A committed Nazi, Luther had been brought into the Foreign Office by Ribbentrop to inject a pro-Hitler spirit that it had been missing. In order to carry out this task, Ribbentrop had formed the "Germany" Department under Luther's direction. The involvement of Nazi Party members in foreign affairs effectively meant working with Himmler, as the SS had become the only guarantee of the implementation of Nazi ideology. During the trial of high-ranking Nazis at Nuremberg, another Foreign Office undersecretary, Carl Friedrich von Weizsäcker, said of the "Germany" Department, "They created their own subdepartments for cases that had nothing to do with the Foreign Office, such as racial politics, Jewish affairs, police issues, and so on." Kiesinger's colleagues in the Foreign Office were not classic diplomatic types but party members, and SS members in particular.

The decree of September 8, 1939, made Ribbentrop, rather than Goebbels, responsible for foreign propaganda, which used transmitters broadcasting from Germany or occupied territories. The department was also supposed to influence or guide foreign radio stations and, if need be, acquire them so that they could broadcast Nazi ideas.

Kiesinger quickly rose through the ranks of this organization, the Rundfunkpolitische Abteilung, which had about two hundred employees in Berlin itself and as many more beyond the Reich. In 1941, Kiesinger was appointed head of Service B, one of the department's two general affairs organizations. He was in charge of the planning and control of guidelines for German radio's foreign propaganda and the restructuring of all propaganda initiatives. As well, he had to coordinate the work of eleven different transmitting offices.

Kiesinger also censored all radio shows to be broadcast abroad. So from 1941 on, he was responsible for the content of Nazi radio programs broadcast in foreign countries. That same year, he joined Interradio. This huge broadcasting company, founded by Goebbels and Ribbentrop, was dedicated to conveying Nazi propaganda abroad. On behalf of the Foreign Office, Kiesinger held a ten-million-reichsmark share in Interradio. He was also responsible for liaising between the Foreign Office and Interradio: if the broadcaster's departments did not apply the directives passed on to them by the regional services of his department, he had the power to force them to obey. Interradio employed seven hundred people, two hundred of them working for the Sonderdienst Seehaus, which monitored foreign radio programs.

Interradio's policy objectives were set out in a document dated November 5, 1941: "Foreign transmitters owned by Germany or influenced by them are, first of all, under the direction of central services in Berlin, an instrument of war in the service of culture, science, and the German economy, and should also actively support the Reich's greater political designs."

So the executives at Interradio were not merely citizens fulfilling their duty as combatants in the civil sector of a country at war, but also the future architects of the new Europe ruled by Hitler.

In 1943, Kiesinger was made assistant manager of the political broadcasting department while continuing to run Service B and becoming the manager of Service A, the second general service. In this way, he became one of the driving forces behind the Nazis' foreign propaganda broadcasts. He was the only man to work in every area, political and administrative, of this extraordinary spiderweb. Kiesinger found himself the all-powerful assistant to SS-Standartenführer Rühle and rubbed shoulders with the new director of the culture department, SS-Brigadeführer Franz Six, just back from Russia, where, as head of the Einsatzgruppen—special death squads—he had overseen the liquidation of thousands of Jews.

During the summer of 1943, Kiesinger made the acquaintance of one of Six's department heads, Dr. Ernst Achenbach, who had returned from a three-year stint in France, where he was at the heart of the *Kollaboration* policy.

When it came to the crucial issue of the Jewish question, Kiesinger took particular care. Obviously, he did not comment on the oppressive measures used against Jews or the Final Solution, but he did stir up anti-Semitic feeling throughout the world. Of course, he had to act appropriately, without making any crudely inaccurate statements.

One of Kiesinger's colleagues, Ernst Otto Dörries, did not understand this method and denounced him to the SS, who kept the letter in his dossier. Kiesinger's concern with striking the right tone in order to optimize the effectiveness of the Nazis' propaganda, however, was shared by the "Germany" Department, the Foreign Office, and the SS.

IN ADDITION TO broadcasts, Kiesinger's department was in charge of disseminating anti-Jewish propaganda to foreign countries via the radio staff at the various German embassies. One of the tasks that Kiesinger carried out particularly well was spreading hatred for the Jews, despite the fact that he pretended not to know what was happening to the Jews in the extermination camps. But he did know. He received "secret" reports on a daily and weekly basis. As part of his job, Kiesinger would have been well aware of the Endlösung, the Final Solution of the "Jewish problem."

And from January 1942, Kiesinger could have heard or read Thomas Mann, who addressed the German people via the BBC and revealed the truth about the concentration camps:

January 1942: *"The news may seem unbelievable, but my source is good. Four hundred young Dutch Jews were deported to Germany to be experimented on with toxic gases . . . They all died."*

September 1942: *"We have now reached the point of annihilation: the insane decision to completely exterminate the Jewish population of Europe."*

IN NOVEMBER 1944, Goebbels enthusiastically agreed to Hans Fritzsche's proposal to bring Kiesinger into the Propaganda Ministry and entrust him with an important position.

Kiesinger, of course, was not a sadistic executioner himself. But the man who incites the sadism of others, who defames a people whom he knows is doomed to destruction, is guilty to an exceptional degree of an exceptional crime.

In May 1945, Kiesinger was taken prisoner by the U.S. Army. After seventeen months of incarceration, he was released at the start of the Cold War and "denazified" by a committee that included his own father-in-law, which nonetheless classified him in the category of Nazis unfit to exercise any political activity. When Kiesinger decided to run for office in Baden-Württemberg, he was obliged to go before his father-in-law's denazification committee once again. After that, his denazification file rather opportunely disappeared.

KURT GEORG KIESINGER, chancellor of the Federal Republic of Germany, lied. He claimed that he joined the Nazi Party only because he hoped, like many other Catholics, to redirect the movement "from within" toward Christian ideals. He stated that, after the bloody elimination of the

SA, or storm troopers, in 1934's Night of the Long Knives, he realized the true nature of Nazism and broke off relations with the Nazis. He specified that he was just a lowly "scientific employee" at the Foreign Office, without any responsibilities.

None of his claims stood up to close scrutiny.

FURTHER DISCOVERIES

As well as the Kiesinger dossier, Serge came back from Germany with information that further strengthened my resolve to be judged by a French court rather than the Youth Office's arbitration committee.

Serge asked the East Germans to check the past of the committee's German judge, and the documents we received left no doubt: Walter Hailer, the man charged with determining the justice of my dismissal, was himself a former Nazi. Ironically, he joined the party on the very same day as Kiesinger, May 1, 1933. His membership number was 3579848.

In 1967, one of the most eminent judges in West Germany and the president of the administrative court of Baden-Württemberg, Walter Hailer had been a regional orator for the Nazi Party and an SA member, with various administrative responsibilities in France and Belgium during the war.

The party's own files for 1936 reveal the official perspective on his capabilities: "Dr. Hailer, thirty-one years old, is considered very favorably . . . No hesitation from a political standpoint." Hailer worked for Franz Six's German Institute for Foreign Studies, which was essentially an espionage organization.

I immediately compiled a dossier on Hailer and sent it to the Élysée Palace and to Jacques Rietsch, the judge appointed by the French government to serve on the Franco-German Youth Office's arbitration committee. Rietsch told me on the phone of his surprise on discovering that his colleague would be expected to judge a case in which he himself was involved.

He was even more surprised when he found out that it was Kiesinger who had appointed Hailer to that position. While he was minister president of Baden-Württemberg, Kiesinger had been asked by the German government to examine the constitution of the Franco-German Youth Office—and had, naturally enough, appointed his friend Hailer to run the arbitration committee.

Alerted by this discovery, I began to wonder if there were other former Nazis in the Youth Office. My instinct proved correct: in the dossier on German criminals at the CDJC, I found the name of Dr. Fritz Rudolf Arlt, who was on the Youth Office's board of directors between 1964 and 1966. I learned that the magazine *Élan* had published an article about Dr. Arlt. I phoned the magazine's editor, Ulrich Sander, who sent me a copy of the article. It was extremely informative.

In 1936, Arlt had written a thesis entitled "Contribution to Racial Psychology," which closely followed the Nazis' racist theories. This brilliant speaker had, "on his own initiative," updated the list of Jews in Leipzig, classified as "full Jews," "three-quarter Jews," "half Jews," and "quarter Jews." This work, which was very useful for the Gestapo's Jewish Affairs Department, provided the basis for Dr. Arlt's next study: "The Ethnological Biology of Leipzig's Jews." With the aid of the SD (the Sicherheitsdienst, the SS's intelligence service, founded and directed by Reinhard Heydrich), Arlt then compiled a list of Silesia's Jews. Arlt was a member of the SS, as well as the Nazi Party. I even discovered later, in the Koblenz state archives, a document from the SD's Jewish Affairs Department that reported: "Dr. Fritz Arlt, a Hebrew specialist, proposed teaching modern Hebrew to members of the SD," enabling them after four weeks of tuition to translate articles from Hebrew. One of his conscientious students was named Eichmann.

But Arlt was no mere theoretician. SS-*Standartenführer* and *Totenkopfträger*—an SS "death's head" colonel—he was notably posted in Katowice, just twenty miles from Auschwitz, as the head of the racial policy department. On November 9, 1941, Heinrich Himmler named him lieutenant colonel in charge of racial questions. In Poland as well as the Soviet Union, Arlt was considered a war criminal.

Arlt resigned from his position as head of the Franco-German Youth Office soon after the publication of the article in *Élan*. There was no scandal. The Youth Office's employees were not informed that one of their superiors had been a Nazi war criminal.

DURING THE WEEKS that followed, I unearthed other former Nazis in the higher echelons of the Youth Office, notably representatives of the Foreign Office: Karl Kuno Overbeck, who was a member of the SA and the policy department of Ribbentrop's ministry, and Luitpold Werz, who was particularly active from 1944 to 1945 in the Inland-Interior II Department, tasked with helping the SS solve the Jewish problem. My dismissal from the Youth Office, then, followed a certain logic. I found out later that the Youth Office had acted under direct pressure from Chancellor Kiesinger's office.

My case was brought to the German parliament on October 11, 1967. During the debate, Mr. Barth, the secretary of state for family and youth, had to answer questions from two Social Democrat deputies:

MR. BRUCK: *Is it true that a secretary from the Franco-German Youth Office was dismissed for criticizing Chancellor Kiesinger?*

SECRETARY OF STATE: *It is true that a secretary from the Youth Office was dismissed following a procedure of which the federal government was informed only after the redundancy letter had been sent by the Youth Office's general secretary.*

MR. BRUCK: *Am I to conclude that the federal government does not approve of this dismissal?*

SECRETARY OF STATE: *It is a complex case. In accordance with the treaty of July 5, 1963, the Youth Office is a bi-governmental, independent body. The federal government is not in a position to exercise influence over its affairs.*

MR. BRUCK: *Could you set out the federal government's position, all the same? I believe that this dismissal is unconstitutional.*

SECRETARY OF STATE: *Once again, while this procedure is ongoing we cannot intervene by giving an opinion.*

MR. FELLERMAIER: *So, once the procedure is complete, is the federal government disposed to outline its own political viewpoint on this matter?*

SECRETARY OF STATE: *Insofar as a political viewpoint can be taken on this particular case, the federal government is disposed to respond after the procedure is complete.*

The federal government never rendered its opinion on the matter.

MY TRIAL BEGAN on February 19, 1968, in the district court of the eighth arrondissement. The previous day, I had phoned about forty journalists, so the French and international press were well represented in the courtroom. There was even a German television crew there.

Le Monde: "Could Mrs. Beate Klarsfeld, a bilingual secretary from the Franco-German Youth Office, be about to lift the lid on Chancellor Kurt Kiesinger's Nazi past?"

And so my message, protesting Kiesinger's Nazi past, reached hundreds of thousands of readers.

THAT DAY, the district court having declared itself incompetent to judge the case, I appealed to the Twenty-First Chamber of the Court of Appeal.

Four months later, on June 18, 1968, the court of appeal confirmed the district court's judgment and sent my case back to the Franco-German Youth Office's arbitration committee. Not only was I not ordered to pay legal fees, but the court demonstrated its sympathy toward me by recommending that the German judge, Walter Hailer, recuse himself, due to the revelation of his Nazi past.

So I was now in the Kafkaesque position of turning to the Youth Office's own arbitration committee for justice—the last legal option open to me. Effectively, by asking the arbitration committee to recuse the German judge, I had to ask Hailer to recuse himself. This is what I did. I also wrote to the French judge, asking him to declare his German counterpart incompetent.

This move—at once desperate and clever—actually worked: in September 1968, Walter Hailer was recused.

This led to a long, complex legal battle that set several precedents. The *Yearbook of the International Law Commission* published two long articles—in 1969 and 1970—about the case and its numerous implications.

In September 1967, soon after my dismissal, I had written to the German justice minister Gustav Heinemann. His secretary of state for justice, Horst Ehmke, wrote to me two months later with some advice that I followed very closely, perhaps more closely than he could have imagined:

> Dear Madame Klarsfeld,
> My personal impression is that an attempt to throw some political light on this complex case would be more likely to prove successful than a protracted legal case or arbitration process.

I realized that he was right: I had to abandon the legal battle and politicize the case in Germany. From that point on, my strategy changed.

A Reunified German

FEBRUARY 1968. The bar of the Bristol hotel is a nerve center for journalists, who come and go from the Franco-German negotiations at the Élysée Palace, returning with news and gossip.

The day ends, and the ministers accompanying Chancellor Kiesinger enter the bar for off-the-record press briefings in a relaxed atmosphere. Franz Josef Strauss, the finance minister, joins the small group of journalists surrounding me. I really dislike Strauss, the tough guy of the German right. It is nearly 9:30 p.m. and he is practically drunk. Strauss willingly answers questions and downs glasses of whiskey. Soon, he is ignoring the journalists' questions and has begun an interminable monologue while holding his head in his hands and staring at the carpet. The son of the German press magnate Axel Springer comes over to tell me that my campaign against Kiesinger is "utterly pointless" and that I should cease talking about his past, as the chancellor has been "democratically elected."

Later that evening, Willy Brandt enters the Bristol's lobby. The journalists rush over to speak to him. He stops in front of the elevators. He is tanned, relaxed, elegantly dressed, very different from the man I met in the summer of 1966. I take the opportunity to remind him about the interview I had requested for *Combat* about his personal memories of living in France before the war. He tells me he will answer my questions soon. He never does.

When the campaign against Kiesinger has grown even more bitter, Brandt's attaché, Mr. Sonksen, will explain to me: "You must understand that Mr. Brandt, as Chancellor Kiesinger's foreign minister and as a member of the coalition, cannot grant you this interview. That would imply that he supported your campaign against Kiesinger."

ON FEBRUARY 14, 1968, I wrote in my regular column for *Combat*:

Europe's democrats should rejoice at the youth rebellion against the resignation, conformism, and culture of consumption. This movement is growing rapidly in the Continent's university towns . . . In the Bundestag, Mr. Kiesinger congratulated the police for their "great patience" in dealing with students, while most newspapers are condemning them [the police] for their excessive brutality . . . Here in France, we should be aware that the battle raging in Germany concerns us all, because one day Germany will be reunified.

It is 9:00 a.m. on March 20, 1968. I have arrived in West Berlin after three weeks spent traveling on my own through the German Democratic Republic. I nervously ring the bell at the house belonging to a theology professor, Dr. Gollwitzer, who is granting asylum to Rudi Dutschke, the leader of the SDS, the radical German student movement. There is no answer.

I keep trying, and at last the door is opened. A girl with disheveled hair looks at me blearily.

"I'm here to see Rudi Dutschke."

"He's asleep, but you can come in."

A few days before this, I had talked to him on the phone, so he knows my name.

The girl calls out, "Beate Klarsfeld is here to see you!"

"Ah, show her in!"

I walk toward the sound of his voice and find myself in a living room with a sofa bed at its center. The blinds are drawn, so it is difficult to see very much. My eyes gradually adjust to the dimness, and I make out Rudi, who is still in bed. Next to him is his wife, Gretel, and between them their baby, Che, still only a few weeks old.

Rudi props himself up on an elbow. He is very natural, direct. Just as he is in public life, when speaking onstage. He has a natural charisma.

I invite him to take part in a meeting I am organizing in Paris: "Young Germans and young Jews joining forces to combat the neo-Nazis." He tells me he would like to, but it is possible he'll have to go to Prague soon, because the situation is growing tense there, so it is not certain that he'll be able to make it to Paris in time for the meeting.

Rudi is very different from the other members of the SDS I have met in recent days. Behind their long hair, flamboyant clothes, and loudly proclaimed sexual freedom, Rudi's friends speak in a convoluted vocabulary of theoretical ideas that barely masks the shallowness of their thinking. They also treat the movement's many young female followers with sexist contempt.

Rudi, by contrast, is clear and precise. He is a leader. With his intelligence, dynamism, and talent for speaking, he could probably have made a comfortable living, but Rudi is not a product of the West German consumer society. He is in exile here from East Germany, where he fought against the excesses of dogmatism. In the West, he has continued to attack the fundamental flaws of the society in which he lives. With charisma and hard work, he has succeeded in making the students of Berlin—and then of Germany—the most politicized in Europe.

MY ACCUSATIONS AGAINST the chancellor had not, up to this point, created the impact I was hoping for in the mainstream French and German press. Every time I went to a newspaper office with my thick dossier in my arms, the journalists and editors all responded in the same way: "Yes, yes, that's very interesting, but what can we do? He's already chancellor!"

It was time to switch tactics. Deciding to draw on the ingenious methods used by Rudi Dutschke's friends, I went to visit Kommune 1, a group of young men and women who proved themselves expert at using humor to mobilize public opinion. For example, they announced that students were about to block traffic on the Kurfürstendamm, a major street in the center of Berlin. Vast numbers of police were deployed and traffic was rerouted. And then a student—just one student, all alone—proudly marched down the deserted avenue.

I'd spent a long time thinking about the best way to ensure maximum press exposure and begun to realize that my dossiers would only have the impact I desired if I could accompany them with some sort of grand gesture. I decided to go to the Bundestag on a day when I knew Kiesinger was due to speak. Arriving in Bonn on March 30, I found a photographer from the German press agency DPA and told him about my plan.

At the Bundestag, I left my coat in the cloakroom and went up to the seats reserved for the public, opposite the lectern where the politicians spoke. I was at the end of a row of seats guarded by ushers. Soon after my arrival, Kiesinger took the stage. This was the first time I had seen him in the flesh. I did not take much notice of his features or his facial expressions. To my mind, a person—particularly a person with an important role in public life—is the sum of their actions, and their physical appearance or private personality means nothing to me.

Of Kiesinger, all I would say is that he was a tall, handsome man of about sixty-five years old (though he looked ten years younger), silver haired, intelligent eyes, the very image of the respectable father figure, with just a hint of sexual attractiveness. As for the private man, this interested me even less than the physical man: I knew that Kiesinger was an irreproachable husband and father who loved animals and once even took his boat out on Lake Constance to rescue a drowning dog. All of this was honorable and might conceivably have given me pause had I taken it into account. But I didn't. If there is one thing I feel certain about, it is that there is no connection between the morality of a man's private behavior and of his public acts.

I had decided to shout at the German chancellor in the middle of his parliamentary speech, but now that I was here, in this large, packed room, I feared I would not have the courage to open my mouth. I watched the clock in the hall and told myself that I had to act before the second hand reached the 12. I stared anxiously as the hand kept moving around the face of the clock. Then suddenly, raising my fists, I yelled very loudly: "Kiesinger, Nazi, resign!" Once I had started to chant this, it was easy to keep going.

The chancellor stopped speaking. Even from afar, I could tell he was disturbed. He looked over in my direction, as did all the deputies in the hall. Meanwhile, the ushers ran toward me. One of them clasped his hand over my mouth and brutally shoved me out of the room and into a small office.

I refused to disclose my identity, and they brought me to the nearest police station. Only there did I agree to answer questions. The chief of police, who had heard about me, ordered a policeman to fetch my suitcase from the baggage locker where I had left it. He detained me for three hours before letting me go.

The next day, the German newspapers published photographs of me raising my fist (which pleased the left) or of my being gagged by an usher (which suggested that the truth was suppressed in Germany). And, naturally, all the papers discussed Kiesinger's Nazi past and the dossier that I had put together. Serge—in Sofia that day on business—saw my photograph on the front page of Bulgaria's most important newspaper. The wall of silence was crumbling.

ON APRIL 11, 1968, three weeks after our encounter, Rudi Dutschke was shot in the head several times at point-blank range. He spent weeks in a coma and was unable to speak for a long time. He survived but was marginalized from German political life, and twelve years later he died from health problems caused by his injuries. His attacker was supposedly a loner, a madman. But there were swastikas in his house, SS badges, a bust of Hitler. This assassination attempt was the fruit of a hate campaign against Dutschke led by Axel Springer's newspapers and by politicians like Kiesinger.

It was the first time a young person had been able to create a movement in Germany, and his enemies realized the danger he represented. Unfortunately, the attack had the desired effect: after Rudi's shooting, the far-left youth movement became rudderless and divided.

The day after the shooting, Germany was in turmoil. Students raised barricades in the streets of Berlin, Hamburg, Hanover, Essen, and Cologne.

The Springer Trust's buildings came under siege. There were violent clashes with police.

I felt close to those young people. Rudi's shooting was proof that his theories were well founded: in Germany, the real danger lay on the right. The day before, Kiesinger had vehemently attacked Dutschke; now, he sent a hypocritical telegram to Rudi's wife, expressing his sympathy. In reality, though, he was gleefully rubbing his hands together, and he was not the only one. I drew from this tragedy just another reason to continue my battle against Kiesinger.

I HAD BEEN in a meeting with some young Germans in Paris that April when we found out about the shooting of Rudi Dutschke. That night, we decided to organize a protest march. The French student leader Alain Krivine promised us his support. He and his followers took charge of printing leaflets. At home, I made banners.

We protested outside the German embassy, where I was surprised to find a thousand students—and a dozen riot-police buses waiting on the opposite sidewalk. There were red flags everywhere. It was still only April, but this was the first sign of the coming convulsion of May 1968.

The students chanted, "Springer, murderer!" A few French students carried signs proclaiming: KIESINGER—NAZI. I was very surprised by this. Was my campaign beginning to bear fruit?

After brief speeches by the leftist leaders Krivine and Cohn-Bendit, the protest was supposed to end, but through word of mouth everyone headed to the Latin Quarter. When we got there, we were greeted by droves of heavily armed riot police. I gave my banners to a German student, who—frightened by this show of force—hid them in a doorway and ran off.

There were a few clashes with the riot police, but for me that was not the important thing. Violence only diverted attention from the political meaning of our actions. It should, I believed, only be used as a last resort and always against those who were actually guilty.

OUR MEETINGS BEGAN attracting larger numbers of students, a fact that did not go unnoticed by the French police. One evening, a student told us that he had seen two men outside the door, dressed like laborers, who kept coming and going and staring at the passersby. We leaned out the window and saw them doing this: they would move about fifty yards away, then quickly return.

One night, most of the Germans who came to our Paris meetings were contacted by phone. An urgent meeting was arranged at the apartment where we usually gathered. When the students showed up, they were greeted by the police, who took them to the station for two or three days and then sent them back to Germany.

In the meantime, I learned that some young activists from the APO (Außerparlamentansche Opposition), a political protest movement, had, during an electoral meeting in Baden-Württemberg, occupied two-thirds of the room and chanted "Kiesinger Nazi, Nazi!" To placate them, the chancellor had declared: "You are young. You never knew Nazism. You have the right to know what your chancellor did during that period." He did not keep that promise.

That same month—April 1968—I also attended a meeting in a large public square in Esslingen, Germany. I took with me three huge suitcases stuffed with pamphlets. One of the students at the meeting told me that I could speak if I wished. I had not prepared anything, but I decided to do it anyway, so I stood in line for an hour.

When my turn came, however, I panicked. That huge square, all those people, all the things I had to say . . . I introduced myself, explained my campaign. I started talking about Kiesinger's past. I probably went on too long. People started losing interest. I announced that I would be distributing leaflets.

Afterward, I rushed to the car and asked two guys to help me distribute the leaflets and handed one of them my precious Kiesinger dossier for a moment. When I turned around, they were gone. They had fled, taking my documents with them. I went back to the microphone and appealed for help; I searched everywhere, to no avail. Were those men right-wing activists or just ordinary thieves? I never found out. Furious, I returned to Berlin.

IN BERLIN, I went to see Günter Grass to invite him to take part in a meeting. He welcomed me into his ivy-covered house, and he let me talk for a while. Then he said, "I don't really want to speak in that kind of environment. For some time now, I have been scandalized by the behavior of those students." He only agreed when I pointed out to him that it was a group of Jewish students whom I wanted him to address.

Subtly, insinuatingly, he asked me about my life, before declaring, "You live in Paris. You sent me a letter with the translation of one of your articles. I advise you to read more in German, because you are losing your native language. You have become very French. It is obvious that you live abroad and that you no longer speak much German."

Everything in his attitude and his tone revealed a man well aware of his undeniable intellectual superiority. And yet, with his wonderful novels, he had helped to liberate German youth of many of its taboos and cultural constraints. His commitment to social democracy had made him, at that time, along with the great Catholic novelist Heinrich Böll, the most famous and talked-about writer in Germany, part of the nation's conscience.

The meeting took place on May 9 in Berlin. With Serge's help, I had carefully prepared my speech. Nearly three thousand students—many of them long haired and bearded—had gathered in the large auditorium of the Technical University.

Günter Grass's speech, strongly attacking Kiesinger, was met with passionate enthusiasm. The tone was set. When my turn came, I was propelled to the microphone.

I told the audience that we had to keep escalating our protest. "To break the wall of silence around Kiesinger's Nazi past, I give you my word today, that I will slap the chancellor in public." The reaction was lively and skeptical. There were shouts of "Naïve!" "Stupid!" "Do it if you dare!" One group chanted, "Promises, promises!"

Günter Grass, who was next to me, did not react at all.

After the speeches, the students were invited to speak. One of them addressed Günter Grass: "Mr. Grass, your words are all very fine, but tomorrow you will be able to show your hostility to the Christian Democrats by coming with us to protest the emergency laws. Are you ready to participate in our great protest march on Bonn—but not by getting there in comfort, on an airplane? You should take the train, sitting on the hard second-class benches, surrounded by students from all over Germany!"

Günter Grass stood up, red-faced with anger. He rushed over to the microphone and yelled, "How insolent, talking to me like that! What does it matter if I take the train or the plane? If that's how it is, I won't go tomorrow." He knocked over his chair, grabbed his papers, and abruptly left the room, to hisses and boos.

A resolution calling on Kiesinger to resign was voted for by three-quarters of the room. It made the headlines in the East German and West German press. I had taken the risk of publicly announcing my intention to slap Kiesinger because I wanted to give the act a premeditated, symbolic quality. I chose the slap after a great deal of thought; that gesture, I sensed, would make a strong impression on the German people.

The next evening—May 10—I caught a train to Bonn for the *Sternmarsch*, the "Star March." The plan was for anti-fascists to converge on the capital the following day to protest the coming vote for the emergency laws that would establish a form of dictatorship by the chancellor in the event of mass violence. The train had been made available by the East German government, and it left the Friedrichstrasse station in East Berlin filled with eight hundred young people—the oldest was maybe thirty—dressed in velvet pants or blue jeans and long green anoraks. Rucksacks and motorcycle helmets were piled up in the nets above the seats.

The protesters proved just as critical of the East German regime as they were of the West Germans. As they went through the stations of the GDR, they yelled slogans like "Bureaucracy leads to fascism and Stalinism!" and "Citizens, stop watching us, come and join us!" while the East Germans stared at them openmouthed with disbelief. Another frequently shouted slogan was "Kiesinger Nazi!"

We entered Bonn at about 8:00 a.m. on May 11, and the law-abiding citizens of Bonn looked just as horrified as their Communist counterparts had been. The Star March was a complete success. The organizers had expected forty thousand protesters, and about sixty thousand ended up parading peacefully through the streets of the capital.

The next day, the barricades went up in Paris. This was the start of the famous May 1968 protests. I set up a Franco-German action committee at the Sorbonne, but it soon became clear to me that the French students were not interested in Germany's problems. And yet, to my mind, the stakes were much higher in Germany than in the streets of Paris.

In *Combat*, on May 4, I wrote, "We must not let the German democrats fight alone. We must help the Social Democratic Party to leave the coalition government and become, once again, the party of hope and honesty . . .

Don't confine the making of history to your own doorstep. Lift up your heads and look clear-eyed at what is actually happening in Europe. Germany needs you."

ON MAY 29, I and a half-dozen others occupied the offices of the Franco-German Youth Office. We got there at 6:00 p.m., three minutes before the arrival of the police, who, in the absence of instructions, withdrew. We asked the employees to leave and hung three huge banners from the windows: FRANCO-GERMAN YOUTH OFFICE OCCUPIED; NO TO THE EMERGENCY LAWS IN GERMANY; FRENCH STUDENTS AND WORKERS IN SOLIDARITY WITH GERMAN STUDENTS AND WORKERS.

Mr. Clément, the director of the French section of the Youth Office, made no attempt to oppose the occupation. The riot police turned up for a second time later that night but disappeared after discussions. I even went down to their bus: they were asking the Ministry of the Interior for instructions on the police radio, but the government seemed unsure what to do. My former colleagues were outraged at the sight of me taking over the offices where I used to sit quietly typing. They were hoping to see me arrested, but it never happened. We withdrew peacefully after twenty-four hours.

The Slap

SUNDAY, NOVEMBER 3, 1968, late afternoon. I walk out of Bahnhof Zoo, the train station in West Berlin. As he waved goodbye to me the previous night at the Gare du Nord in Paris, Serge had been smiling optimistically, but he couldn't hide his anxiety. I have come here to keep my promise. My mother-in-law tried to dissuade me: "You're right, but you could get killed; the police might think it's an assassination attempt."

I wrote and tape-recorded, in French and German, a declaration intended to explain the significance of my action in case I was no longer able to articulate it myself:

> By slapping Chancellor Kiesinger, I wanted to demonstrate that
> part of the German people—its youth in particular—is horrified
> by the presence at the head of the government of the Federal

Republic of Germany of a Nazi who was once assistant director of Hitler's foreign propaganda machine . . .

We do not want that Germany anymore, and Germans who played a leading role in the Third Reich should not be allowed to participate in German political life.

I immediately notice the heavy police presence in the city. At the Republican Club, the headquarters of the student movement, the atmosphere is gloomy. They had planned a major protest, but there are too many police to make that possible, they complain.

The massed ranks of police do not intimidate me, however. It is easier for a young woman to discover the chink in their defenses than it is for a large battalion to do so. I will pass through them, and I will defeat them precisely because I am alone, because I am an individual.

That night, I sleep in a student commune for the first time. The two-story suburban house is surrounded by a large, overgrown yard. A family with one child and two other young couples live on the two main floors; I am lodged in the cellar, which has been converted into an apartment that is well heated and with running water. It is a good place to stay, in spite of the train I have to catch every morning and evening.

"DID YOU SAY COMBAT?"

The secretary frowns as she searches through her records. She does not find my name, obviously. Am I really going to have to turn around and leave after getting through three police checks to reach the press office?

"Could you show me your press card? I have to consult my boss."

The card that Serge gave me is an expired ORTF card, with his photograph replaced by mine.

The secretary returns, smiling and polite: "Unfortunately, we're full up this morning. Too many journalists."

What now? I must find a way to get close to Kiesinger.

ONE OF THE student leaders suggests that I attend a large protest in support of Horst Mahler on Monday morning. Mahler is a young lawyer who is being tried for taking part in the looting of Springer's Berlin offices. He risks being expelled from the bar.

The atmosphere in the streets of Berlin changes as I approach the courthouse. Both camps are agitated. Less than thirty minutes later, the violence erupts. Three thousand students are massed around the courthouse. The riot police move in, and the first Molotov cocktails are thrown. "Get out of here!" calls a young woman in a helmet, gripping the back of a motorcycle as it jumps the curb.

This clash will be one of the most violent ever seen between German students and police, with more than a hundred students and a similar number of police injured.

Sirens scream and tear-gas bombs explode. I get past the police blockade and, on a street corner, hear a young man calling my name. I recognize Reinhard, who came to Paris a few months ago. He leads me into a nearby café. I remind him of the promise I made six months before to slap the chancellor in public, and we talk about the difficulty of getting into the party congress. "You need a photographer," Reinhard suggests. "That way, you'll have a card to get in, and they'll get a great picture of the slap."

He gives me the name of a freelance photographer who works for *Stern* magazine. I call this man—Michael—right away, and we meet that afternoon in his small apartment-cum-darkroom. After hearing me out, he says, "I'm with you. I'll ask my magazine to arrange for an invitation."

The first opportunity is a party being given in the chancellor's honor, at the Hilton Hotel. Good thing I brought a cocktail dress with me.

THE HOTEL IS just as heavily protected as the party congress was, but the invitation card that Michael gave me works wonders. I pass without difficulty through three security checks outside and then through the final check at the entrance to the party. The room is already quite full. On the tables are mountains of caviar on toast, baskets full of little sandwiches. I'm so nervous, I can't even swallow a piece of sausage.

I am not afraid of what might happen to me but of failure—of wasting this opportunity. I try to avoid thinking about the danger. I already feel uneasy enough, knowing that everyone will soon be staring at me. For now, I concentrate on my objective; I try to work out a battle plan, but decide in the end that I will simply have to improvise.

I mingle with a group of journalists, tensing up at the thought that one of them might recognize me. In the hubbub of conversation, I overhear someone standing close to me: "Such a shame. Kiesinger's caught such a bad case of flu that he won't be coming tonight."

It takes me a few minutes to recover my composure, then I run to the Bahnhof Zoo and phone Serge to tell him of my disappointment. The confidence he has in me is absolute, much stronger than my own. Whenever I doubt, it is toward him that I turn. In his eyes or in his voice, I recognize the woman I aspire to be.

ON WEDNESDAY, I go to Michael's apartment to pick up a new card. Kiesinger will speak to his "dear Berliners" tonight at a huge beer hall called the Neue Welt. Around the bar, metal barriers are stretched across the sidewalks. Cars maneuver slowly between barbed-wire stanchions. Police in helmets, wielding long clubs and shields, stand at strategic positions. Riot vans equipped with water cannons are parked in the neighboring streets.

We reach the bar in Michael's car, with the press sticker on his windshield clearing our way. At the final security check, I cling to Michael's arm. They wave us through.

Inside the bar, I am greeted by a reporter, who has interviewed me several times before. "So it's true? You're going to keep your promise?" I beg him to be discreet.

When I see the stage, my determination turns again to bitter disappointment. Kiesinger and his colleagues are sitting behind a table perched on a platform more than six feet high. The two side entrances are guarded by burly security staff.

I think about going up onto the stage, but soon realize that only photographers have access. So I ask Michael if I can borrow one of his cameras. Once I have it in hand, I rush toward the platform, but my way is barred by two guards.

"Your photographer's ID?"

"I don't have it."

They shove me away, and for the next two hours I watch this meeting in a cold rage. The room is full of Christian Democrat supporters, and the atmosphere is feverish. Everything Kiesinger says is met with loud applause and chanted anti-socialist slogans. If I slapped the chancellor in a place like this, I might be lynched. Once again, the opportunity slips through my fingers.

ONLY ONE CHANCE remains. On Thursday morning, at the closing ceremony of the Christian Democrats' party congress.

The day does not start well. Around 9:00 a.m., the photographer tells me he has not been able to obtain an invitation. Even so, he agrees to help me get through the three exterior security checks in his car. We cannot go any farther than this for the moment. He leaves me in the parking lot, hiding in the car.

We have agreed that he will go inside to assess the deployment of security staff and to check on the atmosphere of the room. He will come back as soon as he can to let me know.

The minutes drag by. My fingers and feet are frozen. It has been twenty minutes. What if he doesn't return before the meeting ends? I think about getting out of the car and trying to get through the last security check on my own.

Am I really going to fail again, so close to my goal? I am on edge. Finally, I see him weaving his way between the parked cars.

HE WALKS AHEAD of me, his camera straps hanging from his shoulders. The guards have just seen him leave, and they let him in without checking his pass again. I casually show them a corner of the green press card. I take off my brown coat, which is decorated with a large cross of Lorraine, and leave it in the cloakroom. I am wearing a red skirt with a thick belt and a white turtleneck sweater. I take a pen and a notepad from my purse. Now I look like a journalist.

The vast room is packed. To Michael's relief, I give him back his card.

Margot Kalinke, the social affairs spokeswoman, is giving a speech. No one seems to be listening. On the stage behind her are the president of the meeting and some high-ranking Christian Democrats. Below them, level with the rest of the room, is a long table covered with a white cloth and several vases of flowers. Chancellor Kiesinger sits in the center of a row of ministers. He is writing something; perhaps he is working on the speech he will give an hour later.

There is no space remaining on the press benches, where about three hundred journalists are gathered. I walk down the aisle on the right-hand side of the room. I move forward slowly, pausing every five or six steps to listen to the speech and to take notes.

When I reach Kiesinger's table, I realize it is much wider than it appeared from above. There is no way I will be able to lean across and reach the chancellor. For a few seconds, I hesitate. At each end of the table are two or three guards. I approach one of them, holding up my notebook. I have to improvise.

Suddenly looking up, I pretend to wave at someone on the other side of the table. Then, trying to sound natural, I say to the guard, "My friend's over there. Could I get past?"

He looks uncertain. "It's not a passageway." When I ask again, he tells me more firmly, "Go around the outside. You can't come through here."

I remain in the same spot and smile a few times at my imaginary friend. Tugging at my sleeve, the guard says, "All right, you can go, but make it quick." I walk behind the row of politicians.

As I come up behind Kiesinger, he senses my presence and turns slightly toward me. Suddenly, my nervousness evaporates. I've made it! Shouting "Nazi! Nazi!" I slap him hard as I move past, without even seeing the expression on his face.

After that, all I remember is Bruno Heck, the minister of family affairs and youth, grabbing me around the waist. Behind me, I hear Kiesinger ask, "Is that Klarsfeld?"

I am pushed toward an exit. Before being led away, I have time to hear the room erupt. All the deputies have stood up and are moving chaotically toward the platform. Journalists run through the aisles.

My mind goes blank. I tell myself: I did it! I did it!

I am escorted through corridors and up stairs. The people we pass stare in surprise. One of the policemen holding my arms (and kicking me in the calves as we walk) keeps repeating, in a tone of outrage, "She slapped the chancellor! She slapped the chancellor!"

We enter an office. A policeman writes down my name. "Ah, it's you," he says. "I saw your leaflets in the Kurfürstendamm."

Ernst Lemmer, the chancellor's Berlin representative, comes into the office. As a Reichstag deputy in 1933, he voted to give Hitler full powers. Later, a Nazi propagandist, he glorified the Third Reich in more than two thousand articles. He stands in front of me, leaning on his cane, and says in a seemingly paternal tone, "Listen, my dear child. What good could it do to slap our chancellor?"

"I cannot stand the fact that an ex-Nazi can become chancellor. I slapped him to draw attention to this and to let the whole world know that there are Germans who refuse this shame."

Lemmer leaves the room shaking his head. In the doorway, he turns back and says, "I could be your grandfather."

A few steps later, he gives some journalists his personal opinion on the matter: "This woman, who could be pretty if she weren't so pale, is sexually frustrated." Two weeks later, *Stern* magazine, after printing this quote, publishes a letter of apology from Lemmer: "When I made that remark, I didn't know that Mrs. Klarsfeld was married, with a child, and that her father-in-law died at Auschwitz."

Plainclothes policemen take me out through a secret exit, avoiding the main entrance, which will undoubtedly be surrounded by journalists. We walk through a vast basement, where I am stunned to see a small army of riot police, and come out by one of the side doors. I am shoved into a police car. A few photographers rush over. I see Michael, who makes a V-for-victory sign. He must have gotten a good shot of the slap, I think.

The *Polizeipräsidium* is located in a large building that is part of the Tempelhof Airport, in the center of Berlin. Two detectives interrogate me in detail and make an official report. Then they give me a meal of sausages and potato salad in the cafeteria and allow me to make a phone call. I call Serge at his office, but he's not there. At home, my mother-in-law answers. "He's on his way back here. He called me. He's beside himself. He said, 'I knew she'd do it!' He's going to catch a plane this afternoon. He'll be in Berlin tonight. What should he take for you in case you have to stay in prison?"

I knew Serge would come. I feel certain that nothing bad can happen to me if he is there, and this conviction is strengthened by the strange co-incidence that today is our fifth wedding anniversary.

I also call the office of Horst Mahler, the radical young lawyer. He's not there, but I leave a message. When Mahler arrives, around 3:30 p.m.,

I am taken to another office. The policeman leaves us alone. The first words Mahler speaks to me—in a whisper, in case there are hidden microphones in the room—are "It's wonderful, what you did. Wonderful!"

I realize at this moment that my action will receive the total backing of the German student movement. I am not on my own anymore. Mahler and I spend about twenty minutes working out the key points of my defense.

In the meantime, a courtroom has been reserved and a young prosecutor summoned urgently to the police station. We share a car to the district courthouse, the Amtsgericht Tiergarten. We wait around for half an hour before an usher announces that, given the late hour, the trial will be delayed until the following day.

Back at the police station, I leave my personal belongings at the reception desk, and two policemen escort me to a cell for the night. A female warden tosses me a rough nightgown and some sheets.

The barred door opens and shuts behind me. I am in prison. I make my bed on the wooden plank that folds out from the wall. I lie down and try to remember every detail of the day. Suddenly, the cell door opens and a voice says, "Come now. Your lawyer is waiting for you."

Mahler looks outraged. "They're going to try you immediately. There are several hundred students outside the courthouse. Most of the seats inside have been taken by plainclothes policemen, so only about a dozen journalists have been able to get in."

I KEEP WORRYING that my skirt will fall down, because I had to leave my belt at the reception desk. I am cold, so I put my coat over my shoulders.

I am locked inside a small cage. In front of me, Neelsen, the prosecutor, summarizes the facts of the case. He can't be more than thirty-two. Whenever he utters the words "Chancellor Kiesinger," he sounds so respectful that I keep expecting him to stand up and bow.

I learn that Kiesinger, whose first reaction was to minimize the incident—"I don't press charges against ladies who strike me"—has been pressured into changing his mind by his colleagues. He signed the orders in his car while he was on his way to Tempelhof Airport for the flight back to Bonn.

The prosecutor talks for a long time, in a monotone. He sounds bored and keeps flicking his hair back with his left hand while his right hand makes little whirling motions.

For several months, Mahler has been wearing a suit and turtleneck to work, in protest against the class-based justice system. But he says he wouldn't have worn his robes for this trial, even if he'd had them in his suitcase: "This rushed trial is unworthy."

The prosecutor's first witness is Police Chief Samstag, head of the chancellor's security during the congress.

"What did you see?" the prosecutor asks.

"I saw the accused as she approached the chancellor's table. I noticed that she wasn't wearing a delegate's badge, but she was holding a notepad. A few minutes before this, the chancellor had signed autographs for members of the public. So, given that a member of the security staff had exchanged a few words with the accused and let her pass, I wasn't too concerned when I saw her walk behind the row of ministers."

The superintendent adds a detail that I had preferred not to dwell on beforehand: "The chancellor was heavily protected. There were six armed bodyguards in the room. One of them had already grabbed his gun, but he couldn't shoot because the accused was blocked by the chancellor and the other ministers."

My lawyer demands that Kiesinger be cited as a witness, given that he is claiming he is the victim of "assault and battery."

"That is a ploy to have the trial delayed," Judge Drygalla replies. So Mahler demands that the judge step down, as he is "partisan."

The judge declares, "The court rejects the defense's request, which is designed simply to adjourn the trial."

The prosecutor stands: "We must bear in mind that a representative of our country's government was attacked and proceed to judgment without delay. I ask for a one-year mandatory prison term and a warrant for immediate arrest, otherwise this woman will just hop on the S-Bahn and flee to East Germany. Let me remind you that the accused went to Potsdam to find the documentation she used in her leaflet."

Judge Drygalla remains coolly courteous to me throughout the trial. He does not interrupt me once, not even when I exclaim, "Your expedited trial is very similar to the way the Nazis did things." My defense is that the slap was symbolic, so there was no intention to cause physical harm to the chancellor.

The prosecutor responds, "Must we really point out that a slap in the face is an unpleasant experience? The court does not need proof or the victim's direct testimony to demonstrate that he suffered physical and psychological harm from this slap. Moreover, the victim's identity plays a role in this case that must not be neglected when you pronounce your verdict for a severe prison sentence."

Before retiring to deliberate, the judge says something that worries me: "Germany has already been the theater of violent political conflict, and history later reproached the Weimar Republic for not putting an end to the troubles that confronted it when it had the opportunity."

The verdict is delivered a few minutes later: "One year in prison. The reasons for the verdict to be published in six national newspapers, costs to be paid by the defendant." This would cost me more than fifty thousand marks, a year's salary back then.

Even Mahler, who is used to harsh verdicts, looks shocked. I feel an iron fist closing around my chest, stopping my breath. I cannot believe it. A year, cut off from the world, without seeing Arno or Serge?

I barely hear Mahler as he says, "Do you want to say anything to the court? Don't worry, we'll appeal this, of course."

"I can't go to prison! You have to do something!"

Then rage takes hold of me as I address the judge. "I am outraged by this verdict. A year ago, a former Nazi beat Rudi Dutschke over the head with a steel-tipped cane and was given a fine of two hundred marks." I am panting. With a great effort, I control myself. "And you, you condemn me to a year in prison for slapping a public figure. Well, I think Rudi Dutschke is a public figure, just like Chancellor Kiesinger."

The judge replies, "I am not aware of that case."

Unable to stop myself, I play my last card. "I would ask you to bear in mind that I am a French citizen through my marriage. If you send me to prison, I will ask my lawyer to urgently contact the French governor in Berlin and to see with him if I can be judged under French jurisdiction in Berlin. Maybe in West Berlin, my French nationality will be more important than my West German nationality."

I am touching here on one of the most sensitive areas in the relationship between the Federal Republic and West Berlin. The last thing Bonn wants is the intervention of an occupying power, particularly in a delicate case like this one.

My argument clearly has the desired effect. The judge and his assessors look deeply embarrassed. They leave the room without suspending the trial. This tactic, which Serge developed before my departure from Paris, has hit the mark. When the judge returns, he announces that my sentence is suspended. I am free to go.

I LEAVE THE courtroom flanked by Horst Mahler and a journalist. It is past eight at night. We head directly for the large auditorium at the Free University of Berlin, where several thousand students have been waiting for the past hour.

We are greeted by explosive applause.

I take the stage and ask people to take advantage of the unusual situation I have provoked by intensifying the anti-Kiesinger campaign throughout the country.

Mahler goes next, declaring angrily, "This verdict is unprecedented in the annals of justice in West Berlin."

Some students demand the judge's name, and a few days later I find out through the press that unknown persons have smashed Judge Drygalla's apartment windows by throwing bricks through them, each one wrapped in the *Stern* front page showing the photograph of the chancellor being slapped.

I am taken to a press conference hastily organized by the Republican Club. While I am replying to journalists' questions there, Serge suddenly appears. I am so happy to see him that I rush into his arms, unembarrassed by all the press gathered around us.

IT WAS THE following morning that I realized we had won. Our friends from the commune handed us several newspapers as we ate breakfast. All the front pages were devoted to the slap ("Ohrfeige für den Kanzler"— "She Slapped the Chancellor"), illustrated by powerful images: the chancellor, holding his hand to his face or looking cross a moment later, in sunglasses to cover the red mark near his eye; me, in my cross of Lorraine coat, surrounded by policemen; or in the Bundestag, fist raised, yelling at Kiesinger.

That slap, that last-minute victory, freed thousands of young Germans from the frustrations of a three-day period when all their protests ended in violent clashes with riot police.

Although the newspapers carried the chancellor's spin on events—that I was connected to the student "hooligans" rioting in German cities and that I was wildly obsessed with the chancellor—more space was given to my real motives: Kiesinger's Nazi past and the German youth's refusal to accept such a man as their leader.

Ultimately, no one really believed the story that I was a "hysterical woman," because in the past two years I had written and spoken rationally and consistently on this subject.

In Paris, only a few minutes after my hand had made contact with the chancellor's cheek, Serge was already firing off a press release that contextualized the act: "In slapping Chancellor Kiesinger, my wife was carrying out an act that had been carefully thought out in advance and was intended to highlight the chancellor's Nazi past."

But the crime of lèse-majesté was only one part of the story in that day's newspapers. There was also the scandal of the initial verdict: one year in prison.

These two elements were the subjects of a heated national debate for weeks afterward, in the opinion columns of newspapers but also on their letters pages. There were those who approved of my act and disapproved of the sentence; those who criticized the act and the sentence; those who disapproved of the act and approved of the sentence. Everyone in Germany seemed to take part in this argument, from the man in the street to two of the country's greatest writers: Günter Grass and Heinrich Böll. Even children talked about it: that slap seemed to question the sacrosanct nature of political authority. Should the chancellor be respected because he is the chancellor or because he is a man worthy of respect?

One *Bild* reader said that I deserved to be punished even more severely: "She not only slapped the chancellor, she publicly offended our entire people."

In *Stern*, Wolfgang Ebert wrote: "If what you want to touch is not the man but the position of chancellor, a slap is the only effective method. It possesses a certain symbolic force, probably because the head is considered the noblest part of our body."

Sebastian Haffner, a columnist for the same magazine, wrote that I had broken an old social code: "A slap has traditionally been used to provoke a duel . . . But that is valid only for men. Women's liberation has not changed anything. A woman cannot seek a duel. According to the ancient code of honor, a woman can only slap a man in order to reject his sexual advances."

The widely circulated newspaper *Süddeutsche Zeitung* wrote that "The underlying motive of this struggle led with fanatical obstinacy by B.K., a miniterrorist in a miniskirt, is the favorite dream of all preachers of the truth, denounced by Machiavelli nearly five hundred years ago: the demand that the founding principle of politics is to elevate morality. B.K. demands this morality, without concessions or compromises. An inner force compelled her to give Kurt Georg Kiesinger the slap that was heard around the world."

ON THE OTHER side of the Wall, meanwhile, in East Germany, the mood was one of jubilation. The press was unanimous: "The courageous B.K., in the name of millions of victims, symbolically slapped the old Nazi Kiesinger"; "For the death of a Jew, one day in prison. For a slap, one year." Incidentally, November 7, the day of the slap, was also the anniversary of the Bolshevik Revolution in 1917.

When we arrived in Frankfurt on Saturday morning, I discovered that almost all of the foreign newspapers had given considerable space to the incident, too, despite the fact that Richard Nixon had just been elected president of the United States.

IN WEST GERMANY, meanwhile, center stage in the debate was taken by Günter Grass and Heinrich Böll.

The day I got back to Paris, thirty-six hours after the slap, I received a bouquet of red roses. On the card was written: "Thank you—Heinrich Böll." I felt simultaneously like laughing and crying. Böll, the famous novelist who was so sensitive to human warmth, to the simplest and most powerful feelings of humanity, approved of me.

A few days later, at a speech given for the Ossietzky Prize ceremony, Günter Grass declared:

> No one wanted to see that every day Kiesinger spent as chancellor was a slap in the face for the victims of Nazism [. . .] so a young

woman came from Paris and slapped the chancellor. What rational arguments had not achieved—i.e., front-page news—an irrational act did.

There is no reason to lend Kurt Georg Kiesinger a pair of sunglasses, nor to send roses to Beate Klarsfeld. As much as I am opposed to the presence in the Chancellery of a man who was a Nazi from 1933 to 1945, I am equally intransigent in my opposition to slaps or similar acts of heroism.

A slap is not an argument. A slap devalues the arguments. Kiesinger does not deserve to be slapped; what he deserves is to be asked, always, the same question: "Are you aware that your Nazi past is not only a stain on your term as chancellor, but also on the Federal Republic?"

Heinrich Böll replied powerfully in a column in *Die Zeit* entitled "Flowers for Beate Klarsfeld":

In a magisterial tone, Günter Grass declares that there is no reason to send roses to Beate Klarsfeld. But this declaration seems to me rather presumptuous and annoying. In fact, given its high-handed tone, I would say it is completely inappropriate. I wonder, in all modesty, if it is really Günter Grass's place to judge whether or not I have the right to send flowers to a lady. Well, the answer is that I do have the right, and I am ready to defend it against anyone, no matter how magisterial. I sent those flowers to Beate Klarsfeld for the following reasons:

1. As a logical conclusion to my activities as a writer, whether significant or not.
2. As a personal debt, from a man of fifty-one, who was only fifteen when Hitler was brought into power by the bourgeois politician Von Papen.
3. In memory of my mother, who died in November 1944 during a bomb attack, and who brought together a rare combination of qualities: intelligence, naïvety, instinctiveness, a fiery temper, and a sense of humor! It was she who taught me to hate the Nazis, particularly the kind of Nazi represented by

Mr. Kiesinger: those bourgeois Nazis who do not get their hands dirty, and who have continued, since 1945, to stroll shamelessly through German public life.

4. On behalf of my generation: those who were killed, and those who survived, including all those who cannot allow themselves to send flowers to Mrs. Klarsfeld because, if they did, they would lose their jobs as teachers, lecturers, television producers, publishers, and so on. I can—and do—allow myself to do it, and I am happy to act on behalf of all those with less freedom than me.

   a. Because—see Günter Grass's speech—the criticisms we make, as writers, of Mr. Kiesinger always end up serving the Federal Republic. We play the ludicrous role of "the nation's conscience," to be proudly displayed in other countries, while the heads of government of those countries eat breakfast with Mr. Kiesinger.

      No matter how we pursue our attacks against Kiesinger, no matter the caliber of our weapons, nothing will ever happen to us because we are the "eminent" fools that our government shows so ostentatiously to the public.

   b. Because the primitive psychology of the bourgeoisie always reaches too easily for that word used, unfortunately, by Günter Grass. When I heard about Mrs. Klarsfeld's gesture, it was eleven at night: not a time when it is particularly easy to send flowers to Paris. So I had plenty of time to discuss this with my family, to sleep on it, to discuss it again over breakfast, to think some more, and even then I—half deliberately—let another three hours pass before finally sending my son to the local florist.

      Since then, I have sent more flowers to Mrs. Klarsfeld, and believe me I will send her flowers a third time if the occasion presents itself.

I NEVER HAD to pay for publication of the verdict in the six newspapers cited by Judge Drygalla. In fact, as the verdict mentioned my precise reasons for deciding to slap Kiesinger, it is understandable that the chancellor was not too keen to see it publicized.

I knew I had to go further now. The slap was only the beginning. It was Serge who made me realize the truth of this. "You're like one of those actors who become famous for a role on a TV soap opera," he told me. "To avoid being typecast, they have to be even better in other roles. Very few succeed."

The Kiesinger Campaign Diary

(NOVEMBER 1968—OCTOBER 1969)

D URING THE ELEVEN MONTHS that followed the slap—in other words, until Kiesinger and his party were defeated in the legislative elections of September 1969—I was constantly moving around, rarely staying more than a week at a time in Paris.

The hardest part was leaving Arno when he was sick: flu, mumps, measles. Raïssa would lecture me when that happened, pretending that she didn't want to look after him, so that I would stay. But I had to go; if I'd given in and canceled a protest march or a speech, I sensed that the momentum would be lost. And so I kissed Arno's hot forehead and left him, with a heavy heart, to catch the night trains that saved me so much precious time.

My mother-in-law grasped the enormity of the battle we were fighting then; she realized its importance. And she rallied behind us with all the courage and strength of character that she always showed. She felt it was her duty to lecture me, to warn me of the dangers I was risking, but she always did so kindly, and she always looked after my son.

How many times did Serge and I say goodbye at the Gare du Nord or the Gare de l'Est with a tender kiss that filled me with the strength to keep going? How many times did I wake up, my mouth parched, the pale German landscape rushing past the window, and feel viscerally discouraged by the immensity of the country, its huge factories, its millions of cars, all those strangers whose political morality I was trying to change? What I was seeking seemed, in those moments, so unreal, so unknowable, that I questioned myself: Was it worth the sacrifice of all my energy and the peacefulness of family life? Nazism seemed to belong to the past: the dead were dead, and the sufferings had been lessened by time; I felt alone and very small. So I listed all the advantages that I would gain personally from this campaign; I clung to the love I felt for—and from—Serge, which was constantly growing, and to the trust that so many people had put in me. I focused so hard on these things that I was able to rebuild my world of the night before, and once again I felt inspired.

I was receiving letters from all over the world. Why did so many people who didn't really know me write to me so trustingly? Because my acts embodied the Germany that hated Hitler, the Germany that had accepted the burden of its Nazi past in order to better fight it. That is why there was sometimes such hostility toward me, an emotion born deep inside all those men and women who had not yet accepted that Germany did what it did. The German people had murdered on such a vast scale that the scar in the European flesh was still sensitive: there was so much suspicion of Germany as a nation that any Germans who, rightly or wrongly, were considered exemplary immediately attracted all the trust that foreigners wanted to put in the German people as a whole.

Through the cities and the fields of Germany, I conscientiously pursued the task that I had taken upon myself: from a stage to the head of a protest march, I organized spectacular demonstrations; I wrote detailed dossiers; I held tight to Kiesinger like a dog that won't let go of a thief's ankle, growling and sometimes sinking my teeth into his flesh.

The following extracts are taken from the diary of that campaign:

November 7, 1968—I slap Chancellor Kiesinger.

November 11—Brussels. I arrived from Paris last night with Raïssa, getting here two days before Kiesinger. He is going to speak about Europe to the bigwigs of NATO. I am organizing a meeting of my own that will take place a few hours before this.

November 13—It is 7:00 a.m. Hammering on the door of our hotel room. "Police! Identity check!" My mother-in-law cracks open the door and hands our passports to two plainclothes policemen. "That's not enough. You have to come with us to the ministry. You have fifteen minutes to get dressed and follow us."

As soon as the door is shut, I rush to the telephone. I call one of Serge's best friends, Philippe Lemaître, *Le Monde*'s correspondent in Brussels, and Michel Lang, leader of the Jewish Workmen's Circle in Berlin, who is sleeping in a room on the floor below us. My mother-in-law calls Serge, in Paris, who promises to immediately contact the secretary-general of the International Union of Resistance Fighters, Hubert Halin. He will warn his friends in the Belgian government, particularly at the Ministry of Justice.

More banging on the door. "Hurry up!"

My mother-in-law replies, "We're ladies. We need time to get ready."

We must leave soon. Michel Lang is arrested, too. We are taken to the Belgian police headquarters, where we have to wait for a long time. I am then brought to a small office. Two policemen interrogate me and take down my statement. I am convinced that the purpose of this arrest is to prevent me from speaking, to keep me here until evening and then put me on a train back to Paris. At first, I rage at them, looking at my watch every five minutes to see if I am late for my rally yet. Then I try to reason with them. If they don't let me speak, they will stir up trouble with the students, and it will be an even bigger scandal. I talk about the trip Kiesinger made in 1940 with foreign journalists in Belgium and occupied France to demonstrate the superiority of the German army, and I look at the policeman and say, "You must have lived under Nazism in Belgium. You know what it represents."

They admit that they themselves are former Resistance fighters, "but this is about law and order." The German embassy asked the Belgian authorities to prevent any incidents during Kiesinger's visit. And I am troublemaker number 1.

Around 12:45, a detective enters the office. He hands me a piece of paper and asks me to sign an affidavit that I will leave Brussels as soon as my speech is over. The detective confirms that someone high up in the government has intervened on my behalf.

I jump in a taxi and head straight for the Free University, where the rally has just begun. I am greeted by frenzied applause.

When my speech is over, a delegation of students negotiates with the police so that I can stay in the city until 6:00 p.m. This gives me time to conduct a long interview with *Der Spiegel*.

Kiesinger delivers his speech that evening, and Belgian students turn up to protest. I learn about what happened the next day, in Paris, reading the European press.

A headline in the evening paper *Abendzeitung*: "Kiesinger assaulted. Ohrfeigen-Beate under surveillance." "Beate the Slapper" is my new nickname.

Paris-Presse reports:

As soon as he began to speak, the German chancellor, who was speaking French, was interrupted by chants of "Kiesinger Nazi."

The police intervened, and the chancellor thought the disturbances were over. But ten minutes later, the heckling began again, with added intensity.

Firecrackers exploded from the balcony and leaflets rained down on the audience. These were little squares of paper bearing the words: "National Socialist Party. Kiesinger Kurt Georg. Membership number 2633930. Joined May 1, 1933."

The *Frankfurter Rundschau* adds: "Kiesinger was visibly affected by the protests. The last line of his speech was 'I have, from the very beginning, been a supporter of a federal European state.' He stammered as he pronounced this sentence."

When it was over, groups of protesters gathered outside the building, clashing with a nearly equivalent number of policemen.

So it was that Kiesinger was deeply humiliated before the Belgian government, the leaders of NATO, and the EEC (European Economic Community)—a fact that did not escape the German press, which pointed out that both of these humiliations had been initiated by me.

The next day, the *Süddeutsche Zeitung* published a cartoon that jokingly summed up the situation: an airplane is flying through the sky, and below it is a witch riding a broomstick, with a banner attached to it bearing my name. The caption says: *"Die Quartiermacherin des Kanzlers"* (the chancellors' quartermaster).

West German political commentators began to understand that it was not possible to reduce the slap in Berlin to a mere anecdote. With its international resonance and its follow-up in Brussels, my action was taking on a new significance, and the German people were getting a taste for how embarrassing it could be to have chosen a chancellor whose reputation was being attacked like this, both at home and abroad. According to certain journalists who spoke to the chancellor during this period, the incident in Belgium bothered him even more than the one in Berlin had.

November 15—German journalists lay siege to our apartment. They want to see how this "hysterical" woman lives. Presumably they expect to find a filthy, chaotic commune, so when they come in, they are stunned to see the large foyer and the three living rooms overlooking the Seine. They are so surprised that they imagine the reproductions on the wall must be originals.

They photograph me in the immaculately clean kitchen as I do the cooking; from now on, for them, I am the middle-class woman who, driven by a passion, has temporarily left behind her well-ordered, affluent life. Kiesinger's theory—that I am a professional revolutionary, a mercenary—falls flat.

November 19—I am welcomed to East Berlin by an official delegation bearing flowers. I am lodged at the Hotel Unter den Linden. While eating dinner, I am approached by two young people. They ask me for an autograph, and I sign the menu for them.

November 20—I cause panic in East Berlin when I tell the East German press agency that I will hold a press conference on Kiesinger's Nazi past. My hosts are shocked by this: no foreigner has the right to invite the East German press to an official press conference. It does not happen. All the same, this incident does not dampen the enthusiasm on this side of the wall. I am ceremoniously presented with a scrapbook containing hundreds of laudatory newspaper articles and cartoons that appeared in East Germany after what is described here as my "exploit." How can such a rigidly Communist state shower such praise on an individual act of disrespect toward authority?

November 22—In Dortmund, I attend a meeting for young socialists that also features a speech by Günter Grass.

Grass is not happy at the idea of introducing me. Presumably he is a little frustrated by the publicity that my slap has received. Kiesinger has never responded to his open letters, while my act has made a genuine impact.

A student asks him, "How come you attack Kiesinger for his Nazi past, but Karl Schiller, the minister of the economy, and also a former Nazi who specialized in the economic exploitation of conquered territories, is your son's godfather?"

Furious, Grass answers that the two things have no connection whatsoever. Karl Schiller is his business, not the youth of Germany's. I am disappointed. Had Schiller been elected chancellor, I would have protested in the same way as I have for Kiesinger—something I have already stated, and which the press has highlighted. Former Nazis are not the exclusive preserve of the Christian Democrats; there are some among the Social Democrats, too.

November 23—I record an album entitled *The K. Affair—The Story of a Slap.* The evidence from the Kiesinger dossier is read by actors, while I talk about the meaning of my action and recite a poem I have just written on the subject.

December 1—I am met at the train station by a man holding a bouquet of flowers. This is Mr. Koenig, a journalist who invited me to Munich for a meeting at the Rationaltheater. He suggests we eat lunch at his home. His wife is far from welcoming. After the meal, they have an argument: he doesn't want to help her wash the dishes. I feel very ill at ease and swear to myself not to accept any more invitations to people's homes.

It is only as I'm leaving Munich that I finally understand this gentleman's intentions: he wants to "manage" me, to organize a tour of meetings all over Germany—displaying the slapper like a circus freak show. He would take half of the receipts, naturally, because he believes we ought to be charging people for entry. He even offers me a contract.

I politely brush him off, and he is very surprised.

December 3—I am much more at ease at a "teach-in" at the University of Munich. Tonight, I announce that I will stand as a candidate for the legislative elections in September 1969 against Chancellor Kiesinger, wherever he decides to stand. By doing this, I believe I will be able to avoid prison at the appeal trial that has been brought against me. Any conviction would be interpreted as a dirty trick engineered by my electoral opponent. And it will give my campaign an even-greater impact. Now all I have to do is find a political party for whom I can stand. I have already been expelled from the SPD [the Social Democratic Party of Germany], so I think about the future coalition of small left-wing parties and the Communist Party. I am making my intentions public in order to force their hand.

December 4–7—I speak to the Young Communists in Dortmund.

December 10—I attend a heated debate organized by the MEJ (Jewish Student Movement): "Should Chancellor Kiesinger Be Slapped?" One of the MEJ's leaders decides to come with me to Berlin with a Star of David flag. He wants to protest the recent acquittal of the Nazi judge Rehse. On July 3, 1967, Hans-Joachim Rehse was sentenced to five years in prison for "assistance in criminal acts." The federal appeal court quashed that verdict in April 1968, deciding that, as a judge, Rehse bore the full responsibility for his acts.

Rehse had indeed lent his support to at least 231 death sentences. But instead of finding for the prosecutor, who was demanding life imprisonment for five verdicts given by Rehse during the war "that went beyond the laws of the Nazi terror and constituted murder, pure and simple," the court decided "almost unanimously" that Rehse had acted in good faith, convinced that the verdicts were necessary for "consolidating the Reich."

In his ruling, Judge Oske claimed that a state "cannot be blamed in times of crisis for resorting to exceptional measures of intimidation." To support this, he cited "the recent adoption of the emergency laws in the Federal Republic."

As might be expected, these words caused quite a stir in the audience. On several occasions the reading of the verdict was interrupted by heckles, and a former Gestapo detainee managed to slap Rehse while he was leaving the court a free man.

I pay for the MEJ leader's journey, because he is not able to scrape together enough money to travel in forty-eight hours: I consider it essential to show the German people that Jews are coming from abroad to protest Rehse's rehabilitation.

How many trials where Nazi criminals were acquitted might have had a different, more just outcome if the Jews had demonstrated their determination not to see their people's persecutors go free?

December 14—Ten thousand people gather outside the Berlin-Schöneberg city hall, chanting, "Rehse, murderer!"

The stage is set up in the middle of the square. It's very cold, and I'm bundled up in a leather-and-fur coat. The correspondent for *Pravda* writes: "It was like a scene from the revolution, this young woman speaking in front of a mass of red flags." But he forgets to mention the flag of the Star of David hanging above my head, highly visible in all the photographs in the German press.

I tell the crowd, "When Kiesinger became chancellor, I understood that it marked the start of Germany's reconciliation with its Nazi past; that is Kiesinger's historical role. Through my individual actions, I tried to put an obstacle in his path, but victory can only be won through collective action."

December 18—Serge comes to Berlin. He is here on business for Continental Grain. I spend New Year's Eve without him, however, as he has to take the train to London, where he will expand the Kiesinger dossier through his research work at the Wiener Library.

January 10, 1969—A far-right newspaper has put together an article under the headline "The Beate Klarsfeld Saga" in which they list all the nicknames I've been given by the press. I am, by turns, "the pretty Machiavelli," "Joan of Arc," "the Berlin nemesis," "Charlotte Corday resurrected," "the modern Ravaillac," "Beate the Red," "Saint Beate descended from her red heaven," and "the figurehead for the new Left."

January 22—A weekly Communist newspaper, *DVZ* in Düsseldorf, asks me to be its Paris correspondent. They pay me eight hundred marks per month. I assume this is a form of discreet aid from the East German government, even though the editors of *DVZ* always deny having been ordered to hire me.

February 1—After Bremen, Lebach, Bonn, and Cologne, I give a speech in Duisburg, where it is so cold that I shiver as I turn the pages with my numb, gloveless fingers. After it's over, I go by car to Dortmund, then take the night train to Berlin, where I take part in a meeting at the Free University.

February 3—Serge joins me in Berlin, which is in a feverish state on the eve of the presidential election. Heinrich Lübke, who was the president of the Federal Republic, has been ousted. Accused by the East Germans of having designed the barrack blocks for the concentration camps, he denied being the creator of those sketches. But graphology experts gave the lie to his claim.

The arrival of neo-Nazi delegates from the Bundesrat, roughly West Germany's equivalent of the U.S. Senate, triggers a riot. The student activists of the APO gather in the Technical University and discuss what they should do. But indecision and a dearth of ideas lead, after an hour of speechifying, to an impulsive call to action: everyone heads for the Hotel am Zoo, where many of the leading politicians are staying, only to find the hotel is surrounded by hundreds of riot police. As the protesters yell "Kiesinger Nazi!" they are met with a wave of truncheons.

We hardly dare to believe it, but it's true: Gustav Heinemann has been elected president of the Federal Republic. This is a major setback for the Christian Democrats, whose candidate, Gerhard Schröder, a former SA member, was backed by the neo-Nazi vote.

February 4—I take the early plane from Berlin to Nuremberg. I give a speech in the afternoon, and that evening I lead a demonstration through the streets. A crowd of students boos Kiesinger, and I feel a sort of intoxication when I hear my voice booming from speakers in this city where, thirty years earlier, Hitler readied the German people for a diabolical adventure. I have the impression that my voice is that of another Germany; there is something much greater than myself behind me.

February 14—Arno has come with me to Oldenburg. Today, for the first time, I give a speech to the activists of the ADF (Party for Democratic Action and Progress), which has named me as its candidate in Kiesinger's precinct: number 188, in Waldshut, in the Black Forest. This is a great step forward for me. I stand in front of hundreds of hardened Communist militants, and I sense their hostility toward me. I was imposed on them because my celebrity attracts press attention, and I have the support of the East German government. On the press invitations, my name is the most prominent, as if I'm the sugar coating on the Communists' pill. In fact, I have become the driving force of the ADF in this election, even though I have not received the party's material support. At least the journeys I make on behalf of the party are reimbursed, which makes it easier for me to travel around the country. As an independent candidate, I do not belong to any of the parties that make up this far-left federation. This gives me almost free rein when it comes to speaking my mind.

As the meeting is in full sway, with the ADF's president, Professor Hoffmann, speaking to the audience, the door suddenly opens in a gust of wind . . . and Arno bursts into the room, his underpants around his ankles, shouting loudly, "Mama, poo-poo!" The ADF's driving force slips out of the party congress to attend to a more urgent task . . .

February 20—The neo-Nazis of the NPD [National Democratic Party] are holding their congress, and I am going to attend. If this party obtains 5 percent of the votes in September's election, it will be represented in the Bundestag. The anti-fascists have only one way to stop them: by physically engaging the thugs of the NPD's security staff in fighting, so that they show their true face, which they are attempting to hide behind a mask of respectability. Perhaps the electorate will recoil when it sees this latter-day SA showing its true colors. This dangerous task will be undertaken by the young socialists of the SPD, the APO, and the Communist youth organizations.

Using a *DVZ* press card, I enter the hall and am immediately spotted by two burly bouncers, who shadow me closely.

Adolf von Thadden, the neo-Nazi leader, is stirring up his supporters. I head quickly toward the stage, shouting loudly, "Thadden, you always talk about democracy, so let the real democrats speak!"

The bouncers grab hold of me. Thadden speaks into the microphone: "Gentlemen, gentlemen, you must act properly with ladies! I should count myself lucky that my cheek is farther away from this lady's hand than the chancellor's was when she met him . . ."

Howls of laughter. After a passionate rendition of "Deutschland über Alles," the meeting ends. A Soviet journalist rushes over to protect me because, while most of the crowd moves grudgingly out of the way to let me through, a few thugs come menacingly toward me, yelling insults. I manage to reach the exit, unscathed and relieved.

February 27—From Augsburg, I go to Waldshut, a rural area close to the Swiss border. Local far-left activists want to show me where I should hold electoral meetings.

Is the far left really going to waste its energy trying to win a few votes here when the Social Democrats are in a position to defeat the Christian Democrats with a reasonable program? I remember Serge's explanations of the pre-Hitler period, which made such an impression on me. He told me how the Communists, prioritizing their fight against the Social Democrats, had neglected the threat posed by Hitler and had even sometimes joined forces with the Nazis to undermine the Weimar Republic. Of course, they ended up withdrawing that support, but by then it was too late.

I tell the local militants that I have no intention of wasting my time in empty meeting rooms here, that this is a national campaign, and my role is to appear wherever Kiesinger holds a rally. I must hassle him in the street, outside his hotel, forcing him to be surrounded by police wherever he goes.

March 12—Kiesinger is in Paris on an official visit. I invite a few friends from Berlin. On Wednesday evening, as the five of us are walking in the street, a dozen men rush toward us. They are plainclothes policemen, and they put us in three cars. I am driven to the station in La Muette and released around midnight. But my friends are held overnight and, the next day, are taken to the border and expelled from French soil.

All day long, Serge and I are escorted by police, who wait outside our building in two cars when we are at home. We engage them in conversation; they show us the photographs they have of us. Lots of police have our pictures, presumably because they fear we may try to assassinate the chancellor. One of the policemen jokes with Serge: "We need a new photo of you, because you're a lot thinner in this one!"

April—We work like crazy. For forty-eight hours, I barely sleep. In ten days, I type up the German text of *Kiesinger, or Subtle Fascism*, a pamphlet that Serge and I wrote in conjunction with the historian Joseph Billig. It describes the organization of the Nazis' foreign propaganda broadcasts and defines very precisely what Kiesinger's role was in this capacity. *Kiesinger, oder der Subtile Fascismus* is my weapon for this trial; it receives widespread publicity, and the public realizes that Kiesinger has not published the documentation that he promised, on April 22, 1968, to bring into the open. I, on the other hand, the slapper, have kept my promise and exposed the truth about that past.

April 15—The first day of my appeal proceedings. In front of seven hundred people, I appear once again before my judges for having slapped the chancellor of the Federal Republic of Germany. The Kriminalgericht in the Moabit quarter of Berlin is a large, dark prewar building, encircled by police vans.

Arno, Serge, and Professor Billig are here, along with more than thirty photographers, dozens of journalists, and a few young Germans wearing yellow stars on their chests.

The trial begins with a request for the recusal of the presiding judge, Taegener. My defense team reveals that this judge told a journalist, over coffee in the cafeteria, that the trial would be "over and done with in three hours." After a brief deliberation, the court rejects our request.

I spend a long time on the stand. The judge tries to catch me out, but I manage to evade his traps. One of my replies, which comes to me spontaneously, changes the direction of the trial:

"Mrs. Klarsfeld, why did you decide to use violence against the chancellor of our country?"

"Violence, Your Honor, is when a Nazi chancellor is imposed on German youth."

I talk so much about Kiesinger's past that Taegener, growing impatient, interrupts me with a phrase that the journalists scribble happily in their notebooks: "That's enough. You have already demonstrated that Kiesinger was active in the Nazi regime."

Very soon, the debate becomes political. Joseph Billig is called to the bar, and the dossier on Kiesinger is the sole focus of his testimony.

Joseph Billig was accepted as a witness thanks to Serge, who came up with an original strategy to bring him into the courtroom. Before slapping the chancellor, I went to see Billig—an expert on National Socialism—to find out if Kiesinger's role and actions in the Third Reich gave me the moral right to slap him. After examining the dossier, Billig said yes—and he is in court to explain that response.

When Judge Taegener asks if the witness can prove that Kiesinger was informed about what was happening in the concentration camps, I know I have won: the chancellor is now on trial, not me.

The next morning, my lawyers have not even settled in their seats before the judge announces the adjournment of the trial. He blames this on a lack of time and Kiesinger's unavailability to testify.

The judge and his assessors are gone before we can even react. And so the trial ends in farce. Nevertheless, for us, it is a victory. The newspaper headlines all tell the same story: the chancellor retreats from his battle with Beate Klarsfeld.

May 10—I leave for Stuttgart, where the neo-Nazi NPD is holding its congress this weekend. Serge meets me there.

The NPD's thuggish security staff forms a human barrier around the Palace of Congress; dressed in lederhosen, these burly men hold hands and are bound together by a long chain.

I cannot find enough people to mount a real protest against the NPD, so I decide to take another tack: we will protest the passivity of the Stuttgart mayor in allowing such a gathering. The press is there, and it has to illustrate its stories on the congress, so the likelihood is that it will publish photographs of the neo-Nazi leader Adolf von Thadden onstage. We decide to give the newspapers another, better photo opportunity, one that will push our agenda, rather than that of the neo-Nazis. I suggest that we hang a huge Nazi flag over the city's main square and solemnly declare that Stuttgart is Germany's first Nazi city. It's no mean feat, getting hold of the necessary materials and making the flag ourselves, but in the end we succeed. The photograph of the swastika and our group shouting at the citizens of Stuttgart will be seen all over Germany and the rest of the world with the caption: "Germans protest against the neo-Nazi congress."

May 12–15—Düsseldorf and Mannheim. I become slightly aggressive in the electoral meetings, driven crazy by the tendency of some left-wingers to endlessly split hairs. But the campaign is making progress, all the same: everywhere Kiesinger goes, taunts of "Nazi" follow him.

May 28–30—East Berlin to Frankfurt to Lebenstedt to Hanover . . . and then to Paris, where I collapse, exhausted. How will I keep going at this pace until October?

June 21—In the Potsdam archives, I put the finishing touches on my manuscript on Kiesinger. Back in Paris, I discover that the World Peace Council in East Berlin has awarded me the Grigoris Lambrakis Medal "for her courage and the campaign she is conducting for national independence." That is certainly not the reason for the campaign I am conducting. Still, I am proud to be recognized as a German.

July 5—After several meetings in the north, I arrive in Oldenburg, where Kiesinger is due to hold a large rally for Christian Democrat supporters. I have managed to mobilize about three hundred young people in this town of civil servants and retirees. We have blocked the main door of the Weser-Ems-Halle. The chancellor's helicopter lands in a patch of wasteland surrounded by a high fence just behind the hall. Kiesinger smiles and waves as he emerges, presumably thinking that we must be there to support him. When he realizes his mistake, he continues to wave at us ironically, in order to save face. Serge and I are standing on a car parked next to the fence. Kiesinger approaches us, to a soundtrack of boos and jeers. There he is, right in front of me, only a few feet from where I stand. He sees me and his jaw tenses, his smile vanishes. He stops and stares at me. My arm is raised and, like all the others, I am shouting what I was once the only one to shout: "Sieg heil" and "Kiesinger Nazi!" He looks as if he would like to say something to me, but then he makes a weary gesture with his hand that seems to express the impossibility of a dialogue. Shaking his head, he walks past us and enters the hall through a back door.

A journalist with access to the chancellor's office in Bonn told me: "Kiesinger's friends have often said to him: 'Let us organize a meeting with this woman; there must be a compromise you can make with her.' Kiesinger always replied: 'No compromise is possible with that woman.'"

July 24—Frankfurt, where I am present for a fierce brawl between the NPD's thugs and some student protesters. I get out unharmed, but others are not so lucky. The injured are mostly students, their noses and jaws broken by bike chains or lead pipes. Faced with Hitler's direct descendants, those brave anonymous young people did their duty as Germans. It is from them that I draw my strength, my determination. *Stern* publishes dozens of photographs showing the brutal aftermath of the violence, and this surely has an effect on public opinion: the neo-Nazis receive only 4.6 percent of the vote, and so they will not have a representative in the Bundestag.

August 14—I take Arno with me on an electoral campaign in my precinct because Kiesinger will be campaigning here next weekend. I try to find a group with a car so that we can follow the chancellor around. We drive in an Opel Kapitän at first, then use a Volkswagen bus lent to us by a sympathetic cheesemonger; it transports six students, lots of leaflets and posters, and tomatoes and eggs, which we plan to throw at Kiesinger.

First stop: Uhlingen. This little village is so sweet and simple-looking. The stage in the little village square is hung with flags and garlands. For the seven hundred inhabitants, today is a celebration.

Kiesinger gets out of his helicopter and is greeted by young girls in regional costumes, each carrying a bunch of flowers.

Serge, Arno, and I are standing, with seven friends, on a bench so we can see what is going on. As soon as Kiesinger begins to speak, we shout out: "Nazi!" Arno, standing next to me, yells the word at the top of his voice. Suddenly, some thugs rush up behind us and tip over the bench. We are thrown to the ground. Kiesinger, watching this, says angrily, "It's always the same faces that we see . . . I have nothing against the opposition, but if these people wish to destroy the state, we won't let them get away with it."

On the way to Waldshut, where the day's last electoral rally will take place, we stop in a little village to stock up on old eggs and crates of rotten fruit, which we pile up in the car. The town of Waldshut has been beautifully decorated, and the inhabitants are all dressed in their best clothes. We arrive separately and stand here and there in the crowded town hall. The security guards look nervous.

As soon as Kiesinger opens his mouth to speak, about forty people stand up, arms raised, and boo him.

Kiesinger is surprised by the number of protesters. The audience seems too shocked to react: nothing like this has ever happened before in this traditionally right-wing town. Kiesinger stammers a few sentences that no one can hear and, red-faced, goes back to sit down.

When the meeting ends, I am harassed by the locals.

"It's shameful," one woman tells me, "bringing up your child to be a fanatic. He should be asleep now, the poor thing. He must be exhausted."

A crowd gathers around us.

I say, "It's strange how, during the war, you never took pity on all those Jewish children who were crammed onto trains before being murdered at Auschwitz . . ."

The woman does not respond. She beats a quick retreat, and the others slowly disperse.

"Oh, these Jews!" says one man, in a rage. "It's a shame we didn't exterminate all of them!"

The press covers these incidents, which are repeated day after day. Arno becomes a celebrity: the "youngest politician in Germany." I am now the mother who campaigns against the chancellor, with her son in her arms.

August 19—Berlin. A press conference, Arno beside me. My book on Kiesinger, with a preface by Heinrich Böll, has just been published, six days before my second appeal trial.

After I meet with Karl Gerold, the owner of the newspaper *Frankfurter Rundschau*, a friend of Willy Brandt and a longtime anti-Nazi, he gives me an entire page of his paper for an article on Kiesinger and the Final Solution. Gerold himself publishes a powerful editorial, under the headline "Kiesinger—Never Again." "We write in the conviction that our people will remember the dead, victims of Nazism. Those dead whom Kiesinger supposedly knew nothing about. What is certain is that the ex-Nazi Kiesinger must never be chancellor again."

Kiesinger, meanwhile, has asked several historians to write his side of the story, but they have all refused: Gerhard Schulz, from Tübingen, and Eberhard Jäckel, from Stuttgart, as well as the writer Golo Mann. Hans

Buchheim, a professor at the University of Mainz, at first agrees and then pulls out, citing the unacceptable working conditions: the chancellor wanted him to work only with the documentation he himself would supply and not to consult other sources.

August 25—The day of the second appeal trial. First, we must find out whether Kiesinger is going to testify in person, as he is the plaintiff and the victim and as this is, at last, his chance to publicly refute my accusations so close to the elections. Judge Taegener reads out a letter from the chancellor in which he explains that his electoral campaign leaves him no time to appear in court.

The judges know they cannot send me to prison, because it would cause a scandal if the chancellor's electoral opponent were locked up, so they must prove themselves generous in order to undermine my pugnacity. I have already decided to make short work of this trial, which no longer offers me any advantages. I declare that, in the chancellor's cowardly absence, I refuse to answer any of the judge's questions: "I will not go on with this farce. For me, the trial is over." My lawyers also refuse to plead. After that, it is all wrapped up very quickly. The court delivers the verdict everyone expected: a four-month suspended sentence.

On September 8, Georges Pompidou, the new French president, will go to Bonn on an official visit, so Serge and I pack a suitcase full of the newly printed French edition of my Kiesinger book and distribute copies to all the high-ranking political staff who will accompany Pompidou to Germany.

September 7—In Bonn, two young women from the ADF and I distribute a crate of red books to about a hundred journalists who are waiting for a press conference. The door is ajar, and no one pays us any attention. To speed things up, we leave five copies at the end of each row of seats. By the time the security staff realizes that what we are handing out is not an official document but an anti-Kiesinger pamphlet, it is already too late: most of the journalists are reading it. We are removed from the room, followed by a few correspondents who have yet to receive a copy.

On our way out, we pass Günter Diehl. Pleased with our success, I hand him a copy of the pamphlet, which he pushes away. "Diehl Nazi!" I yell. Surprised, he turns around, and at first cannot think of anything to say. Then, finally, he shouts, *"Kommunisten, Bolschewisten!"*

Günter Diehl was one of Kiesinger's closest collaborators during the war. This spokesman for the chancellor's office was also a Nazi with expertise in psychological warfare and subversive propaganda.

My action in Bonn makes the Germans smile, but it also makes them think: now they know that the French leaders are aware of their chancellor's wartime activities.

September 20—Karlsruhe. With hundreds of young protesters, we lay siege to the Gartenhalle, where Kiesinger will speak. I can no longer discreetly enter any hall in order to contradict him. There is always someone who recognizes me and shouts "Kiesinger's enemy!" and shows me the door.

Ravensburg, Waldshut, Rheinfelden, Esslingen . . .

September 26—Serge joins me, along with Petia, our cocker spaniel, who will act as my bodyguard during the final two days of the election campaign. In Waldshut, we are passing a crowd of Kiesinger supporters when a woman holding an ice cream launches herself at me. First, she plants the ice cream in my face; then, while I am temporarily blinded, she begins punching me. Petia starts barking very loudly. Serge turns around, drops his pile of leaflets, and comes over to push the woman away.

Albbruck, Waldshut, Dogezn, Unterbruckringen, Trengen, Säckingen, Görwihl, Hochsal . . . All day long, we visit these villages, where Kiesinger gives speeches, and we protest against him. Sometimes Serge and I are alone in the front row, constantly interrupting the chancellor. The gorillas from Kiesinger's Junge Union are furious that they cannot intervene; but the press is there, and it would damage the chancellor's image if anything untoward were to happen to us.

September 28—Election Day. As a candidate, I am entitled to be present at the assembly for the counting of votes and announcement of the results. Two or three security guards keep an eye on me, and I am surrounded by journalists. They ask me what I expect, and I am honest: the ADF, my party, will not win more than 1 percent of the vote.

I feel a hand on my shoulder: it is the chief of police in Bonn. He expresses his reservations about my opinions but offers me his "personal congratulations" for my "courage." A few Christian Democrats make the same remark to me that evening. I have often noticed the almost-exaggerated respect that right-wing German men have for a woman who stands up for her beliefs.

The ADF ends up with only 0.7 percent of the national vote, but I don't care. The results that matter to me all go our way: the NPD does not get its 5 percent, so there are no neo-Nazis in the Bundestag; Willy Brandt is the new chancellor; and Kiesinger, blamed for the failure of the Christian Democrats, loses his place as the party's federal president to his younger rival Rainer Barzel.

WILLY BRANDT'S ARRIVAL in power brought me a serene joy, a satisfaction that nothing could disturb. It was the confirmation that I had not fought in vain, that my cause was not locked in the past but oriented toward the future. Kiesinger, defeated, was instantly forgotten. For me, at any rate, the page was turned.

I felt certain that I had played my part—modest but tangible—in this victory for the forces of progress. Would I have had the strength to keep fighting against Kiesinger if he had been reelected? I doubt it. Weariness would have overcome me.

I was anonymous again, to my great happiness. I had time to be a mother to Arno, a wife to Serge. My husband and I would go to the local movie theater two or three times a week and devour two films in a row. I felt rejuvenated in the glow of having accomplished this great task.

And that memorable handshake between Kiesinger and Brandt during the handover . . . how I savored that! The fallen Nazi's tense smile as he forced himself to put a brave face on defeat, as he gave way to another and very different German—from a Germany that Nazism had not managed to destroy.

ACHENBACH'S TURN

O N MARCH 30, 1970, the *Süddeutsche Zeitung* announced that Ernst Achenbach, a deputy for the liberal FDP (Free Democratic Party), was a candidate to succeed Fritz Hellwig as the German member of the European Commission in Brussels and that he would soon be officially appointed to that post by the West German government. I had already come across this Achenbach in my research into Kiesinger. In my files, I found a note dated June 28, 1940, from the Foreign Office's cultural department. Addressed to the German ambassador in Paris, this note specifies that the embassy's secretary, Dr. Achenbach, will be responsible for the political content of German broadcasts in occupied France.

And then I came across another familiar name—Dr. Sonnenhol, the head of that department. Only a few weeks before, the West German president, Dr. Heinemann, had personally intervened to block his nomination as foreign secretary due to the fact that his role had been more policelike than diplomatic during the years 1943 to 1944. So maybe it would be possible to block Achenbach in the same way?

According to *Der Spiegel*, Achenbach's candidacy for this post was the result of a deal made just after the September 1969 elections between Walter Scheel, leader of the liberal FDP, and the right wing of Achenbach's party. It was one of the conditions imposed by the right for their support in Willy Brandt's appointment as chancellor. Having become foreign minister in the new government, Scheel had sent an emissary to Paris to smooth the former Nazi's path. "If the French agree," he said, "then the Dutch and the others will follow."

I was under no illusions. This path-smoothing exercise had been performed very craftily: a few witness statements about Achenbach's kindness, a few reminders of his pro-French statements over recent years, the highlighting of his position as vice president of the Franco-German parliamentary group, his perfect command of the French language . . . it was possible to make him look like the ideal candidate.

But beneath this façade lay the reality of his past, and it was up to us to expose it. So it was that Serge and I visited the CDJC once again . . .

WE DID NOT find many files on Achenbach there, only a protest from the Resistance when Achenbach entered the European Parliament a few years earlier. That pamphlet repeatedly described Achenbach as a "Nazi diplomat," but there were no details. Fifteen hours of determined research enabled us to write, on the night of April 1, a six-page note, in French and German, which formed the basis for my open letter to Achenbach published in the *Frankfurter Rundschau* three days later: "Dear sir, I believe that your activity under the Third Reich, your convictions at that time, your role at Nuremberg and in the Naumann affair make you unfit to represent the Federal Republic of Germany in Europe."

In that letter, I revealed previously unpublished details of Achenbach's career in France. A Nazi Party member from 1937, Achenbach had been part of the German embassy in Paris just before the war, where he worked as a political adviser to the ambassador Otto Abetz. In his statement to the French intelligence agency on November 22, 1945, Abetz declared, "The embassy's most important section was the political section led by Mr. Achenbach." In Nuremberg, on August 23, 1947, Schleier, the embassy's number two, admitted that the most important political issues, notably those concerning Franco-German collaboration, were dealt with by Abetz and Achenbach.

Too often, we tend to imagine the German diplomats under Hitler as distinguished gentlemen attempting to soften the extremism of the Gestapo. This is completely false. The embassy leaders, like those of the Gestapo, were highly educated men in their early thirties. When the center of gravity shifted from the embassy toward the Gestapo, SS leaders like Helmut Knochen and Herbert Hagen smoothly replaced Abetz and Achenbach in their role as decision-makers on Nazi policies in France.

This was the same Achenbach who, on August 13, 1940, put the finishing touches to Germany's absolute control of French newspapers, radio, cinema, publishing, and theater. The same Achenbach who had a front-row seat for the meeting between Hitler and Pétain.

The German embassy was behind the first racial discrimination measures in France. It constantly pressured the Vichy government to adopt legislation in compliance with the racist Nuremberg Laws. It was one of the first instigators of definitive liquidation via deportation to the East. It was the Gestapo's strongest supporter in the conception and application of anti-Jewish measures on French territory, working hard to remove the diplomatic obstacles preventing the Gestapo's Jewish Affairs Department from detaining or deporting such and such a category of foreign Jews and trying repeatedly to overcome the Italian authorities' reluctance to persecute the Jews in their zone of occupation.

On February 28, 1941, Achenbach attended a meeting, in the company of Abetz, Achenbach's subordinate Theo Zeitschel, and SS-Obersturmführer Theodor Dannecker, head of the Sicherheitspolizei, the Sipo-SD's service IV-J, which led to the creation of the ominously efficient General Commission on the Jewish Question, the official mouthpiece of the Vichy regime.

The embassy's political section was remorselessly hostile to Jews in France. This was demonstrated during the first deportation: a convoy of a thousand French Jews arrested in retaliation for attacks on Wehrmacht soldiers. Martin Luther, the Foreign Office undersecretary, cabled the German embassy in Paris on March 11, 1942: Heydrich had given him details of the plan "to transfer the one thousand Jews arrested in Paris on December 12, 1941, to the Auschwitz concentration camp. These are all Jews of French nationality. I would be grateful if you would let me know if you have any objections to the execution of this action." It was Achenbach's political section that, via his subordinate Nostitz, formulated the very brief and fateful response that same day, under the heading "Secret": "No objection to the planned action against the Jews."

On March 18, 1942, the embassy's political section expressed its satisfaction at the appointment of a high-ranking SS member as the head of the German police in France, "which will have favorable consequences for the Final Solution of the Jewish problem." A little later, when it became mandatory for Jews to wear a yellow star on their chests, there was a propaganda campaign of leaflets and posters. The embassy took part in this with a poster containing the words: "The Jew kills in the shadows. To know him, we must mark him."

ON AUGUST 26, 1942, a member of the Gestapo's Jewish Affairs Department wrote a note following a phone call from SS-Sturmbannführer Herbert Hagen, who worked directly for SS general Karl Oberg, the "Butcher of Paris." Hagen said that Achenbach had called him because he wanted to be kept updated on the exact details regarding the deportation of stateless Jews. Achenbach had to provide a report on the situation to the Foreign Office in Berlin.

In 1971, Ernst Achenbach was Herbert Hagen's lawyer. The pair of them are connected by their complicity in the anti-Jewish actions in Paris.

In 1943, Achenbach returned to Berlin, where he worked in the Foreign Office under Franz Six. He ran two sections in the cultural policy department. It was at this point that Achenbach got to know an assistant manager working in a neighboring department; like his, that department was renowned for giving positions to young, intelligent, efficient Nazi activists rather than career diplomats. The name of that assistant manager was, of course, Kurt Georg Kiesinger.

Even after 1945, Achenbach did not give up. In 1953, he was implicated in the Naumann plot, where he played an active role liaising between Goebbels's former propaganda undersecretary and major industrial corporations in the Ruhr. Achenbach's objective, thwarted at the time by the British government, was to infiltrate Nazis in all West Germany's political parties, so that they could return to power through democratic means.

That same year, Achenbach wrote an introduction for a book by Abetz, who was in prison in France at the time: "Can we seriously talk about the Franco-German entente if one of the main combatants in the vanguard of that entente, the Reich's ambassador in Paris during the war, is still behind bars? Nothing better demonstrates the moral grandeur of that man who, despite the injustices committed against him, still and always asks his German friends to hold true to the ideal of the Franco-German entente."

It is interesting to compare this text with another document signed by Abetz on July 2, 1942, which reveals the true "moral grandeur" of Nazi diplomats:

> The information from Berlin that the Hungarian government has now agreed that the measures applied to the Jews here [in France] should be extended to stateless Hungarian Jews has been brought to the awareness of the SD's Jewish affairs secretary. The embassy salutes this development . . . Last, concerning the deportation of forty thousand Jews to the camp in Auschwitz, the embassy replied as follows:
>
> In principle, the embassy has no objection to the deportation of forty thousand Jews to the camp in Auschwitz. From a psychological standpoint, the impression will be more effective for the majority of the French population if the evacuation measures are initially aimed only at foreign Jews and apply to French Jews only if the number of foreign Jews is insufficient for the required contingent. Such a measure does not in any way indicate that French Jews should be given a privileged status, as obviously in the course of the purification of Jews from all European countries, the French Jews must also be eliminated.

The photocopies of all these documents were already in my possession. Serge had quit his job at Continental Grain three months earlier, and we were living on his unemployment compensation. This money rapidly disappeared as we put coins into the photocopier in the post office, and I had the impression that we were dropping our entire family budget into an infernal slot machine.

But we felt compelled to do it, as we were—to our despair—the only ones who would act in the way that circumstances demanded: quickly, with a lot of hard work and the necessary funds.

Once the dossier was complete, I set about distributing it. To politicians, first of all: I sent a copy to the president of the European Commission, to the foreign ministers of Holland, Italy, and Luxembourg, to Willy Brandt, and to the prime ministers of Belgium and Great Britain. In Paris, I went to the Élysée Palace, where an assistant took possession of the dossier with the promise that it would be closely examined. A few months later, the French foreign minister wrote to me about Achenbach, in response to a letter in which I asked him to exclude the former Nazi from the Franco-German parliamentary group: "I will take the opportunities I am given to express the feeling we both share." But politicians only act if the press kicks up a stink. To make the press take notice, two main conditions must be met: first, they must have a dossier in their hands; then you must create an event that will enable the journalists to publish their point of view. A political editor once gave me this cynical advice: "Shove Achenbach out of a window, and I'll publish his dossier."

On April 4, I spent all day doing the tour of international press agencies, French daily newspapers, and representatives of the biggest European newspapers. Not only did I give them the dossier, but I talked to them about it: I had to persuade them to read it rather than just dumping it in a drawer.

A few days before this, we came to a decision. There was an association of EEC employees who were former Resistance fighters and concentration camp prisoners, and its leaders would go to see journalists in Brussels, dossier in hand, and convince them of their argument. This plan was executed perfectly. On April 6, the AFP (Agence France-Presse, the third-biggest news agency in the world) transmitted the news of the association's protest throughout its global network, specifying that its dossier contained a document "in which the Germany deputy proposed the arrest and deportation of two thousand Jews."

After articles appeared in *Le Figaro* and *Le Monde*, I set in motion our plan to internationalize the story. I sent a telegram requesting meetings with the Dutch foreign minister, the Belgian prime minister, the president of the European Commission, and the German government's spokesman. Accordingly, in the space of twenty-four hours, press agencies in Holland, Belgium, and Germany sent dispatches, all repeating the same information: that there were hostile reactions to Achenbach in view of a dossier on the diplomat's Nazi past. When the European newspapers received three dispatches on the same subject on the same day, they would realize that something big was happening, and they would give the story more space.

While I flew to Holland, Serge went to Brussels to meet with EEC employees who wanted to know more about the dossier. Arno went with him, as my mother-in-law wasn't free to look after him. Naturally, that was the day Arno suddenly started suffering with a toothache. So Serge, while discussing these serious matters, had to rub our son's gums with a special gel to keep him from drowning out their conversation with his moans and cries. I reached Brussels in the early afternoon and took over the care of Arno, while Serge handled the day's photocopying.

On April 9, the international press reacted as we had hoped. There were articles in *Die Welt* and the *Süddeutsche Zeitung*, while *Il Messaggero* in Italy ran the headline "Shock and Outrage in Brussels: Nazi Criminal Applies for EEC Position."

Back in Paris the next day, we continued our research.

THE CRUX OF the Achenbach case was its single most spectacular document: the famous telegram signed by Achenbach himself, sent from Paris on February 15, 1943, to the Foreign Office in Berlin:

> On February 13, 1943, around 9:10 p.m., Lieutenant Colonel
> Winkler and Major Nussbaum of the general staff of the Third
> Detachment of the Luftwaffe were shot from behind while they
> were walking from their office to the Louvre hotel in Paris [. . .]
> Lieutenant Colonel Winkler was hit by three bullets and Major
> Nussbaum by two. They both died that night after being taken to
> the hospital. [. . .]
> As an initial retaliation, the plan is for two thousand Jews to be
> deported to the East.
> Achenbach

This document seemed to amplify Achenbach's direct responsibility for the retaliatory measures. Knowing how the Nazi machine worked in occupied Paris, I assumed that the decision Achenbach mentioned in this telegram had not been made by him and that he was simply passing on information that had been given to him. If he told the press this, he would have appeared as the victim of a conspiracy. Thankfully, Achenbach had already defended himself publicly over this document when it was first published in 1953. The FDP deputy, under scrutiny at the time over his involvement in the Naumann affair, had explained himself in an open letter. But instead of simply claiming that he was only passing on information, Achenbach went further. "General Heinrich von Stülpnagel only asked for this telegram to be sent to Berlin in order to avoid the execution of hostages in retaliation. I transmitted the message and covered Stülpnagel." In *Der Spiegel*, Achenbach added, "We had to make a lot of noise and, thanks to that, all went well." In other words, all went well, and the Jews were not deported.

This was the version that Achenbach tried to give the press on April 11 and 12. But why had this accomplished lawyer waited so long to respond to my allegations? He could have sued me for defamation after the publication of my open letter. Instead, he took refuge in silence.

Now, returning to the 1953 defense, he claimed that his telegram was merely a bluff, that the two thousand Jews had never been arrested or deported. So, in fact, this telegram might even be regarded as an act of resistance!

We had to prove that this deportation measure, supposedly suggested as a bluff, had not only been planned but carried out. For three days, we dug deep into the archives, sometimes following leads that ended nowhere and sometimes chancing upon documents that had previously gone unnoticed by historians.

It was through this investigation that we were able to really understand the mechanisms of the Sipo-SD—the umbrella organization combining the Gestapo (the secret state police) and the Kripo (the criminal police)—something that would prove extremely useful to us when we later went after Nazi criminals such as Lischka and Hagen.

THE EMBASSY'S POLICY regarding the selection of hostages to be shot in retaliation for attacks on Germans was decided by Abetz and his political adviser Achenbach. According to them, it was best, in the interests of the German people, to avoid the idea that the French were rebelling against collaboration. Abetz advised taking Jews and Communists hostage.

When Abetz was informed that the embassy's proposed measures had been approved by the Führer, he is reported to have said, "These measures correspond with the principles set out in my written report of December 7, chapter 4."

After that, the embassy took part in writing communiqués to Berlin about the bloody retaliations. Among these, I found a twelve-page report by Achenbach dated March 17, 1943, that featured dozens and dozens of names of those who were shot.

But what became of the "two thousand Jews" for whom all went well, according to Achenbach? On February 23, 1943, SS-Obersturmbannführer Kurt Lischka, the *Kommandeur* of the Sipo-SD in Paris, informed his counterpart in Brussels that "I told the chief of police in Paris that, in retaliation for the killings, two thousand Jewish men aged between sixteen and sixty-five must be arrested and transferred to the Jewish camp at Drancy." The next day, Röthke, head of the Gestapo's Jewish Affairs Department in France, reported to Lischka on his meeting with Thomas Sauts, from the chief of police's office: "Sauts replied that the arrest of two thousand Jews [. . .] has begun. More than fifteen hundred Jews aged sixteen to sixty-five have already been detained in the two zones."

A report by the French Federation of Jewish Organizations confirms the arrest of foreign Jews aged sixteen to sixty-five in the former free zone, their roundup at the Gurs camp, and their transfer to Drancy on February 26 and March 2, 1943.

Those two convoys were sent to the extermination camp in Sobibor, where the two thousand deportees were immediately murdered, with the exception of two groups of about fifty younger men, who were sent to the neighboring camp of Maidanek. In 1945, only four survivors remained from convoy 50 and six from convoy 51.

OUR INVESTIGATION WAS conclusive. Achenbach had lied; he had even attempted to claim credit for an act of resistance when the truth was that he had taken part in a decision, made by Kurt Lischka the day after the attack on the German soldiers, that led to the arrest, deportation, and extermination of two thousand Jews in the space of less than a month.

We sent our conclusions to Brussels. On April 11, the German commissioner, Wilhelm Haferkamp, published a statement making clear that, if Achenbach were appointed, he would resign.

ALTHOUGH ACHENBACH TRIED to cling to his promised position after that, the battle was over. Professor Dahrendorf was appointed to the European Commission in his stead. On May 29, when Dahrendorf's position was made official, the government began its search for someone to succeed him as parliamentary undersecretary in the Foreign Office.

Eager for revenge, Achenbach resurfaced: he informally applied for this job. Thankfully, we had kept a photocopy of a "secret" document dated February 11, 1943; the signatory of this note to SS-Obersturmbannführer Röthke had not been identified. As we had an example of Achenbach's signature in our possession, we had no difficulty in recognizing it at the bottom of this document, which gave the necessary diplomatic green light to the Gestapo for "the application of anti-Jewish measures in the new occupied zone."

On the morning of May 30, I arrived in Bonn with about a hundred photocopies of this document and a similar number of a press release in which I summarized the story of the two thousand deported Jews. I distributed these documents to the press and to the relevant government departments, and then immediately returned to Paris. On June 1, 1970, Karl Moersch was appointed as Dahrendorf's successor. Achenbach's consolation prize was a position as the FDP's parliamentary spokesman on foreign policy.

I have never met or even seen Ernst Achenbach.

SERGE

BESIDE BEATE

D URING THOSE TURBULENT years, I did my best to support Beate in her campaigns, gradually detaching myself from my professional life to engage in militant activism where time was of the essence. Beate's dismissal from the Franco-German Youth Office had made me so angry that I felt compelled to act. I was French; my father was murdered at Auschwitz; my wife was French by marriage; she worked in Paris and had been fired from her job because she publicly denounced the fact that a former Nazi propagandist was the chancellor of Germany. If my father had had enough courage to fight back in Auschwitz, I could not simply give up. Beate was ready to fight, so I would fight with her.

In 1970, I was one of about twenty employees at Continental Grain made redundant for economic reasons. Almost immediately, I was hired by the Crédit Lyonnais. Walking through the bank's vast lobby, however, I felt myself gripped by anxiety: if I worked here, I would not leave until my retirement. I had to save my soul, which would disintegrate in this world to which I did not belong. And so I quit after only one month in the job.

THIS WAS A turning point in our lives. We left Paris for West Berlin, where I became a volunteer correspondent for *Combat*, writing under the pseudonym Henri Daru.

We went back to Paris after a few months spent in a fascinating city, where we met Andreas Baader, Ulrike Meinhof, and other future terrorists. I remember having a bitter argument with Beate's former lawyer, Horst Mahler. He intended to engage in violent action, and I was trying to dissuade him, in vain. Those political militants wanted nothing less than a revolution; they had supported our actions, but they did not want Willy Brandt, the reformist whose accession to power they had helped bring about. They felt betrayed. Violence now seemed to them the only way they could impose their will. Some of them died violent deaths; others spent years in prison; a few gave up the struggle. Mahler, the group's ideologue, was incarcerated for a long time before repositioning himself as a right-wing extremist, fanatically anti-Jewish and anti-Israeli.

Back in Paris, we moved in with my mother, who was happy to be reunited with our little family. Arno slept in her bedroom, while Beate and I shared the other room. We were poor but free—and ready for the long campaign that awaited us.

East Germany was closed to us now, as a result of Beate's protests in Warsaw and Prague, and in the west our margin for maneuver was very narrow. The right loathed Beate and her slap; the far left was anti-Israeli; the Social Democrats were divided: they respected Beate but did not have the courage to openly state that the Franco-German legal agreement—allowing criminals condemned in absentia in France to go on trial in West Germany—should be ratified. The Christian Democrats would vote against this measure, and the FDP liberals—who were part of the coalition government with the SPD—would argue against it under the influence of Ernst Achenbach, who remained a powerful figure within the party due to his representation of big business.

In 1971, a long article on Beate in the *Nouvel Observateur* led the FSJU (United Jewish Welfare Fund) to offer me the position of head of its vacation centers for a six-month trial period, but only on the condition that I not publicly take part in Beate's activities. I accepted because we needed the money, but I did wonder how I could respect that condition and also why I should. This was a large Jewish organization, and our objective was the judgment of Nazi criminals; what was the need to be discreet about it? I soon appeared in the media as Beate undertook several journeys around Bolivia, and I had to explain the situation to the written press, radio, and television. To his great regret, the director of the FSJU said he felt obliged to put an end to my trial period. The president of LICA intervened on my behalf with the FSJU, who paid me a year's salary. Not only was this a relief, but it allowed us to become totally committed to our political activities.

IN FEBRUARY 1971, when we began our campaign to bring Lischka and Hagen to justice, and to put an end to the legal dispute between France and Germany that went back to the Second World War and had still not been resolved, we did not know that our patience would be tested so severely. It was not until February 1980 that we were finally able to conclude the case.

When we started that campaign, there were only the two of us. By the time it ended, a thousand orphans of Jewish deportees had gathered around us. From an individual initiative, we developed it into a collective movement and, in so doing, created the vehicle and the group that would help us achieve our common goals in the decades that followed.

BEATE

PROTEST IN POLAND

I N 1970, I began to look eastward. If Willy Brandt were to make history, that was where it would be made. But it was also from that direction that we heard the rumble of anti-Semitism, growing disturbingly loud.

When the German elections were over, I phoned Mr. Dmowski, a Polish diplomat who a few months earlier had invited me to visit his country. I was ready to go; I was interested in seeing the sights, of course, but I also wanted to communicate with the youth of Poland. I wanted to speak at Auschwitz. Though I called him several times, the invitation never came to fruition.

Not long before this, on October 5, 1969, I was invited to East Berlin for the celebrations commemorating the twentieth anniversary of the creation of the German Democratic Republic. There was a series of receptions. I wore a white cocktail dress—stylish but modest—that attracted the attention of the gathered Communist leaders. This was one of the rare circumstances where I felt genuinely seductive, probably because I was one of very few women allowed into this small circle of men. There was one moment I particularly savored: seeing the looks of stupefaction, almost of bitterness, on the faces of the West German Communist Party leaders and the leaders of the ADF, when an official came to find me in the large reception hall of the State Council and led me to the VIP section where Walter Ulbricht and the Politburo were welcoming the leaders of the socialist countries.

Ulbricht warmly shook my hand. The attention I received from this little man, the embodiment of Communist Germany, was due to the intransigence I had shown toward Kiesinger. A member of the Central Committee told me that he had been present when Ulbricht was informed about the slap: "It was November 7, the anniversary of the Soviet revolution. We were in the middle of a meeting in Ulbricht's office when a secretary came in and whispered to the president that you had just publicly humiliated Kiesinger. Our discussion then turned to that subject. I vividly remember what Ulbricht said about you: 'That is a courageous woman. We must support her.'"

After two years of clashes and hostility, I could not relax completely in the company of politicians. The compliments and friendly smiles bestowed on me by these East European leaders—Stoph, Honecker, Brezhnev, Husák, Zhivkov, Kádár, and others—made me feel good, but I did not belong to this system. I remained convinced that the German nation could only express itself through acts of political morality.

It was a very enjoyable evening all the same, the kind of evening young girls dream about, the kind of evening I had dreamed about myself. I was filmed dancing in the arms of a white-haired Soviet marshal in full uniform. The six-year-old German girl who had watched in terror as the Cossacks invaded the village where she and her mother had taken refuge in 1945, could she ever have imagined that one night she would find herself waltzing with one of the leaders of the Red Army? Commitment to a cause can never be absolute; it always leaves a small breach through which you can follow your own adventure, like a mildly fascinated spectator.

IN OCTOBER, I returned to Berlin for two conferences: the first on the NPD and the second on what stance to take regarding Willy Brandt. I shared the opinion of most of the student movement's members that we should immediately bring an end to our infighting. However, some more radical left-wingers—among them my lawyer, Horst Mahler—were opposed to this idea. Serge tried to bring them round, but in vain.

At the end of 1969, I decided to start writing about non-French subjects for *DVZ*. I went to The Hague for the European summit. I wanted to be there for Brandt's entrance on the international stage and to let the Dutch people know that the youth of Germany were behind their chancellor.

The first inter-German summit was due to take place in Erfurt on March 19, 1970. I absolutely wanted to be present for that historic moment. But my foreign-press authorization from East Berlin was late in arriving. Very few foreign journalists were allowed to attend this conference. In desperation, I flew to East Berlin at my own expense and insisted on gaining access until I was finally given the precious piece of paper. I then hitched a ride to Erfurt with two journalists from the Gamma agency. I helped them get through police checks, as neither had received their accreditation.

On the platform of the train station in Erfurt, I stood only a few yards away from Willy Brandt and the East German prime minister Willi Stoph as they shook hands like two men who respect each other and are reunited after a long separation. It was an exhilarating moment for me: the meeting at Erfurt put an end to Bonn's claims to exclusively represent the interests of Germany. It was also a point of no return on the path that led to the legal recognition of the GDR as a sovereign state by Bonn and the West—a landmark on the journey toward reunification.

As Brandt came out of the station, I was so close to him that he happened to see me—and his serious expression broke into a smile.

In the afternoon, I followed Brandt to the Buchenwald Memorial. It was extremely cold, and snowing. The monument is located on a small hill above the city of Weimar. Brandt was accompanied by the East German foreign minister Otto Winzer. They headed toward the commemorative tower, which had been wrapped in the East German flag, and then toward the crypt. Some soldiers from the East German army had formed an honor guard in front of the monument. There was a military band, too. Brandt, preceded by soldiers carrying flowers, went down into the crypt while the band played the West German national anthem—for the first time, I believe, on East German soil. Brandt and the East German leaders honored the dead for the same reasons: these were Germans who had fought against Hitler. For both sides, this was no mere ceremony but a genuine return to their roots.

After Brandt had left the crypt, I went down there, my arms full of flowers handed to me by East German leaders. As I placed the flowers next to one of the walls, I read this phrase engraved upon it: THE DESTRUCTION OF NAZISM AND ITS ROOTS IS OUR AIM.

ON MAY 24, 1970, I was in Kassel, West Germany, for the second summit between East and West Germans. This thaw in relations between the two republics did not take me by surprise. My logic was simple enough: no great people has ever remained divided indefinitely; the Jewish people were able to recover their homeland after two millennia, despite being persecuted and small in number; therefore, the German people would also be united once again.

My vision was not utopian. For that reason, I had to remind people in the East, as I had done in the West—and not only with words but with acts—that they were subject to urgent moral imperatives with regard to their ideological commitments. After what happened under Nazism, shouldn't every German feel a duty to combat anti-Semitism, to help keep former Nazis away from positions of power, and to prevent the "rehabilitation" of Nazi criminals?

That was why I went to Austria on May 15 to oppose the presence of Hans Schirmer as the West German ambassador in Vienna.

A Nazi Party member (number 3143496) from May 1, 1933, Schirmer had worked in Goebbels's propaganda ministry and had been Kiesinger's superior from 1939 to 1943. He had also been the director of the Radio Mundial agency, an international propaganda broadcasting network that disseminated the idea of a "new Europe" all over the world.

Walter Scheel, the West German foreign minister, had declared, "The Austrians have already forgotten the Anschluss." And he was right. No matter how much I stirred up the Austrian press or questioned Chancellor Kreisky at his press conference, nothing had any effect. Bruno Kreisky replied to me that refusing an ambassador was an act of hostility toward the country he represented and that it was the responsibility of the host country to verify its diplomats' pasts and decide if they were acceptable.

I tried again on June 17, at the Austrian Socialist Party's congress. This time, I had brought some leaflets with me—as well as Arno, since my mother-in-law was staying in Bucharest with her sister.

We were outside the front door for the opening ceremony of the congress. It was raining, and we were soon soaked. Arno was horsing around in the rain, so in an attempt to calm him down I gave him a few leaflets and asked him to help Mama by handing them to people. Instead, he had great fun soaking them in puddles, scrunching them up into wet paper balls, and throwing them at the delegates.

I was hoping the Austrian socialists would take a stand against Schirmer, but the exact opposite happened. During that congress, they protested aggressively against Simon Wiesenthal, who criticized them for letting former Nazis into government. The security guards escorted me from the building. I was furious.

From Vienna, I went on to Bucharest, to introduce Arno to his great-aunt. Ten days later, I had to return to Berlin. All these trips were costing us a fortune, so I went to the East German embassy and pleaded my case. They immediately gave me a Bucharest-Berlin ticket on the Interflug airline. In East Berlin, I was offered a free vacation in the GDR with Arno. This offer had been made to me by the East German government before, but I'd never had the time to take them up on it. This time, though, I accepted— and, from August 5 to 20, the two of us stayed at the Hotel Panorama in Oberhof.

The only trip I'd made in East Germany before this had been in March 1968. For three weeks, I had traveled around the country alone. The East Germans trusted me: I was not forced to follow a particular itinerary but could go where I pleased. In Oberhof, it was very different: we stayed in a palatial hotel surrounded by a very bourgeois East German clientele, wealthy people who expressed no political opinions and with whom I felt no connection whatsoever. My only friend there—and a great love of Arno's— was a cleaning lady named Marion.

I had plenty of time to think while I was there. In Poland, anti-Semitism had come back into the open, with the blessing of the Polish authorities. For more than a year, I had been promising myself that I would raise the issue of anti-Semitism in front of the Polish youth. Up to now, I had not been able to keep that promise.

In East Germany, too, the nation's youth had to be armed against anti-Semitism, not through words, but through a trial of strength with the East German authorities. In the GDR, it was not the party leaders who were anti-Semitic but senior civil servants then aged forty-five to fifty-five who had grown up under Nazism. They had not been like Walter Ulbricht, marching alongside the Red Army, or Erich Honecker, locked up in a Nazi prison, or Hermann Axen, a Jew imprisoned in a French camp and then deported. Many civil servants do not resemble their leaders; it was among these people that the anti-Semitic menace was spreading. I had always sensed a faint hostility toward me from them, just as I had from men of that generation in West Germany.

East Germans listened to West German radio stations; they watched West German television. They would hear about my arrest after I carried out my plan, as they would hear about my motives. They would be very surprised, and they would read the East German party's line in their newspapers. Either that, or the party would make the decision to destroy my reputation through defamatory newspaper articles. Or recognizing the truth of what I was saying about Polish anti-Semitism, they would remain silent on the issue.

Anyway, I was well aware that, after the action I was planning, silence would descend around me in the GDR; that the West German Communists would quickly distance themselves from me; that the newspaper I worked for, *DVZ*, would do its best to fire me.

What I planned to do was not anti-Soviet or anti-Communist, however; it was not about finger-pointing at the Poles; it was a question of not remaining silent or inactive in the face of tyranny.

I carefully assessed the risk I would run, because I had no wish to be a martyr. As with the slap, I would do all I could to avoid prison. The Poles would never believe that I had acted alone. When they learned about the moral support I had received from East Berlin, there was a good chance they would imagine the GDR was in some way behind my actions in Warsaw. For the Polish government, then, the best solution would be to rapidly expel me from Poland—and I was happy with that, on the condition that Western press agencies would immediately spread the news of my arrest.

I WROTE A leaflet in German and French, and had it translated into Polish. I then made two hundred copies of this trilingual text.

I also had to get hold of a Polish entry visa. At the Polish military mission in West Berlin, a bureaucrat had me fill out various forms. I exchanged my marks for vouchers that would enable me to pay for my hotel room in Warsaw. Then the same bureaucrat spent a long time examining my French passport. "You're a journalist?" he asked. That was what I had written on the form. "Come back in two weeks to collect your visa."

That same day, I went to the Polish embassy in East Berlin. This time, I was more prudent. I took care to engage in a long conversation with the bureaucrat, who knew about my anti-Nazi activities. And yet he still frowned when he spotted that fateful word.

"So you're a journalist?"

Very quickly, I said, "No, I used to be, during the election campaign, but now I'm just a housewife."

"Then write 'no occupation,'" he suggested, and gave me the visa.

NINE P.M., AUGUST 25. The train moves slowly through the suburbs of Berlin. For the first time, I feel palpable fear. The protest I am planning to make tomorrow morning in Warsaw is very different from all those I've organized in Western countries. In Poland, people have rotted in prison for less than this.

There is a man in his forties sitting on the seat facing me. For a few moments, he stares at me. He does not speak until well after our departure. He works in the East German embassy in Warsaw. I breathe a sigh of relief.

"Do you know Warsaw?" he asks.

"No. I'm going there to do some sightseeing for a few days."

"I would be happy to act as your guide. My family lives in East Berlin, so I have plenty of time."

This invitation is awkward, because if the diplomat is seen in my company, it could seriously affect his career after what I am going to do tomorrow.

We arrive in Warsaw early in the morning. Again, the diplomat wants to help: Please, let him find me a hotel. I politely refuse.

TIME IS SHORT. I find a youth hostel, but it has no vacancies. The desk clerks do agree to look after my suitcase, though.

I only have a few hours to alert the Western press agencies. I feel very small and vulnerable as I rush through this unknown city. My taxi driver cannot find the address of the AFP correspondent. The minutes tick by. I ask him to drop me—I'll find it myself. But I can't, and in the end I have only one solution: call him. The phone rings and rings. Just as I am about to give up, someone answers. But he does not speak French, and I don't know a word of Polish. In hesitant German, the man explains that he is a carpenter doing some work in the AFP's office. Thankfully, I at least manage to get him to give me directions.

After waiting for a good hour, I finally see a short man arrive. He speaks French with a strong accent. So the AFP's correspondent is Polish? In that case, I cannot possibly tell him about my plan. He questions me.

"I'm a French tourist. One of my husband's friends works for the AFP in Paris, and he advised me to come and meet you so you could give me some information about the city."

He appears surprised by this, and not very convinced. I can't keep up this pretense. I decide to take the plunge.

"Are you French? I mean, do you have French nationality?"

He stares at me wide-eyed. "Yes, but why?"

"That changes everything. I want to let you know about something. Can we talk here?"

"No, no, we'd better talk in my car."

I feel slightly more reassured when I notice that his car has French license plates. I explain the action that I am planning to carry out around noon. He does not seem too thrilled about this. The punishment is severe. All the same, he does agree to be present. "All I'm asking you is to go there and witness my protest. You don't have to speak to me, just send the information to Paris."

FINAL PREPARATIONS. I go into the restroom of a café to tie a chain around my waist, over my dress. The other end goes through the buttonhole of my coat.

Noon. On the Marszałkowska, in the center of Warsaw, the sidewalks are packed. I carefully choose a tree that looks strong enough. It is close to a stoplight and faces a very wide and busy crosswalk. Perfect. The cars—more of them than I had imagined—come to a halt a few yards from where I stand. Pedestrians walk past on either side of me. It's time.

Quickly but discreetly, I take out my chain. It almost slips out of my hands. I hadn't realized I was trembling. I wrap the chain around the tree and padlock it. But what should I do with the key? People are swarming around me. That tiny key in my palm seems to weigh a ton. My first reflex is to swallow it. Dumb idea. Keep it in my mouth? I try, but it's an unpleasant sensation. I look around for a sewer. Nothing nearby. Clearly I haven't thought of everything. I could simply throw it on the ground, but what if a passerby were to see it? Only one solution remains: I drop it behind the railings that surround the tree and then put my foot on it.

People are starting to notice me. I move around as much as the chain allows and hand out my leaflets. People slow down to take them from me. In less than ten minutes, all two hundred leaflets have been distributed. I keep one copy and hold it to my chest, so that the others can read what it says:

Polish citizens,
    The elimination of the Jews that is still going on in Poland is not part of a struggle against supposed Zionist traitors—it is simply ANTI-SEMITISM. These new persecutions are damaging the reputation of Poland and of socialism all around the world. In reality, they have been engineered by the enemies of socialism, who are trying to seize power by acting like demagogues.
    Poland suffered terribly under Nazism, but do not forget that in Auschwitz and Treblinka millions of Polish Jews were exterminated while the rest of the population remained passive. Only the Polish Communists and socialists fought against that genocide in an organized way. Follow their example and demand that your government put an end to its measures, which are forcing the last Polish Jews—among them many patriots and socialists—to flee their homeland. I am not a Zionist, nor even a Jew; I am a German anti-fascist.
    B.K.
    Lambrakis Medal, awarded in 1969 in East Berlin by the World Peace Council

I spot a policeman going into a phone booth. He comes out, still staring at me. A few minutes pass. A Jeep stops on the sidewalk, and the people in the crowd in front of me are shoved out of the way by two policemen. One of them grabs my arm and tries to lead me away. He doesn't get very far. Young people smile openly as I show the policeman my chain. Disconcerted, he walks around the tree, then demands the key. *Klucz*, he repeats five or six times.

Eventually, he goes back to the Jeep and rummages around in the trunk. The second policeman stays close to me. I am careful not to move my foot, in case he sees the key hidden beneath it. People crowd around, and the policeman tries to push them back, in vain. Angrily, he grabs hold of a young man who is reading my leaflet and confiscates his identity papers.

The other policeman returns, with a pair of wire cutters. He frees me without difficulty. While all this is happening, I notice the French journalist on several occasions. I am led away to the Jeep, along with the young man, and we are driven to the police headquarters. There, I am taken to various offices before they find a superintendent who speaks German. The usual interrogation ensues. The police officers are courteous. They do not understand the reason for my public protest.

"Do you have any other leaflets?" they ask.

"Yes, in my bags. I left them at the youth hostel."

We go there in the car. On the way back, another policeman attempts to convince me that anti-Semitism is no longer a problem in Poland.

Back in the police station, a senior civil servant takes over, telling me unceremoniously, "You have committed a serious crime. As a foreigner, you have protested against a democratic country. You will be taken to court, and you may be sentenced to two or three years in prison."

"Do what you think is right."

My lack of anxiety seems to take him aback. He leaves me alone for more than two hours, then returns.

"We have decided to expel you. We have taken into consideration all that you did before the mistake that you made today."

At the airfield, they take the money from my bag and use it to pay for my ticket to Paris. The superintendent then hands me over to the French pilots. I leave Warsaw sitting in the cockpit of a Caravelle airplane. A few minutes later, the crew invites me to sit in first class and offers me a glass of champagne to celebrate my happy escape. Serge and Arno fly from Bonn to

Paris, reaching Orly Airport a few hours after me, and we celebrate Arno's birthday at home.

WE DID NOT have to wait long for the first press reactions. A West German Christian Democrat newspaper wrote: "A globetrotter in the name of socialism and anti-fascism, this young woman is perhaps a little eccentric; it is possible to laugh at this Amazon who loves a good fight, but she is always consistent in her political opinions, and she is obviously not biased—because she sees the flaws in Communist countries, too, and denounces them."

I went back to Berlin, hoping to seize the moment. The main goal of my protest was to win over the youth of East Germany, so I wanted to get a feel for the reaction in East Berlin. First, I went to my mother's house in West Berlin; I had imagined for an instant that she might change her mind about me, since the right-wing press had written something favorable about me for the first time. Wrong! She seemed to be allergic to any form of public protest whatsoever.

As I crossed the east-west border on the S-Bahn, at the Friedrichstrasse checkpoint, I felt slightly apprehensive: Would they let me through without any difficulties? My fears were unfounded: everything went smoothly, and I went to see one of my friends who worked in radio and who had been the first person to help me establish relations with East Germany. I was about to show him the leaflet I had handed out in Warsaw, thinking it would come as a surprise, but he told me he had already read it. He said that the press agency dispatches had caused a degree of shock among East German journalists, even if they didn't show it.

Next, I contacted a bureaucrat at the Ministry of the Interior who had helped us when we were researching Kiesinger's past.

"I wanted to meet you. Could Serge and I come to your office?"

"I don't think that will be necessary after what you did in Poland," he replied coldly.

"But why shouldn't I denounce anti-Semitism in Poland?"

I was trying to start a discussion, so I could explain my position, but it was no good.

"Your view of the issue is from the wrong historical standpoint."

The conversation was over; the bridges were burned. Would I have better results with the editors of the East Berlin newspaper *BZ am Abend*, for whom I wrote regular articles? When Serge and I arrived, we saw the head of the foreign-news department, so I asked him if the piece I had sent three weeks earlier was going to be published. "We can no longer publish anything by you," he replied. "We did not agree with your protest, even if it's true that there are problems in Communist countries. Our opinion is that those problems should not be exposed, as it provides more ammunition for the capitalists."

This flat rejection revealed the gulf that had opened up between us. The fear of heresy led to the most cowardly kind of dogmatism.

I tried one last time, going to the East German anti-fascist association. We began with a lot of small talk, as if they were trying to avoid discussing the elephant in the room. When I showed them the leaflet I had distributed in Warsaw, the old Resistance fighters looked embarrassed. One of them said, "Yes, we heard about your protest. Everyone's talking about it, but only in whispers; not many dare to speak openly about it. Lots of our friends approve of what you did, because there's been a problem for a long time that shows itself during the memorial ceremonies at Auschwitz or in the Warsaw Ghetto. Only delegations from the Eastern countries attend those ceremonies. We have tried to change things through discussions with our Polish comrades, but it hasn't made any difference."

It was during this period that my relations with East Germany deteriorated. I went back one more time with Serge. They made us wait at the border for two hours before finally announcing that we no longer had the right to enter East Germany.

A FEW WEEKS after my protest, Willy Brandt—the first chancellor of the Federal Republic of Germany to visit Poland—chose to kneel at the Warsaw Ghetto memorial, to the great displeasure of the Poles and also of many Germans.

Later, when Brandt received the Nobel Peace Prize after overseeing treaties that normalized the Federal Republic's relations with the Soviet Union and Poland, tears came to my eyes—and I am not someone who cries easily. Of all the things I have done, one of those that brings me most joy is working on behalf of Willy Brandt and having put my trust, for once in my life, in a politician. Brandt's vigorous and courageous *Ostpolitik* and the human relations that he facilitated between West Berliners and East Germans have already earned their place in history.

THE EAST GERMAN authorities' sudden reversal did nothing to shake my deepest convictions. I continued to believe that the sole solution to the German problem was the official recognition of both states of the German nation. Germany's absence from the United Nations struck me as deplorable, too. It was time that East Germany and West Germany joined the UN simultaneously.

I would make my opinion public a few weeks later, on October 23, 1970, on the twenty-fifth anniversary of the United Nations Charter, to be commemorated at the UN headquarters in Geneva. At the time I was in West Berlin, and it was a telephone call that made my mind up: Michel Lang's mother told me that there was a rumor in German far-left circles that I was a CIA agent. Not only that, but our predecessor in the spacious fourth-floor apartment we had just left in order to live with my mother-in-law again—the apartment that would soon be used to shoot *Last Tango in Paris*—was the head of the CIA in Paris; that, at least, was the claim made in a Soviet pamphlet that gave his name and address. I was appalled. But then, when I thought about it, such an accusation seemed logical. The way in which the different systems—capitalist and Communist—defend themselves against those who denounce their excesses is always pretty much the same. Two years earlier, the far-right press had stated that I was a Stasi agent, in the pay of Walter Ulbricht. The newspapers explained how each time I went to East Germany I would receive my instructions directly from him. Now it was the far left that was attempting to smear me. I would not let this calumny go unchallenged; I would respond in my own style—with a simple, clear, public act, proving that my political beliefs had not changed.

To realize my plan, I needed leaflets and two large German flags. I found the address of a flag-making factory in the phone directory. I was pretty surprised when the flags actually arrived, though: each one was eight feet by five feet. I had planned to attach them to broom handles, but that was obviously not going to work! I had to buy two seven-foot flagpoles. Carrying them on a train from Berlin to Geneva was far from easy!

At the station in Geneva, there were press photographers waiting for me on the platform: I had told them I'd be arriving. Still carrying my unwieldy package—the two flags were wrapped in brown paper—I took a taxi with a convertible roof to the UN headquarters.

I don't know who denounced me, but the UN's security staff had been warned about my visit and instructed not to let me enter. Thankfully, they were on the lookout for a young woman carrying two flags, or perhaps a group of students arriving on foot. Consequently, they paid no attention to taxis. That was how I was able to enter the gate without any problems.

As it happened, there was a crowd of delegates on the front steps. Without wasting a second, I unwrapped my parcel. A young man offered to help me. I nailed the two flagpoles, arranged so that they crossed each other, to the façade near the entrance and then immediately began handing out the two hundred leaflets. It did not take long for the UN's security guards to react. They confiscated my flags, but not before the photographers were able to immortalize the moment.

IN THE FALL of 1970, I also went to London to protest the British home secretary's plan to expel Rudi Dutschke. I went to see journalists at all the major newspapers on Fleet Street, pointing out that Dutschke had been gravely wounded by a pro-Hitler fanatic.

Articles appeared, and Harold Wilson—the leader of the opposition Labour Party—promised to intervene. He did so, but it made no difference. Dutschke had to go into exile once more, this time to Denmark, where he would die without fulfilling the destiny he deserved.

And Now for the Czechs . . .

I N DECEMBER 1970, two of the people accused of attempting to hijack an airplane to escape the Soviet Union were sentenced to death. In tandem with LICA and thousands of Jews, I took part in the protests in Paris that followed this verdict.

Three weeks later, I was asked to speak at the Maison de la Mutualité. The room was packed. Among the other speakers were Jean-Paul Sartre and Eli Ben Gal, the European representative of the Israeli party Mapam. When my name was announced, there was a loud burst of applause. I was very touched by this. Later that evening, Ben Gal came up to me, shook my hand, and said, "This is the first time in my life that I have shaken the hand of a German. But after all you have done, I can and I must." He wrote a short dedication for me on the program for the event: "To Beate, who brought something unique into my life: the hope, one day, of a reconciliation between our two peoples and, while we wait for that far-off moment, a real friendship."

How far I had come since that day in the summer of 1966, at a kibbutz in Galilee, when a young woman explained to me that they did not allow Germans to live with them! To be allowed into the hearts of the Jewish people, to be able to shake a Jew's hand without any ulterior motive on his part, we as Germans had to do more than simply leave them in peace.

That night in the Mutualité, a journalist from a German press agency was taking notes. He sent a complete account of the meeting to Hamburg, expressing how moved he was by seeing a German woman welcomed so warmly by so many Jews. That paragraph was censored from his article: German readers must not be made aware that the scandalous path I had taken in public life could have ended in the respect of Jews, a respect that most Germans were far from earning.

I spoke with more emotion than usual that evening, perhaps because the battle was about to move to a new front: Czechoslovakia.

The expulsion of many Jewish socialists from Poland, the insidious persecution of thousands of others who do not want to leave their country, the inferior status reserved for the majority of Soviet Jews, the obstacles that prevent them from living and expressing themselves as Jewish nationals or emigrating, the recent trial in Leningrad and its terrifying verdict: all of this is anti-Semitism. Likewise the venomous attacks on former Czech leaders of Jewish origin. We must be clear about this! All of this is anti-Semitism, and it will only spread and strengthen unless the Communists, socialists, and anti-fascists here in the West openly and wholeheartedly throw themselves into the battle against it!

The western Communists denied the fact that many Soviet Jews wished to emigrate to Israel; in Brussels, in February 1971, I even heard a delegation of Soviet Jews state that there was no Jewish problem in the USSR. And yet it was obvious that the problem did exist and that it would take more than denial to make it go away.

But words were not enough; the situation demanded action. I could not be content merely to write press releases and sign petitions. Particularly as the East German party newspaper, the *Neues Deutschland*, had just taken up an anti-Semitic position by approving the death sentence of the sixteen refuseniks (all but two of them Jewish) who had attempted to escape the USSR by stealing a civilian aircraft, in what became known as the First Leningrad Trial.

If the East Germans were subject to such brainwashing, I felt obliged once again to make a public protest against that hateful policy in a way that would reach the people of East Germany. A number of former Nazis had found jobs in the GDR's propaganda department. They were not in positions of great power, but they still had influence. And the occupation of Czechoslovakia, the persecution of Jews in the Soviet Union, the GDR's good relations with the Arab countries . . . all these things gave those ex-Nazis the opportunity to rear their ugly heads.

In early 1971, anti-Semitism was growing stronger in Czechoslovakia. The Bratislava edition of *Pravda* attacked "Jewish intellectuals who were able to occupy a number of influential posts in Czechoslovak cultural life." On January 13, Radio Prague broadcast the conclusions of the Czech Communist Party's Central Committee accusing Zionist elements of having played a considerable role in the events that led to the Soviet invasion. Whenever a former leader of Jewish origin was mentioned, the radio announcer used certain set phrases, such as "an admirer of Lev Davidovich Bronstein, better known as Trotsky." A trial of twenty-six young Trotskyites was due to take place on February 8. They were accused of "attempting to overturn the socialist regime, not only in Czechoslovakia but in other socialist countries, including the USSR"—a monumental accusation.

I decided to protest outside the courthouse on the opening day of the trial. This date seemed particularly propitious, as the East German prime minister was traveling to Czechoslovakia the day before, to take a rest cure in Karlovy-Vary. It was highly likely, after my arrest, that Gustav Husák, the secretary-general of the Czech Communist Party, having met me in East Berlin, would turn toward the East Germans for advice on what to do with me. And I felt pretty sure that the East German government would not want its youth to find out I'd been sent to prison, because that would almost certainly provoke a wave of protests, particularly among the country's students. And they couldn't hide the truth from them, because they were able to access news from West Germany. With Willi Stoph being in Czechoslovakia at the time, his opinion would probably be decisive. So he and his fellow East German leaders would be caught in a dilemma: to abandon a

German woman in prison, knowing that she was telling the truth, or to intervene on her behalf despite the trouble she was causing them.

But first I had to get a visa. As it was possible that the Czech secretary in the Paris embassy might know my name—and what I had done in Warsaw—and consequently be suspicious of my intentions, I decided to turn up at the consulate with Arno, playing the role of a snobbish middle-class woman who wanted to embark on a pleasure trip in a slightly "exotic" country. Arno did his part, climbing on the furniture and making a mess of the secretary's neatly stacked paperwork, and the secretary quickly got rid of us, handing me a visa without any questions and even booking me a hotel room. I bought a Paris-Vienna-Prague-Cologne-Paris plane ticket and packed my suitcase with three hundred leaflets, written in French and Czech.

It was hard to leave my family. My mother-in-law was frantic, fearing that I would be drowned in the Vltava, as had happened to a leader of the American Jewish Joint Distribution Committee in 1968 at the hands of the Czech secret service. Serge had trouble concealing his anxiety, too. For once, Arno knew nothing about it all.

I left Serge at Orly Airport. As I walked away from him, I turned my head, and the two of us stared intensely at each other. I believe that couples who deliberately live with a shared ideal and in a climate of danger are much more likely to see their love increase over time. To me, that is what living together really means.

I LAND IN Vienna on Saturday, February 6. From there, I will take the train to Prague. The police checkpoints in airports are far more rigorous than those in train stations, and there is a strong possibility that my leaflets will be discovered if I go through airport security. I have to wait an hour at the airfield in Vienna because the customs officials sees my name on a blacklist.

After finding my hotel, I call Simon Wiesenthal. He meets me that evening in a café. I tell him about my plan, and he gives me some new information, notably that the Trotskyists' trial will not take place on February 8 because the Czech authorities fear it will provoke protests at the Young International Communist Conference in Bratislava.

Wiesenthal approves of my plan, but he is very worried. "Czechoslovakia is not like other countries; the police are really tough. There's a real risk that you'll end up in prison for a long time."

My greatest fear, however, is not being able to inform anyone of my arrest, and simply disappearing. Of course, I have the addresses of Western journalists in Prague. Once again, I will have to contact them without raising suspicion. Serge and I have agreed that, if I succeed in talking to one of those journalists on Sunday evening, I will send a telegram to Paris stating: "Got here safely. Beautiful city."

On Sunday, I catch my train. The three hundred leaflets are hidden in the lining of a small bag. This bag is full of food, notably a Camembert cheese so ripe that its smell will, I hope, dissuade even the most conscientious customs official from digging any deeper. I have also bought a huge bouquet of flowers that I will carry while looking vacuous. My aim is to be above suspicion.

It all goes as planned. The young policeman smiles at me as he glances distractedly at my passport. He takes a brief look inside my suitcase but doesn't even glance at my bag of food. I do, however, have to get rid of an Austrian architect who seems determined to show me around Prague, unaware that his tourist itinerary would probably end with a visit to the local prison.

From the Flora Hotel, I take a taxi to the apartment building of a German journalist. He lives quite far from the city center. It is already pretty dark. The buildings have a sad look. I climb the stairs to the third floor and ring the bell. No one answers. I sit on the top step to wait. One hour later, I leave; I don't have time to just wait around. I need to organize a contact with the press that evening.

I go to see a Reuters English correspondent, who lives in the city center. After listening to me, he explains that there is no anti-Semitism at all in Prague. All the same, I give him the time and place for the meeting. The place I have chosen for my protest is the university's philosophy department, to which most of the students accused in the trial are attached.

As I doubt the Englishman's reliability, I go to see a German journalist who works for a Cologne radio station. His wife is there alone, as he is at the Young International Communist Conference in Bratislava. She calls a cameraman from a West German television channel, and we spend the rest of the evening together in a café. Here, at last, I can speak freely: the young woman was obsessed by the fear of hidden microphones at her apartment. Getting back to my hotel room at one in the morning, I send the coded telegram to Serge. I sleep badly that night.

On Monday morning, I leave the hotel around ten o'clock and walk through the streets of Prague for two hours. It has been snowing, and the streets are covered with muddy slush. I take refuge in a café to warm myself up. I sit there tensely, surrounded by young people talking cheerfully.

At noon, I walk to a large square outside the philosophy department and take out my leaflets. On the back of each one, printed in large lettering in Czech, it says: "Against re-Stalinization, against repression, against anti-Semitism." On the front, the same text is printed in both French and Czech:

Citizens of Czechoslovakia,

I am not a Jew; I am a German anti-fascist. In the name of all the forces of the left, I led the campaign of young Germans against the Nazi chancellor Kiesinger. I was sentenced to a year in prison for slapping him.

Today in Prague, as I did on August 26, 1970, in Warsaw, I am calling on the citizens of an Eastern country to oppose the frenzy of anti-Semitism that is being whipped up in the socialist nations by the supporters of re-Stalinization.

Under the influence of Stalinists, Czech propaganda continually claims that the 1968 occupation was caused by the pernicious and anti-Czech role of "Zionists." This propaganda continually underlines the Jewish origin of certain liberal leaders; they are trying to convince you that there is no difference between a Jew and a Zionist agent. All of this is not anti-Zionism, it is anti-Semitism. They are looking for a scapegoat.

We must not let this anti-Semitism discredit socialism. The only solution for Western anti-fascists who are not blinkered is to act openly against it and against those who propagate it—as in the USSR, where Jews' national rights are flouted; as in Poland, where the ultra-nationalist Moczar entered the Politburo while Jewish Communists are driven out of their country; as in the German

Democratic Republic, where the *Neues Deutschland* dares to unreservedly back the death sentences handed out at the Leningrad trial.

Citizens of Czechoslovakia, do not allow yourselves to be contaminated! Fight against anti-Semitism!

A student reads the text, then asks me in German if it is really me, Beate Klarsfeld. "We know all about your campaign against Kiesinger, we talked about it a lot in class. What you're doing is extraordinary. But be careful, the police here are very harsh. You should leave right away." He takes twenty leaflets from me, promising to distribute them to his friends.

After three-quarters of an hour, I go to Wenceslas Square. It is full of people, but they all seem wary; I really have to insist before anyone takes a leaflet from me. A few minutes later, a policeman enters the square. He has seen what I am doing. I immediately give him a leaflet. He goes into a nearby phone booth, and I see him read the words on the leaflet out loud. Not long after that, I am brutally manhandled by another policeman, who tears the leaflets from my hands and shoves me into a police car. There is a long discussion on the car's radio, and I am driven to a large modern building in a narrow street. I assume this must be the police headquarters, though in fact I never find out where exactly I was held.

I sit in a small office opposite a fat superintendent in a dark suit, about fifty years old with a round, rather jovial face that appears to grow harsher with each question he asks. He speaks to me in fairly good German. He empties my bag out on the table and, after taking my ID papers, spreads all the objects out. Then he phones to ask for an interpreter, and we wait for nearly an hour in silence.

Finally, the door opens and a man in his sixties enters: he is pretty thin and wears a very long dark gray leather coat with a belt, like a Gestapo commander. I get goose bumps. This is the official interpreter, a former Austrian. They start the interrogation, which is extremely methodical and lasts several hours. A secretary records all the questions and answers on a typewriter. The superintendent wants to know everything: Who wrote the leaflets? Who translated them? What machine was used to print them? Who gave me the money? Why are there so many East German visas in my passport? Who are my friends in the GDR? Are they aware that I am currently in Prague? Most of the time, I just tell him the truth, which makes things easier. On the walls is a poster protesting the imprisonment of the American radical Angela Davis.

The first phase of the interrogation ends. The superintendent, a detective, and the translator take me to the hotel to search my bags. On the way there, we walk through a courtyard lined with barred windows. The impression is so suffocating that I say to the superintendent while we wait for the car, "You'll have to release me tomorrow, you know, like they did in Poland, because you can't allow anti-Semitism to go on trial."

"No, no," he tells me, "that might work for Poland, and as it happens I completely agree with you, because there's a definite anti-Semitism in Poland: it's not organized by the government; it's just rooted in the Polish people. It's not like that here. You should have come on a visit and asked around; we could have shown you the country, and you would have realized that there is not anti-Semitism here. And you wrote [on your leaflet]: 'Against re-Stalinization, against repression.' But without Stalin, the Nazis would have won, and the Jews would have been exterminated."

"I know they're not the same, anti-Semitism in Poland and anti-Semitism here. I know that the Czech people are not anti-Semitic. But there is a team in the government, notably in the propaganda department, that is scapegoating the Jews, trying to make them out to be the cause of all your problems."

"Why did you repeat the same protest in two Eastern countries? Surely you must realize that this repetition is fatal for you. We are going to be much firmer with you this time; you have slandered our country; you have acted against Czechoslovakia. You're going to have to stay here for a while."

I am becoming increasingly anxious. I am cut off from the outside world. In the West, I would have a lawyer to defend me. But here in the East, what do I have?

THREE POLICEMEN SURVEY the hallway while we go up to my room. They empty my suitcase and my travel bag. They search under the mattress, under the blanket, and in the cupboards, where they find some leaflets that I'd left there; they even lift up the carpet and inspect the bathroom.

Suddenly, I notice that the man who is searching my suitcase has put his hand beneath the liner and is taking something out. He discovers a dozen pieces of microfiche, and the police start holding the pieces under a lamp, trying to decipher what is written on them. These microfiche contain lists of names of Czech Jews killed by the Nazis during the war and awarded posthumous honors by the Czech government; I brought them here intentionally to infuriate the police. Serge found them at the CDJC. We expected the police to research the names immediately and, after realizing their true meaning, to understand that we were mocking them: after all, discovering hidden microfiche is the dream of all detectives. In fact, none of the police will ever mention those microfiche to me.

I am hungry, having skipped breakfast. The hotel has a luxurious dining room, and delicious smells keep wafting up from the kitchen. I decide that I may as well have one last good meal, and the superintendent agrees to my request. The four of us sit at a table, surrounded by foreign tourists. The policemen order only a beer each—they will pick up sandwiches on the way back to the station—but I choose a shashlik from the expensive menu and a half bottle of wine.

It is past 8:00 p.m. by the time we get back to the office. The policemen are all eager to go home for the night, so the interrogation is postponed until the next morning. They tell me that I will spend the night here, in a basement cell. I leave all my personal belongings in another office, where they are carefully sealed inside an envelope, and then I am taken to a kind of filthy cellar. All I have on me is one handkerchief, which I will end up using as a washcloth.

I am feeling pretty happy after everything that's happened today, and I am expecting to find a bed in my cell, as I did in Berlin. Instead, I discover a dark little hole, twelve feet by fifteen, with three women—two thin and one fat—already lying on mattresses on the floor. My mattress is still rolled up against the wall. There are no sheets, only a stiff, dirty, stinking blanket. The women speak only Czech. One of them helps me to make my bed. Like them, I lie down fully dressed. Their panties and tights are drying by the window. I sleep better than I did the night before.

At 6:00 a.m., someone hammers on the door. One of the young women gets up and knocks on the wall. I don't understand why until water suddenly spurts from a small pipe that sticks out of the wall. It is in a corner and is separated from the rest of the cell only by a torn curtain that no longer closes properly. Next to it is a bucket so disgusting that I assume it must be a chamber pot. But no, this is the bucket that holds all our water for the day. These Czech women are clearly used to this: they carefully use every drop of it. First they brush their teeth, then wash their faces; after that, they clean their laundry. They really are remarkably well organized. One of the women even cleans the cell with the last bit of grayish water. Then we roll our mattresses against the wall and fold our blankets.

All our guards are men. They watch us through a peephole in the door. The young women wear short skirts, and the one who cleans the cell does not put her panties on until she is done, so I imagine the male guards are enjoying themselves.

The cell's window looks out on the courtyard I walked through the day before. It can't be opened very much, and the stench coming from the corner behind the torn curtain makes me want to throw up. In the middle of the cell are a table and some stools. The walls were painted gray a long time ago, and the floor is covered by torn linoleum. At 6:30 a.m., breakfast arrives: some very sweet white coffee and a thick slice of stale black bread.

I wait for them to come and fetch me. They keep interrogating the fat girl from our cell, and each time she returns she is in floods of tears. She tells the others all about it, and they try to calm her down. The youngest one—the one who cleaned the floor—cheerfully sings Western pop hits to herself. I wish I knew how long she has been here and what she is here for, but the language barrier makes conversation impossible. From time to time, the women bang on the door. Almost every time the guard arrives, they ask him for a cigarette. They laugh and flirt with him, and he lets them have one. The rest of the time, they make their own cigarettes using old stubs, some bread crumbs, and a bit of dust; they savor each drag.

The day goes by slowly. At noon, we are given cabbage soup with a bit of meat in it, but it's so salty and greasy that I eat only a few mouthfuls; I don't want to get a stomachache in a tiny cell like this.

In the afternoon, my back starts to hurt from sitting on the stool for so long. So I unroll my mattress and lie down on it. A few minutes later, the door opens and the guard shouts something at me. I know what he wants, but I pretend not to understand. When he comes back and sees me still lying there, he storms into the cell, grabs me by the arm, yanks me to my feet, and hurls the mattress against the wall.

I am beginning to worry now. Last night, they told me I would be interrogated this morning, but no one has come to see me all day.

Around 6:00 p.m., the cell door opens again. The guard calls me over and leads me out. He shoves me into the little office where I left my belongings; they are returned to me. In a bigger office, I see one of the policemen from last night, sitting on a chair. A young, prematurely bald man sits behind a large table; he is better dressed than his colleagues. In barely comprehensible German, he tells me, "You are going to be expelled from Czechoslovakia immediately. We have prepared everything. A car is waiting for you outside, and it will take you to the nearest Austrian border."

In a corner of the room, I see a camera pointed at me. On a low table, the spools of a tape recorder turn round and round. The young man opens a file and takes out a sheet of paper, which he begins to read in Czech. He questions me. I say I don't understand what he is saying; he summarizes the text in German.

All I gather from this is that I have broken this or that Czech law, and I am now banned from entering this country for the next four years. He gives me a pen and asks me to sign the paper. When I leave the office, I am followed by another man, who carries a portable camera. But apparently he doesn't like the scene he has shot, so he makes me do it again three or four times. I am allowed to wash in a bathroom, this time surveyed by a woman. When I have gotten dressed and picked up my bags, I walk outside, still pursued by the cameraman.

Outside the building, on the other side of the narrow street, a large black car awaits, with a driver and a policeman inside. I get in the backseat with the woman from the bathroom and another policeman. We have to repeat this scene several times for the cameraman. I wonder if he is new at the job or if he is shooting the scene from different angles. Around midnight, we arrive at a small border post in the middle of a forest. It is very cold, and there is a thick layer of snow on the ground. After a few formalities, two policemen and a uniformed customs guard escort me toward the Austrian border.

Suddenly, the policemen come to a halt. They do not say a word. Ahead of me, there are a few lamps and then nothing—just darkness. The customs officer explains that he cannot go any farther. I walk, alone, through the snow, heading for a tiny light that I can just make out in the distance. This turns out to be an Austrian border post, even smaller than the Czech one, a single room. When I enter, the two Austrian customs officers look up at me in astonishment.

"Did you come by car?" they ask.

"No. I walked."

"But where did you come from?"

"I've just been expelled from Czechoslovakia."

"Expelled?" They laugh. "Well, you're lucky they didn't keep you there!"

They are staunchly anti-Communist and fully prepared to help me find a room for the night.

This has just been organized when, at 12:25, their replacement arrives. The two guards explain the situation, and the new man picks up my passport and examines it. He speaks with the other two. "You should have asked for authorization from the police in Vienna before you gave her an entry visa." He takes them aside, and I hear the name "Kiesinger" mentioned several times. Obviously, they are not going to get a response from the Vienna police at this time of night. I try to argue, but the new customs officer pays no attention. I have to spend the night in that border post, lying on two chairs.

At 6:00 a.m., the response from Vienna arrives: I can enter Austria. I reach Vienna by bus and train, and from there I call Paris. I reassure my mother-in-law that I am fine, and she tells me that Serge has gone to Bonn as planned. I catch a plane to Frankfurt, and another one to Cologne, and finally see Serge at four that afternoon.

THE NEWS OF my arrest had not filtered out of Czechoslovakia. Serge had called the hotel where I was staying but had found out only that I was no longer there. Because of the telegram I sent, he knew I had made contact with the press agencies in Prague, so he called their Paris offices and asked them to question their Prague correspondents about me. That was how he learned about my arrest. On Tuesday morning, it was in all the newspapers, which perhaps played a part in my expulsion. I learned later that Willi Stoph had immediately intervened on my behalf; I like to think that he had a sudden fit of conscience, though maybe he simply didn't want his Czech vacation to be ruined.

ON MARCH 2, the Czech leader Gustav Husák criticized my "bad behavior" in Prague, probably because the anti-Communist radio station, Radio

Free Europe, had created a buzz around the incident and because I had explained in an interview broadcast within Czechoslovakia the reasons for my protest.

My role is not to make people happy; it is to tell the truth as strongly as possible—bluntly, even savagely, if necessary. But having been banned from Czechoslovakia, Poland, and East Germany, I was now about to be arrested in West Germany, too.

SERGE

No More Impunity for Nazi Criminals in France

WHEN THE GERMAN ARMY withdrew from French territory, so did the German police. Among these men were the leaders of the Sipo-SD, which included the Gestapo.

This department's sinister reputation spread so quickly that the name "Gestapo" was often used to describe the entire Sipo-SD. While French military tribunals were able to judge the few German criminals they managed to capture, the majority kept their distance from the French occupation zone in Germany and often lived under a false identity. Some of them had been policemen or intelligence agents before 1939. After 1945, they were protected by their former colleagues who had remained in—or returned to—the ranks of the German police. As for the leaders of the new West German intelligence service, the BND (Bundesnachrichtendienst), now devoted to the struggle against communism, they had—with the United States' blessing—hired as many "anti-subversive" specialists as they could find. These specialists were former members of the Gestapo and the SD, which explains why so many Nazi war criminals were able to come out of hiding and live with impunity. From 1948 on, all those who had gone to ground in the Soviet zone headed for the American zone, where well-paid employment awaited them.

The SS general Franz Six, sentenced at Nuremberg to twenty years' forced labór for the mass murder of Jews and Russian civilians, was soon freed. Reinhard Gehlen, appointed by the Americans as leader of the BND, hired Six to be one of his highest-ranking assistants.

There is a tendency to assume that men like Six were not hunted down after the war because they were too old. But that is to forget that Nazis put a great emphasis on the energy of youth. Franz Six did not turn forty until 1949, while Helmut Knochen, his protégé, was only thirty-one when Heydrich named him head of the Sipo-SD in occupied France.

Brought back to Paris in 1947, Knochen was judged at the same time as General Karl Oberg, head of the SS and the German police in France. Given the vast scope of their crimes, the only possible verdict was the death sentence. The earlier the trial occurred, the more likely the sentence was to be carried out. But Franz Six, a powerful man once again, remained loyal to his friend Knochen. At that time, the United States held considerable sway over France, so Knochen and Oberg did not appear in court until 1954. They smiled smugly as their verdicts were read out. Yes, they were sentenced to death, but they knew they would not die. And, indeed, their sentences were commuted to life imprisonment. In 1962, the thaw in relations between de Gaulle and Adenauer, the French and West German leaders, led to Oberg and Knochen being pardoned and returning to Germany after seventeen years in prison.

The vast majority of German war criminals were never even arrested. In 1954, when the Federal Republic of Germany became practically independent, the problem of those criminals' punishment became acute. Many of them had been sentenced in absentia by French military tribunals. In total, between September 1944 and October 1954, 1,026 Germans were convicted in absentia for war crimes. The French authorities feared that, if the German courts became competent to judge these cases, they would be extremely lenient toward them. With so many Nazis still working as judges, men sentenced to death were likely to have their cases dismissed or their sentences suspended. For that reason, in article 3 of the convention of October 29, 1954, France made it impossible for the German courts to be competent to judge cases in France concerning German war criminals. As soon as this convention was signed, the criminals in question just went back to Germany.

France demanded that the German government extradite these criminals, but the Federal Republic's lawyers pointed out that article 16 of the law approved by France when it was an occupying power stated that the West German government could not extradite its own citizens.

After attempting to find its way out of this legal maze, the French government finally located a loophole, in the form of a judgment by the German supreme court on February 14, 1966, providing for the possibility of concluding a special agreement to remove all obstacles to the administration of justice. Grudgingly, the Bonn government agreed that the German judicial system should once again become competent to judge those in absentia verdicts. The signature of that agreement was delayed for a long time for spurious reasons: none of the German chancellors that followed— neither Adenauer nor Erhard nor Kiesinger—really wanted to deal with this problem, preferring to let time pass so that the criminals would escape the justice of men.

THERE WERE JUST the two of us; we had to follow the same path we had taken in the Kiesinger affair. Once again, we were facing a clash with West German political society. We had to compel the German parliament to ratify the legal agreement signed with France on February 2, 1971, when two of the three parties represented in the Bundestag were opposed to it and the fate of the liberal–social democrat coalition hung in the balance. When we had obtained this ratification, which would transform the agreement into law, we would then have to force the German justice system to do its duty: to try to sentence these criminals.

As with the slap, we decided to raise awareness of the problem with a momentous act: we would abduct the former Gestapo officer Kurt Lischka and bring him back to France to be tried. Our cause was legitimate, but once again it was David versus Goliath. Our strategy was simple, if delicate: act illegally and repetitively, but with tact, in order to give ourselves a platform. We knew we risked prison, but in doing so we would create a situation in which the real criminals remained free while the victims' representatives were punished for acts that paled in comparison with those committed by the criminals. If we could hold firm, public opinion would swing our way and would demand the ratification of the agreement, even though the French government had long ago given up on the possibility.

BEATE

Hunting Lischka

I MET WILLY BRANDT again in January 1971, during his official visit to Paris. The meeting took place at the German embassy.

During my anti-Kiesinger campaign, I had been banned from the embassy. This situation did not change after Brandt became chancellor: the consulate even refused to renew my German passport. Furious, I called the government's assistant spokesman, Rüdiger von Wechmar, whom I'd gotten to know when Brandt met Willi Stoph in May 1970. I hated having to use my connections in this way, but it was the only language that those bureaucrats understood.

AT BRANDT'S PRESS CONFERENCE, I raised my hand.

"Chancellor Brandt, when will the impunity of German criminals sentenced in France come to an end?"

"Soon, soon, *gnädige Frau*. A few days from now, the two governments will sign a new agreement that will put an end to the current situation."

When the conference concluded, Brandt walked over to me. What he said went straight to my heart. "Your courage is refreshing. We were talking about you today, in fact; we were surprised that your work is still going on, because we'd thought it would end when Kiesinger left office. Your critical commitment in the East and the West is very positive."

In fifteen months in power, Brandt had left his mark, particularly in terms of foreign policy. He had pulled West Germany out of its rut.

Ten days after I returned from Prague, I received a phone call from Yaron London, an Israeli television representative in France. He wanted to talk to me about my recent protests. The interview took place in his apartment, as we had moved to a smaller place a few months before this, for economic reasons, and our house was a mass of toys and piled-up case files.

When the interview was over, London asked me about my plans for the future, and I told him about our intention to bring the most prominent Nazi war criminals to justice.

"Their trials would be an opportunity to understand the police mechanism that led to the deportation and death of more than seventy-five thousand Jews from France and to establish who was responsible for it. And if we can bring to justice those few big fish, we will be able to prevent all the little fish in Germany from being rehabilitated. Any proceedings that end in a case being dismissed or an acquittal would lead to German public opinion accusing the French judicial system of having wrongly condemned those 'German patriots.' But the rehabilitation of Nazi criminals can only sully Germany's reputation. We must force German society to examine its conscience, however uncomfortable that makes it."

"Who are the biggest Nazi criminals in France who have not yet been punished?"

"There are two: Kurt Lischka and Herbert Hagen."

"And where are they?"

"Living peacefully in Germany."

"Whereabouts?"

"Lischka, who was the number one Nazi policeman in France, lives in Cologne. When I was going through his files, I noticed that he had been head of the Gestapo in Cologne from January to November 1940. So I thought that, if he were still alive, he would probably have chosen to live in a city where his former subordinates and colleagues worked in the police and government. I called the operator in Germany and asked if there was a Kurt Lischka in the Cologne phone directory. Ten minutes later, they called me back: 'Yes, there is a Kurt Lischka. His number is 631 725, and his address is 554 Bergisch-Gladbacher Strasse.'"

"It was that easy?"

"Yes. It's only in detective novels that ex-Nazis live in constant fear in Patagonia. Apart from the Eichmann abduction, which was organized and carried out by Israeli government services, there has never been any illegal action against Nazi criminals."

As we were talking, I thought of something that Serge once said about Lischka: "Think how powerful a man like Lischka must feel. He's responsible for the deaths of so many Jews, he's sentenced to life imprisonment in France, and yet he puts his name in the phone book. How much contempt must he have for Jews? We have to react, Beate. You as a German, and me as a Jew."

When I told London that we were planning to write an article about Lischka and Hagen for *Combat*, he suggested we make a film as well. "We could show it in Israel as part of an in-depth news show called *Panorama*."

Thrilled, I agreed, and on February 15, Serge finished writing the screenplay for the *Panorama* program that would last twelve minutes if we succeeded in filming Lischka and Hagen. Four days later, my article was published in *Combat*. And two days after that, we were in Cologne, ready to get to work.

AT 8:00 A.M. on Sunday, February 21, we parked our car opposite Lischka's apartment building, on the far side of the wide street where he lived. It was a three-story building in a suburb of Cologne, and he lived on the top floor. The day was gray and rainy, and the streets were deserted.

We waited for six hours for him to emerge, but nothing happened. We went to eat lunch, and I called his phone number to find out if there was anyone home. When his wife answered, I hung up. We decided to ring his doorbell. He must have been watching us through his window, however, and, seeing a cameraman, opted not to respond. So we rang all the bells in the building, and someone eventually came downstairs and opened the door to us. We explained that we were there to see Mr. Lischka. They let us in and told us he was on the third floor.

We walked upstairs. His door opened. Mrs. Lischka appeared: her hair was blonde and stylishly cut, her expression cold. I explained that we had come to interview her husband for a French television show. After a moment of thought, she invited us into a small room, probably the dining room, and called out to her husband, "Kurt, come and see!"

Kurt Lischka entered the room. I told him that Mr. Klarsfeld was a French journalist and he wanted to interview him. I was his translator. Lischka asked to see Serge's press card, then asked me for my name. As usual in such situations, I used my maiden name. Lischka got to his feet and stood next to his wife. He was very tall, with a large pink head and sparse blond hair, and he spoke in short, dry sentences. He wore slippers, pants, and a cardigan. I was watching him closely when I announced Serge as "Mr. Klarsfeld," but Lischka did not react. I translated Serge's questions word for word.

"After the signature of the Franco-German agreement, I did some research into Nazi criminals judged in absentia in France. You were at the top of the list, Mr. Lischka. But before starting a campaign against you, we came here to ask if there was anything you wanted to say in your defense."

"I have nothing to tell you. If I am ever asked to account for my actions in a German court, I will do so, but only in a German court. To you and to the French courts, I have nothing to say."

"Do you acknowledge that you were assistant head of the Sipo-SD in France, head of the Gestapo in Paris, and one of the main organizers of the persecution of the Jews in France?"

He responded to this with icy silence. His expression was closed, hostile. Serge asked him, "Would it interest you to see the orders you signed? Perhaps you thought they had been destroyed, like most of the German archives were; but at the CDJC, the archives for the Gestapo's Jewish Affairs Department have all been kept, and your signature is at the bottom of several documents. You will be tried and, I hope, convicted."

Lischka was interested in those documents. I handed him a few photocopies. His wife leaned over his shoulder to see, and we noticed the sheets of paper tremble in Lischka's hands. He read the pages attentively, one after another. He looked like he was in shock. We left soon afterward.

SERGE

The Kurt Lischka Dossier

I N BERLIN, REINHARD HEYDRICH, head of the RSHA, the Reich Main Security Office, is concerned: Paris is the weak link in the police chain that he is tightening around Germany's recently conquered territories. He summons Heinrich Müller, the Gestapo chief, and the two of them discuss the subject. I imagine their conversation:

"I need someone in Paris, to work with Knochen. A supremely competent man who can take over the Gestapo there."

Müller thinks about this, then barks out, "SS-Sturmbannführer Kurt Lischka!"

"He's running the Gestapo in Cologne, isn't he?"

Heydrich remembers this tall, blond officer, a perfect Aryan specimen. "Yes. He's an excellent organizer and one of our leading specialists on the Jewish question. Just turned thirty. Very dynamic."

Müller knows what he's talking about. Lischka was in charge of the deportation of twenty thousand Jews to the Polish border, which ended with many of them—babies in particular—dying there because they did not have Polish passports and so were not allowed to enter the country. It was this tragedy—in which his parents died—that inspired the young Jew Herschel Grynszpan to assassinate a Nazi diplomat in Paris: the incident that sparked off the infamous Kristallnacht in November 1938.

BORN IN BRESLAU in 1909, Kurt Paul Werner Lischka entered the Gestapo in 1936. A hard worker, he was quickly promoted. In 1961, the Israeli prosecutors asked Adolf Eichmann, "Who created and directed the RSHA's Jewish Affairs Department IV-B4 in 1939?"

"Regierungsrat Kurt Lischka. He was Theodor Dannecker's direct superior at the time."

Dannecker, under Lischka's direction, was responsible for the implementation of the Final Solution in France, where he was head of the Gestapo's Jewish Affairs Department.

OUR WORK AT the CDJC began with the need to identify Lischka's signature and, in particular, his signed initials. This latter was important because numerous initialed documents do not bear the signatory's name. In this way, we were able to reclassify many documents whose signatures had been cataloged as "illegible" as well as some others that had been wrongly attributed to Dannecker, who wrote down Lischka's notes and orders. Our conclusion: the Parisian Gestapo *was* Lischka.

In fact, the entire German police apparatus in France was in Kurt Lischka's hands. He was, notably, all-powerful when it came to executing hostages and torturing prisoners.

ON JANUARY 20, 1941, there was a conference on the Final Solution, where Lischka and Dannecker represented the Sipo-SD. A contemporary document recounts:

SS-Sturmbannführer Lischka indicated that, as far as the new measures applicable to Jews in France were concerned, the goal was to solve the Jewish problem in Europe following the directives put in practice in the Reich. To this end, the plan was to create a central Jewish Office in France that would take care of the following tasks:

1. Dealing with all police questions regarding the Jews (inventories, files, surveillance).
2. Economic control (elimination of Jews from economic life; collaboration in the reassignment of Jewish businesses to Aryans).
3. Propaganda (anti-Jewish propaganda in France).
4. Institute of Anti-Jewish Studies.

ON APRIL 2, 1942, Lischka refused an exceptional request from the German embassy to release Roger Gompel, a Jew they considered "notable," stating that he could not make any exceptions "otherwise the French will think that there are no German anti-Semites except for the Führer himself."

Two weeks before this, Lischka had written to General Speidel, former chief of staff to Field Marshal Rommel:

Following our proposal, the RSHA has declared itself ready to accept five thousand Jews from France in addition to the one thousand Jews from Compiègne . . .

A large number of the Jews to be deported can be taken from the Drancy camp, and the camps near Orléans, Pithiviers, and Beaune-la-Rolande.

It will therefore be possible to begin replacing these Jews in the camps and to carry out further roundups in order to thin the ranks of Paris's Jewish population.

LISCHKA

On May 15, 1942, Lischka wrote to Eichmann about the Sipo-SD's need for train carriages to transport Jews. Despite pressing military demands, the heads of the Gestapo expended all their considerable energy obtaining trains that would cross Europe loaded with Jews. And obtain them they did.

Contact was established with Lieutenant General Kohl, head of the railway department (ETRA). Kohl is an implacable enemy of the Jews and he has guaranteed that we will have the carriages and locomotives necessary for their transportation. Consequently, at least ten trains will soon be in a position to leave France . . . I would like to be informed if and when a large number of Jews can be received and at which camp.

Given that further roundups are necessary and that the room available for them is limited here, I would be grateful for an immediate delivery of five thousand Jews.

STURMBANNFÜHRER LISCHKA

The word "delivery" was frequently used by Lischka during and after the war, as he became an authorized signatory for a cereal company, and the bureaucratic and logistical mechanism for the delivery by train of wheat and Jews is practically the same.

Lischka left France on October 23, 1943. Back in Berlin, he was promoted to the position of Gestapo department head. Implicated in the execution of Czech Resistance fighters, Lischka was imprisoned in Prague before being freed in 1950.

TWO DAYS after our visit to Lischka, we return to 554 Bergisch-Gladbacher Strasse in the Mercedes belonging to our cameraman Harry Dreyfus. It is 7:00 a.m. and very cold. At 7:50, Lischka leaves the apartment building. We are hiding behind a fence near the metro station. He is dressed in a long coat, hat, and glasses and carrying a black briefcase; he looks exactly like someone who once worked for the Gestapo.

Lischka comes toward the station but crosses the road as soon as he spots us. He speeds up, and we follow him, filming him as we go. Suddenly, Lischka stops and then sets off in another direction, and then in another, while we stay close on his heels. Then he breaks into a run, and so do we. Kurt Lischka, suddenly confronted with his own past, is now fleeing down the streets of his own town.

The sequence we filmed that day produced a big emotional reaction when it was broadcast in Israel, and it is still shown on television even now whenever the fate of Nazi criminals is discussed.

The next day, we leave at 6:00 a.m. for Warstein, about 125 miles northeast of Cologne, to film Herbert Hagen. Beate had called his house the previous night and spoken to his wife. "Would your husband agree to be interviewed by a French journalist?" The answer, it turned out, was no, and "My husband does not understand why you would want to interview him." Beate ended the conversation there.

We arrive in Warstein at 8:30 a.m. and park our car about a hundred yards from Hagen's house. There, we wait for five hours before Beate, who is starving, goes off to a café, and we see a man in a tweed jacket emerge from the house and head toward a crowd of people gathered to watch a passing parade. Thinking it is Hagen, we run after him. But when we get closer, we realize our mistake. This man is too young to be the former Nazi. We walk back toward the car, but just as we are passing Hagen's house, the door opens and a man in a coat, hat, and glasses comes out, walking quickly down the front steps and into the garage. He gets into a large Opel, and Beate, who has come back from the café, throws herself in front of the car as it rolls out of the garage, blocking it on the driveway. "Mr. Hagen? Is that you, Mr. Hagen?" He looks up, says yes, and then notices the camera trained on him. He opens the car door and moves threateningly toward us. Then just as he is about to grab the camera, he changes his mind and composes himself: if he were to damage the camera, we would file charges, and his name would be in the press.

Beate points at me and says in German, "This gentleman is a French journalist; he wants to ask you a few questions." Hagen gets back in the car and waits for his wife. Then he speaks to me in fluent French, sounding outraged.

"Monsieur, you have no right to film me in my street, outside my own house."

"Mr. Hagen, there are Germans who were given life sentences for doing more than filming in the streets."

"But, monsieur, I am not in hiding. I have been back to France more than twenty times since the war."

"It's a shame the French police didn't notice your name, otherwise you would have been arrested. What I want is to ask you a few questions, in particular whether you acknowledge having been the head of the Gestapo in Bordeaux, General Oberg's right-hand man, head of the SS and the German police in France, and head of the SD's Jewish Affairs Department."

"Monsieur, I have nothing to say to you," he replies, with a tense smile. "If you wish, you could get in touch with my son, who is a journalist in Cologne."

Then, sitting behind the wheel of his car, he adds, "All I want is to be left in peace."

When his wife and teenage daughters walk out past the car, Hagen drives after them, offering me a final, icy "Goodbye, monsieur."

THAT NIGHT, REMEMBERING what he said about his son, Beate calls the house in Warstein. Mrs. Hagen answers. "We know who you are, Mrs. Klarsfeld. Call my son: he'll give you all the explanations you need. He's a left-winger, like you."

After doing some research into us, Jens Hagen agrees to meet us. He is a thin young man, casually dressed, with a long beard and long hair. He writes for left-wing newspapers. In English, he tells us, "I'd like to know what you can tell me about my father. I don't know very much, because there are some things he never talked with me about."

I take out the Hagen dossier and show it to him. "These are documents that he wrote and signed during the Nazi era."

Shoulders slumped, utterly silent, he begins to read. As he turns the pages, he looks shell-shocked. Clearly, his father had never told him the truth.

"My father was an idealist," he says. "He was led astray, but he's not a criminal. He never killed anyone. My father was so anti-militaristic that when he was in Yugoslavia, he didn't even carry a weapon when he led raids against the Resistance."

Beate replies, "I disagree. I think your father was so militaristic that he deliberately didn't carry a weapon so his men would think him brave and be more ready to follow him."

Jens turns back to the documents. The more he reads, the more he realizes the evidence is undeniable. He even sheds a few tears over that pitiless dossier.

The Herbert Hagen Dossier

H ERBERT HAGEN WAS born in 1913. At age twenty-three, this brilliant student of Professor Franz Six joined the SD.

Six offered Hagen a position as head of Department II-112. The aim of that section was the war against the Jews. Hagen accepted. His talents as a journalist were also useful to Six in his capacity as head of the Institute for Foreign Studies, an organization that reported to the SD and whose newspaper published numerous articles bearing Six's byline but written by Hagen. Books such as *World Jewry: Its Organization, Its Power, Its Politics*, published by the Nazi Party under the pseudonym Dieter Schwarz, were the fruit of a collaboration between Six and Hagen. Hagen's predecessors had assembled a hard core of anti-Jewish fanatics; Hagen's subordinates included Dieter Wisliceny, future exterminator of the Jews in Hungary and Czechoslovakia; Theodor Dannecker, future exterminator of the Jews in

France, Bulgaria, and Italy; and Adolf Eichmann, future architect of the Final Solution.

Hagen successfully bureaucratized the ideological nature of the anti-Jewish work. The SD was later revealed to be a more effective enemy of the Jewish people than the Gestapo. During his interrogation in Jerusalem, Eichmann would state: "Hagen was a reasonable man, with a broad perspective and a good general culture. He was excellent at assimilating a problem and creating a summary of it. He was Six's close personal friend, and he became his writer. Every six months, Hagen would write a long activity report for Department II-112, each one remarkable for its clarity and attention to detail."

Due to a series of circumstances, we were practically the only people to consult those notes: at the CDJC in Paris, there was a cardboard box filled with Hagen's personal files, which he had forgotten when Paris was liberated. Those files were not examined until after Eichmann's trial. Hagen was the master spy working against the Jewish world, compiling endless files on them. He informed men and institutions of the Nazi viewpoint on the Jews so that they could accomplish their tasks in accordance with Hitler's wishes.

During the first six months of 1938, Department II-112 organized twenty-three conferences: Eichmann spoke once, Dannecker four times; Hagen spoke on eighteen occasions about Jewish issues. Eighteen conferences in six months. Hagen used all his legal and police skills in the service of this task. Eichmann and Hagen were very close friends. Eichmann would address letters to "Lieber Herbert" and sign them "Ady."

That intimacy dated back to an extraordinary journey the two men took together to Palestine in order to deepen their knowledge of the Jewish world and examine the possible benefits to the Third Reich of a Jewish state. Eichmann repeated at his trial in 1961: "Hagen was my boss . . . I was Hagen's subordinate." Their trip was the result of discreet contact between the Nazis' intelligence agency and an agent for the Haganah, a Jewish paramilitary organization, which was presumably eager for German emigrants to move to Palestine. Eichmann and Hagen met the agent, Feivel Polkes, in the Kranzler café, but the talks were never followed up, with the two SS men concluding that Palestine's Jews were resolutely opposed to the Reich. The anti-Jewish persecutions of 1938 put an end to any such contact.

Through carefully developed methods, Department II-112—led by Hagen and Eichmann—examined Jewish movements all over the world, setting up permanent intelligence agents in Paris, New York, Cairo, Jerusalem, Prague, Bucharest, and other cities. Section II-112 amassed files and experiences that would be used in the Reich's conquered European territories to attack various Jewish communities with an efficiency that still surprises Holocaust historians.

In October 1938, Hagen went to Vienna and Prague, where he delivered some advice: "Now would be a good time to engineer a widespread action against the Jews." He went back to Prague in May 1939, after the Czech capital had been occupied, and on June 30 he outlined his plan: "Show the influence of Jews in Czech politics, culture, and economics. That way, we will be able to name and shame the leaders responsible for tolerance toward the Jewish influence [an effective way of getting rid of Czech politicians still in power]; show that a converted Jew remains a Jew in his character."

When Himmler reorganized the police into the RSHA, Hagen was given the job of leading section VI-2: "Judaism and anti-Semitism." In June 1940, SS-Standartenführer Helmut Knochen arrived in Paris at the head of a Sonderkommando, a special commando of twenty men, the hard core of the Sipo-SD in France. Questioned in Nuremberg, Knochen replied, "It was Heydrich himself who put me in charge of that mission. SS-Hauptsturmführers Hagen and Dietl were with me."

Knochen soon entrusted his right-hand man, Hagen, with the crucial task of establishing the Sipo-SD on the Atlantic coast. On August 1, Hagen was named *Kommandeur* of the Sipo-SD in Bordeaux, where he quickly deployed his anti-Semitic zeal: the city's chief rabbi testified in 1944 that "within days of the occupation, about two hundred German Jews were taken for who-knows-what reason to camps in Gurs and Saint-Cyprien."

On December 8, 1941, Hagen decreed: "All Jews must be detained, irrespective of their age." Moreover, Hagen's former assistant, Dannecker— who had since become head of the Gestapo's Jewish Affairs Department in France—wrote to SS-Obersturmbannführer Lischka on January 13, 1942: "SS-Sturmbannführer Hagen informed me yesterday that the internment of Jews in the Basses-Pyrénées and the Landes in concentration camps is necessary for military reasons as well as for the extension of the anti-Jewish measures." The next day, SS-Obersturmbannführer Lischka informed the military command of his decision to follow Hagen's advice.

Hagen extended his zone of action as far north as Brittany, establishing the Sipo-SD in the Atlantic region's main cities in order to prevent or suppress all French opposition and in order to organize the arrest of Jews.

On May 5, 1942, Heydrich sent General Karl Oberg to Paris to oversee the SS and the German police in France and appointed Herbert Hagen to be Oberg's personal adviser. This was a huge promotion for Hagen. Not yet thirty, he was for a time also the head of department VI of the Sipo-SD in France. That department specialized in intelligence gathering on foreign governments, the French government, and French political parties.

Hagen is the perfect example of the "desk killer." No, he did not get his hands dirty; no, he was not a sadistic torturer; but his fanatical intelligence, used in the service of evil, defined the guidelines and the structures within which men like Barbie committed their atrocities. Hagen's notes, written in light-filled offices overlooking the Bois de Boulogne, trace the journey taken by the Jews toward their bitter end in Auschwitz.

Hagen was perfectly aware of what happened to the Jews. He was informed of their arrests and transfers: every document Oberg received passed through Hagen's hands.

ON JULY 2, 1942, there was a meeting among Oberg, Knochen, Hagen, Lischka, and Bousquet; Hagen kept the minutes. That meeting was about the Vél' d'Hiv roundup. Hagen also presided over the meeting on July 17, in which the fate of the children arrested during that roundup was decided. They were all deported.

Herbert Hagen was one of the last German criminals to have been convicted in absentia in France. On March 18, 1955, he was sentenced to life imprisonment.

JENS HAGEN PULLED himself together after examining his father's dossier. He began by explaining to us that his mother was sick, that his family was poor, that we should spare his father, that he had changed.

"We are happy to consider the possibility that your father has changed. Anyone can change. But for that we would need proof—and it is very easy to supply it. The best thing would be if your father were to turn himself in to the French authorities and ask to be tried. He would be a valuable historical witness, because he was present at the origin of the anti-Jewish persecutions. Eichmann and Dannecker were his protégés. He knows a lot of things. It would be extremely positive if he were to appear in court in France. And it would prove that he really has changed. He can help today's society to understand how he became the SS Herbert Hagen of the 1940s. In that case, we would defend the Herbert Hagen of 1971, who would almost certainly not go to prison for his crimes. But if he doesn't turn himself in to the French authorities, that means he hasn't really changed."

Jens told us he would pass on our proposal to his father. Beate and I smiled at each other after he left: we were not naïve; we knew we would never hear back from him. But, from a legal standpoint, we had to at least try this approach before entering the fray of battle.

It was, incidentally, very interesting to see how a supposedly left-wing journalist, the son of one of the biggest Nazi criminals, judged the generation that preceded his. Apparently, his feelings as a son outweighed all other considerations.

AND SO, IN three days, we had filmed both Lischka and Hagen. On March 4, 1971, I went to Ludwigsburg, near Stuttgart, to speak with Adalbert Rückerl, prosecutor general at the Office for the Investigation of War Criminals in Germany.

Dr. Ruckerl looked through the dossiers on Lischka and Hagen. Soon afterward, he recorded a declaration:

These deportations of Jews took place for racial reasons. In accordance with our legislation, these are base reasons [niedrige Beweggründe], which means that, by virtue of current German criminal law, the cases in question can be pursued; there is no statute of limitations. Foremost among the persons liable to such prosecution are Lischka and Hagen. I am of the opinion that we must arrest those at the summit of the hierarchy, responsible in whole or in part for these events; it is these men that we must submit to the impartial justice of the German courts.

Now, to help us in our battle and to strengthen our resolve, we had this declaration from the most competent German to judge such matters, affirming that Lischka was at the very top of the list of Nazi criminals. This time, we were ready to move from words to action.

Operation Lischka

THE PROBLEM NOW was to put together a small team: we needed at least three extra men in order to carry out Operation Lischka.

We found two of them by pure chance. Talking about the situation in a restaurant, we were overheard by the two Jewish men at the next table, who interrupted our conversation to announce they would be proud to help us. Their names were Marco and David. Not only that, but Marco knew a photographer, Élie Kagan, whom he thought might well agree to take part in the abduction. He gave us Élie's number.

Beate and I met him in a bar in the eighteenth arrondissement. Élie could not believe that a man who had signed the order for the Vél' d'Hiv roundup could be living peacefully in Cologne under his own name. But we showed him the Lischka dossier, and he was soon convinced.

The five of us began our preparations by studying the plans that Beate had put together. It was all very professionally done, with a detailed map of the area and observations of Lischka's habits, what time he left the house in the morning, and so on.

We also needed to equip ourselves with the necessary materials. First, we needed a club to knock out Lischka. Élie showed us his. It was so tiny, we all laughed. Élie got angry. "You don't know anything about it! I can bring down a mammoth with a little club like this!"

Still, we also needed a more intimidating weapon. Élie had an old pistol; we rendered it harmless by removing the hammer. But at least, if things went badly, we would be able to show that we meant business. I also bought a pair of handcuffs and rented a Renault 16 for our expedition.

We left Paris on the night of Saturday, March 20, arriving in Cologne at 3:00 a.m. That morning, we ate breakfast together, but by the time we went to pick up our second rental car—a five-door Mercedes 220, the most common car in Germany at the time—we were already a few hours late. That delay was fatal: Hertz had rented the car to someone else.

In the end, we had to be content with a three-door Mercedes 280, a luxurious cream-colored automatic. This vehicle had Frankfurt registration plates, too, which made it especially conspicuous, and the lack of back doors made the logistics of the abduction a whole lot harder.

We had come up with a good plan, and now we began to rehearse the ballet of cars that would enable us to abduct Lischka. From the place where we snatched him, we would drive the Mercedes to a little forest nearby. Here, we would transfer Lischka to the Renault. The forest was completely isolated, and to get there you had to take narrow roads, making it easy to find out if we were being followed. Yet once we reached the spot where the transfer would take place, we were only about five hundred yards from the highway that skirted Cologne and would take us to the Belgian border.

On Sunday, we checked out these locations and finalized our plan of action. We left the apartment. David drove the Renault, and Marco the Mercedes. Almost immediately, the two cars became separated, and it took half an hour before we found each other again outside the apartment. We skipped lunch that day, which annoyed Élie. Our photographer had an extraordinary and somewhat exasperating capacity to focus on pointless details, while the rest of us were obsessed with the risky operation we were about to carry out. We decided to prepare ourselves psychologically: each of us had to repeat every tiny movement we would make, in order for it to become second nature.

In hindsight, we clearly didn't prepare thoroughly enough, because, when the time for action came, nothing at all went according to plan.

TO PRACTICE CAPTURING our victim and shoving him into a car trunk, we went to the beautiful forest near Cologne. We found a quiet spot deep in that forest, as obviously we did not want to be seen. David played the role of Lischka. One of us had to grab Lischka under his arms while two others took his legs. The driver would remain behind the wheel. Everyone carried out their task to perfection, and David found himself locked inside the trunk within a few seconds. Only then did we remember something important, however, as we heard David yell from inside the trunk, "But I've got the keys!"

Thankfully, it turned out that the trunk could be opened with a lever inside the car. We had a moment of panic before we realized that, though: it would certainly have been hard to explain to a locksmith why there was an Orthodox Jew locked inside our trunk . . .

Our trials were not at an end, however. When we got back to the apartment, the owner called us to say he was coming back earlier than expected, so we wouldn't be able to stay there. We had to find a hotel, but we knew we couldn't give our names, as that would put the police on our trail. Beate found us a hotel on the Hansaring, and as it happened the young bellman had heard about her before and was sympathetic to her cause. While she chatted with him, we slipped upstairs to the room without filling out the usual forms. Inside the room, we got the club out again and began joking around as we trained for the next day's kidnapping. We had barely fallen asleep when Beate told us it was time to get going. It was 6:00 a.m. She was in a bad mood because it was too early to get breakfast at the hotel, and she would have to go into battle on an empty stomach.

Arriving outside Lischka's apartment at 7:00 a.m., we took up our positions. We had to stand on either side of a tree-lined street that Lischka walked along every morning to catch his tram. I hid in the doorway of a church, while David hung about outside some garages. We had parked the Mercedes on the sidewalk. While we waited for Lischka to emerge—he was supposed to leave his apartment building at 7:25 a.m.—we became anxious at the sight of all the people catching the tram only a few yards from where we stood. In our panicked state of mind, their presence struck us as extremely compromising.

Élie was supposed to grab Lischka from behind and immobilize him; Marco, who was pretending to fix the Mercedes's engine, had to help him out while David approached Lischka from directly in front, threatening him, and I surged out from the side. Beate's job was to give the signal when Lischka left his apartment by taking off her fur hat.

There was an incessant coming and going of cars. Men, hands on steering wheels, waited there for their wives and children. I had left the Mercedes's engine on. Suddenly, Beate lifted up her hat. A tall man whom we immediately recognized walked past the street corner and came up alongside the Mercedes. Marco, seeing that Élie had not moved, was taken by surprise and realized that the opportunity had been lost. Lischka kept walking. When he reached the tram station, he turned around furtively, as if he had spotted us, and we all felt a stab of despair. On top of everything, it started raining. Sheepishly, we drove the Mercedes to the center of Cologne. No one dared speak or even look at one another. The air was thick with guilt and failure.

After parking the car outside the cathedral, we ate breakfast in the hotel opposite the train station. There, I tried to lift everyone's spirits. I explained that, even if we failed to kidnap Lischka, the aim of the operation was to raise public awareness about Lischka and to make former Nazis realize that they were not safe anymore. So the minimum objective was to at least attempt the abduction. Even if we didn't manage to get him over the border, a failed kidnap attempt could still be considered a success as long as it caused a big stir.

Beate's research told us that Lischka took the 1:25 p.m. train home. We decided to try again in the afternoon, hoping that Lischka had not seen us that morning.

All the same, we were worried. If he had spotted us, he might come back armed or with friends or accompanied by the police. Who knows, he might even shoot us, given that it would probably be considered "legitimate self-defense."

AT 12:45, we are back outside the tram station, determined to act this time, with no thoughts of discretion or caution. The car's engine purrs as we stand next to it and chat. We are trying to act like four policemen, there to arrest a criminal—which is, in a sense, what we are.

A flood of passengers pours from the tram stop every ten minutes. We watch them anxiously. Suddenly, Lischka appears, detaching himself from the crowd as he walks toward us. Marco rushes up to Lischka, who is about a hundred feet from the car. Two seconds later, I run over, too. We are each holding one of his arms, and Marco is yelling, *"Komm! Komm!"*

Unthinkingly, Lischka takes a couple of steps toward the waiting car before he notices that something very strange is going on. David and Élie arrive, and Élie hits him over the head with the club. We realize we are unlikely to be able to drag him all the way to the car. He is impossibly heavy. Passersby see what is happening and come up to us, while Lischka, terrified, screams, *"Hilfe, Leute, Hilfe!"* He stands sturdy as an elephant as Élie hits him again, then slowly crumples to the ground. But we are surrounded now. One of the passersby shoves a police badge in our faces. He must think we're colleagues of his. Thankfully, he is not armed. We ask him, in French, to leave.

I am starting to fear that the Mercedes will be blocked in when we get to it. There are so many other cars around, and I left the keys in the ignition of the empty car. All it would take is for one of the spectators to remove the key, and we would be caught in a trap. I yell, "The car! Let's go!"

Élie is still holding Lischka's hat, and the little policeman runs after him, saying, *"Den Hut, bitte, den Hut!"* Élie does not understand that he just wants the hat. He turns back to him, and the policeman points to the hat in his hand. Élie gives it to him, and the policeman says, *"Danke schön!"*

Lischka is lying on the sidewalk. Inside the car, I calm down. Beate now has the platform to launch a campaign against Nazi criminals. Three minutes later, we are in the little forest, and we have switched cars. We are supposed to wait here for Beate, but we hear police sirens in the distance and decide to leave her to her fate. I feel certain she'll make it to the train station without any problems. We throw the syringes and vials of chloroform out the window as we speed down the highway. When we reach the border, everything goes smoothly. As for Beate, she simply catches a train back to Paris.

BEATE

WHO IS ON TRIAL HERE?

W E CAREFULLY STUDIED the legal aspect of transporting Lischka to France. Serge examined the case of Colonel Argoud's abduction from Munich, which set a precedent.

The conditions of the return to France did not constitute a major obstacle to the retrial of someone convicted in absentia: *Male captus, bene detentus* (Captured in irregular conditions, but detained in regular conditions).

Once we had attempted to abduct Lischka, the real battle began: getting the story in the German press. The next morning, I called a newspaper in Cologne, the *Kölner Stadtanzeiger*, and told them my name was Mrs. Schmidt: I lived on Bergisch-Gladbacher Strasse, and I had witnessed an attempted kidnapping the day before.

"Some young people clubbed a man over the head. I can't believe it: the police got involved, and yet this morning there's nothing in the papers."

The journalist replied, "Yes, there is: look at page two, at the bottom.

There's a little piece on it there: 'Four persons unknown attacked a shop-keeper early yesterday afternoon and then fled.'"

After that, I called another local paper, the *Kölner Rundschau.* "Hello, this is Mrs. Schmidt. I live at 559 Bergisch-Gladbacher Strasse. Yesterday, I witnessed an incident in Maria-Himmelfahrt Strasse. There's nothing about it in your newspaper, and the *Kölner Stadtanzeiger* just talks about a shopkeeper attacked by four unknown people. But the attackers were for-eigners, and the man who was attacked—I know this because I live nearby—is the former head of the German police in France."

"That's very interesting," the journalist told me. "We'll look into it."

We called several newspapers, providing them with the same informa-tion. Then Serge phoned the German press agency, explaining that he was a French journalist and that there were rumors in Paris that the former head of the Sipo-SD in France had escaped an attempted kidnapping, and his newspaper was after the details of the event. So it was that a group of journalists began demanding information from the Cologne police. Around 1:00 p.m., we learned that there was going to be a police press conference on the subject that afternoon.

Later that day, I called again, this time using my real name. The jour-nalists, who by now had worked out what was going on, ironically ad-dressed me as "Mrs. Schmidt." But our ploy had worked. The police had told the press that the Mercedes they'd found in the woods had been rented by a French person born in Bucharest. They did not divulge Serge's name, out of fear that it would be connected to mine and that the press would turn it into a big story. The police must have imagined that we would remain silent in order to avoid getting into trouble; they did not yet understand that our goal was to raise awareness in Germany of the impunity enjoyed by Lischka and his accomplices, even if that led to legal action being taken against us. I gave the journalists the precise details of the abduction and the victim; that same day, I sent them dossiers on Lischka. For days afterward, there were headlines featuring my name and Lischka's all over the German press.

Phase two of our plan involved drawing attention to Hagen. Forty-eight hours later, while the Lischka affair was still rumbling on, I sent out a press release via the Associated Press announcing that several hundred criminals like Lischka still lived free and that, unless the Bundestag ratified the convention, we would abduct other criminals whose names and addresses we knew. Our next victim would be Herbert Hagen, in Warstein. We gave details about his Nazi past, and his photograph, which we distributed to all the newspapers, appeared in the next day's pages alongside his curriculum vitae. Hagen immediately called the police.

IF I HAD simply taken my dossiers to the newspapers' editorial floors, none of this would have happened. For several days, the German press went into paroxysms of outrage over this menace to German citizens.

And so the whole issue of these criminals' impunity—little known prior to this—was at last exposed in the press. In the *Vorwärts*, the Social Democrats' party organ, Wolf Scheller wrote: "Since March 22, several gentlemen of a certain age . . . can no longer sleep peacefully; they do not answer the telephone, or let their wives say that they are absent."

Simon Wiesenthal supported us: "Although the Federal Republic is not South America, I do understand why these young people are losing patience." His was not a view shared by many West German columnists, however, many of whom seemed irritated that a woman should be involved in such actions. Peter Herold, in the *Tagesanzeiger*, was categorical: "The woman who slapped Chancellor Kiesinger has become a criminal. The Klarsfeld affair is a case of political pathology."

Through journalists who were in contact with the examining magistrate, Dr. Bellinghausen, I learned that, at least for the moment, no arrest warrant had been put out for Serge or me. Questioned about this on March 31, Dr. Bellinghausen replied, "I am not obligated to believe what I read in the newspapers."

Clearly, the German justice system was hesitating to issue an arrest warrant for fear that it would cause an even bigger scandal. I knew that if I forced the issue by going to see Dr. Bellinghausen, he would either have to let me go, which would suggest that the situation involving war criminals in West Germany was so outrageous that the government did not dare to crack down even on those who acted illegally against them, or he would have to arrest me, in which case the war criminals were continuing to enjoy impunity while their militant anti-Nazi accuser went to prison in their place.

So I went to Cologne, accompanied by Ralph Feigelson, a former French Resistance fighter and Auschwitz survivor, who wore his concentration camp uniform, decorated with medals. With his imposing physique and impressive beard, I knew Ralph was extremely photogenic, so we went to the DPA press agency. Several journalists, photographers, and cameramen followed us from there to the courthouse, where more photographers and cameramen were waiting for us.

We went to see the prosecutor.

"I know," said Mr. Bellinghausen. "I heard about your arrival in Cologne."

"Mr. Bellinghausen, I have come here, accompanied by Mr. Feigelson, first of all to bring you these dossiers. I also wanted to let you know that what was written in the newspapers is completely true: I am responsible for the attempted abduction of Lischka."

"I have a warrant for your arrest in my desk drawer. Mrs. Klarsfeld, you are under arrest."

BACK IN PARIS, Ralph Feigelson described this scene in LICA's house newspaper:

> The prosecutor Joseph Bellinghausen and his assistant received us courteously. They looked pale and embarrassed, but not surprised. After Beate presented them with the dossier, I asked for Lischka to be arrested immediately. The prosecutor, who looked like he was too young to know much about the war, said he was not competent to try the case. Beate was translating for me as he spoke because I only learned German in Auschwitz, so I find it hard to understand and even harder to speak. So, when he talked about the arrest warrant, I thought for about half a minute that he was going to have Lischka arrested! But he was talking about Beate Klarsfeld. The German state is charging B.K. with "a serious attempt at illegal confinement, complicity in assault and battery, and organization of a criminal association," for which she faces up to twenty-three years in prison.

I was transferred to the Ossendorf Prison, a few minutes from the city center. My cell was on the first floor, and it overlooked a grass courtyard with a few flowers. It was an individual cell containing a bed without box springs, a wardrobe, a sink, a toilet, a barred window, a table, and a chair. I was allowed to write, to read three books per week (though no newspapers), to listen to the radio from 6:30 a.m. until 10:00 p.m. Everything was fine, clean, bearable—except for the loss of freedom. And the food, which, while it looked better than the meals I'd been given in Prague, tasted just as vile. I was allowed two thirty-minute walks per day. Most of the other women in the prison were prostitutes, though there was also an East German spy. We talked a lot during our walks (except for the spy, who always walked on her own), and some of the girls told me secrets: "One of my clients is a judge; he's old, and he always asks me to tickle him beforehand because that gives him strength, but really I'm the one who needs tickling, because it's not much fun with him. He pays well, though. Anyway, I should probably write to him. He might be able to get me out of here sooner . . ."

They were all very kind to me: I had slapped the chancellor; I had not been afraid to attack SS officers; and I'd been to prison before.

In the first few days, my only communication was with my lawyer, Klaus Himmelreich, a young Christian Democrat supporter whom I'd chosen by chance when I was arrested. Horst Mahler, my usual lawyer, was not in a position to recommend anyone to me, as he'd spent the previous six months in prison. Always very friendly and dressed to the nines, my new lawyer specialized in car accidents and saw my case from a purely legal standpoint. His attitude changed after he met Serge in Belgium, particularly as he was regularly threatened: "How can you defend that Klarsfeld woman?"

I had no contact with Serge, and I felt lost, suddenly cut off from the world. And yet, paradoxically, prison also relaxed me after so many weeks of physical tension. I did worry about Arno, though.

A day or two after my arrest, I was summoned to the courthouse for the examination of my case. I sat across from Dr. Bellinghausen and his assistant, Mr. Wissborn. While the prosecutor was notably well groomed, his assistant had a scruffy look; he was in charge of pornography, which meant his duties generally consisted of reading all the pornographic magazines that were published. Whenever he looked at me, I had the impression that he was trying to remember which magazine he had seen me in.

The examination took place in a relaxed atmosphere. I was given coffee and sandwiches, and the prosecutor even cracked a few jokes. But I had experience with German prosecutors: they tend to be very pleasant as a way of making people talk.

My objective was to make sure that all Lischka's functions as a high-ranking Nazi were recorded in the minutes of our interview. Their objective was to limit the conversation to the legal parameters of my particular case, dissociating Lischka's past from the man he was now. Whenever they said "Lischka," I added "The head of the Gestapo's Jewish Affairs Department," and I would stop speaking and cross my arms if this was not written in the minutes. My case file ended up being huge, about twelve or thirteen pounds of paper.

During my sixteen days in detention, my lawyer asked on two separate occasions for my arrest warrant to be suspended and for me to be freed until the trial in July. Both times, the court refused. The judge, Mr. de Somoskeoy, had already given his personal opinion: "An act like Mrs. Klarsfeld's can only be explained by a mental deficiency." He insisted that I should be examined by a psychiatrist, and I replied that a society that rehabilitated murderers like Lischka was more worthy of psychiatry. The judge concluded, "Then the psychiatrist will attend your trial and will make his report based on his observations of you."

WHILE I WAS jailed, the SS anthropologist Bruno Beger was tried in Frankfurt for procuring and preparing the eighty-six Auschwitz prisoners who would be killed in order to furnish bones for Professor Hirt's pathological anatomy collection at the Reich University of Strasbourg. After being transported to Natzweiler concentration camp in August 1943, the victims were gassed, boiled, and then dismembered. Beger's sentence: three years in prison.

Meanwhile, Serge was organizing a campaign to support me. After mobilizing former Resistance fighters and deportees, he was able to obtain a suspension of the arrest warrant, so I was—temporarily—free. In order to save face, the court demanded thirty thousand marks in bail. (To give you a point of comparison, the bail for SS Ludwig Hahn, head of the Sipo-SD in Warsaw, was eight thousand marks.)

When I was released, a guard in his early fifties came up to me and shook my hand. "I was worried that I wouldn't see you walk out of this place.

You did a good thing, a very good thing. I hope Lischka will take your place here one day."

SERGE TOLD ME later what had happened during my imprisonment: "At the instigation of Mr. Pierre-Bloch, the various organizations of Resistance fighters and deportees, Communists and non-Communists, came together for the first time in years. At their third meeting, they formed a National Liaison Committee to seek out and punish war criminals. I also got in touch with some of the youth movements. The Revolutionary Jewish Organization occupied the German embassy and covered it with stickers saying 'Free B.K., imprison Nazi criminals.' Then they chained themselves to the embassy railings. And one day, we received a call at home from a gentleman named Mr. Lichtenstein. He told us he was worried about you, that he had fled Germany during the Nazi persecutions, and that if they ever gave you bail, he would pay it. And he kept his promise."

Mr. Lichtenstein always said that what he did was "normal." Serge and I know just how exceptional it was.

WHILE STILL IN my cell, I received the greatest reward I could imagine: a beautiful justification of all my protests carried out in the name of the German people, in an article by the philosopher Vladimir Jankélévitch in *Combat*:

So B.K. is in prison and Dr. Lischka, SS-Obersturmbannführer, is free to go about his business unmolested. B.K. is in prison, but the head of the Gestapo in France, Knochen, a doctor of philosophy, is free to philosophize and to live his bourgeois life without having to spare a thought for the hundreds of thousands of poor victims whose bones are rotting in the ground. For now, the indifference of the German justice system is winning out over the courage of Chancellor Brandt. The apparent illegality of an act of protest is used by the Cologne prosecutor to conceal the horrifying responsibilities of a war criminal.

It is not difficult to understand why German neo-Nazis are so worried about B.K., so eager to silence her. B.K. is, alone, the conscience of a nation that would rather forget its past, would

rather enjoy the benefits of its prosperity, its "economic miracle."
All Germany's shopkeepers, its captains of industry, its tourists and
soldiers, seem stunningly oblivious. Or is it that their consciences
are clean? They think they do not owe us anything: no
explanations, no apologies; they don't even understand what we
want from them. Which makes B.K. doubly precious to us . . .

She is fulfilling the promise made to us by the judges at
Nuremberg, which they did not keep: "pursuing the greatest
criminals in the greatest crime in history until the ends of the
earth." Her cause is our cause. Her exemplary struggle is a triumph
of perseverance, lucidity, and passion, and it has the potential to
rehabilitate the youth of Germany.

As a German citizen, she has bravely accepted the responsibility
for horrible crimes she did not commit; though innocent herself,
she has taken on the weight of her people's guilt. And yet those
crimes were not hers: they were the crimes of vile, fat, sixty-year-old
men who currently run German politics and industry.

[. . .] And in spite of everything, B.K. has not decided that those
crimes have nothing to do with her. That is wonderful . . . B.K. has
chosen tribulation and danger. And so, for us, she represents hope,
the possibility of reconciliation, the first great opportunity for
forgiveness.

[. . .] And the same thing applies to her other protests: slapping
an unrepentant chancellor, making a scene in parliament, chaining
herself in the streets of Warsaw and Prague to bring attention to
anti-Zionism and anti-Semitism before the indifferent eyes of the
crowds there . . . These are, assuredly, "scandalous" acts. But these
scandalous acts, disturbing the good conscience of passersby,
highlighted another scandal—an infinitely more serious scandal
hidden by the forces of law and order: the scandal of the
unpunished crime amid this triumphant prosperity. Acting
scandalously to make people see the real scandal: that is the
dangerous role B.K. has taken on, not in words, but in deeds.

I WAS ALSO encouraged by the attitude of the East German government.
Friedrich Kaul, the GDR's official lawyer, asked to take part in my defense.

When he saw me in Cologne, Kaul told me, "Mr. Honecker gave written orders for me to defend you. Without that, I would never have been able to overcome the objections of all the senior civil servants who are against you. I also wanted to pass on Mr. Honecker's greetings and his respect for you." That respect meant a great deal to me, as I had earned it despite—or because of—my protests in Warsaw and Prague and my attacks on East German anti-Semites. It came from a man who had not, like me, spent two weeks in a pleasant, clean prison but had been locked up by the Nazis for ten years.

I informed Kaul that Serge was attempting to obtain an Israeli lawyer to represent Lischka's Jewish victims at this trial. The GDR was extremely hostile to Israel at the time, but Kaul did not take offense. Perhaps he didn't believe that the Israelis would support me. It was true, after all, that the newspaper of the West German Jewish community, the *Allgemeine Wochen-zeitung*, had not been in agreement with the World Jewish Congress or the Jews in France, who had actively supported me: "This situation [the impunity of war criminals] does not give B.K. the right to act as a spokesperson for Jews and persecuted people, and to seek personal publicity in this intolerable manner."

But I was not acting in the name of the Jews. Serge was acting in the name of the Jews, and I was acting in the name of the Germans. Anyway, it seems normal to me to assume that, as they were being murdered, those six million Jews would have preferred that their murderers—and the people who ordered those murders—should be punished rather than protected by the spokespeople for German Jews.

ISRAEL

N EWS OF MY arrest made very little impact in Israel, to begin with. Serge wrote to the Israeli embassy asking for an Israeli lawyer, but we waited in vain for a response. So Serge sent an open letter to the most important journalists in Israel, and this drew results. Several journalists came out in favor of me, the first one being Israël Noiman in *Davar*:

Open letter to a hardened criminal—the silence surrounding the B.K. affair is a scandal.
　　Dear Beate and Serge,
　　I had hoped that more famous and more important people than me would do something more impressive and useful for you than writing a letter. But, to my stupefaction, nothing has happened. That is why I am writing you this letter. Perhaps it will help to wake from their torpor those who ought to act and protest on your

behalf? The silence here in Israel cannot be allowed to continue. It is an insult to the victims of the Holocaust. There are many organizations in this country representing Holocaust survivors, but none of them have bothered to publicize the scandal of Beate being arrested for denouncing the fact that Nazi war criminals are living peaceful, comfortable lives even after being convicted of their crimes. Presumably those organizations are too busy planning ceremonies to commemorate the Holocaust and cannot find the time to deal with a matter of such insignificance.

May you be blessed, Beate, for your actions. You will not be alone in the dock of that Cologne court. We will be with you, either in person or in spirit.

[. . .] The state of Israel must not be absent from that courtroom in Cologne, because your trial is ours.

In May, we learned that the National Lawyers' Guild in Israel had decided to pay for a lawyer to defend me. Serge went to Israel in order to explain all the details of the case to the union.

But first we had to pay for the flight, and we were penniless. Most of our meager budget went to our telephone bill, which was huge after the many calls to Germany. Serge went to see the director of the CRIF (Representative Council of Israelites in France), an umbrella organization of French Jewish associations, and told him, "I came because I believe it is normal that the Jewish community in France should pay for this ticket, given that Lischka is the man who organized the Final Solution in France."

"In principle, I agree. But from a budgetary viewpoint, it's difficult."

"Did you know that the head of the Gestapo's Jewish Affairs Department used to come frequently to this building? And I can assure you that he had great difficulties finding enough trains to deport the Jews from France, but he managed somehow. Three weeks before Paris was liberated, when German soldiers were in chaotic retreat, he was able to obtain a train to deport more than a thousand Jews, hundreds of them children."

Very soon after that, Serge's plane ticket was paid for.

SERGE, WHO DID several interviews for Israeli television and radio, constantly repeated, "We do not need an Israeli lawyer to defend Beate but to attack Lischka." Shmuel Tamir, a deputy in the Knesset and a former Irgun commander, volunteered and was given the job by the union.

Tamir had some very useful experience of such trials. In 1953, as a young man, he had defended Michael Greenwald in the Kastner affair. Greenwald was an Austrian Jew who had denounced Rudolf Kastner—then a spokesman for the Ministry of Trade and Industry—as a traitor, a Nazi collaborator who had helped carry out the Final Solution in Hungary, liquidating 430,000 Hungarian Jews. This seemed inconceivable, as up to this point Kastner—who had moved to Israel in 1952—had been regarded as a hero, having stood up to the demands of Eichmann, who had appointed him as head of the Hungarian Jewish community. Tamir conducted an aggressive campaign, gathering from Europe and America enough documentation to prove Kastner's responsibility. Kastner thus lost his defamation case and was murdered in March 1957 on a Tel Aviv street.

Kastner had been saved from ultimate disgrace by the false testimony of SS-Standartenführer Kurt Becher, Himmler's special representative in Budapest, who had actively participated in the extermination of nearly half a million Hungarian Jews. In that way, Becher was even with Kastner, who had given positive character references for the Nazi after the war, allowing him to escape prosecution for war crimes. Becher knew that Kastner would be obligated to cover for him, otherwise Kastner's role in the slaughter of the Hungarian Jews would have been revealed by Becher. If that had happened, we would have learned how Kastner had persuaded thousands of Jews to peacefully report to the "labor camp" at Auschwitz. Kastner could hardly be unaware of what awaited them there; he also knew that many Hungarian Jews might have been able to save themselves if he'd sounded the alarm.

On February 17, 1958, Israel's supreme court formally stated that "Kurt Becher was a war criminal, not only in the technical sense of the word, but in its most terrifying aspects." The money taken from rich Hungarian Jews was banked in Switzerland by Becher before the end of the war. Once he was acquitted, thanks to Kastner's testimony, he was able to recover this money and use it to found a cereal business in Cologne in 1950. This firm developed very quickly, and by 1971 SS-Standartenführer Becher had become one of the richest men in Germany. Coincidentally, SS-Obersturmbannführer

Kurt Lischka, having returned to Cologne in 1950, had become the authorized signatory for Krücken, another cereal company.

SERGE HAD BEEN fired from Continental Grain, the multinational cereal corporation, one year before our Cologne adventure. Michel Fribourg, an American Jew of French origin and owner of this corporation, at that time controlled 15 percent of the global trade in grain. In May 1971, we learned—practically at the same time—that Kurt Lischka was working in the cereal trade and that Kurt Becher, the German cereal king, had been one of the most prolific liquidators of the Jews. Continental Grain worked actively with both Becher's and Lischka's firms. Soon afterward, Serge sent the dossier on these criminals to one of Fribourg's partners, requesting that he ask his boss to end business relations with those German firms. The partner told Serge that there was no hope of this happening. The company's attitude was simply "business is business." We knew that merely denouncing this attitude would have no effect, so we decided to try a different tactic.

In November 1971, the international press, all the world's largest cereal firms, and the highest-ranking executives at Continental Grain received two dossiers written in English, entitled "Nazi Criminals Running German Cereal Companies: No. 1 Kurt Lischka, No. 2 Kurt Becher." Each document consisted of a detailed dossier and was preceded by a statement from Fribourg:

I was recently shocked to learn that certain firms with whom the Continental Grain group had been doing business were managed by Nazi criminals who led the extermination of the Jewish population in several European countries. I ordered an investigation. Today, I am able to make available to all the companies in the grain trade and to the international press, the dossiers of Kurt Becher and Kurt Lischka, whose freedom is an affront to the sense of justice felt by any honest man at the bottom of his heart. Out of respect for the innocent victims of such mass murderers, I have decided to cease trade with their firms, and I have no doubt that the rest of the business world will adopt the same attitude.

This statement was followed by my own: "I would like to express my gratitude to Mr. Michel Fribourg, who enabled me to assemble this documentation. I honor the decisions he has taken and the full awareness he has of his responsibilities as a Jew, as an American, and as a man."

No one doubted the veracity of these statements. It seemed completely normal that a Jew, one of the richest men in the world, would react this way. Everyone knows that the Jews cannot forget or forgive Nazi war criminals. Well, the truth is that they can and do! But, all the same, this is such a widely held assumption that we decided to take advantage of it to achieve our ends.

And they were achieved very quickly. The executives at Continental were proud to have "a boss who dares to break relations with Nazi criminals"; Becher was outraged by this unexpected blow. Whatever happened next, we would be the winners from this operation: either Fribourg accepted all these compliments and actually broke off relations with Becher and Lischka, or he would continue to work with them in spite of everything. In the latter case, people would believe that he was yielding out of weakness or cowardice. Fribourg's lawyers demanded that I declare that their client had nothing to do with the statement attributed to him. I refused, and they threatened to sue me for forgery. Well, they could hardly sue me for defamation, could they? I had made Fribourg look like a hero. And how could a Jew take to court a non-Jewish German and, in so doing, affirm his desire to do business with the murderers of his own people? I would have had a field day. Fribourg retreated. His representatives made it known that "he never made that statement to Mrs. Klarsfeld, that the quality of the managers of the two German companies had been brought to his attention, and that his company was maintaining its business ties with the firms in Bremen and Cologne."

And then he continued working with Germany, or at least with Kurt Becher.

Henry Bulawko, president of the Association of Jewish Former Deportees in France, wrote to Fribourg: "I am convinced that you did not know about their past. That being said, now that you have been informed about the 'quality' of your German partners, it is incumbent upon you to break off relations with them—and even to do so publicly."

Fribourg never replied to Bulawko or to the Jews of Auschwitz. Those men, women, and children whose ashes were used to fertilize the wheat fields of Poland counted for nothing next to Becher or Lischka.

PASSING THE BATON

AFTER BEING RELEASED from prison in Cologne, I returned to Paris on April 22. It is difficult to describe how it feels to be reunited with your family after escaping from danger. Proportionally, there was less space for each of us in our little apartment than I'd had in the cell at Klingelpütz, but I was so happy! As always after my escapades, there was a pile of housework waiting for me, but I attacked it with gusto and a smile on my face.

On April 25, I was invited to attend the LICA congress, led by the energetic Jean Pierre-Bloch, who had brought together a group of young people with character. I liked them immediately. They were unpretentious, brave, and determined to act, not just talk. They even paid their own expenses, with the wealthiest ones helping the others.

On May 11, 1971, six LICA militants—Pierre-Bloch among them— went to the Bundestag in Bonn, where they interrupted the political debates by shouting, "Punish the Nazi criminals!" and handing out pamphlets written in German and French, calling on the German parliament to ratify the February 2 legal agreement that would allow Nazi war criminals convicted in absentia in France to go on trial in West Germany.

This spectacular protest made a huge impact in the Federal Republic. It was the first time French Jews had ever made their voices heard in Germany.

Six weeks later, another group of LICA activists traveled to Germany. This time, I went with them. Our objective was to occupy Achenbach's office in Essen. I had gone to scout the premises a few days beforehand. I told the press what was going to happen. The aim was to show that Achenbach—Hagen's lawyer and the spokesman for war criminals in the Bundestag—would not file charges against those who accused his client of involvement in the deportation of French Jews. Most of the seven French people with whom I traveled were under twenty, and this was their first time in Germany: they were nervous, so I looked after them.

To my relief, there were journalists and cameramen waiting outside Achenbach's office when we got there. That guaranteed us coverage in the newspapers and on television. Within minutes, two large Nazi flags were hanging from the first-floor windows, and a sign written in German was stuck to one of the panes: OCCUPATION BY FRENCH PEOPLE OF THE NAZI-FDP ACHENBACH'S OFFICE.

After guiding my comrades to Achenbach's office, I slipped away before the police could turn up. It was crucial that I wasn't arrested this time, because I was out on bail. If the police had gotten hold of me, I would have had to go back to prison.

A wanted notice was put out for me, but I managed to catch the first train to Belgium, changing at Aix-la-Chapelle and crossing the border with my French passport.

Now I had to help my friends get out of prison. After occupying the building for half an hour, the seven protesters had been taken to the central police station in Essen. They were held for twenty-four hours; then the four minors were expelled from Germany, while the three adults were thrown in prison until their trial began, six days later.

The day after the occupation, all the newspapers ran with the story of young French protesters in Achenbach's office. Why didn't all those journalists criticize this "illegal act"? Because the moral legitimacy of the act was immediately made clear by Achenbach's reaction. An innocent man would have demanded that the dossier on his activities be made public; he would have filed charges not for breaking and entering but for defamation; he would also have filed charges for forgery of those documents on the Jewish question where his name was mentioned. Achenbach did none of these things, and everyone in Germany—particularly those in power—took note of the fact. The protest in Essen enabled us to take another step toward the ratification of the convention on Nazi criminals.

HUNTING KLAUS BARBIE

K LAUS BARBIE WAS the epitome of the Nazi criminal: the man who arrested and tortured the famous French Resistance hero Jean Moulin, who sent the forty-four Jewish children in Izieu to their deaths, who fled to the ends of the earth to avoid capture. It took us sixteen years to bring him to justice.

So long after the events, the question of punishing criminals convicted in France appeared pointless to some people, inspired only by a desire for vengeance, even futile. This was absolutely untrue. It was not a question of turning back to the past but of expressing a country's democratic will.

Even after the Barbie affair entered our lives, we did not give up our systematic protests against desk killers such as Lischka and Hagen. On January 13, 1972, we went to Herbert Hagen's comfortable house in Warstein, accompanied by five young people, one former deportee, and several journalists. Armed with flyers summarizing his career, showing his photograph, and giving his address, we plastered the entire house with the leaflets. The police arrived soon after we began, but they did not intervene. In the afternoon, we went around town, handing out the flyers and engaging in lively discussions with the citizens of Warstein. Some of them approved of our actions; others thought it was "ancient history" and should be left alone. But all of them were made aware of Hagen's past, as were thousands of other people when the protest was broadcast on television and radio and covered in newspapers. Thanks to what was known as *die Klarsfeld-Gruppe*, Herbert Hagen's SS secrets were brought to light.

Meanwhile, I was feeling a great material strain: there were four of us living in a two-room apartment, its floors covered in dossiers; the future was uncertain and the present filled with threats of violence, almost on a daily basis. But if Serge and I gave up, who would oppose the Nazi criminals' rehabilitation? We had to overcome the obstacle of our poverty, and so we did.

OUR CONFRONTATION WITH Klaus Barbie began on July 25, 1971. I was doing research at the CDJC that day, trying to work out a precise organization chart for the German intelligence departments in occupied France, when the center's director, Mr. Mazor, handed me a document he had just received: "I think you might find this interesting." It was a photocopy of the decision rendered on June 22, 1971, by the Munich prosecutor Dr. Wolfgang Rabl to close the Klaus Barbie file. This decision had not been made public. As I read the ten-page explanation for closing the file on the "Butcher of Lyon," twice sentenced to death by Lyon's military tribunal, I gradually realized the consequences of this act. The German courts, aware that the Franco-German legal agreement of February 2, 1971, threatened all the former Nazis now living peacefully in West Germany, aimed to use the Barbie case to set a legal precedent; it was also a way of testing the French people's determination to pursue Nazi criminals. If they let Barbie be rehabilitated, then all the other Nazis who had terrorized France would undoubtedly follow suit.

It was a flagship case, and we had to fight relentlessly to have the case reopened in Munich.

I TRANSLATED THE ten pages of the prosecutor's argument that night; this would constitute the first element in our case file. Serge and I decided to base our campaign on three approaches: gathering and disseminating the most complete documentation possible on Barbie; using this dossier to mobilize public opinion in France and West Germany; and using the reactions in the Lyon region to the closing of the file to confront the Munich prosecutor with his error of judgment and force him to rethink it.

After a few days of intense research, I had put together a solid file of sixty pages. This dossier was then sent to the international press agencies, all the main German and French newspapers and magazines, the Resistance groups in Lyon, and the relevant authorities in both countries.

It was imperative that we kick up a storm in Lyon. If Rabl's decision did not provoke angry protests in the city where Barbie had committed his crimes, the Germans would think that the people of France shared the Munich prosecutor's opinion of the case.

On July 27, I went to the Parisian offices of the Lyon newspaper *Progrès* and informed the journalist André Severac about the case. The next day, the paper ran a large article headlined "German Prosecutor Abandons the Case Against Klaus Barbie, Head of the Gestapo in Lyon and Torturer of Jean Moulin."

There were numerous follow-up stories in the following days, with local groups as well as prominent figures expressing their indignation. On August 1, I went to Lyon to persuade the people there not only to protest but to fight. An article in *Progrès* appeared the next day, quoting me:

"You, the people of Lyon, must not accept the decision of Munich's prosecutor to suspend the case against Klaus Barbie, the former Gestapo chief who shed so much blood and so many tears in your city and the region around it. And I, a German woman, am telling you this . . ." The documents given to us by B.K. speak for themselves. They are photocopies of orders signed and countersigned by Klaus Barbie regarding the arrests and deportations of hundreds of Jews rounded up in Lyon and its surrounding region.

"But if the German witnesses have lost their memory of events back then, here there are men and women who bear the scars of those cruel, unfading memories. They can testify, and not based on hearsay. There are, alas, very few survivors from the sinister cellars on Avenue Berthelot or the deportation camps. "Those survivors,"

B.K. says, "those people who were tortured by Klaus Barbie, must come forward and tell their stories. The case against him has only been suspended. If we can gather enough precise witness testimony, we can have it reopened."

In the following weeks, articles began to appear in the Parisian press, too, climaxing in a piece in *Le Monde* on August 17, which concluded: "The recently publicized decision by the Munich prosecutor to close the case file on Klaus Barbie, the former Gestapo chief in Lyon, has provoked numerous protests in France. In a press release, LICA described the "profound emotion" its members had felt on learning of the decision and called on all organizations associated with the Resistance to join together in a large protest march on September 3 and 4 in Lyon. A delegation of former Resistance fighters and deportees will also travel to Munich early next month."

The Barbie campaign was under way in France.

NEXT, I HARASSED the Parisian correspondents of the big German daily newspapers and took particular care to inform the Munich press about the case. A long article appeared in the *Frankfurter Rundschau* under the headline "German Justice Again Seen in a Bad Light: Outrage in France at Decision to Discharge Barbie": "The Munich prosecutor's office can expect a turbulent next few weeks. In the French press—on the right and the left—questions are once again being asked about the genuineness of West Germany's desire for justice to be served on a sad chapter in the Franco-German past."

I returned to Lyon on August 21 to push for progress on the Munich delegation. The date was set for September 13, and several of the delegates would have their expenses paid by LICA.

While I was in the region, I went to visit my son, who was at a summer camp in Le Chambon-sur-Lignon, a town famous for having protected fleeing Jews during the Second World War. With Arno, the sunshine, and the kind people of that town, it felt like paradise regained after the purgatory of running a campaign, with all its frustrations and dead ends and its constant fear of failure.

On August 24, Serge came across a document for the deportation convoy of August 11, 1944, drawn up by the research department of the International Red Cross: this convoy took to Auschwitz the last Jews in Lyon to have escaped deportation or execution. Three hundred and eight names were on that list, alongside the forty-two names of Jews summarily killed in the Gestapo's cellars, with the dates of each execution. Barbie was directly responsible for the fate of all these Jews. The Lyon newspaper *Progrès* published the lists in their entirety.

The delegation took shape on September 3 during a meeting at a Resistance organization. It wasn't easy, as many of the potential delegates were facing practical problems of finance and organization, but I did my best to raise enough money to pay for their travel expenses. I pointed out that the impact of this protest was likely to be all the more powerful, as it would occur the day before a Franco-German legal symposium in Bonn, attended by the French minister of justice René Pleven, to whom I had written asking him to raise the issue with his German counterpart.

During my speech, one of the Resistance members stood up and addressed the others: "Wake up, will you? When a German has to tell you to do your duty, there's something wrong!"

In Munich, the prosecutor's office, prompted by the prospect of this delegation, announced that, if new evidence could be produced, the dossier could still be reopened. Serge and I began meticulously researching Barbie's past at the Center of Contemporary Jewish Documentation.

Many of our leads turned out to be dead ends, but we did eventually find a more promising one. Serge noted that the General Union of Israelites in France—the organization created at Kurt Lischka's instigation, to represent the Jewish population with the French and occupying authorities—had a liaison office with the Gestapo's Jewish Affairs Department. In 1943 and 1944, this liaison office was run by a Jewish former lawyer from Berlin, Kurt Schendel. His was an unpleasant job, as it involved direct contact with the two supervisors of the Final Solution in France: SS Heinz Röthke, head of the Gestapo's Jewish Affairs Department, and Alois Brunner, Eichmann's assistant. Brunner ran a special commando tasked with accelerating the rate of arrests and deportations, and Röthke took care of the administrative aspects of the work.

Alois Brunner disappeared in 1945. As for Heinz Röthke, who was just as active and responsible, he died a natural death in 1968, after a prosperous career as a legal adviser in Wolfsburg, West Germany, despite being sentenced to death in absentia in France. Röthke did not spend a single minute of his life in prison.

WE THOUGHT THAT the former lawyer Schendel, with his SS contacts like Brunner and Röthke, would be able to provide information on Barbie and on how much the regional Gestapo leaders knew about the fate of the Jews sent to Auschwitz. Prosecutor Rabl had concluded that there was nothing to prove that Barbie knew what would happen to those Jews he sent to Drancy. This was the official version of the Final Solution, limiting those who knew the truth about the Jewish genocide to a microscopic minority of Nazi dignitaries and thus absolving the German people as a whole.

We found Kurt Schendel's phone number in the Paris directory. We called several times but got no answer. Not until September 6, when the voice on the other end of the line confirmed that, yes, he was *that* Kurt Schendel, and he had just returned from vacation. And, yes, he remembered Klaus Barbie, even if he had never met him.

We met Dr. Schendel, and on September 8, he made a statement in German:

My observations during the year I spent around department IV-B and the numerous conversations I had with all those people, as well as the insinuations of other German departments, gave me the irrefutable conviction that all the heads of department IV-B, except perhaps those at the very bottom of the ladder—in other words, certainly Röthke, Brunner, and the heads of the Jewish sections in the Sipo-SD's regional *Kommandos*—knew exactly what fate awaited the deported Jews.

I saw reports in which Barbie pursued the Jews with particular zeal. In late 1943 or early 1944, I was present at a meeting with the UGIF's board of directors for the southern zone. There was much talk at this meeting about the executions of Jews arrested by Barbie and later shot without a trial. One of the delegates said they had constantly tried to intervene in favor of the arrested Jews so that they would, at least, not be shot. Barbie responded to this request with the words: "Shot or deported—what's the difference?" This remained in my memory: at the time, we could not understand those words, but our anxiety about the fate of the deportees was certainly heightened. Brunner sent his assistant, SS-Oberscharführer Weiszel, to Lyon for a few months, and Weiszel—who had been a member of Brunner's special *Kommando* in Thessaloníki—could have given Barbie eyewitness reports on what happened to the Jews who were deported to the east.

This statement seemed to us a significant document. But we had to find the UGIF director to whom Barbie had said, "Shot or deported—what's the difference?" Because, in this precise instance, Dr. Schendel's testimony was only hearsay.

Serge looked at all the minutes for the UGIF's board of directors, checked the list of directors' names, and made a lot of phone calls to try to find out what had become of them all. But twenty-eight years had passed . . .

IN THE MEANTIME, I found out that the organizers of the trip to Munich had gone to see the German consul in Lyon. On hearing that I was involved in the protest, the consul had recommended that they limit the number of their delegates to twelve and that they keep their distance from me so as not to be compromised by proximity to a scandalous woman. From the embarrassed voices of the organizers on the phone, I guessed that they had been persuaded of this and that they would adopt an extremely respectful attitude toward the German authorities.

I had already organized everything in Munich, called all the region's newspapers, television channels, and radio stations, alerted the anti-fascist associations, so that there would be a big welcoming committee at the airport when we arrived. The Germans were expecting the "French Resistance": a group of people who would demand justice. They were expecting flags, medals, anger, and determination, not just a dozen French people who looked like any other group of tourists. Given the delegation's state of mind, I now believed that the trip's likely repercussions were very limited. In a confrontation like that, only a show of strength could make the prosecutor change his mind. And this was shaping up to be more of a show of weakness.

Once again, the archives of the CDJC proved a precious source of help. Among the children arrested by Barbie in the Jewish orphanage at Izieu, there were three brothers: Jacques, Richard, and Jean-Claude Benguigui, aged thirteen, six, and five, respectively. They were immediately transferred to Drancy, as Barbie indicated in a telex on April 6, 1944, to IV-B in Paris: "In the early hours of the morning today, the Jewish children from the orphanage in Izieu were deported. In total, forty-one children were arrested, aged between three and thirteen. Furthermore, the arrest of the entirety of the Jewish staff was successful; this comprised ten people, five of them women. No cash or other valuable objects were recovered. The transportation to Drancy took place on April 7, 1944."

I found the names of the Benguigui children on the list for the convoy of April 13, 1944, to Auschwitz, where they were murdered. We found the name of Alexandre Halaunbrenner—the brother of some other children from the orphanage, deported by Barbie—in the directory. He knew Fortunée Benguigui, the mother of the three boys. She lived on Rue des Franc-Bourgeois, in Le Marais. I went to see her. Mrs. Benguigui had herself been deported to Auschwitz on July 31, 1943, where she was horribly tortured in the medical experiments block. While she was in the camp, she had harbored the hope that her children were safe in that secret orphanage, but, in the spring of 1944, she saw a pile of clothes discarded by people who had then been gassed and recognized a sweater belonging to her son Jacques, knitted for him by his grandmother in Algeria.

I explained to Mrs. Benguigui that the man responsible for the deaths of her children had had his charges dropped in Germany, and I asked her if she felt strong enough to go to Munich with me. She did.

So there would be a show of strength in Munich after all.

A FEW DAYS before our departure, Laure Moulin, sister of the Resistance hero Jean, sent me a letter that encouraged me: "I don't know how to express my admiration for the unswerving courage you have shown in your battle to ensure that your country acknowledges the Nazis' errors and crimes, and that it sends them to prison forever."

Protest in Munich

THE DAY BEFORE our departure for Munich, I was invited to dinner by one of the delegates. It was all very convivial until my host explained to me that I would not be part of the next day's delegation. The French foreign minister had asked the delegation not to damage Franco-German relations in any way and had told them the only way to achieve anything was through diplomacy.

There were forty-eight of us in Munich the next day, mostly former Resistance fighters, plus a few young activists from LICA. Mrs. Benguigui met us there. As the bus arrived at the French consulate, one of the delegates pulled me aside and whispered, "Please don't enter the consulate. We've arranged it that way with the consul."

"All I have to say," I replied, "is that I have a French passport, I am not under anyone's orders, and I have just as much right as you to enter the French consulate."

The names of the twelve "official" delegates were announced, and they stood up and walked into the courthouse. I could not hold back my indignation, knowing that German journalists would be there and that they would be expecting about fifty protesters. "It would be shameful for some of us to stay here," I told the others. "We must all go in together." Nobody was convinced. The chosen twelve went in.

The young activists and I did manage to at least herd the others out of the bus so that they could stand in front of the door of the courthouse, but the effect of this protest was so much less than it could and should have been.

Inside the office of the prosecutor general, Dr. Manfred Ludolph, the delegates handed him a memorandum "formally requesting" that he reopen the investigation.

While this was happening, Mrs. Benguigui and I went into the courthouse and, prevented from seeing Dr. Ludolph, gave his secretary the dossier containing copies of the documents signed by Barbie and Dr. Schendel's witness statement.

When the other delegates went back to Lyon, Mrs. Benguigui and I remained in Munich, determined to act because the situation demanded it. Two women: one Jewish, the other German. Our sole weapon: the only photograph of her three children that Mrs. Benguigui possessed, which I'd had blown up, and two signs that I'd made in our hotel room. Our plan was simple: tomorrow, we would take up position on the steps of the courthouse, and Mrs. Benguigui would go on a hunger strike while holding the photograph of her children.

The next morning at nine, in the cold and rain, we were outside the courthouse, standing on some crates that I'd found in a grocery store. I'd also bought Mrs. Benguigui some thick socks and warm slippers. Above Mrs. Benguigui, her sign, written in German, read: I WILL GO ON A HUNGER STRIKE UNTIL YOU REOPEN THE CASE FILE AGAINST KLAUS BARBIE, THE MAN WHO MURDERED MY THREE CHILDREN. My sign read: PROSECUTOR RABL REHABILITATES WAR CRIMINALS.

Our photograph was in all the German newspapers the next day, accompanied by long articles in favor of our initiative. The French consulate was alerted, and the vice-consul brought Mrs. Benguigui a blanket. The police came to tell me that my sign constituted a criminal offense. I didn't take it down. In the end, the prosecutor general decided to negotiate with us. The police escorted us to his office.

Dr. Ludolph was a very well-dressed man in his early forties who greeted us with cordial politeness.

"What is it that you want?"

"The case against Barbie to be reopened."

"For that, I would need conclusive proof."

"Have you read the dossier I gave to your secretary yesterday?"

"I have not yet had time."

"Well, you should do that now."

When the prosecutor general read Dr. Schendel's witness statement, he exclaimed, "This is important! If Dr. Schendel's informer can be found and can confirm that Barbie used those words, then I promise I will reopen the case."

"Give us that commitment in writing."

"My secretary has already gone home for the day."

"That's all right—I used to be a secretary myself."

I sat behind the typewriter as Dr. Ludolph dictated the official letter confirming his promise. I immediately communicated this letter to the German press, which published it the next day:

> Dear Mrs. Benguigui,
>
> [. . .] Concerning Dr. Schendel's statement of September 8, it seems to me necessary to find the witness who reported the accused's words—"Shot or deported—what's the difference?"—to Dr. Schendel. If this witness can be found and he confirms that these words were spoken by Barbie, I will reopen the case, as that would prove that the accused knew that the Jewish victims were going to be killed.

For the first time since the death of her children, Mrs. Benguigui felt she had done something for them. She had proved that she could take action, better than many others, who merely gave speeches.

LUCK WAS STILL on our side. Serge found the key witness in the phone directory. His name was Raymond Geissmann, and he was a lawyer at the court of appeal who worked for both the Israeli and West German embassies, a fact that only strengthened his value as a witness. And, yes, he was the same Raymond Geissmann who, in 1943 to 1944, had been director of the UGIF's southern zone in Lyon.

Geissmann received us in his office. Did he remember Barbie? Of course, and it was indeed to him that Barbie had spoken that terrible sentence after the summary execution of several Resistance fighters in the Gestapo's cellars. And, yes, he had been to UGIF board meetings. He immediately dictated a statement to his secretary:

> Some of my colleagues and I were summoned to the Gestapo or went there ourselves when we were trying to save such or such a person from the claws of the Sicherheitsdienst after they had been arrested.
>
> In that way, we met either Barbie or his subordinates [. . .]. We all shared the absolute conviction that those torturers knew exactly what happened to our fellow Jews once they were arrested. I remember seeing Barbie foam at the mouth as he expressed his hatred for the Jews, and the expression "Shot or deported—what's the difference?" was indeed spoken by him. I heard him say it myself and I reported it to my Parisian colleagues.

On October 1, I went to Munich with Jean Pierre-Bloch, the president of LICA, and the two of us gave Dr. Ludolph the German translation of this statement. The prosecutor general immediately dictated his decision to his secretary and gave us a copy of it:

> Munich, October 1, 1971
> Case number 123 Js 5/71
> Subject: Criminal investigation by the Prosecutor's Office of the
>   Landgericht of Augsburg against Klaus Barbie as an accessory to
>   murder.
> The case will be reopened on the point that he is accused of having
>   participated in the homicide of French citizens of Jewish origin
>   by deporting them from France toward the East.

On the point of Barbie's repression of the Resistance, Dr. Ludolph remarked that the Lyon Resistance fighters had not yet sent him the witness statements they had promised, but that, for him, "it was time to turn the page." In the name of the French Resistance, Jean Pierre-Bloch replied that the page would only be turned when Barbie was put on trial for the crimes he had committed in France.

Dr. Ludolph had no choice but to reopen the investigation. I tried to guess what strategy he would adopt next. Barbie's case was highly unusual: he was one of the few criminals to have fled Germany. In helping to find him in the country where he had taken refuge, the German courts essentially handed the matter over to the French authorities, the only ones in a position to demand extradition, as the German courts were not competent to try him until the February 2, 1971, agreement was ratified. So as far as the Germans were concerned, this was a test of the French government's determination to pursue German war criminals. If the French failed the test, then why should the Bundestag bother to ratify the agreement? And even if it did ratify it, why should the German courts demonstrate severity in punishing the country's war criminals?

Dr. Ludolph handed us two photographs of Barbie taken in 1943, one in profile and the other face-on. He also handed us a photograph of a group of businessmen sitting around a table. One of them looked very much the way you might expect Barbie to look twenty-five years later. "This was taken in La Paz in 1968," the prosecutor general told us. "That's all I can tell you for now. You have proved yourself very efficient so far, so why don't you help me identify this man?"

BARBIE, A.K.A. ALTMANN

B ACK IN PARIS, we went public with the information that Barbie was probably living in Bolivia. We had the photographs copied and sent them to Lyon in the hope that witnesses would come forward and identify him.

Jean Pierre-Bloch went to see the French foreign minister Maurice Schumann on October 8 and asked him to intervene with the Bolivian government so that it would find and extradite Barbie. He also gave him the photocopy of the German prosecutor's decision to reopen the case and the famous photograph of the group of businessmen. It would then have been very easy for the French authorities to find Barbie: all that needed to be done was to send a copy of the photograph to the embassy in La Paz and then for one of the embassy's employees to make the rounds of the few expensive hotels in the Bolivian capital, asking porters and barmen if they recognized the man in the picture. We would have had the man's identity by the end of the day. But none of this happened.

I gave a copy of the group photograph to an editor at *France-Soir* in the hope that its publication would bring forward witnesses to Barbie's current identity. A few days later, the editor told me, "Our legal advisers said we shouldn't publish this picture because, if the man in the image turns out not to be Barbie, he would be in a position to sue us."

One morning in October, I went to the headquarters of the Paris police's criminal investigation division at 36 Quai des Orfèvres. I did not have an appointment, but I explained to the employee at the anthropometrics department that I had some photographs to analyze. Eventually, I was taken to the office of the department's chief, a man in a white shirt who greeted me warmly. He was a former Resistance fighter, and he knew my name. "I can only do a superficial examination, and I cannot give you a written report," he cautioned. I expressed my gratitude. For the next half hour, he inspected the three photographs and then told me, to my immense relief, "Yes, there is a very good chance that this is the same man: same ears, lobe turned outward, especially the right ear, which is rare. The shape of the left frontal bone is highly unusual, and the folds at the end of the lips are identical."

I sent Dr. Ludolph an account of this examination. On October 12, his assistant, Prosecutor Steiner, wrote me a letter expressing the prosecutor general's willingness to work in tandem with me on this case.

At the end of the month, I sent Dr. Ludolph several witness statements from people who had met Barbie and who recognized him, with varying degrees of certainty, as the man in La Paz. On November 2, *L'Aurore* published the photograph of Barbie alongside the anthropometric examination and affirmed that this was indeed Jean Moulin's murderer. "This is the first time," the newspaper wrote, "that B.K. has been able to pursue her crusade with the blessing and even the support of a West German judge, when she is still on bail herself. A paradoxical situation for prosecutor general Ludolph's new assistant!"

A few weeks later, the prosecutor asked me if I would be willing to get in touch with a German living in Lima who had seen a businessman recently arrived from La Paz and believed that it was Barbie. This German had seen the 1943 photograph of Barbie in a recent article in the *Süddeutsche Zeitung*, which he received in Lima. His name was Herbert John, and he was a manager at Editoriales Unidas, a publishing house owned by the very wealthy Luis Banchero Rossi, the "Fish-Meal King of Peru."

On December 16, Prosecutor Rabl, the man who had made the initial decision to drop the case against Barbie, wrote to me: "The prosecutor's office has come into possession of recent photographs that probably show Barbie. I have asked the Department of Anthropology and Human Genetics at the University of Munich to draw up a report on the question of this man's identity. I would be very happy if you could, after receiving this report, come to Munich to discuss in detail what should happen next."

Rabl put me in touch with Peter Nischk, a friend of Herbert John's who lived in Munich. On December 28, Nischk sent us Barbie's current name and address: "Klaus Altmann, c/o Fritz Schwend, Santa Clara via Lima, Casilla no. 1, Carretera Central, km. 14."

We had been monitoring all press articles relating to Bolivia and Peru for several days now, and the omens were not good: in *Le Monde*, we learned that France was attempting to appease Peru's hostility to French nuclear testing. All the same, Serge phoned General Bourdis, chief of the prime minister's military office, on December 30. Bourdis had been Serge's superior in 1961 and 1962 when Serge was doing his military service. They met discreetly, and Serge gave him all the details that we had about Barbie.

Serge told a military office adviser that there were two factors regarding the possibility of extradition, one of which played in our favor and the other against us. The first was the wave of negative sentiment recently aroused by something the president of the Republic, Georges Pompidou, had said about the Resistance. By acting vigorously to extradite Barbie, the president would be in a position to end that negativity. The other factor was the French desire to appease the Peruvian government over France's nuclear testing. Then Serge came to another difficulty, one that he had recently learned about during a phone conversation with Herbert John: "Fritz Schwend, Barbie's friend, is a CIA agent; he was also a Nazi war criminal sentenced in absentia by the Italian courts to twenty-one years in prison. Now the owner of a chicken farm, Schwend was responsible for developing the system of postal censorship in Peru. He has eyes and ears everywhere. If France demands Barbie's extradition, Schwend—and consequently Barbie—will know about it within five minutes."

And yet it was important that France show its determination to relentlessly pursue Nazi criminals. In any case, Barbie would probably manage to flee Peru, even if we did all we possibly could to prevent that.

LATER, PEOPLE WOULD often ask us, "Why didn't you kill him? You could have caught him off guard." None of these people would have committed the act themselves.

Our goal was to compel the legal system to try these criminals and to prevent the rehabilitation of Nazi criminals who had operated in France. To achieve that, we had to focus on a few of those criminals, the most important ones: Lischka, Hagen, Barbie. Their names would provoke a passionate debate, thus preventing these monsters from living their lives in peace and quiet. If Barbie were identified, it would strengthen the public's conviction that Nazi crimes must not be swept under the carpet and forgotten. Killing Barbie would have achieved nothing. At most, the newspaper articles would say, "A man suspected of being Klaus Barbie was found murdered yesterday." It would have been nothing more than an act of vengeance.

A few days later, we found out that Luis Banchero Rossi—Herbert John's boss—had been murdered in his own home in Chaclacayo. The prime suspect was his gardener's degenerate son. But we knew that Altmann and Schwend were neighbors of Rossi and that Altmann had been seen on several occasions with the gardener's son.

In the meantime, on January 8, 1972, Serge and I went to Xavier Vallat's funeral. We did not go to mourn this man, who had been the first commissioner general for Jewish Questions under the Vichy government. We went to protest all those who were there to celebrate his merits and falsify the truth. We were the only protesters, but our presence was a reminder that Vallat's anti-Jewish acts had not been forgotten. We stood outside the church in silence, wearing yellow stars on our chests, holding a copy of Dr. Billig's reference work, *Le Commissariat général aux Questions juives* (*The General Commission on the Jewish Question*). Vallat's friends insulted us, and some even spat at us. But the chief of police refused to force us to leave.

On January 12, I received a letter from Prosecutor Rabl, who informed me: "The identity report from the Department of Anthropology and Human Genetics has just reached me. Its conclusion is that there is a very strong possibility that the businessman Klaus Altmann in La Paz, Bolivia, represented in the photographs, is in fact Klaus Barbie."

Five days later, we sent the new photographs of Barbie that I had received from the Munich prosecutor's office to *L'Aurore*, along with the latest information. The newspaper published them on January 19 under the headline "Will France Bring Him Back?" This article had the impact we were hoping for: in France, former Resistance fighters and deportees demanded that the government extradite him. In Lima, Altmann furiously denied that he was Barbie. Numerous articles followed, asking if Altmann really was Barbie. Still, the French government did nothing.

On January 21, Dr. Ludolph sent me more information concerning Altmann's personal data. That afternoon, Jean Pierre-Bloch and I gave a press conference in Lyon to provide an update on the investigation. Geissmann, the lawyer who provided the key-witness statement, and some of his friends decided that—as they had been lucky enough to survive Barbie's persecutions—they ought to do what they could to bring the torturer to justice. So they paid for me to fly to Lima.

My departure was set for the night of Thursday, January 27. But I needed to take written evidence with me, and Dr. Ludolph's information had all been provided verbally. At 2:00 a.m., he finally called me back and agreed to provide me with an official dossier. At seven the next morning, I caught a flight to Munich, and at ten I arrived at Dr. Ludolph's office. We worked together until seven in the evening. He found out all he could for me about the issue of extradition between France and Peru, which was made possible by the laws of October 23, 1888, and July 28, 1924. We finalized a dossier signed by the prosecutor general of Munich, which established irrefutably that Altmann and Barbie were one and the same. Four key proofs were given in the dossier:

1. Klaus Altmann's daughter, Ute, was born on June 30, 1941, in Kassel. The registry office for Kassel does not list any Ute Altmann. On the other hand, Ute Barbie—Klaus Barbie's daughter—was born on June 30, 1941, in Trèves.
2. Klaus Altmann's son, Klaus-Georg, was born on December 11, 1946, in Kasel, near Leipzig. The commune of Kasel does not exist, but in Kassel, on December 11, 1946, in Dr. Kuhn's clinic, Klaus-Jorg Barbie, son of Klaus Barbie, was born.

3. Klaus Altmann's wife is called Regina, and her maiden name was Wilhelms. The series of amazing coincidences continues: Klaus Barbie's wife is also called Regina, and her maiden name was Willms.

4. Last, the thoroughly convincing anthropometric examination conducted by Professor Ziegelmayer at the University of Munich was detailed in a sixteen-page report. I translated it on the plane back to Paris.

MY PLANE LANDED in Paris at 11:00 p.m. on Wednesday night. Serge and I spent an hour on the phone booking a seat on the flight from London to Lima the next morning, because Serge realized that if I moved up my journey, I would have a full day in Lima—the Friday—when all the offices would still be open and I would be able to act.

Then we went to the newspaper *France-Soir*, where the proof of Altmann/Barbie's identity did not seem to interest anyone. At the AFP press agency, they photocopied the dossier but did not send a dispatch. Once again, the dossiers alone did not have any effect. The next day, Serge would send this dossier to the head of the French military court.

I also learned from reading Ludolph's dossier all about what Barbie did between 1945 and 1949, particularly his activities working for the Americans. Later, I would send my notes to Allan Ryan, who was leading an official investigation in Washington into the links between Barbie and the American special services in Germany, so that the United States could formally apologize to France for its behavior regarding this Nazi criminal. Barbie had even been the subject of a wanted notice on April 25, 1949, for stealing jewelry. The text of this notice was a masterpiece of irony: "Klaus Barbie, five foot six, dark blond hair, thin lips, sunken eyes, distinctly Jewish features, speaks literary German, courteous manners."

At 2:00 a.m., I went to bed, exhausted. It was too late to see Arno now, and I would have to leave before he woke up. At 4:00 a.m., Serge got me up. We heard on the radio that Barbie had left Lima by car and was headed toward Bolivia. We calculated that he could not reach the border until Friday afternoon. By then, I would be in Lima. And, if necessary, I would pursue him to La Paz.

On the flight to London, I reread my notes on Barbie. When I got to the airport, however, the policeman inspected my passport, then consulted the long list of names of people sought or suspected by the British authorities. He asked for my ticket, took my passport, and disappeared. I began to fear I would miss my connection. The reason for this treatment was the campaign against Rudi Dutschke's expulsion that I had waged in London. "Just get a policeman to watch over me while I wait for my flight," I told them. "That way, you won't have to worry." Finally, they let me through.

On the way to Lima, I read Barbie's dossier and slept. Thanks to the time difference, I landed in Peru at 10:00 p.m. the same day. It was hot and humid; I was wearing a heavy winter coat, but here it was summer. There had been a mistake in the dispatches—they'd given my arrival time as GMT instead of local time—so there were no journalists waiting for me at the airport in Lima. Even my informer, Herbert John, wasn't there.

I managed to get hold of Albert Brun, the AFP's correspondent, and he came to fetch me. A thin, tanned man in his early fifties, he was accompanied by Nicole Bonnet, the *Figaro* correspondent. I took a room at the Savoy, showered, changed my clothes, and went down to the bar with my dossier to join a group of journalists. I showed them the proof that Altmann was Barbie. Albert Brun translated my explanations into Spanish. It was 2:00 a.m. before I finally got to bed.

Around nine the next morning, I met Herbert John on the front steps of the hotel. He was in his thirties, very tall with stooping shoulders, blond haired and blue eyed, and he looked nervous, ill at ease. He kept glancing fearfully around him, giving me the impression that we were being watched. He promised to put me in touch with the Bolivian police so that I could give them my documents. At the AFP office, there was a constant flow of journalists consulting the Barbie dossier. Everyone seemed completely convinced. That day, the Peruvian newspapers began a campaign: "The German Nazi Hunter Proves That Altmann Really Is Barbie."

I gathered from my conversations that Peru did not wish to become involved in a conflict between France and Bolivia and wanted Barbie to return to Bolivia. Also, thanks to "Don Federico"—a.k.a. Fritz Schwend—Barbie could count on solid support from the Peruvian special services. Around noon, a friend of Herbert John took me to the military police, where I explained the situation to a general and asked him to arrest Barbie before he crossed the border. He photocopied my dossier and promised to pass it on to the relevant ministry. Then I went to the government's press office: all the employees there knew that Barbie was going to cross the border. They looked with interest at my documents. They all admitted that Altmann was Barbie, but they did not perform the crucial act of closing the border to him. Instead, they phoned the intelligence service, which was located across the street. There, I met a colonel, who listened to my story, photocopied the dossier, phoned the border post, and asked if Barbie's car—a Volkswagen with the registration plate HH CD 360, registered under his son's name in Hamburg—had crossed the border. It had not. From there, I rushed to the French embassy, where I spoke with Mr. Chambon, the ambassador, a former deportee who gave me a warm welcome and embraced me in front of the press. I gave him a copy of the documents, and he was instantly convinced.

The phone rang: the consul in Puno was calling to tell him that Barbie had crossed the border at noon, accompanied by two Peruvian policemen who handed him over to the Bolivian police. So the request that the ambassador had just made to the minister of the interior—to arrest Barbie while we waited for an official demand for extradition—would go no further.

I returned to the AFP, where I continued working with the press and television people until midnight. That work was crucial, as the Peruvian press would be read in Bolivia.

The next morning, I caught a plane to La Paz. I was on Barbie's trail.

Unmasking the Butcher of Lyon

THE LITTLE AIRPORT in La Paz is located thirteen thousand feet above sea level. I am herded by about twenty photographers, cameramen, and journalists into a small office that is normally used as an infirmary. There, I give an improvised press conference while a doctor treats a young woman whose plane has just landed.

When the press has left, I am taken to another office, where three plainclothes policemen make me fill out forms. I do not have a Bolivian tourist visa, and I am not here as a tourist. They keep my passport, promising me that I will get it back when I reach the hotel. In fact, it is another three days before I see it again.

I was expecting summer heat, but it is cold in La Paz. Loud music blares from a stadium behind the hotel where I'm staying: cymbals, trumpets, a repetitive rhythm. Added to the altitude, this racket gives me a violent migraine. But I continue speaking to the parade of journalists that files through my first-floor hotel room.

The next morning, reading the newspapers, I come upon the headline: *"No Es Altmann, Es Barbie!"* The proof of this statement is printed over several pages.

The next day is Monday. I go to the French embassy in the morning, but the ambassador refuses to see me. I head to the building next door, which houses the Ministry of the Interior. A soldier prevents me from entering and keeps repeating, "Mañana." In the hotel, some journalists arrange a meeting for me with Rodolfo Greminger, the immigration secretary, and try to get me a meeting with Colonel Hugo Banzer, Bolivia's head of state (and dictator). I meet Greminger that afternoon, a European-looking man in his early thirties. He seems guarded. I leave him my dossier so that he can photocopy it.

At my hotel, I see the famous French TV journalist Ladislas de Hoyos and his crew.

I still have a headache and not much appetite—and the meals served in the hotel restaurant do nothing to whet it. I settle for a few avocados and some fruit puree.

I talk to journalists in my room until late at night. I explain to them the truth about the Gestapo, Nazism, the French Resistance, the death camps. This seems to me an essential task in La Paz, irrespective of the issue of extradition. I have heard and read a lot about the Banzer regime in Bolivia; by denouncing the fascism of the past, I feel as if I am helping the Bolivians to connect what is happening now under Banzer with what happened in the thirties and forties under Hitler.

On Tuesday morning, I go to see Greminger, the immigration secretary, who gives me back my passport and my documents. Then he hands me a newspaper in which he has underlined in red pen some of my declarations to the press. He tells me I should not be talking to journalists when I have come to Bolivia on a tourist visa, which had eventually been granted, even though the authorities knew I had come for the Barbie case. And yet I sense that he is more sympathetic toward my cause than he was before. He tells me that he is preparing the Barbie dossier for the committee he heads and that he will pass on his report to the supreme court, which will decide Barbie's fate. Greminger takes Altmann's passport from a drawer and shows it to me. I read the date of birth: October 25, 1913, the same

ABOVE: Raïssa Klarsfeld, student in Berlin, in 1925 (AUTHORS' PERSONAL COLLECTION)

RIGHT: Arno Klarsfeld, foreign volunteer, in 1939 (AUTHORS' PERSONAL COLLECTION)

ABOVE: Hélène Künzel with her daughter, Beate, in 1943
(AUTHORS' PERSONAL COLLECTION)

LEFT: Kurt Künzel, Wehrmacht soldier stationed in Belgium, in 1940
(AUTHORS' PERSONAL COLLECTION)

Arno Klarsfeld and his children
at the Chateau de Masgelier
in May 1941

BELOW: Arno, Georgette, Serge,
and Raïssa on the Promenade des
Anglais, in Nice, in May 1943

April 2, 1968—
Beate interrupts
the Chancellor at
the Bundestag in
Bonn: "Kiesinger,
Nazi, resign!"
(PHOTOGRAPH ©
ULLSTEIN BILD-DPA)

December 1972:
Régis Debray
and Serge Klarsfeld
with their Bolivian
friends
(AUTHORS' PERSONAL
COLLECTION)

Serge presents the press with photographs of the former SS officer
Alois Brunner. (PHOTOGRAPH © KEYSTONE FRANCE)

Beate shows a reproduction of Klaus Barbie's Bolivian military
special services card. (PHOTOGRAPH © PETER TURNLEY / RAPHO)

1972: Beate and Serge outside the Pailharès cemetery on the day of
Xavier Vallat's funeral (PHOTOGRAPH © ÉLIE KAGAN / BDIC)

October 23, 1979: Opening of the Kurt Lischka trial in Cologne
(PHOTOGRAPH © ÉLIE KAGAN / BDIC)

Protest on the steps of the Cologne courthouse (PHOTOGRAPH © ÉLIE KAGAN / BDIC)

The Association of Sons and Daughters of Jews Deported from France (FFDJF) protests against Le Pen. (PHOTOGRAPH © ÉLIE KAGAN / BDIC)

December 5, 1976: Serge makes a scene in the infamous beer hall where an attempted assassination of Hitler took place in 1939. (PHOTOGRAPH © ÉLIE KAGAN / BDIC)

Beate protests in Santiago, Chile, against Walter Rauff. (PHOTOGRAPH © JOSE ARGUTO / AFP)

Beate leads a protest in Vienna against Kurt Waldheim. (PHOTOGRAPH © RUDOLF BRANDSTATTER / AFP)

The French president François Hollande promotes Beate to the rank of
Commandeur of the Legion of Honor and Serge to Grand Officier.
(PHOTOGRAPH © PHILIPPE WOJAZER / AFP)

Beate and Serge at the Shoah Memorial in 2011 (PHOTOGRAPH © JOEL SAGET / AFP)

as Barbie, not October 15, as "Altmann" claimed in Lima. Greminger asks me to bring him certain official documents from Munich concerning Barbie's life and Nazi career. I promise I will.

As I am coming out of Greminger's office, I am accosted by a policeman, who takes me to see Major Dito Vargas, the head of the Bolivian intelligence services, who is notorious for his cruelty. I have heard that he tortures people himself and summarily executes guerrillas after first chopping off their hands. He is not yet forty, and I silently hope, when I see him, that he never will be. He is well dressed and has a large, fat face and slicked-back black hair. Our interview is translated by a policeman who speaks English. Smirking sarcastically, Major Vargas informs me that, as a foreign tourist, I am not entitled to use the Bolivian press to mount a campaign.

I reply with equal sarcasm, "I don't need to see the press anymore because I've already seen them all and they've informed the Bolivian people of almost everything I had to say." He brings the interview to a swift end. Presumably he is not used to women standing up to him.

In the lobby, I am told there is a phone call for me. It is a member of the French embassy, arranging to meet me at my hotel; as a precaution, we will not meet in my room. This diplomat, who is Jewish, has followed my previous protests. He confirms that I was not seen by the ambassador because I am not here on an official visit. But the embassy employees are curious to study my documents.

That afternoon, I hear on the radio that the French ambassador has demanded Barbie be extradited. I am relieved. In the middle of the night, I am woken by a phone call from the correspondent of a U.S. press agency: I will be expelled the next day for breaking the rules of tourist behavior.

The next day, Greminger asks me to leave that same day for Paris, via Lima. He books me a seat and tells me to return to see him at 2:00 p.m. In the meantime, Ladislas de Hoyos interviews me on the main road overlooking La Paz. I am told that Colonel Mario Zamora, the minister of the interior, has just announced that I have been expelled. But when I see Greminger again at 2:00 p.m., he denies this. "You have not been expelled, but I need those new documents. Only you can bring them to me. I have decided to work with you, and I have just explained that to the press."

His press release that afternoon makes clear that "Mrs. Klarsfeld has left of her own free will." Two policemen take me to the French embassy, where I pick up my dossiers. Back at my hotel, I call a few journalists and take a reel of film given to me by Ladislas de Hoyos, so that I can bring it to Paris. He feared that if the police found the film in his possession, it would be confiscated—or worse.

In Lima later that afternoon, two police detectives take me to an office. The order has been given not to admit me to the city: "We are here to ensure your safety, because there is a risk you might be killed by neo-Nazi organizations if you enter the city." Herbert John confirms to me that Fritz Schwend, with whom Mrs. Barbie is staying, has declared that, if I return, they will "take care of" me. But I want to sleep in a bed, not on a chair in a muggy airport. "Give me a revolver," I tell the policemen, "if you're really worried about me. I know how to look after myself." They refuse, and I spend a long, sleepless night in a glass-walled office.

The next morning, I board an Air France jet. When the captain is informed of my presence, he invites me into the cockpit and opens a bottle of champagne in my honor.

DURING THE DAYS that follow, I enjoy a few moments of relaxation with Serge and Arno. I also do a lot of housework. Whenever I go away, I am always obsessed with the problem of my men's laundry. They are both rather careless when it comes to looking after themselves. It may seem absurd that such considerations preoccupy me while I am hunting SS killers on the other side of the world, but it's true: I constantly worry about whether Arno will have clean underwear, whether Serge's shoes are dusty, whether Raïssa will be able to find the dry-cleaning ticket that I left next to the television set . . . It is a source of joy and relief to be able to catch up on these tasks.

I call Dr. Ludolph to tell him I am back in France, and he informs me soon afterward that the French military court is going to take over for me: the West German foreign minister has just been in touch to ask him to speak with two French judges on Monday. All the same, I go to see him because I have just learned that Barbie has been arrested in Bolivia for fraud; the state development agency claims that he owes them a large sum of money. If a minority of Bolivian leaders are hostile to Barbie, we must help them by providing the Bolivian police with as much evidence as possible. Unfortunately, the French justice system is a slow-moving machine, so it is better if I return to La Paz myself, taking the documents I have just been given by the Munich prosecutor's office, documents that will prove beyond doubt that Altmann is Barbie.

FOR THE PEOPLE of Peru and Bolivia at the time, the reality of what the Nazis did was practically unknown. I had to show them that Barbie was not, as he claimed, merely "a soldier doing his duty." He had told a reporter from *Pueblo*: "During the war, I acted as any army officer acts in such circumstances. I acted the way Bolivian officers acted when they were fighting Che Guevara's guerrillas." I had to highlight the mass murder of civilians and the liquidation of the Jews. The Bolivians needed to see more than just documents and photographs; they had to be brought face-to-face with the evil of Nazism through the words and tears of someone who had suffered directly at Barbie's hands. All I needed now was to find enough money for the flight tickets and living expenses and then find the right person to accompany me—and convince him to make the trip.

The day I went to see Dr. Ludolph in Munich, I had food poisoning. I did not feel or look too good, but he showed me the evidence I had asked for, notably the four Barbie children's birth certificates, the proof that Barbie was classified as a police officer during the war, rather than a soldier, and specimens of Barbie's handwriting. We worked until 7:00 p.m. Unfortunately, Dr. Ludolph no longer had the right to give me photocopies of this evidence, as he had to pass it on officially to the French military judges. Otherwise, I could have been in La Paz with those documents by Thursday, February 10. Going through official channels, the documents would take at least ten days to reach Bolivia.

IN PARIS, BARBIE was front-page news again. Ladislas de Hoyos had managed to interview Barbie in prison. Confronted with the image of their torturer, Barbie's victims recognized him despite the passage of so many years.

From now on, for the French people, there was no longer any doubt: Altmann *was* Barbie. I felt simultaneously happy and furious: indisputable evidence was more or less ignored, while questionable witness testimony won the argument. I do not have a good memory for faces, even those I have seen a short time before, so I tend to doubt the claims of those who can be certain after twenty-seven years. All the more so, as it was perfectly feasible that the outcome might have been different: what if those witnesses had not recognized him, despite the fact that Altmann really was Barbie and that the Munich prosecutor general had stated that he believed "with a 100 percent certainty that would convince any German court"? In that case, what would have happened?

Among the witnesses who came forward was Mrs. Simone Lagrange, who was interrogated by Barbie in June 1944, when her name was Simone Kadousche:

I was thirteen years old. When we arrived at the Gestapo building in Place Bellecour, they put us in a fourth-floor room—and that was where I saw Barbie for the first time. He walked toward my parents and me, delicately stroking a large gray cat, and—without raising his voice—asked my mother if I was her only child. Mama replied that she had two younger children, but she didn't know where they were. Barbie then approached me and politely asked me for my little brothers' address. I told him I didn't know. He gently placed his cat on the table, then suddenly slapped my face twice, telling me that he would find them himself. On June 7, I was taken back to Place Bellecour, where Barbie was waiting for me. Another interrogation began. He said to me in a kind voice that, if I gave him the boys' address, he would send the three of us together to the hospital in Antiquaille, that we would be well cared for and we would not be deported. Again, I told him that I didn't know where they were, so he moved closer to me. I had very long hair at the time. He rolled this around his hand, then abruptly yanked me toward him. Then he started slapping me, for about fifteen minutes. It hurt a lot, but I didn't want to cry. Finally he let go of me and I found myself on the floor. He kicked me in the belly until I got up, and escorted me to prison himself. He told my mother that she was heartless, letting her daughter be hit like that, and that, if she talked, there would be no more interrogations. Then he slapped her a few times. We saw each other again on June 23, 1944, the date when we were transferred to Drancy, along with our mother, prior to our departure for the concentration camp in Auschwitz, where Mama was killed on August 23, 1944. As for my father, he was murdered on January 19, 1945, as the camp was being evacuated.

Serge met Mrs. Lagrange during a protest outside the Bolivian embassy. She immediately expressed her interest in going to Bolivia with me.

On February 12, 1972, Barbie was released. *Le Figaro* stated optimistically: "Barbie is not about to be tried in a French court, but Altmann is suffering trials of another kind. For him, from now on, every hour of the night will be like that first hour of dawn dreaded by all those men he sent to be executed."

This article was a mistake, because its subtext was "Reader, don't worry, the criminal will not get away. He won't have long to enjoy his villa, his swimming pool, his family. The inexorable machine of justice has been set in motion, and Barbie will eventually receive his due punishment, so there is no need to make any effort at all." By confusing our desires with reality, we lead the public astray, silence their demands, and earn the contempt of those smirking Nazi monsters.

In reality, Klaus Barbie regularly went to the bar of Lima's Crillon Hotel to savor a few whiskies in peace. No one was trying to kill or kidnap him.

THE ROLE I PLAY is much bigger than I am. Inside me, there is the black of a Barbie or a Kiesinger; there is the gray of those who, out of indifference or cowardice, resign themselves to the impunity of Nazi war criminals or the repression in Prague; and there is also the off-white of those who, though they are not resigned to such horrors, are content to sign petitions in order to appease their troubled consciences. And yet, what count are acts—black or white—and the choice of principles that lead one inexorably to act in a way that is black or white. Each man's fate is determined by his acts. He becomes white, black, or gray, no matter what shade his soul originally might have been.

On February 15, Georges Pompidou wrote to Hugo Banzer: "Time erases many things, but not all. So the French people cannot accept that crimes and sacrifices be forgotten, because if they are, then justice is tarnished." I agree entirely with these words.

I WAS GIVEN two plane tickets to Bolivia by Francine Lazurick, the manager of *L'Aurore*. Mrs. Lagrange, on the other hand, would not go with me: "I was asked not to go there yet, so as not to compromise the course of justice."

I decided to ask Mrs. Halaunbrenner instead. She was nearly seventy years old, and Barbie had ruined her life. She still had a son, Alexandre, and a daughter, Monique, but her husband, her eldest son, and her two other daughters had all been exterminated by Barbie. I took a statement from Alexandre:

> In 1943, our family consisted of my father, Jakob; my mother,
> Itta-Rosa; my elder brother, Léon (thirteen); my three sisters, Mina
> (eight), Claudine (four), and Monique (three). Between 1941 and
> 1943, we were held in several camps in the southern zone. On
> August 26, 1943, we were put in a residence under surveillance in
> Lyon. At 11:00 a.m. on October 24 of that year, the Gestapo
> knocked on our door. There were three men: two of them tall and
> in their forties, the third younger (he looked about thirty to my
> child's eyes) but obviously their boss. His face has remained
> engraved in my memory ever since that moment; it has haunted my
> dreams and my sleepless nights. When I saw the photograph
> published by *Die Weltwoche* on September 10, 1971, I recognized
> him instantly, as did my mother, who was sitting next to me.
>
> My brother Léon, who was very tall for his age, came home
> about 6:00 p.m. When he walked into the apartment, they
> searched him, then decided to take him along with my father. My
> mother began to howl in Yiddish that they should let my brother
> go. We were all crying and shouting, but in vain. When my mother
> tried to stop them from being taken away, Barbie took out his
> revolver and struck my mother's hand with it. The next day, we
> stood in the street waiting for our brother and father to return, my
> sisters clinging to my mother's dress. We then saw a German army
> van stopping outside our house, presumably to take us away. So we

pretended to be just passing, and left everything behind us. A few weeks later, on December 14, we learned through a friend that my father was dead in the hospital. My mother and I went around to all the hospitals in the city but found nothing. Then I thought of looking in the morgue, and that was where we found my father. He had been shot by a firing squad at the Gestapo's headquarters: seventeen machine-gun bullets in his neck and chest. My brother Léon was deported. He worked in the Polish mines until he died of exhaustion. Two of my younger sisters, Mina and Claudine, were placed by the UGIF in the Jewish orphanage at Izieu. We thought they would be safe there. But Barbie did not spare them. My sisters were deported on June 30, 1944, and were killed upon arrival in Auschwitz.

I persuaded Dr. Ludolph to give me a copy of the photographs of Mrs. Barbie in 1940 that he had just discovered. While I was in Munich, I also met my informer, Peter Nischk, who would die soon afterward—he was found drowned in an Italian lake. Herbert John, his friend, was certain that this was no accident.

I took the plane back to Paris that evening. On the flight, I examined the photographs of Mrs. Barbie, comparing them with one taken in 1972. She had not changed in thirty years: a few wrinkles, nothing more. The resemblance left no room for doubt. When I showed the pictures to Serge at Orly Airport, he ushered me into a taxi. It was nearly midnight when we arrived at *L'Aurore*. The page layout was changed at the last minute. The two photographs were inserted, followed by a long article headlined "The Final Proof."

I returned to La Paz only a few weeks later, this time accompanied by Mrs. Halaunbrenner.

WE LEAVE PARIS on Sunday, February 20, 1972, and spend one day in Lima. I fear that we will be turned away from Bolivia. There will be less risk of this if the Peruvian press prints this latest proof and Mrs. Halaunbrenner's story. Sending us away would be equivalent to refusing to hear what we have to say. The French consul is at the airport with a group of journalists, eager to see the photographs and hear our words. Mrs. Halaunbrenner responds with dignity and simplicity to the reporters' questions. The consul takes us to the Savoy, where he tells us that the ambassador is in Europe. In spite of Schwend's threats, I do not really fear any reprisals by the neo-Nazis here; attacking me would provoke a major campaign against them. The next day, our story is front-page news in the papers of Lima.

On Tuesday morning, at the airport, we are stopped at the check-in desk and told that a dispatch has arrived from La Paz: we do not have the right to leave and must contact the Bolivian embassy. We pick up our suitcases and catch a taxi to the embassy. The ambassador informs us that we must ask the foreign minister and the minister of the interior for an entry visa, and we must pay for the telex ourselves.

Back at the Savoy, I send two telexes—and another one to Rodolfo Greminger, reminding him that he had asked me to return to La Paz. Now we must wait—and hope. The press supports us: "The Bolivians protect Barbie by preventing his accusers from seeking justice."

Around 5:00 p.m. the next day, I receive a phone call from the AFP press agency: the Bolivian minister of the interior has sent out a press release announcing that Colonel Banzer has personally granted us an entry visa; the Altmann dossier is currently being studied at the Foreign Ministry (and not the Ministry of the Interior anymore), and the legal authorities will make their verdict in due course. I take the telex from the AFP to the Bolivian consulate, where I am told that they have not received any such notification. The consul, Ricardo Rios, is a close friend of Barbie, and he grins as he gives me this news. I have barely made it back to the hotel when Rios calls me again: the consulate has just received our authorization.

On Thursday, at noon, we arrive in La Paz.

I worry about the effects of the altitude on Mrs. Halaunbrenner, but she seems to cope with it better than I do. A young man enters the airplane just after it lands and warns me that I will be repatriated immediately if I make any press statements. I try to get hold of Greminger, but apparently he has had his wrist slapped: "I am no longer involved in the Barbie case; you should talk to the vice–foreign minister, Mr. Tapia, instead." I arrange a meeting with Mr. Tapia for Friday afternoon.

Everything seems to be in Barbie's favor here. A government spokesman announces, "There is no need to extradite Klaus Altmann. President Banzer believes that he has sufficient evidence to consider the problem settled." A few days before this, a renowned Bolivian lawyer (and Foreign

Ministry adviser), Constancio Carrion, proclaimed, "Bolivia is an inviolable asylum. Even the worst crimes, in Bolivia, have a statute of limitations of eight years. So Altmann-Barbie's crimes are ancient history." Carrion is also one of the lawyers defending Barbie.

On Friday morning, we are invited to lunch at the city's finest restaurant by the *Los Angeles Times* reporter. "When I interviewed Colonel Banzer on Wednesday," he tells us, "I told him what a bad impression it would make internationally if he prevented two courageous women from entering Bolivia. That is why he changed his mind. He is very sensitive to American opinion; apparently, the CIA pays him seven dollars per day for each prisoner incarcerated for political reasons."

That afternoon, we meet the vice–foreign minister, Jaime Tapia, and submit the new evidence to him. Mrs. Halaunbrenner tells him her family's story; he warmly pats her shoulder and promises to do everything he can, but we know not to expect too much from the country's legal system.

On Saturday, February 26, I make some discreet inquiries of journalists and discover that they have been told not to mention our presence in Bolivia. When I suggest that I hold a press conference, they are delighted, particularly when I bring up the idea of confronting Barbie's victims with the filmed interview of "Altmann" produced by Ladislas de Hoyos.

On Monday morning, I phone all the journalists I know to invite them to a press conference at 11:00 a.m. I have to act quickly. At 10:15, half a dozen plainclothes policemen enter the hotel. Two of them approach me in the lobby and ask me to follow them. I ask if I can pick up a few things from my room, and two other policemen stand guard outside my door. Inside my hotel room, I call our Jewish friends so they will come and look after Mrs. Halaunbrenner, who is worried about this new incident. I also talk to Albert Brun and ask him to explain the situation to the journalists if I am not back by 11:00 a.m. Major Dito Vargas gives me a formal warning: if I give that press conference, I will be expelled immediately.

I return to the hotel in the police Jeep at 10:50 and, in a large conference room, we give a press briefing to about thirty journalists. The film is projected. I hand out the photographs and the dossiers prepared by Serge. I review the case. Mrs. Halaunbrenner speaks next, and the journalists are visibly moved by her story. Just as she finishes speaking, at 12:15, the policemen who had escorted me before come back in and take me away again. I am locked in a small, grimy office, and I wait there for nearly five hours.

Then the head of the Policía Internacional, Hernau Arteaga, releases me with the strong suggestion that I should keep my mouth shut from now on: "This is your last warning. Next time, you'll be arrested."

The next day's press is full of Barbie stories: not only reports of our press conference, but entire pages devoted to the extermination camps, revealing the dark truth concealed by Altmann-Barbie's ordinary-looking face.

Bolivian people swarm around us, offering their consolations to Mrs. Halaunbrenner, assuring us of their support, demanding that Barbie be extradited.

Just after breakfast, two familiar faces appear. I stand up, resigned, and am taken once again to the local police station. I spend the day in the same office. I keep asking why they are holding me, but in vain. Finally, a detective, who speaks a little bit of French, becomes exasperated by my repeated questions and replies in the language of Descartes, "You piss us off, so we piss you off! That way, you get the hell out of here!" Now that I know where I stand, all I have to do is patiently wait until the end of the working day. When the employees go home, they set me free, just like they did the previous day.

In the meantime, the French ambassador has made an official request—at our prompting—for a confrontation between Barbie and Mrs. Halaunbrenner. Of course, Barbie refuses this request. So Mrs. Halaunbrenner brings a civil case against him for murdering four members of her family. The second lawyer we contact, Manuel Morales Davila, begins legal proceedings. We file Mrs. Halaunbrenner's charges with a notary, and then he tells us his fee: seven thousand dollars. Realizing that this is a deliberate tactic to prevent us from taking the case to court, I declare to the press that "Bolivian justice is too expensive for us." I remember hearing a prescient proverb in La Paz: "Beware Chilean women, Peruvian friends, and Bolivian justice."

On Saturday, we have a day of relaxation at Lake Titicaca before we begin a public protest. I buy some chains and two padlocks in preparation.

On Monday morning, I make sure everything is in order with our passports and exit visas, then book two seats on the La Paz–Lima flight for later that day. Around noon, we wrap the chains around our waists and wrists. We have two signs in Spanish. Mrs. Halaunbrenner's has a photograph of her family and words that translate as: BOLIVIANS, LISTEN! AS A MOTHER, I DEMAND JUSTICE. BARBIE-ALTMANN, THE MURDERER OF MY

HUSBAND AND THREE CHILDREN, MUST BE TRIED FOR HIS CRIMES! The other sign reads: IN THE NAME OF THE MILLIONS OF VICTIMS OF NAZISM, EXTRADITE BARBIE-ALTMANN. We walk over to the offices of Transmaritima Boliviana, where Barbie works as a manager. The building is located on the Prado, the busiest road in La Paz. We chain ourselves to a bench, opposite the offices, and hold up our signs. A crowd gathers; traffic slows to a crawl. A traffic jam develops. No one here has seen a public protest since Banzer's police state clamped down on freedom of speech after last year's August putsch. The news is broadcast on the radio. A police Jeep arrives; its occupants read the words on the signs, and then it drives off again. At 4:00 p.m., a van stops near our bench, and plainclothes police get out and push through the crowd of spectators. They confiscate our signs and then run off. Some young Bolivians and an Israeli man passing through La Paz make new signs for us, and we continue as before.

A journalist hands me a microphone and asks me to explain the significance of the chains. "These are the chains that link the Bolivian regime to Nazism," I reply.

It starts to rain. We have been sitting on our bench for six hours now, and we have been seen by most of the city's population, as well as the diplomatic corps. An employee from the French embassy stops by to tell us, "What you're doing is pointless." But he is wrong: this protest will have a major positive impact. We have raised people's awareness of the situation, laid the groundwork. The Banzer regime is far from stable; perhaps its successors will see this case differently after the work we have done here.

When evening comes, we catch our plane and spend twenty-four hours in Lima, which is pleasantly warm after La Paz. We go to the hairdresser because we both want to look good for the television cameras that will await us at Orly Airport.

We land in Paris on the afternoon of Thursday, March 9, after eighteen days in South America.

THE LETTER BOMB

P OETICIZE YOUR LIFE," Serge had written to the young German woman he met in the spring of 1960. "Raise it to the level of a transcendent experience." Without him, without his unflagging energy, what could I have achieved? Another man would probably have demanded that I cut myself off from Germany; Serge helped me to really become a German.

A series of brief trips to Germany allowed me to complete my list of the leaders of the Nazi police machine in France. Maybe I thought I was stronger than I actually was? On my way back from one of these trips, I was blocked in Strasbourg by a general strike. At 2:00 a.m., I had to leave my sleeper carriage and stand outside in the cold for a long time, waiting for a seat on another train. Soon after returning to Paris, I lost the baby I had been carrying inside me for the last three months.

On May 10, I went to Cannes with Arno. I would give a speech, and then the two of us would spend three days relaxing. This trip proved timely in more than one way, as it allowed us to escape death.

A few hours after our departure, at 5:00 p.m., the concierge brought up a parcel that the mailman had dropped off, addressed to "Mme Beate Klarsfeld." My mother-in-law put the parcel on the table, intrigued by the fact that the postmark ("Paris, May 9, Avenue de Wagram, 12:30") did not match the sender's address ("Samuel Ségal, Les Guillerettes, par 34-Gignac"). She became suspicious and decided to wait for Serge to come home. He got back at 6:30. He began by opening the first layer of kraft paper, revealing a soft cardboard box. Inside this, wrapped in tissue paper, was a package in brightly colored wrapping paper bearing the label of the confectioner "Marquis." Serge tore off this paper and discovered a pale-orange cylindrical box with the word "Sugar" on it.

"I was surprised," he told me that evening on the phone. "Who could be sending us sugar? When I examined the paper more closely, I saw some tiny black grains, like dust. My mother thought it might be black sugar. I put a grain on my tongue, and it tasted acidic. Then I moved a match flame over a few grains that I'd put in the sink. The flame seemed to grow bigger before dying. My suspicions were confirmed. I called the operator and asked about a Samuel Ségal in Gignac. No one was listed under that name. So I called the gendarmerie in Gignac, and one of the policemen there checked for me and reported that he could not find anyone called Ségal nor a place named Les Guillerettes. Finally, I called the confectioner Marquis: no, they did not sell boxes of sugar. I put everything in a shopping bag and took it to the police station in Auteuil. I explained to the police, who were skeptical to start with, that this might just be confectionary, but that it could also be a bomb. The police chief called the bomb squad, and they X-rayed the box in their van. When he saw that there was a detonator, the engineer ordered traffic blocked from both streets near the station for fifteen minutes. This gave them enough time to saw the box open and empty it. There were ten ounces of nails inside, plus enough explosives to kill the person who opened the box and anyone standing near them."

A few months later, Dr. Fully, head of the medical organization in charge of all French prisons and a former Dachau deportee, received the same type of parcel and opened it. The explosion killed him and the concierge who had brought him the package.

SERGE

Shooting Lischka

To MAKE PROGRESS in Germany, we needed to create shock waves. The first kind of shock wave was the illegality of our protests, which had to be psychologically violent. That violence was justified if it enabled us to highlight the legitimacy of our protest and our call for justice. To achieve that, we had to be the ones who took the brunt of the violence—being arrested, going on trial, being sent to prison—while the real criminal remained free because the German parliament refused to vote for a law that would allow him to be tried. The second form of shock wave consisted in finding the Nazi war criminals who operated in France and showing how their impunity permitted them to take honorable, respectable jobs.

In October 1972, we started working on both of those forms of shock wave simultaneously. Our research led us to Dr. Heinrich Illers, an SS captain, Lischka's assistant, and head of the Paris Gestapo in 1943. In 1942, it was he who chose which men were to be shot at Mont-Valérien; in 1944, it was he who organized the "convoy of death" that took Resistance fighters to Dachau. In August 1944, he ordered two deportation convoys from Compiègne, despite the intervention of the Red Cross, which pointed out the Nordling-Choltitz agreement made between the Swedish consul and the German military command. One point of that agreement was that there would not be any more convoys of deportations. "The only orders I take are from the head of the SS," he replied.

Illers had disappeared, and the French military courts had abandoned the case because they could not identify him. When we noted in one document that he was named as "Dr. Illers," we went through the lists of lawyers and judges, and there discovered "Dr. Heinrich Illers," presiding judge in the social affairs court in the Land of Lower Saxony and . . . expert in problems relating to victims of war.

Now we needed his photograph. We asked a young German woman, Lisa, who had looked after Arno two years earlier and who lived in Munich, to go to his house.

When she got there, she saw Illers doing the gardening and asked him if she could take a photograph of his beautiful house; he agreed. We made dozens of copies of the picture, and one week later his image appeared in *Der Spiegel*.

To make sure that this man really was the same Heinrich Illers, Beate called him.

"I'm writing a dissertation about the German military administration in France. Were you part of that?"

"Yes."

"Could I ask you some questions about the hierarchy of the Sicherheitspolizei? Helmut Knochen was the chief, correct?"

"Yes."

"And Kurt Lischka was his assistant, as well as being *Kommandeur* in Paris?"

"Yes, that's right."

"So who was Lischka's assistant and the head of the Gestapo in Paris?"

"Karl Bömelburg."

"That's not what it says on the organization chart I have on my desk. Bömelburg was the head of the Gestapo in France. In Paris, the head of the Gestapo was Dr. Heinrich Illers."

"Unmöglich!" (Impossible!)

I was close to Beate during this conversation, and I listened carefully to Illers's responses. That last shouted word was so loud and sincere-sounding that I was impressed, even if I didn't believe him.

TO DRAMATIZE OUR revelation, I decided to secretly enter West Germany, where there was a warrant out for my arrest due to my participation in the attempted abduction of Lischka, and to hold a press conference in Bonn— at the Hotel am Tulpenfeld, a journalists' hangout near the Bundestag. At that time, Bonn was West Germany's political capital. In order not to be arrested at the border, I booked a sleeper carriage on a night train and used the passport of a friend of mine who was the same age as me. I was accompanied by a former deportee.

I knew that passports were checked at the border and the police would not check that the passenger matched the passport. Beate, who was not wanted by the police in West Germany, sent out invitations to journalists specifying that, even though there was an arrest warrant out for him, Serge Klarsfeld would hold a press conference at 2:00 p.m. during which he would make certain revelations.

At precisely two o'clock, I made a theatrical entrance to the conference room, accompanied by Heinrich Böll, Beate's firmest supporter and a future Nobel Prize winner. As soon as I reached the microphone, two policemen presented me with the *Haftbefehl*, the arrest warrant. They were perfectly polite.

The journalists wanted to hear what I had to say, and the two detectives agreed to wait until the press conference was over. They stood close to me while I spoke, and their blurred images were printed in all the newspapers the next day. Beate handed out the dossier we had prepared on Illers. His photograph would be on every front page.

When the press conference was over, the detectives took me to a courthouse cell in Cologne. The judges recommended that I be released on bail, but I refused to spend even a single mark. As they absolutely did not want to keep me in prison, they decided that the bail paid a year ago by Beate should be divided in two: half for her, half for me. This was completely irregular, but it allowed them to get rid of me without delay.

That day, Heinrich Illers retired from his job. One investigation was opened against him in Paris, now that he had been identified, and another in Germany.

Our charming, intelligent, and daring friend Lisa, happy to have contributed to the cause, decided to work alongside us. Her support would prove extremely valuable to us, particularly in Bolivia.

ON DECEMBER 15, 1972, I was back in Bonn, this time accompanied by ten former deportees, who were there to support the ratification of the Franco-German legal agreement. At their head was Georges Wellers, president of the Auschwitz III–Monowitz association and editor of *Le Monde Juif* (*The Jewish World*) magazine; Julien Aubart, who was deported at twenty and who became my best friend until his death in 1977, at the age of fifty-three; and two of his comrades from Auschwitz, Henri Pudeleau and Henri Wolff, who also supported us until their premature last breaths. These three—Aubart, Pudeleau, and Wolff—were our moral guarantors. They mobilized dozens of camp survivors to protest in Germany. That day—the day when Brandt's new government was introduced at the Bundestag after the legislative elections—we protested in the forbidden zone. A mob of policemen descended on us, but they didn't dare use violence in front of all the deputies and journalists. I took advantage of this fact to send a few of their helmets flying before they managed to subdue me. At the police station, the ex-deportees were asked the routine question "Have you ever been arrested before?" and each one answered with the date and reason for his arrest by the Gestapo and his camp identification number. That evening, the police escorted us to the border.

ON FEBRUARY 11, 1973, I was with Julien Aubart in Hamburg to unmask August Moritz, a Gestapo member in Paris, Orléans, Marseille, and Lyon. He was celebrating his sixtieth birthday that day. SS Untersturmführer Moritz had arrested the Jewish French politician Victor Basch and his wife and delivered them to the Milice—the French militia—who summarily executed them. Moritz agreed to speak with us. He defended himself by stating that he was now on the far left and that he had rebuilt the archives of the VVN, the Berlin-based association for victims of Nazism; that he had even been to hear Beate speak at the University of Hamburg in 1968; that he had spent four years in prison as an East German spy; last, that he was innocent and his conviction in France was unjust. I suggested he give himself up to the French authorities, and he refused: his first duty, he said, was to his family, his job, his reputation. I then asked him if he had had any responsibilities regarding the Jews. He assured me he hadn't. I handed him photocopies of a dozen documents bearing his signature; they were addressed to the head of the Gestapo's Jewish Affairs Department in Paris. For example, on January 10, 1943, Moritz had asked him, "To which camp should we send the Jews we have arrested?" After a long silence, Moritz admitted that he had signed these documents. "But I never killed anyone." I pointed out that the Jews were sent to the gas chambers by a vast police and administrative machinery. Hitler, Himmler, and Eichmann had not killed a single Jew between them in the strictest sense, but they had helped the death machine function.

A legal investigation was opened on his case.

ON MAY 7, 1973, guided by Beate—who was six months pregnant at the time—Julien Aubart, Henri Pudeleau, and four young LICA members walked up to Lischka's office, behind the central train station in Cologne. Our two friends, wearing concentration camp uniforms, tied themselves to the windows and shouted, *"Lischka! Nazi Mörder!"* People stopped to stare. Some police came and roughed up Julien and Henri. Almost as soon as they were inside the police station, the police started punching them. It takes courage for those who have survived the camps to voluntarily end up in the hands of German police with no respect for the victims of their Third Reich predecessors. After one night in a cell, our two friends and their four accomplices were tried and sentenced to pay the Krücken firm—Lischka's employer—the sum of two thousand marks to repair the office's windows. They never paid anything.

Our strategy was to repeatedly show, through our illegal protests, that there was a clash between our desire to have the Franco-German legal agreement ratified, allowing Nazi war criminals to be judged in West Germany, and the desire of the German politicians to protect those criminals by not ratifying it. The balance of power was not in our favor, but protest after protest, we strengthened our cause.

On June 13, Julien and I were in Bonn to distribute fifty dossiers on

Ernst Achenbach, who had just been nominated rapporteur of the Franco-German legal agreement within the Bundestag's foreign affairs committee. It was he who would decide, on behalf of that committee, whether or not to ratify the agreement. We gave out dossiers to everyone on the committee, but that did not prevent them from voting for Achenbach.

In West Germany, the twenty-year statute of limitations was supposed to begin with the creation of the Federal Republic in 1949. Crimes against humanity were exempt from this statute of limitations except if they had happened prior to 1949. In 1969, after a lively debate and under international pressure, the statute of limitations for crimes against humanity was pushed back ten years; this meant that in 1979 parliament would have to make a decision on the subject. So Achenbach's pressure group was already active, attempting to convince the German deputies that "thirty years were enough."

ON AUGUST 15, 1973, our daughter, Lida-Myriam, was born, eight years after Arno. It was another responsibility, of course, but we were very happy.

I was now able to devote myself full-time to our battle. As of May 1972, I was unemployed. I was one of the few at that time—France was going through its last period of full employment—to claim benefits at the mayor's office in the seventeenth arrondissement. In the fall of 1974, when I claimed benefits for the last time, there was a long line of unemployed people behind me.

IN ISRAEL, WHERE I went with Jean Pierre-Bloch a few days after the end of the '73 Yom Kippur War, I realized how close the country had come to defeat. Israel was saved by the sacrifices of the tank commandos in the Golan and Ariel Sharon's strategic genius. I also learned that Israel's discreet diplomatic approaches to Bonn, intended to hasten the ratification of the Franco-German legal agreement, had come to nothing.

I was in despair; this was the only period when I really doubted. I decided to show the German government that, if they did not ratify the agreement, they would bear the responsibility for a tragedy: we would kill Lischka or Hagen, or some other Nazi criminal, and the Bundestag would be to blame. But first I had to prove that I was serious. Lischka was licensed to carry a weapon, so I chose him as my target.

On an icy day in December, I stood in the train station in Cologne, a revolver in my pocket—a Walther, which Julien had procured for me. Beate and my mother had tried to dissuade me, but I was resolute.

I waited for Lischka to come out of his office, then I followed him to his car and rushed at him, revolver in hand. He was wearing gloves, and he didn't have time to draw his weapon. I pointed my gun at his forehead; he collapsed onto the hood of his vehicle. His eyes were full of terror; he believed his time had come. I pulled the trigger. But the gun was not loaded. I laughed, and then ran back toward the train station. He did not get up and follow me, and none of the passersby who had witnessed the scene reacted. In the station, I caught a train that crossed the Belgian border and deliberately sat in the same compartment as the policemen who were there to check passports.

The next day, the presiding judge at the court of Cologne and the prosecutor general received a letter in which I begged them to warn the relevant authorities, emphasizing that they could not avoid a terrible scandal if the agreement wasn't ratified and if the German courts did not try Lischka and Hagen. The response was not long coming: a new arrest warrant was put out for me. All the same, I knew that my fake murder was a step forward, and my morale returned to its normal level.

Would I have killed someone if we had not succeeded in bringing those men to trial? I believe I would have. My determination to go all the way in order to ensure that our cause did not fail was the same determination Beate had felt when she risked her life to slap the chancellor, surrounded as he was by bodyguards ready to shoot anyone who attacked him.

When you commit to a great, just cause, you cannot give up without, in some way, giving up on yourself. If I'd done that, I would never have recovered. If hope had brought me to a dead end, despair would have opened the road. But at what price? The destruction of my soul, in all probability, because no one kills with impunity, even if the person they kill is a murderer living with impunity.

The Failed Abduction of Barbie

IN THE FALL of 1972, the French Marxist philosopher Régis Debray got in touch with us. For him, even more than for us, Barbie was a link between the Nazis' European reign and the oppressive regimes in 1970s Latin America. Debray had been friends with Che Guevara; he had been sentenced to death in Bolivia, saved by the intervention of General de Gaulle, and freed after five years in prison. We felt we had a great deal in common with him. Like us, he was disliked by many of the 1968 militants because they thought he gave a "bad example." Like us, he had the courage to go beyond words and postures and to risk his life for his beliefs.

Beate and I met Régis Debray at the Café de Flore in Paris. We got along well and decided to cooperate on the following basis: we would attempt, using the South American connections of Régis and his Venezuelan wife, Elisabeth, to kidnap Barbie and bring him back to France via Chile. Régis told us that the man he considered best qualified to carry out this operation was a former left-wing journalist and prefect from Bolivia, now exiled in socialist Chile.

His name was Gustavo Sánchez Salazar. He was forty-five years old. Régis assured us that he was absolutely trustworthy. We invited Gustavo to Paris, and he arrived on October 20, 1972. Together, we hatched a plan. Gustavo knew some young Bolivian army officers opposed to the country's military dictatorship. He suggested that I go to Chile, bringing five thousand dollars so that they could buy a car and abduct Barbie on the road from La Paz to Cochabamba, where he went regularly because he was part owner of a sawmill in the area. Gustavo's men would ambush Barbie's car, abduct him, and transport him to the Chilean border. After that, it would be up to us to find a way to get him to France, using the support of Chile's leaders, who were friendly with the Debrays.

I could not enter South America with my passport: the name "Klarsfeld" was too closely linked to Barbie's. So a friend from high school, Michel Boyer, lent me his passport; when I opened it, I noticed that the stamp on the photograph was placed almost identically to the one on my passport. So Daniel Marchac, my surgeon friend, used his scalpel to remove the photographs from both passports and swap them. Only a close examination would reveal the forgery. I became Michel Boyer, and I learned to copy his signature.

Once I got to Santiago, Régis guided me. We rented a tourist plane that took us to the north of Chile, on the Bolivian border. On a dirt track, we waited for Gustavo and a Bolivian officer named Carlos, who would drive the car that they would buy with the money I was bringing them. Beate and I had raised the five thousand dollars from the small group that had gradually gathered around us during our campaigns. I handed over the briefcase; we all shook hands and then went our separate ways.

Back in France, I waited for the date of the operation to be set. But three dramatic events occurring one after another reduced our hopes to ashes. First, an accident destroyed the car we had bought; Carlos lost control of the vehicle as he attempted to swerve around some llamas that had strayed onto the road. Soon afterward, in March 1973, Barbie was arrested. While his extradition file was being examined by the Bolivian supreme court, he went to Paraguay for a few days. Fearing that Barbie would flee to Asunción and that the French government would blame its Bolivian counterparts for negligence, the Bolivians kept him under close guard, meaning that he could not be abducted. Last, just when Barbie was released, after the demand for extradition had been refused, Chile's socialist president Salvador Allende was overthrown by General Pinochet and died during the coup d'état.

In Brazil, reading a back issue of *Le Monde*, I learned that it was now possible for someone with a diploma from Sciences Po to enter law school in the third year without having to pass an examination. This news reassured me: it was not too late, at thirty-seven years old, to go back to my studies. It would be another challenge, of course, but the law was one of the few professions open to me that would prove useful in accomplishing our mission.

BEATE

Arrested in Dachau, Tried in Cologne

A RREST WARRANTS AND voluntary arrests were part of our strategy. The next symbol of our struggle was my arrest inside the Dachau camp.

There had been a warrant for my arrest in Germany since I took our group to protest in Cologne in May 1973, so it would be easy to get arrested. But what we wanted was for the Israeli government to demand my liberation and to announce that it was infuriated not only by the fact that the Germans were arresting me, but also by the place where the arrest would take place and by the date: it was Yom HaShoah, Holocaust Remembrance Day.

I left Paris on April 16, 1974, accompanied by two of our loyal supporters: Henri Pudeleau and Henri Wolff. They stood beside me in Dachau, in their concentration camp uniforms. In Munich, the police received an anonymous tip-off: "Beate Klarsfeld, who is under an arrest warrant, is in the Dachau camp right now." A few minutes later, several police cars turned up. Three policemen entered the camp and arrested me before a crowd of journalists and photographers. I was taken to the Bavarian state prison, and the next day four policemen drove me from Munich to Cologne, where I once again found myself in the Ossendorf Prison.

The next day, in Tel Aviv, protesters outside the German embassy yelled, *"Nazis in, Beate out!"* Israeli politicians from the left and right came out in support of my cause. On April 23, there was another protest outside the German embassy in Paris. But none of this altered the situation. I feared that the German courts would postpone my trial until October and that I would spend the next six months in prison; that way, they would be able to sentence me to six months and free me at the same time, which would satisfy German public opinion. I was not exactly enthused by this prospect, particularly as one of my cellmates was a former extermination camp guard. On May 2, fifty former deportees took a coach from Paris to protest outside my prison, where they left fifty red, white, and blue bouquets before heading to the Bundestag.

The same day, the interim French president Alain Poher expressed his "profound distress" over my detention, while in Israel a petition calling for my release was signed by several hundred thousand people. In prison, I received hundreds of letters of support from Israel. *Le Monde* published a petition signed by some very famous names, including Jacques Chirac and François Mitterrand.

In prison, while the Baader-Meinhof girls trashed their cells and clashed with the guards, I was faultlessly polite and kept my cell meticulously clean. Willy Brandt had just been forced to resign because of the Guillaume affair, when his trusted aide Günter Guillaume was found to be an East German spy. Christel Guillaume, the spy's wife and accomplice, was sent to Ossendorf, where she was put in the cleanest available cell—mine.

On May 6, in spite of Henry Kissinger's arrival in Jerusalem, a special session of the Knesset was held to deal with my case. The session ended with a unanimous resolution, sent to the Bundestag, demanding my immediate release and the ratification of the Franco-German legal agreement. As my lawyer, Shmuel Tamir, was also a politician and wasn't free to leave Israel for some time, he was replaced by another renowned lawyer, Arie Marinsky, who immediately set out for Paris to prepare my defense with Serge.

Marinsky and my German lawyer, Jürgen Stange, went toe to toe with the intransigent judge, Victor de Somoskeoy, who saw only a breach of the law. After eight hours of intense negotiation, Marinsky obtained my temporary release in return for Israeli politician Benjamin Halevi's guarantee that I would return for my trial in early June. Marinsky told the *Jerusalem Post*: "Beate Klarsfeld is in real danger. The German legal machine can be inflexible to a scarcely imaginable degree. It might seem unthinkable that an idealist like Beate Klarsfeld could be imprisoned, while some of the cruelest criminals in history, like Lischka, remain free . . . The Germans cannot stand the idea of one of their own people reminding them of things they would rather forget. There is a conspiracy of silence in Germany."

After three weeks in prison, I was reunited with my family, free once again to look after our house and go shopping at the Porte de Saint-Cloud market. I had often been compared to Antigone, but Antigone was single. I was married with two children, one of them an eight-month-old baby. The real heroine was my mother-in-law.

MY TRIAL BEGAN in Cologne on June 25, 1974. These were the key moments:

June 25—Many of my supporters protest outside the courthouse. The judge has not yet decided whether he will allow the defense witnesses.

June 27—During the trial, the judge spots my lawyer, Marinsky, handing two notes to the Israeli consul. He demands that the notes be read out loud. Marinsky agrees. The first one says: "Is there any mail for me?" The second one says: "Could you go out and buy me some aspirin?" Marinsky goes on, "If I ask for or receive instructions, it will not be from Jerusalem, but from Bialystok, where my entire family was murdered by the Germans."

The same day, the new French president, Valéry Giscard d'Estaing, intervenes in my favor. He sends a letter to the German foreign minister stating that he is concerned about my trial, asking for the French witnesses to be heard by the judge, and reminding him that the Bundestag has still not ratified the Franco-German legal agreement of February 2, 1971. The judge agrees to hear the French witnesses.

July 1—The courtroom is packed. Jean Pierre-Bloch is there, as are many of my supporters, including some Jewish students who have traveled here from Paris. Lischka is on the stand. The judge denounces the French president's letter as "an intrusion on the court's independence."

Questioned by Marinsky, Lischka remembers nothing or refuses to answer. The audience rises: "Murderer! Nazi!" There is total chaos. The trial becomes front-page news.

July 2—The judge, having read this morning's newspapers, is much more careful. Georges Wellers is called to testify about the sufferings of French Jews. Joseph Billig details Lischka's Nazi career. Their testimonies are important, but the German journalists are not really interested. We need a new shock to get their attention back.

July 3—The judge again complains about the French president's "intolerable" intervention. The lawyer appointed by the court to join my defense counsel stands up in support of the judge: "This is a tactic reminiscent of the Nazi period." I protest: "This man is not my lawyer—he's the judge's lawyer!" At the end of the deposition by René Clavel, a former Resistance fighter, the judge accuses him of having parodied the Nazi salute while taking his oath. Turmoil in the courtroom: the police manhandle former deportees and Resistance heroes.

Achenbach tells the media in French and German, "We demand a general amnesty for humanitarian and Christian reasons. As the Bundestag's rapporteur for my committee, I will carefully examine the proposal for ratification, and that will take time—a lot of time."

July 5—The judge decides that, due to recent events, the trial will take place behind closed doors. I get to my feet: "Those incidents only happened because of the inhumanity with which you are handling this trial." Furious, he wants to sentence me to prison for contempt of court.

The prosecutor asks for a six-month suspended sentence.

Marinsky's defense speech is remarkable. He explains why an Israeli lawyer had to be there to defend me, what I represent for the Israelis, what Lischka represents for Germany, the crimes he committed and why it is necessary to put an end to his impunity by ratifying the agreement of February 2, 1971. He concludes with these words: "I pray also that a new Germany shall take root and that this plea for justice shall be heard."

My last words to the judge are "You have a unique opportunity to show the Bundestag that it is its duty to ratify the agreement and strengthen the meaning of justice in our country. For me and my friends, it wasn't easy to break the law in order to obtain justice. It won't be easy for you to acquit me when you know that I committed an illegal act, but if you do, you will demonstrate that, unlike so many other German judges before you, you were able to see beyond the letter of the law."

July 8—The day before the verdict. At the Franco-German summit between Helmut Schmidt, the new chancellor, and Valéry Giscard d'Estaing, Schmidt announces—to everyone's surprise—that he has promised the French president that the agreement will be ratified before the end of the year. This was supposed to be an economic summit, but it has turned into a legal one instead.

July 9—The verdict is delivered at 2:00 p.m. I am sentenced to two months in prison, with no obligation to serve the thirty-seven days I have already spent in prison (sixteen in 1971; twenty-one in 1974) and with no obligation to go to prison now for the remaining twenty-three days, as my case must be submitted to the federal court of Karlsruhe. Outrage in the courtroom, where my supporters sing "La Marseillaise."

The conclusion of the next day's editorial in *Le Monde* struck a powerful note among the politicians in Bonn: "It is not with the Germany of Lischka and the Cologne judges that the French people wish to make a European union, but with the Germany of Willy Brandt and Beate Klarsfeld."

On July 10, outside the German embassy in Paris, more than two thousand people chanted their support for me. Surrounded by policemen, Serge standing close to me, a huge bouquet of flowers in my arms, I was the center of attention. But I wasn't fooled: I had known too many days after moments of triumph when Serge and I had found ourselves alone, or almost, when the time came to take the next, tricky step.

RATIFICATION WOULD TRANSFORM the Franco-German legal agreement into law; it had been named "Lex Klarsfeld," which was the most sincere tribute I could imagine.

There was an international backlash to the verdict against me: Achenbach was forced to resign his position as rapporteur for the Bundestag's foreign affairs committee, and his political career went into decline. The press conference I held in Bonn on New Year's Day 1975—during which I gave every German deputy a special edition of the *Le Monde Juif* devoted to Achenbach—prevented him from taking part in the debate on ratification in the Bundestag.

At that debate, on January 30, the Free Democrat–Social Democrat coalition held firm, and ratification was voted through. And yet, that was not the end of the story. The right-wing Christian Democrats planned to vote against the measure in the Bundesrat, roughly West Germany's equivalent of the U.S. Senate, where they had a majority. All we could do now was to keep making revelations about the Nazis.

On February 4, in Jerusalem, I gave a press conference at which I revealed that the man in the West German Foreign Office in charge of preparing Euro-Arab talks was Hans Schirmer, Kiesinger's predecessor as assistant director of the Nazis' foreign propaganda unit, which used to broadcast messages to the Middle East, such as "The Jews are the mortal enemies of the Arabs [. . .] Your salvation can only be delivered by the Axis powers, who are ready to rid you of the Jewish plague." Soon afterward, Schirmer retired due to ill health.

On February 21, 1975, the deputies in the Bundesrat voted unanimously for ratification.

Campaigning in Damascus

Klarsfeld to Protest over POWs
Nazi Hunter Beate Klarsfeld boarded a plane for Damascus last
night with a message for President Hafiz al-Assad protesting the
treatment of Israeli prisoners of war and the Jewish minority in
Syria.

Her message, which she intends to present to Assad and his
ministers, reads in part:

"Wherever Jews happen to be persecuted, it is our German duty
to intervene on their side. In recent years, dreadful treatment was
inflicted upon the Jewish community in Syria, and today, the most
awful uncertainty is arising insofar as Israeli war prisoners are
concerned—considering the fact that dozens of their comrades,
after being captured in the Golan Heights, were savagely
slaughtered.

"Such barbarities, together with Syria's refusal to publish a list of the survivors, do not redound to the honor of Syria.

"Should my demarche be fruitless, let me remind you that thirty years ago, the people I belong to brought deep shame on their name by waging a total war against the Jewish people. Do not let the crimes committed by Hitler's Germany serve as examples to the Arab people.

"Instead of dreaming over ways to annihilate a small and peaceful state . . . [you should] search patiently and sincerely with Israel for the routes toward a just peace for all the belligerents."

—*Jerusalem Post*, January 17, 1974

JANUARY 16, 1974. My plane lands in Damascus. The situation in the Middle East is more poisonous than ever, particularly in Syria, where the Baathist regime's long-standing support for the Palestinian cause is putting the Syrian Jewish community under increasing pressure.

I am not too worried when I get off the plane in Damascus, probably because I have, once again, obtained a visa using my maiden name. Back in France, however, my family is extremely anxious on my behalf. Only a couple of hours after settling into my hotel room, I receive a call from Serge, who is beside himself at knowing that I am alone in a country where there is very little sympathy for our struggle. He is right: I have to act quickly and resolutely.

A taxi takes me to the presidential palace, where I wish to convey my message in person to the Syrian president Hafiz al-Assad. He is busy with weightier matters, however, and one of his advisers asks me to come back a few days later.

In my hotel room, I am visited by the Palestinian correspondent of an American press agency, then the Damascus correspondents of AFP and Reuters. They are clearly hostile to my campaign in Syria.

That evening, I try to call my family to break the oppressive atmosphere of solitude and silence, but the line is dead. I am cut off from the world. It takes the intervention of the French ambassador, who comes to visit me in my hotel room, to rescue me from my state of isolation.

There is still no word from the Syrian government, in spite of the adviser's promises. I am hoping that Colette Khoury—a Syrian writer with a bourgeois Christian background who is very close to certain circles of power—can help me in my mission. She made the first move, suggesting that we meet soon after my arrival.

We chat in my hotel room. The conversation is friendly to begin with, but she soon launches into violent anti-Israeli diatribes, and we end up with a dialogue of the deaf. On my second evening in Damascus, I am invited to meet a few officials at a dinner given by Khoury. Two visions of the world, two political interpretations of contemporary history and the tragic fate of Europe's Jews, collide, without ever overlapping. Between them, no doubt, like an unbridgeable chasm, is the Palestinian tragedy.

Early the next day, there's a knock at the door. Bureaucrats from the Ministry of the Interior enter my hotel bedroom and announce that their superiors believe I have tested their patience long enough. A car is waiting outside for me. My bags are loaded into it, my bill is paid by the president's office, and I am driven to the airport.

IN MARCH OF the same year, families of prisoners held in Syria welcomed me with bouquets of flowers when I traveled to Israel with Serge. One war, two camps. I chose mine a long time before this. We met the Israeli prime minister Golda Meir on March 23. Soon after that, she wrote:

Courage, Conviction, Compassion, Decency, Justice and Self-Sacrifice to the point of personal danger—these are words that come to mind when one hears the name Beate Klarsfeld. With an unmatched and fearless integrity, this young, unusual non-Jew has dedicated herself to seeking out and sweeping out the residue of Nazism wherever its obscene criminals still abide. Her passionate humanity has led her to identify herself in the most personal sense with Jews everywhere who, thirty years after the destruction of the Nazi death machine, are still victims of discrimination and persecution. To Israel and the Jewish people Mrs. Klarsfeld is a "Woman of Valor"—a title that has no peer in Jewish tradition.

In a world in which appeasement has again reared its ugly head at the expense of moral values and human dignity, the personal example of Beate Klarsfeld serves as one woman's personal assertion of the supremacy of Right and Justice.

AFTER MY TRIAL in Cologne, the mayor of Jerusalem, Teddy Kollek, invited Serge and me to bring our children for a vacation at the Dalia kibbutz. For four consecutive summers, I would spend a month in various kibbutzim.

IN OCTOBER 1974, I went to the seventh Arab League summit, which was taking place in Rabat, Morocco, where I wanted to express my exasperation with the systematically bellicose attitude toward Israel of Arab governments, both in words and in deeds. I handed out leaflets calling on the countries in that region to "let Israel live in peace":

> I came here because there has to be at least one person to protest [. . .] against a policy whose objective is the destruction of the Israeli state. Thirty years ago, Hitler's Germany exterminated six million Jews. As a German woman, I must fulfill my duty to tell the Arab nations: do not follow the example of which my country is guilty. Let the Jewish state live in peace. This country is a refuge for survivors of the Holocaust, for Jews expelled or oppressed by Soviet communism, and for the Jews who have had to leave Arab countries in greater numbers than the Palestinians exiled in 1948. In the Palestine of the Balfour Declaration, there is a place for the Israeli state and for a Palestinian state.

The Moroccan security services were on high alert for the summit. Marco, who took part in the aborted abduction of Kurt Lischka three years earlier, and who had lived in Morocco, came with me. Our airplane landed in Casablanca on the morning of October 26. In our bags were 250 copies of my leaflet. We rented a car and passed the numerous checkpoints on the road to Rabat without any difficulties. We were even able to park near the Ministry of Information without raising suspicion. This would not last. In the meantime, though, we were able to achieve what we had set out to do. I handed out my leaflets while Marco remained at a distance, disappearing as soon as the police finally noticed me. I was escorted into the ministry, and a high-ranking police officer began a long interrogation. He was hoping to uncover a conspiracy, propaganda printed in Morocco, accomplices waiting nearby. He examined my passport, which contained six Israeli stamps, and became visibly irritated by the slackness of the border police, who had not even spotted them at the airport. He got really mad when he found out that I had come with Marco, who had vanished. He issued an order for Marco's arrest, while I was taken to the police headquarters for mug shots, fingerprints, and more questions.

While Marco returned to France via Tangier and Spain, I spent the night on a bench in the police station, guarded by two officers, before being put on a plane back to Paris the next morning.

Le Monde, L'Aurore, and *Le Figaro* ran stories about my arrest. One month later, in Jerusalem, the Israeli foreign minister Yigal Allon gave a reception in our honor, declaring that "Beate has done more than my whole ministry."

ON JANUARY 13, 1975, we organized a press conference in Berlin to make public the new documents collected by Serge on Ernst Achenbach, who was still resolutely defending his old Nazi friends from prosecution. I gave the Achenbach dossier to five hundred German deputies. My goal was to force Achenbach to resign from his position as head of the Parliamentary Association for Euro-Arab Cooperation by revealing that one of his closest colleagues in his law firm was Horst Wagner, formerly head of the Jewish Affairs Department in the Third Reich's Foreign Office. He had, in particular, worked with the grand mufti of Jerusalem to prevent thousands of Jewish children from being saved. Achenbach resigned soon after this.

Next I went to Cairo, for reasons similar to those that had taken me to Damascus a year earlier. I wanted Egypt, ruled by Anwar Sadat, to distance itself from Achenbach, to forge new relations with its Israeli neighbor, and to intercede with the governments of Syria and Iraq to ensure that their Jewish minorities were no longer persecuted. I left without a visa but was allowed into Egypt anyway. My intention was to travel from there to Beirut, Baghdad, and Damascus in order to spread my message. Sadat's minister of information received me in his office and appeared to listen very courteously to what I had to say, but the Syrian customs guards refused to let me enter their country, so I caught a plane to Beirut, where I was granted a forty-eight-hour visa.

In the Saint Georges Hotel there, I met up with journalists from the Associated Press and the French-speaking Lebanese newspaper *Le Jour.* We had not been in discussion for more than five minutes when five men from the Lebanese security services stormed into my room. The two hotel employees who accompanied them picked up all my belongings and stuffed them into my suitcase. The scene that followed—I was getting used to it by now—took place in a security services building, where a bureaucrat unexpectedly congratulated me on my Barbie campaign . . . before asking me to bear in mind the Israelis' mistreatment of Lebanese people in the south of the country. After that, it was the sinister, monotonous ritual of the night in the police station, lying on a bench, and then the car to the airport, where the police did not let me out of their sight until I had boarded a flight to Rome. And from there a connection to Paris.

SERGE

In Search of Irrefutable Proof

I N 1974, AS our activism was in full swing, I had to devote part of my time to studying the law. Everywhere I went, I took my books with me, opening them whenever I had a spare moment. My first objective was to obtain my master's degree.

That year, Jean-Michel Charlier, who wrote the story lines for the popular Western comic-book series *Blueberry*, asked me for ideas for a television documentary series entitled *The Black Files*, which would tell the stories of important historical figures who had not been in power. I suggested Otto Strasser, who was close to Hitler and later fought against him, and Menachem Begin, whom I admired and who, the previous year, had been the only Israeli politician to warmly welcome Beate, despite his hostility to the Germans.

I interviewed Otto Strasser in Munich and found a bitter, ill-tempered old man. It was hard to imagine him as one of the leaders of the Nazi Party.

Menachem Begin, on the other hand, whom Beate and I met in Jerusalem, represented not only the past for me but the future. I wrote the script for my television documentary *Begin and the Irgun* by focusing on three key moments: the attack on the King David Hotel; the Acre Prison break; and the Deir Yassin massacre.

AFTER GETTING MY master's in June 1974, I had to cram four years of penal, civil, commercial, and administrative law into the space of a few weeks in order to pass the extremely tough bar exam. All while traveling and campaigning for the judgment against Lischka and Hagen.

I remember a whole night spent studying in a hotel room for my oral exam, attempting to understand an accounting book that I had never even opened before that. Thankfully, it all went well.

This was a happy moment, for my family and for me. Not only had my political activism caused us no problems, but it had given me the motivation and strength to pursue a career that would allow me to be free and respectable while also earning good money and being able to better defend our cause—since the trial of the Nazi criminals was moving closer with the ratification of the Franco-German legal agreement, which finally went through in February 1975.

We now had to formulate a strategy for the application of the Lex Klarsfeld by the German justice system, which had thus far made no effort to persuade the country's politicians that it was ready to try Nazi war criminals. Gehrling, the prosecutor general who had filed charges against Beate, would be tasked with filing charges against Lischka and Hagen if he decided that the dossier warranted criminal charges, and if the grand jury believed that they would lead to a successful conviction. Our job was to fill the dossier with irrefutable proof that the accused were personally aware of the fate of the deportees.

For Lischka and Hagen, I took the eleven volumes I had gathered containing photocopies of thousands of German documents relating to the Final Solution in France, arranged chronologically. Then I listed all the documents signed by, initialed by, addressed to, or mentioning the names of Lischka and Hagen. In that way, we were able to identify two documents that made it clear that Lischka knew the truth about the Final Solution.

The first document was dated May 13, 1942. It was a report written by Dannecker, the head of the Gestapo's Jewish Affairs Department, to the attention of Knochen and Lischka. He had met General Kohl, the Wehrmacht's director of rail transportation in France: "During our conversation, which lasted an hour and a quarter, I gave the general an overview of the Jewish question and the policy concerning the Jews in France. In that way, I was able to note that he is an uncompromising enemy of the Jews and that he approved 100 percent of the Final Solution of the Jewish question, the aim of which is the absolute destruction of the enemy."

Lischka initialed this document.

The second document, also initialed by Lischka, is dated July 20, 1942. Dannecker reported the following words to Knochen, Lischka, and Oberg, the head of the SS and the police: "The head of the Camp des Milles [internment camp] provided some interesting information on this problem. He noted that, whenever there is a possibility of it, the Jewish emigration company HICEM will pay almost any sum to enable Jews to leave the country. Which shows how aware the world's Jews are that all the Jews under German power are headed toward their total destruction [*restlosen Vernichtung*]."

For Hagen, the proof was easier to find: it was he who trained Eichmann and his henchmen, and it was he—in France, beside General Oberg—who pushed hardest for mass deportations.

WE THEN DISCOVERED a third figure from the SS in France. His name was Ernst Heinrichsohn. At twenty-two, he had been Dannecker's assistant. We noticed on one of the documents that he had been studying law. So we got hold of the list of all the lawyers in Germany—and bingo! Heinrichsohn was a lawyer and notary in Miltenberg, Bavaria, as well as the mayor of the neighboring town of Bürgstadt.

I took the train to Munich with Julien Aubart, our friend and a former deportee. There, our friend and assistant Lisa joined us, and we rented a car. Julien had seen Heinrichsohn in the camp at Drancy, so he was in a position to recognize him. In 1942, the German had been a tall, handsome, blond man who, according to witnesses, took a particular pleasure in personally organizing the deportation of very young children. Three thousand of them were sent away in six convoys between August 17 and 28. In

Miltenberg, Lisa phoned Heinrichsohn's law firm and was told that he was in court. We waited outside the courthouse and eventually saw a well-dressed blond man emerge and get in a car. Julien thought it was him, so we followed in another car.

To confirm that this was the right man, we decided to make it obvious that we were following him. Before long, he turned around and saw me sitting next to a man of roughly his own age, Julien, who was glaring at him. He accelerated, turning left, then right, in a vain attempt to shake us off. Then, suddenly, he stopped outside a police station and ran inside. Now we had no doubt about his identity. He must have been afraid that we were going to shoot him.

THE TRIAL OF these three men—Lischka, Hagen, and Heinrichsohn—would be enough for us to settle the Franco-German legal dispute. If the trial took place, it would be difficult for the German courts not to convict them. And if the German courts seemed reluctant to do so, we would do what we always did: commit illegal acts of obvious symbolic value. As for other Nazi police leaders, we had to find some among them who were still alive in order to demonstrate the necessity of trying the men who had commanded them.

Fritz Merdsche was the *Kommandeur* of the Sipo-SD in Orléans, with authority over four French départments, including the internment camps at Pithiviers and Beaune-la-Rolande. In these camps, thousands of children were forcibly separated from their mothers and sent to Drancy, and from there to Auschwitz. In August 1944, on the eve of the Liberation of Paris, when the Gestapo in Bourges was unable to transfer thirty-nine Jews (including eleven women) to Drancy, its chief Erich Hasse phoned Merdsche to ask him what he should do. The response was immediate: "Liquidate them." They were thrown alive down some deep wells on a farm in Guerry. Merdsche was twice sentenced to death in absentia. When we found him, he was the editor of one of the most important legal journals in Germany, having retired from his position as a judge in Frankfurt. He would die in his own bed after being charged by the German courts.

Hans-Dietrich Ernst was sentenced to death four times in absentia. He had been *Kommandeur* of the Sipo-SD in Angers from 1942 to 1944, with authority over eight départements. He was responsible for the deportation of 8,463 people, nearly half of whom did not survive. He was living in Leer, in northern Germany, where I went to identify him. Another lawyer and notary. He was expelled from the bar and charged, but he died—from a fall downstairs—before his trial began.

Count Modest von Korff had been *Kommandeur* of the Nazi police in Châlons-sur-Marne. In October 1942, he ordered the deportation of Jewish children whose parents had been arrested and deported three months earlier. He was the only one of these men to appear before the criminal court in Bonn. He had reached the top of the bureaucratic ladder: ministerial director at the Ministry of the Economy in Bonn.

There were numerous other examples. For each individual case, we had to compile precise dossiers, photocopy all the documents, seek out plaintiffs, gather their statements, transmit the dossiers to the relevant prosecutors in Germany, and communicate the information to the media in a way that would ensure its dissemination. Beate translated everything into German.

WITH THE AID of Maurice Pioro, president of the Jewish Deportees Union in Belgium, we also tackled the problem of the impunity of the two men in charge of the deportation of twenty-five thousand Jews from Belgium and northern France, Ernst Ehlers and Kurt Asche. In Brussels, we gave a speech, in which we revealed to the Jews in the local community center that SS colonel Ehlers was alive, his crimes having gone unpunished.

On May 7, 1975, Beate took seven young Jews from Brussels to Schleswig, in the north of Germany. They entered Ehlers's apartment while he was out. The police arrested the youngsters while Beate fled with the driver of one of the two cars. She returned safely to Brussels, while her accomplices were released after a few days. But the campaign against Ehlers had begun. Joseph Billig and I prepared a historical assessment that would prove decisive, after numerous legal twists and turns, in indicting Ehlers and Asche in May 1977.

In the meantime, right after the incident in Schleswig, we sent a commando of young people to smash the glass façade of Lischka's Cologne office. We wanted to make the German courts understand that it was time for them to do their duty. To keep the incident quiet, a hasty trial was arranged, and the judge fined the youngsters before ordering them to be escorted to the border. A week later—after the broken windows had been replaced—a second commando went back and smashed them again. This time, the nine activists—among them a rabbi named Daniel Farhi—were imprisoned.

After three days behind bars, they were released to await their trial, which promised to be a major legal event. It did not take place until May 1976: the German courts were just as reluctant, then, to try us as they were to try former Nazis.

ON FEBRUARY 4, 1976, while I was still wanted for arrest in Germany (dating back to 1971), I turned up at the public prosecutor's office in Frankfurt. After informing the press of what I was doing, I handed the prosecutor general the dossiers for Fritz Merdsche, Hans-Dietrich Ernst, and Ernst Heinrichsohn. As Merdsche had been head of the Nazi police in Orléans, I was accompanied by Mr. Rébillon, the city's chief of police and a former Resistance member, as well as by my friend Julien. Once again, the judges had to choose between an arrest that would cause a scandal and allowing the law to be broken without sanction.

The prosecutor duly noted the dossiers I had given him and then executed my arrest warrant. I made the usual statements to the press and spent the night in the courtroom cell. The next day, two policemen took me by car to Cologne. At the prison in Ossendorf, where Beate had also been incarcerated, I was welcomed like a visiting dignitary: the director greeted me at the door, delighted to see me after my wife's stay there, and I was searched but allowed to keep most of my belongings, including a towel that they did not even unfold. My cell had a radio and was as clean as a hotel room. The next day, the French consul brought me cookies, chocolate, and cigarettes, which I handed out to the other prisoners. Knowing I would be arrested, I had brought with me the first volume of Plato's works. An attentive, in-depth study of the book might take several months. I had time to read only two dialogues before being freed.

The date of my protest was chosen deliberately: a few days before the Franco-German summit. My incarceration was an embarrassment to the authorities, and it had to be dealt with before the summit began. So while the German courts were clearly in no hurry to try former Nazis, they demonstrated exceptional swiftness in judging me. My trial took place at the courthouse in Cologne on February 9. I told the court that, as soon as

I was free, I would break the law again in order to obtain justice. But my declaration did no good: Judge Liptow refused to keep me in prison. He expressed his understanding for our motivations, sentenced me to a two-month suspended sentence, and released me.

The third episode in the window-smashing saga at Lischka's office took place on May 19, 1976, the day of the trial of nine people charged with committing the same crime eleven months earlier. It was a "mammoth" trial, as the Cologne press described it. And they were not wrong: a total of eighteen lawyers were present on the first day, as well as five translators. A considerable outlay for the German taxpayer.

For us, this day was an opportunity to make the German courts understand that we would not accept the existence of this trial, due to the nonexistence of the trials of Nazi criminals who had operated in France, and that we would keep reoffending until Lischka and his accomplices were brought to justice. For that reason, at six o'clock that morning, a commando of fifteen people was sent in a specially hired bus to Lischka's office, where they once again smashed the windows. They wore orange jackets and ski masks to hide their identities and broke the glass with iron bars.

Three hours later, they were at the courthouse, where they joined a second bus full of activists. Everyone wore a yellow star and a badge of the French flag. Our banners, written in German, were held up before the television cameras: TRY LISCHKA, NOT FRENCH ANTI-NAZIS; WE'LL KEEP COMING BACK UNTIL THE GERMAN COURTS BRING THE NAZI CRIMINALS TO JUSTICE.

The courtroom was too small for all our friends, and more than forty of them had to remain outside. After demanding, in vain, that the trial be moved to a larger courtroom, they occupied the access stairway under the direction of Julien Aubart, the first man to be tried for attacking Lischka's office in 1973. For more than an hour, they chanted "Auschwitz! Dachau! Buchenwald!" in voices so loud that they could not be drowned out.

I went to the police station and introduced myself as Gisèle Guerchon's defense lawyer. A baker had identified her as being one of the protesters he had seen smashing Lischka's windows a few hours earlier. Gisèle denied actively participating in the assault, while declaring her solidarity with all the French people who had traveled to Cologne to support Rabbi Farhi. Gisèle, a mother who had lost her father in Auschwitz, would spend the night on a stone bench in a filthy prison cell, surrounded by prostitutes. The next day, she was transferred to Ossendorf Prison.

Meanwhile, at the trial, while the judge attempted to stick to the facts of the case, the accused all highlighted their reasons for acting the way they did, and Rabbi Farhi delivered a speech so eloquent and moving that the young judge, Günter Kaumanns, declared, "The court shares your emotion."

While the main trial continued, Gisèle Guerchon was tried in another courtroom, meaning that two trials for identical crimes were being carried out simultaneously in the same building. The two cases overlapped when Elisabeth Hajdenberg testified that the baker who had supposedly identified Gisèle was the same man who, on July 1, 1975, had torn the yellow star from Rabbi Farhi's chest and trampled it underfoot. The baker offered an unconvincing denial of this accusation, before eventually admitting that he didn't remember what had happened and that it was possible he had done this. Which meant that Gisèle had been identified solely on the word of an anti-Semite. The judge, an elderly man, hesitated but delivered the outrageous verdict, agreeing to the three-month suspended sentence demanded by the prosecutor. There was uproar in the courtroom: Julien Aubart leaped to his feet, embraced Gisèle, and, his voice shaking with emotion, accused the judge of having convicted an innocent woman. I grabbed the French flag—a piece of evidence in the trial—from the judge's table and, in order not to leave it intact in the hands of a German judge, I broke the flagpole, shouting, "I won't let you take my country's flag!"

The main trial, meanwhile, was getting bogged down in the testimonies of expert witnesses called to establish the toxicity of the smoke grenade used in the attack on Lischka's office. In Paris, Cologne, Brussels, and Tel Aviv, there were numerous articles detailing the events of this dual trial.

I testified on May 24, taking full responsibility for the instigation and preparation of various actions against Lischka's office, actions that would, I made clear, continue if Lischka were not made to stand trial. I accused the public prosecutor's office of deliberately dragging its feet over the trial of those accused of implementing the Final Solution in France. I asked the judge to acquit us, in order to prove that a German judge could finally see where the real crime lay: in the continued impunity of these Nazi criminals. The prosecutor, Wissborn, asked for a three-month suspended prison sentence. Then Elisabeth Hajdenberg took the stand: "For the first time since 1945, a rabbi is being tried by a German court. The world is watching this trial, awaiting your verdict, because this is about something bigger than some broken glass and a bit of smoke. For us, that smoke was a distress signal that we wanted to send to Germany, to make sure that those criminals do not remain free, unpunished, respected, to make sure this does not all start again one day . . . You must acquit us. To convict a rabbi and a survivor of Auschwitz would be an outrage to the six million who were killed for being Jewish."

Rabbi Farhi's statement was even more powerful: "We came to your country not for our sake but for yours: to help you recover from this terrible accident of history. The prosecutor said that he did not understand how a rabbi and philosopher could be involved in this action. Your Honor, you must understand that it took something very important to make me descend from philosophy to political action, and, I repeat, we are determined to commit this crime again and again until those criminals are brought to justice."

The judge retired with his assessors for three-quarters of an hour before delivering his verdict: general acquittal, with fines to cover the material damages. In his summation, Judge Kaumanns affirmed that he had no doubt about "Lischka's responsibility for the murder of many French people and the deportation of the Jews of France."

For the first time, a German judge had heard us. We had finally succeeded in piercing the defensive wall of German justice.

AFTER ALL THESE turbulent events in Cologne, I settled down to the more methodical task of researching ex-Nazis. I was preparing three dossiers. The first, written in German, consisted of 136 documents, most of them written or signed by our three targets; we would send this to the German press and members of parliament. The second dossier was our bill of indictment: I provided Joseph Billig with all the documents I could get my hands on and, after discussing them with me, Billig wrote *The Final Solution of the Jewish Question: Essay on the Principles in the Third Reich and in Occupied France*, which demonstrated the importance of the roles played by Hagen, Lischka, and Achenbach. We also distributed this book, written in French and translated into German, to the German press and members of parliament. The third dossier was born of my determination to see the criminals' victims represented at the trial. Not just a few witnesses, but all the surviving deportees. I spent a long time researching those names in Paris, Brussels, Auschwitz, and New York. For I am not only a Nazi hunter; my task, above all, is to find and identify all the Jews who died in the Holocaust.

To each friend of ours who was willing to help, I gave a list, a thousand index cards, and a shoe box. Their job was to write down the full name, date and place of birth, and identification number of every deportee and to classify the files in alphabetical order. The lists were difficult to decipher, the task an arduous one.

We made progress, however, despite all these obstacles. Not only were the deportees in each convoy organized alphabetically and the convoys listed in chronological order, but I created a dossier for each convoy and inserted into it every document I could find that made reference to that convoy. I also wrote a history of each convoy, reconstructing the historical context for when it left France.

At the Tel Aviv airport in September 1975, a man of about thirty-five approached us, offering help. We heard from him again back in Paris: his father had been deported in convoy 4, his mother in convoy 22; she just had time, as she was going downstairs from her apartment, to hand her two-year-old son to a non-Jewish neighbor. That child grew up to be the man who had met us at the airport: Henri Golub, who rediscovered his Jewish identity when he traveled to Israel. He wanted to do anything he could to help us. He called his relatives, organized meetings, raised funds. And he was only one of many. Little by little, through our actions and through our preparation of the Memorial of the Deportation, we gathered around us a group of Holocaust orphans.

WHILE MUCH OF our time was devoted to this research, we did remain active in other ways. In Germany, far-right parties like the Deutsche Volksunion (DVU), whose members were in fact neo-Nazis, were riding high at this time, organizing large rallies in city centers. We wanted to stop them in their tracks. But how?

There was a DVU rally planned for December 4, 1976, in Munich, at the famous Bürgerbräukeller, site of the Beer Hall Putsch of 1923 and the attempted assassination of the Führer in 1939. We decided that ten of us would go to Munich, with the aim of my getting on the stage. This would inevitably lead to violent retribution. And so, with the press watching, a Jew would be publicly beaten by Nazis and neo-Nazis for the first time since the end of the war. This would, we hoped, mobilize public opinion against the aggressors. Our friend the photographer Élie Kagan came with us.

The room was enormous—about two hundred feet long and ninety feet wide—and filled with long tables that were covered with beer mugs. Our group sat down at a table near the back. There were about eight hundred people in the room, the majority aged fifty or over: former Wehrmacht soldiers and SS officers, happily swapping photographs of the good old days.

Kagan, looking like a Nazi caricature of a Jew with his red beard, long hair, and leather jacket, went from table to table with his camera, and I was almost weeping with laughter at the looks of bemusement on the Nazis' faces. As the night's speakers took the stage, to ecstatic applause and Nazi salutes, I stealthily took out my Star of David armband and slipped it over my sleeve.

Taking advantage of a moment's inattention on the part of one of the security staff, I ran up the steps to the stage and strode over to the table at its center. The evening's featured speaker—former Luftwaffe ace and hard-line Nazi Hans Rudel—could not believe his eyes when he saw the Star of David on my arm. I knew he had lived in the United States, so I spoke to him in my rudimentary English: "Mr. Rudel, I ask of you the right for a Jew to speak; my name is Klarsfeld." He didn't respond, so I repeated my question. The security guards surrounded me, and I was thrown to the bottom of the steps. I picked myself up and calmly walked into the crowd that rushed around me. They were so eager to hit me and spit in my face that they were pushing one another out of the way.

Knowing exactly what was going to happen, I seemed impervious to the blows as they landed on me. In the middle of the room, I was seized by two men . . . to my great relief. These were friends of mine, posing as neo-Nazis so they could safely escort me from the hall. When Beate saw me being attacked, she started to scream, "Nazis!" Immediately, a man grabbed her by the throat. Luckily, our friends managed to rescue her, too. Outside, the police refused to go inside the beer hall with me so I could point out some of my assailants.

The incident was mentioned on that evening's radio and television news, and the next day there was an avalanche of newspaper articles accompanied by photographs showing the crowd of Nazis attacking me. We had succeeded: a wave of indignation rose up against the Nazis.

We pursued our campaign to prevent the DVU from being allowed to use city-center venues to hold its rallies. It worked: wherever they went, the neo-Nazis were forced to organize meetings in small suburban halls, and they did not gain the 5 percent of the vote necessary for them to have representatives in parliament. The *National Zeitung*, the Holocaust-denying neo-Nazi newspaper, raged against Israel, the Jews, and our band of terrorists, *"die Klarsfeld-Bande."* The result? In the middle of the night, when no one was in the building, a bomb destroyed the offices of the *National Zeitung*. Amid the rubble were found leaflets bearing only the names "Auschwitz, Sobibor, Treblinka." A few hours later, I arrived in Munich and made a statement to the press and police. "I had nothing to do with this, but I am going to explain to you why it happened." I had been in Paris when the explosion occurred, so they let me go free.

IN 1976, SS colonel Joachim Peiper was murdered in the French département of Haute-Saône, where he lived. The police did not find out who was responsible, or did not want to find out. Soon afterward, a few French and German journalists were invited to a mysterious press conference in a room of Paris's Grand Hôtel. When they were all gathered there, they were ushered into a communicating room, where they found themselves facing seven men in ski masks. One of them, speaking in a faint Yiddish accent, said, "Peiper—that was us." Some of the others pulled up their sleeves and showed the journalists the identification numbers tattooed on their forearms. Photographs were taken. The journalists were then given a very detailed dossier on a particularly despicable Nazi criminal named Christmann, who was living in Bavaria: the dossier listed his address, his car, the place where he worked, and his daily routine, not to mention all his crimes. This little scene was designed to convince the German courts that, if they did not bring those Nazi criminals to justice, they would be responsible for more murders.

BEATE

BATTLING DICTATORS IN
ARGENTINA AND URUGUAY

BRINGING NAZI CRIMINALS to justice was Serge's most important cause, just as the campaign against Kiesinger had been mine. I fully participated in his protests, but I knew that Serge was leading the campaign and that he would never give up, no matter what it cost him; he would not rest until Lischka and Hagen had been tried.

From the mid-1970s on, for the next fifteen years or so, I would tour the United States and Canada once or twice a year, giving speeches. This provided us with the money we needed to live and to continue our campaigns, but it was pretty grueling. In 1980, for example, between November 4 and December 10, I successively visited New York; Washington, D.C.; Syracuse; Baltimore; Norfolk, Virginia; Cincinnati; Madison, Wisconsin; Bloomington, Indiana; Los Angeles; San Francisco; Richmond, Virginia; Winnipeg, Manitoba; Montreal; Houston; Buffalo, New York; Sarasota, Florida; Miami; and Dayton, Ohio.

One day, while I was in the middle of one of these tours, I discovered that I had been nominated for the 1977 Nobel Peace Prize by fifty-seven members of the Knesset—among them Abba Eban and the future prime minister Menachem Begin—and by forty-four university professors. I was the first non-Jewish German to receive this honor. I knew I had to live up to it.

MOST OF THE governments in South America were still dictatorships at this time. I had already experienced life in a dictatorship during my visit to Bolivia—and I knew I had been lucky to get out of that country alive. Monika Ertl, the young woman who killed the Bolivian consul in Hamburg—Roberto Quintanilla, one of the men responsible for the murder of Che Guevara—was executed with a bullet in the head after her arrest in 1973, one year after my visit. She had two passports, one Bolivian and one German. The Bolivian police wanted to avoid the diplomatic hassles they'd had with me, so they shot her on the spot.

On May 2, 1977, at the height of the Argentine government's bloody repression, I flew to Buenos Aires. I wrote an open letter to the Argentine authorities, protesting the country's growing number of human rights violations, but most of the press refused to publish it. Only Mr. Timmerman, the editor of the *Buenos Aires Herald*, who would, shortly afterward, be arrested, tortured, and imprisoned for a long time, had the courage to print it:

> Five years ago, I went to Bolivia to expose Klaus Barbie, a symbol of the link between the Nazi oppression in Europe and the dictatorships enslaving people in parts of South America. Since then, sadly, the torture chambers, the concentration camps, and the summary executions have spread to Chile, Uruguay, and Argentina.
>
> It is my duty as a German anti-fascist, a French citizen, and a LICA leader, to protest human rights violations wherever they occur: yesterday in Warsaw, Prague, and Damascus; today in Buenos Aires; tomorrow in Montevideo.

I knew I was risking my life by protesting in these places. But to me, it seemed inadequate to protest in front of an embassy when there was the possibility of taking my campaign to the country itself to give my words real meaning.

SERGE

The Document

B Y THE SPRING of 1978, our *Memorial to the Jews Deported from France* was ready to be printed, but we did not have enough money to do it ourselves. We needed the help of an organization or a patron in order to publish this 656-page book, structured in a format comparable to a phone directory.

The person in the best position to help us, due to her role in the Jewish community, responded that she could not take care of the book's publication because "the Ministry of War Veterans has always spoken of 100,000 to 120,000 racial deportees, and your study contains only 76,000 deportees, 3,000 who died in camps in France, and a thousand who were summarily executed; a total of 80,000 victims."

I replied, "You should be relieved that the number of victims is lower than imagined. The truth is indivisible: for example, the plaque at the

Vélodrome d'Hiver must be corrected because it mentions the internment of 30,000 Jews on that site, yet the German and French reports that I discovered at the police headquarters indicate 13,152 arrests, with 8,160 interned at the Vél' d'Hiv (1,129 men, 2,916 women, and 4,115 children). History must be precise and rigorous." My argument did not convince this person, however, because she did not want to be convinced.

Beate phoned Henri Micmacher, the founder of the bridal-wear shop Pronuptia, several of whose relatives appeared on this terribly long list. We met him, and he agreed to pay the printer of his catalogs to publish five thousand copies of the *Memorial*.

When people first read the book at the Twelve Hours for Israel gathering in May 1978, hundreds of them broke down in tears or fainted as they read the names and exact fates of their parents, siblings, and friends. I think the creation of that book was perhaps our single most important act.

In *Le Nouvel Observateur*, the philosopher Vladimir Jankélévitch wrote a wonderful article on the *Memorial*:

> Serge Klarsfeld's *Memorial*, perpetuating the memory of the seventy-five thousand Jews deported from France, is notable first of all for the immensity of the work that it represents, and for the pitiless, methodical, meticulous rigor that it required. But it is also notable for the enormity of the suffering evoked by these lists. Even though we knew all this, we didn't know anything. Even though we say it over and over again, we still haven't said anything.
>
> Serge Klarsfeld has understood that words will always fall short of the horror, that our indignation, however natural, can never measure up to that vast massacre. So he has chosen objectivity and the terrifying precision of enumerations and statistics, knowing that precision and objectivity are in themselves the most implacable indictments.
>
> This extremely dry work takes on an exceptional moral importance. The human being bears a name, and it is the name that makes it a human being; it is not lost in the anonymity of the species, like an abandoned dog. But those bureaucrat executioners, determined to dehumanize these "subhumans" as completely as possible, began by destroying their identity as a prelude to the

incineration of their bodies. The deportee became nothing more than a number, impersonal and interchangeable . . . Above all, in *Memorial*, there is memory: benign memory. Serge and Beate, my friends, you are the knights of benign memory.

We also received many letters from readers. The most significant was from a woman named Annette Zaidman:

> Thank you! Thank you a million times over for this *Memorial to the Jews Deported from France*, as well as for all your actions. I have spent three nights reading only part of this "book." Through my tears, I found twenty-five people I knew from my childhood.
> As a daughter, sister, niece, cousin, and friend of deportees, I would like to offer you more than my gratitude, more than my sympathy and my heartbreak.
> I offer you my complete dedication. What can I do to support your actions? Please tell me. For me, this is not only a wish, but a duty.

Annette, whom I went to see with our friends Henri Golub and Simon Guerchon, was the manager of a photocopying store on the Champs-Élysées. Her machines were at our disposal for years. Her limitless devotion led her to help us create the Association of Sons and Daughters of Jews Deported from France (FFDJF). A new challenge was about to begin, and a new power was about to drive forward the memory of the Holocaust: the power of the orphans.

THE IMPACT MADE by the *Memorial* was such that, in June 1978, when we were organizing a trip to Bavaria to protest the Nazi war criminal Ernst Heinrichsohn, we had to hire two buses with beds inside so all eighty of us could travel through the night to our destination.

In Miltenberg, to attract the locals' attention, we gathered outside Heinrichsohn's office, and one of us, the herculean Olivier Friedler, smashed the lawyer's plaque from the wall with a sledgehammer. Faces appeared at windows, people spilled into the street; Beate told them about Heinrichsohn's

Nazi past; they seemed unimpressed by this. He had a reputation as a good lawyer and a good mayor. The police turned up and asked to speak to our leader. I stepped forward. The interrogation took place in their car. They received their instructions by telephone and let us leave in peace.

On November 9, for the fortieth anniversary of Kristallnacht, we went to Cologne for a peaceful protest. Holding up large banners, we demanded that Lischka be brought to justice. It was he who organized the transfer of Jews arrested that night to concentration camps. It was freezing cold; we marched from Lischka's home to his office, and we stood outside the synagogue where services took place. Not one of those German Jews who attended the service came out to meet us; they turned away as they walked past our banners, ashamed and upset by our presence, fearful that our protest would harm their position in the town.

THE "COLOGNE TRIAL," as we were already calling it, was fast approaching. That summer, the prosecutor general drafted his bill of indictment against Lischka, Hagen, and Heinrichsohn, but it still had to be approved by the president of the fifteenth criminal court in Cologne, Mr. Hutmacher. On June 6, 1979, we made one last effort: first, a protest in the courthouse in Düsseldorf, where a trial of several SS officers had been going on for months. During this trial, some of the defense lawyers had behaved very badly toward the Jewish witnesses, mocking them or verbally abusing them. Accompanied by a large group of protesters from Jewish youth movements, we went by bus from Düsseldorf to Cologne, where our protesters occupied the first floor of the courthouse. All of the judges came to witness this unprecedented scene.

On June 19, 1979, I once again went to Cologne in order to meet the judge and the prosecutor general and to give them my opinion on the bill of indictment. The trial was set for October 23.

We methodically organized more than three hundred plaintiffs, helping the German lawyer who would represent us in Cologne prepare his argument. Representation by a German lawyer was mandatory, and we had to cover his fees ourselves. Or we would have had to but for the Israeli prime minister Menachem Begin, who decided to pay them for us.

I was fully prepared for this legal marathon, which would, I knew, be the decisive event of my life. I could not afford to lose it. I imagined every eventuality and how I would adapt to each, every possible defense maneuver and how to block it. Of all the trials we would face, this one was the most important: the trial of the men who actually commanded the Final Solution in France.

Targeting Bousquet and Leguay

MEANWHILE IN MADRID, in October 1978, Louis Darquier de Pellepoix, the former general commissioner on Jewish affairs, made some outrageous remarks—for instance, "At Auschwitz, they only gassed fleas"—which provoked an indignant reaction from the press and public.

In 1972, Darquier made preparations to visit his sick brother in France. Though his address in Madrid was known to the French authorities, France had never demanded his extradition. The radical intellectual Pierre Goldman came to see me, a few days before he was murdered, to talk to me about the possibility of kidnapping Darquier. It would have been a very difficult operation. Darquier's remarks provoked me to take a different approach.

Since 1975, I had been collecting documents on the role of the Vichy regime in the Final Solution. René Bousquet, who had been secretary-general of the Vichy police, had already been tried and more or less acquitted: it was impossible to try him twice on the same charges, unless there was new evidence. But Bousquet's trial dossier was in the National Archives, and I did not have the necessary authorization to consult it.

In New York, Beate tracked down the whereabouts of Jean Leguay, Bousquet's delegate in the occupied zone. Leguay had moved back to Paris; he would be our judicial target. And while we waited for new evidence to emerge, we would attack Bousquet out of the courts.

THE VICHY REGIME's collaboration with the Nazi police on the Jewish question essentially took place in 1942, when Germany looked almost certain to win the war: forty-two thousand Jews were deported in six months, compared with thirty-three thousand between January 1943 and August 1944. In both the occupied zone and the free zone, the regular French police and the French gendarmerie took on the role of arresting Jews on behalf of the Germans. Most of the police's negotiations with the occupying powers were conducted by the leaders of the French police, spurred on by the General Commission on the Jewish Question.

The members of this high-ranking political staff involved in anti-Jewish actions, under the authority of Marshal Pétain, were Pierre Laval, René Bousquet, Jean Leguay, Louis Darquier de Pellepoix, Jacques Schweblin (Jewish affairs police), and Jean François (director of the police headquarters). These were the men who, almost exclusively, met with the chiefs of the Nazi police—Oberg, Hagen, Knochen, Lischka, Dannecker, Röthke, Heinrichsohn—when it came to organizing the arrest of Jews, their delivery from the free zone, and their deportation to Auschwitz.

We found a German diplomatic letter describing the Paris visit of Reinhard Heydrich, head of the RSHA and the chief organizer of the Final Solution. This happened in May 1942. Prior to that, there had been only one single deportation convoy, on March 27, 1942. Heydrich informed Bousquet, the head of the French police, that he would soon be able to provide trains for deporting stateless Jews interned in the occupied zone. And Bousquet's response was, essentially: Could you also take the stateless Jews we've had interned for more than a year in the free zone?

As for Leguay, Bousquet's delegate in the occupied zone, he took part in two Franco-German police meetings on July 7 and 10, 1942, during which the Vél' d'Hiv roundup was organized. He led the delegation of high-ranking French police officers who, on July 17, repeatedly insisted to Hagen and Röthke that the thousands of children (almost all of them French) of Jews arrested on July 16 and 17 should be deported along with their parents. It was the French police who separated these children from their parents and who held them in terrible conditions in Beaune-la-Rolande and Pithiviers. (Some of the children had already died after ten days in these camps.) It was the regular police who transported them to Drancy, where they were herded by gendarmes, under the delighted gaze of Heinrichsohn, and deported. None of those four thousand children ever returned.

Vichy's supporters claim that, if Laval had not given the Germans all these stateless and foreign Jews, France would have been governed by a German or by an even-more-collaborationist Doriot-Déat government. This is completely false. There is no trace of any such threat in any German document.

In fact, if Pétain and Laval had been brave enough to refuse to order the French police to serve the occupying powers in their persecution of the Jews, the Nazis would have had no choice but to back off. Their priorities lay elsewhere. The men at the top of the collaborationist pyramid also had the possibility of resigning. Leguay did the work he was asked to do, and in return he received a promotion.

After the Liberation, Leguay was interrogated by a purification commission that possessed none of the documents relating to the anti-Jewish actions. He claimed that he had met Dannecker only twice, whereas we had seen the minutes of six such meetings. He claimed that he had refused to yield to Dannecker's demands when asked, in early July, to arrest "twenty thousand French Jews," and he did not even mention the Vél' d'Hiv roundup. Leguay's impudence allowed him to enjoy a good postwar career: after being sent to the United States in 1945 by the Ministry of Industrial Production, he entered the private sector and became an executive in the cosmetics and pharmaceuticals industry in New York, London, and Paris.

As for Bousquet, his trial, in 1949, skimmed over the Jewish question. He was given the minimum sentence, which was lifted due to his "services for the Resistance." He then became an executive at the Indochina Bank.

IN 1975, BEATE tracked Leguay down in New York. We had decided to wait until the Nazi police criminals had been indicted before starting a campaign against their French collaborators. Lischka, Hagen, and Heinrichsohn were officially indicted in the summer of 1978. That fall, we began our offensive against Bousquet and Leguay, focusing our legal efforts on Leguay, who had never been tried.

On November 1, 1978, *Le Monde* obtained an interview with Jean Leguay:

LE MONDE: *Do you still claim that the "arrest of twenty thousand Jews by the Paris police did not take place"?*

LEGUAY: *There was no roundup of twenty thousand French Jews. They were foreign Jews.*

LE MONDE: *So, in your opinion, arresting foreign Jews who had taken refuge in France—and their French children—is a less serious offense?*

LEGUAY: *Listen, at the time, we had to obey the Germans. There were German Jews, Polish Jews. The French government defended its own people. That's normal.*

On November 10, 1978, I held a press conference to announce that I planned to file charges against Leguay. In my statement, I declared, "I believe that politicians and the public should demand that they resign from the various posts they currently occupy. They've lived in peace for thirty-five years. Well, now it's time for them to pay for their crimes!"

On November 15, 1978, on behalf of several relatives of victims of the police operation led by this man, I filed very detailed charges against Jean Leguay for crimes against humanity. Simultaneously, I made public my dossier on Bousquet. We protested outside Leguay's home in Paris. This caused a big stir, and it was probably that evening that we decided to create the FFDJF to represent the French sons and daughters of those deported by the Vichy regime.

Bousquet's situation unraveled very quickly. After protests, he was forced to resign from his position at the Indosuez Bank, at UTA airlines, and from his numerous directorships, supposedly so that he could devote time to defending himself from the charges brought against him.

In the meantime, on March 11, 1979, Jean Leguay became the first French man to be officially charged with crimes against humanity. I learned this news very close to the building at 15 Rue d'Italie in Nice, where my father had been arrested. In the front window of the bookstore a few yards down the street from our old home, I saw the headlines in *France-Soir* and stood there in shock. It was a great comfort for me to discover such incredible news in that particular spot, especially as the trial of the Nazi criminals in Cologne was soon to begin. France's hard-line anti-Semites reacted to this development by publishing the addresses of the Jewish plaintiffs in the weekly far-right newspaper *Minute*, sparking a wave of abusive and threatening phone calls.

I was grateful for the assistance of Charles Libman, an experienced trial lawyer and former Resistance fighter, in the Leguay case. When it came to direct contact with the investigating judge, Martine Anzani, who had instantly grasped the importance of the dossier and who had shown the courage to pursue the case irrespective of outside pressure, everything was fine, but I had no experience with how things worked in the Palais de Justice. Charles Libman's help was indispensable in guiding me through that labyrinth of jargon and required forms.

The Cologne Trial

A T HOME IN PARIS, around 1:00 a.m. on July 6, 1979, we heard an explosion. We were not sleeping. In the underground parking garage, our car was blown up, and all the cars around it were damaged. We found out later, after the investigation, that there had been an explosive device equipped with a timer, presumably intended to explode in the morning, as I was taking our daughter, Lida, to kindergarten. We received lots of death threats during this period.

The organization Odessa claimed responsibility for the car bomb and sent us a letter threatening further reprisals: "We warn you: our German comrades are waiting for you in Cologne. They will be armed and their determination will be as absolute as the hatred they feel for you. They have taken the blood oath: if Klarsfeld comes to our city, we will kill him!!! So, Mr. Klarsfeld, do you still intend to go to Cologne? Yeah? Then go ahead! GO AHEAD!!!"

So I went.

THE TRIAL BEGAN on October 23, 1979.

At 6:45 a.m., three hundred deportees and children of deportees marched through the streets of Cologne, chanting and holding up banners demanding that the Nazi criminals be convicted. The atmosphere in the courthouse was chaotic. The courtroom where the trial was due to take place was far too small: there was room for only seventy journalists, who had come from all over the world, and about fifty members of the public. There was soon fighting between the protesters and the police tasked with maintaining order.

That first day was a successful one for us. The clumsiness of the German legal authorities justified the morning's protest, which was designed to show that the Jews of France could put an end to this trial if they were unhappy with the way it was going. Furthermore, the reduced capacity of the courtroom enabled us to fill it for each hearing, bringing together for the first time in German legal history the Jewish victims, the Nazi criminals, and their judges. Also for the first time, the judges were the kind of people we had been demanding: four men and one woman (the judge, Heinz Fassbender, his two assessors, and two jurors) under forty-five years of age. And another first: the criminals were there, all three of them, and they came to each hearing.

When we realized that the judge was hostile to the defense lawyers' delaying tactics, we decided to give him the chance to show another side to German justice. From the second hearing on, the protests grew calm. This made a big impression on the media and on German public opinion.

Sometimes, however, I would deliberately provoke outbursts from the crowd. As Kurt Lischka's two lawyers rolled out a series of pointless legal arguments against the way the trial was being run, there were howls of protest from the crowd gathered outside the courthouse. Even though the guards closed all the windows and drew the heavy red curtains, it was impossible to silence the shouts of *"Lischka Mörder, Hagen Mörder, Heinrichsohn Mörder"* that went on for more than four hours.

All of the witnesses, with the exception of the French people summoned by the court, had been members of the Nazi police. Presumably the judge hoped to obtain the truth by questioning them. But we knew that they would simply claim that they had not done anything wrong and that they knew nothing about the activities of the three accused. That was why I surprised several of these witnesses with evidence of their wrongdoing; for example, when Söllner, a Gestapo member from Alois Brunner's team, stated that he had not seen any children at the camp in Drancy, I proved that more than twenty-five hundred children had been deported during his time at the camp.

During the hearing for Nährich, who had been the chief of the German military command's police, Judge Fassbender realized that he was on the wrong track. He got nothing from that witness. When my turn came to question him, I asked, "Did you classify the Jews into categories in the camp at Compiègne? Did you prepare the escorts for convoys? Did you draw up rulings on the need to wear yellow stars?" Nährich answered no three times. I then presented him with a series of documents written and signed by him, which proved the exact opposite. The judge told him to leave without taking an oath, otherwise he would be forced to charge him. Then he asked me if I had any documents relating to the other witnesses. I gave them to him. When confronted with these documents, Kübler (liaison officer with the French police), Illers (head of the Gestapo in Paris in 1943), and Moritz (Gestapo member in Paris, Marseille, and Orléans) all refused to testify so as not to be forced to lie under oath.

While Laube (who drew up the list of hostages to be shot) and Knochen (head of the security police) claimed to be sick, Jüngst (Oberg's aide-de-camp) testified in favor of Hagen. His words made a big impression because he appeared sincere and admitted he did not like Hagen much as a person. I asked him, "Do you know if Hagen put any pressure on Vichy to denaturalize the Jews?" No. "Did you write reports on the Jewish question and send them to the Gestapo?" No. "Can you recognize your own signature?"— and I handed him a report on the Jewish question that he had sent to the Gestapo, relating Hagen's attempts to denaturalize the Jews. And that was the end of Jüngst.

This trial was notable for two essential elements that distinguished it from other trials of Nazi criminals. Not since 1945 had hundreds of Jews come (from abroad!) to attend the trial—in Germany—of one of their persecutors. The only Nazi who'd had the privilege of being judged among Jews before was Eichmann, in Jerusalem. But now his boss Hagen, who took him to Palestine in October 1937, and his predecessor as the head of the Gestapo's Jewish Affairs Department, Lischka, were also surrounded by

Jews. All those nights we had spent on the train from Paris to Cologne with the sons and daughters of Holocaust victims had been worth it.

The trial's second distinction was the existence of so many documents from the CDJC in Paris. Those documents had come from the Gestapo's anti-Jewish section in France, and they were extremely important. They constituted the basis of my documentation and allowed us to establish the precise responsibilities of each accused man.

One of the highlights of the trial was the moment when the three French plaintiffs gave their moving and terrifying testimonies about the deportation of thousands of children separated from their parents and herded onto trains like animals. During these testimonies, even some of the defense lawyers' eyes filled with tears, but the criminals remained impassive: Lischka continued to shield his face with one gigantic hand while endlessly taking notes with the other; Hagen sat utterly immobile, while Heinrichsohn slumped over, red-faced. Mrs. Daltroff-Baticle and Mrs. Husson, who together took care of the deported children at Drancy, recognized the photograph of Heinrichsohn, taken in 1942, from among a hundred or so pictures of other Gestapo members. Like those two witnesses, Georges Wellers was categorical: it was definitely Heinrichsohn who supervised the majority of Auschwitz convoys in 1942.

Lischka chose not to say a word or to cooperate with the court in any way whatsoever. Hagen refused to respond on the pretext that these matters were confidential and he would need special authorization to speak about them.

On January 31, 1980, we organized a massive protest in Cologne: a special train left Paris, while buses carried people from other parts of France. Around fifteen hundred French Jews marched from the train station to the courthouse. The last time that many Jews had been seen on German streets was during the arrests that followed Kristallnacht.

Prosecutor general Cohnen's closing speech asked for prison sentences in line with those defined in the Bismarck penal code. The actual sentences were even a bit more severe: twelve years for Hagen, ten for Lischka, six for Heinrichsohn. The verdict of the Cologne trial came as such an immense relief, particularly as it was followed—to the surprise of the German people—by the incarceration of the three convicted men.

"Relief" is the right word, because this was not a matter of satisfaction. There could be no punishment, no matter how severe, commensurate with the gravity and scale of the crimes committed by Lischka, Hagen, and Heinrichsohn.

Thirty-five years after the end of the war, it was not easy for judges and juries to condemn their fathers' generation. But they did, and that was the proof that even the most overdue Nazi trials can produce positive results, on both a legal and a historical level. It was the proof that the German people were ready to assume their responsibilities to the Jewish people and that they were increasingly opposed to racist totalitarianism. It was on that point that I concluded my closing speech: "It is true that the road we have had to take to reach this trial has been difficult for us and for you; but you should know that, throughout this long journey, the Jews of France have never lost confidence in the German judicial system."

The *Jerusalem Post* commented:

The verdict is also a personal victory for Beate and Serge Klarsfeld. In more than ten years of private effort they flushed the three men out of their hiding places in prosperous civilian jobs in Germany itself. They almost singlehandedly forced the German Bundestag to pass the legislation making it possible to retry the men in German courts, after they had all been sentenced *in absentia* in French courts.

At the prison in Ossendorf, where several of our group had been briefly imprisoned in order to ensure that he would go there one day, Heinrichsohn found it hard to accept swapping his position as mayor and lawyer for a prison cell, which he shared with Lischka (but not Hagen, who was incarcerated at the prison in Bochum). In a letter to his cousin, Heinrichsohn wrote:

Like you, I would never have believed it possible that I would be arrested or convicted. I really didn't do anything wrong. I am innocent. But that does me no good at all. I was convicted and now I am imprisoned. So I must bear my fate. I am a victim of my generation. In my place, anyone else would have acted in the same way.

Heinrichsohn died soon after his release.

JUSTICE AND MEMORY

IN THE IMMEDIATE aftermath of the Cologne trial, we continued proceedings against Ernst Ehlers and Kurt Asche, responsible for the deaths
of twenty-five thousand Jews in Belgium; against Arnold Strippel, who
hanged twenty Jewish children in the basement of a school at the Bullen-
huser Damm in Hamburg; against Jean Leguay; and then against Maurice
Papon and the Holocaust denier Robert Faurisson. We also continued to
keep watch over Klaus Barbie in Bolivia, waiting until the moment was
right to demand his extradition.

Frustrated by the inability of Michael Marrus and Robert Paxton, the
authors of *Vichy France and the Jews*, to gain a precise understanding of the
chronology of the Final Solution in France due to a lack of new documentation, I started to prepare the book *Vichy-Auschwitz*. Around this time
we realized it was up to us, the Sons and Daughters, to organize the first
single-day group pilgrimage to Auschwitz. This involved the rental of two

planes, one Polish and the other French. We also resolved to erect a stone memorial in Israel for the eighty thousand French Jews exterminated during the war, to be surrounded by eighty thousand trees—the Forest of Remembrance—and for the names and personal details of those eighty thousand victims to be engraved on the monument.

ON THE FIRST day of the Ehlers-Asche trial—November 26, 1980, in Kiel, northern Germany—we marched through the streets of the city to the courthouse with a group of Jews from Brussels. Ehlers, head of the German police in Belgium, committed suicide before the trial started, electrocuting himself in his bathtub; his wife had killed herself just before this. Asche's trial took place over the course of thirty-six days during a seven-month period. I participated in nearly half of those days. Asche, head of the Gestapo's Jewish Affairs Department, was convicted on July 8, 1981, and sentenced to seven years in prison.

Arnold Strippel had already spent twenty years in prison for other crimes and could not, according to German law, be incarcerated again after another trial. His war crimes, however, were so vile that we wanted the German courts to charge him, so that the deaths of those Jewish children, rounded up from all over Europe for use in medical experiments and hanged in a school basement, would not simply vanish in the mists of time.

So I went to Hamburg, where I had filed charges against Strippel, and explained to the prosecutors that I had been harassed in Paris by people who reproached me for seeking a legal outcome to the case when what they wanted was to exterminate Strippel. To back up this bluff, we had to send several people who, one by one, walked around close to Strippel's home, attracting the attention of the police—who could not arrest them, as they had not actually done anything wrong. The Hamburg prosecutor was impressed by these ominous signs and ended up charging Strippel. Soon afterward, he died, a free man, but accused of the heinous crimes that he committed.

Bringing Barbie Back to Lyon

A FTER OUR FAILED attempt at kidnapping Barbie, we kept constant watch over him. How? It was our friend Lisa who helped us. This time, she had to go to Bolivia, approach Barbie, and try to find out whether he intended to stay in the country or not.

Her plan of action was simple: elegantly dressed, she would go to the German club in La Paz, where she would engage in conversation with one of the regulars; she would play the part of a right-wing German woman who had just visited Machu Picchu in Peru and had come to Bolivia to see Lake Titicaca. When the moment was ripe, she would mention that she'd heard that Klaus Barbie lived nearby. And that is exactly what happened. The German man she talked to, an industrialist, said that he knew Barbie well and, three days after her arrival in La Paz, Lisa was invited into the Barbie family home, where she ate dinner with them. She found out that Barbie was happy in Bolivia and felt very comfortable under Colonel Banzer's regime.

Lisa kept in touch with the Barbies, and later she would return briefly to La Paz on two occasions to make sure Barbie had not changed his mind about leaving Bolivia.

In August 1982, I publicly reproached the French courts for not yet having charged Barbie. Based on the 1964 ruling that the statute of limitations did not apply to crimes against humanity, the investigation against him had to take into account the new facts we had uncovered, which had not figured into his 1954 trial in absentia: the abduction of forty-four children in Izieu, the Rue Sainte-Catherine roundup, and the deportee convoy of August 11, 1944. We filed charges against Barbie, supporting our case with very precise documentation of these new facts. This was necessary for France to be able to approach Bolivia once again. In fact, our protest was effective, and Barbie was charged in Lyon.

IN EARLY 1982, Lisa flew to Bolivia again to review Barbie's situation. The country's military regime was tottering, but Barbie did not seem overly concerned about Bolivia's political problems, as he was focused on his personal difficulties: the death of his wife in 1982 and of his son, Klaus-Georg, just before that. His daughter, Ute, had moved to Munich, where she worked as a secretary to Hans Rudel, who had crossed our path back in 1976 at the Bürgerbräukeller.

Barbie was very active in Bolivia's military special services during the crackdowns that followed each coup d'état or sudden change of dictator. And there was a whole series of these changes in the late 1970s and early 1980s, each new dictator basing his support on the army. Finally, the military lost all credibility, and the Bolivian people pressured Congress into naming Hernán Siles Zuazo the new president in October 1982.

That same year, a Bolivian exile told us that he was going back to Bolivia and that he would attempt to assassinate Barbie. We wished him good luck. Soon afterward, he called us from La Paz and told us that he was abandoning his plan because the dictatorship was crumbling and there was a possibility of acting legally against Barbie. Now the ball was in our court. I got back in touch with Régis Debray, who was now, along with Jacques Attali, one of President François Mitterrand's two main advisers. In his memoir *Verbatim*, Attali summarized what happened next:

August 3, 1982. Serge Klarsfeld has just reminded Régis Debray of how, in 1973, the two of them attempted to abduct Barbie.

October 5, 1982. Hernán Siles Zuazo, the democratically elected president of Bolivia, is sworn into office. Klaus Barbie is perhaps accessible once again. Régis Debray continues to negotiate with the Bolivian minister of the interior, his friend Gustavo Sánchez [Salazar]. Klarsfeld has an idea: if the Bolivians deliver Barbie to Cayenne [in French Guiana], we can pick him up there.

October 27, 1982. Régis Debray meets with Serge Klarsfeld and informs the president. Klarsfeld believes that either we can obtain Barbie's extradition or the Bolivians can expel him. The president [of France] agrees to begin proceedings.

January 26, 1983. Barbie is arrested in La Paz, as planned. Debray is working on a plan with Klarsfeld and Sánchez. The Bolivians will bring their prisoner to Cayenne, where we will take delivery of him.

February 3, 1983. Jean-Louis Bianco, general secretary of the French presidency, is organizing the French military expedition that will bring Barbie back from Cayenne. For Serge Klarsfeld, this represents ten years of struggle finally crowned with success.

IN LA PAZ, our friend Gustavo had become the state secretary for security and the Bolivian president's trusted right-hand man. On February 4, 1983, the president appointed him vice-minister of the interior, so that he would have the authority to extradite Barbie to France. Barbie, meanwhile, was being held in San Pedro Prison for refusing to pay an old debt of ten thousand dollars. When at last he decided to settle up, he did not have enough money to cover the accumulated interest, so Gustavo was able to keep him behind bars until the moment when he was ushered directly from prison to a Hercules C-130 military airplane, which took him to Cayenne. That same day, the Bolivian cabinet had decided to expel Barbie, strip him of his Bolivian citizenship, and label him an undesirable alien.

On February 5, 1983, Barbie returned to France. Beate and I were greatly relieved after ten years of tension and the fear that we would not realize our goal.

We found ourselves in a media storm, the subject of innumerable interviews. The French president François Mitterrand granted us both the Legion of Honor in 1984, and that same year the glamorous Farrah Fawcett played Beate in an acclaimed made-for-TV movie entitled *Manhunt: The Beate Klarsfeld Story.* My role was played by Tom Conti. Twenty-four years later, another TV movie, *The Hunt,* also told our story, this time starring Franka Potente and Yvan Attal.

Despite the sense of celebration, we knew that we had to prepare meticulously for the coming trial.

I HAD BEEN asking the president's office for some time to give me the green light to try to find the original telex regarding Izieu. Dated April 6, 1944, this document concerned the Jewish orphanage and the transfer of the children to Drancy the following day. To convict Barbie, we would need this original document.

The Izieu telex had been borrowed for the Nuremberg Trials from the archives of the Center of Contemporary Jewish Documentation. It had been photocopied by the court's reprographics unit, and I had managed to obtain three authenticated copies: one in The Hague, another in Washington, D.C., and the third in Nuremberg. The original telex could not be found at the CDJC. I was given permission by the president's office to search anywhere I liked. I tried the archives of the Foreign Ministry's legal department, but to no avail.

At the National Archives, the director of the contemporary section allowed me to see all the archives they possessed for the years 1940 to 1944. I was dumbstruck by the sheer number of dossiers that no researcher had ever seen before, including all of the documents pertaining to the investigations that led to the trials of Bousquet, Darquier de Pellepoix, Bussière (the Paris police chief), and Hennequin (director of the municipal police). This material aided me immensely in writing *Vichy-Auschwitz,* enabling me to explain in detail for the first time how the Final Solution unfolded in France.

I worked feverishly for several weeks, recopying entire documents. It was a source of great satisfaction for me to become a historian again, knowing for certain just how necessary my task was. Time ceased to exist: I would enter the archives and spend whole days in 1942.

As for the original telex, I located it in early 1984, after receiving permission from the Center of Contemporary Jewish Documentation to search the basement, where dozens of boxes filled with various archives had been put after the CDJC had moved from a different building. Inside the second box, the CDJC's archivist and I opened a dossier entitled "Abetz" and found inside it, in excellent condition, the Izieu telex.

What had happened? In 1949, for the trial of Otto Abetz, a historian at the CDJC had taken this document to the investigating judge to prove the nature of the German crimes perpetrated when Abetz was the ambassador in Paris. Back at the CDJC, the dossier had not been reopened, and the document had not been put back in its correct place. And when the center moved to a different building, the dossier had ended up in the basement. To me, this discovery really seemed like a miracle, and for a moment I picked up my dialogue with God, interrupted forty years before.

THE FIRST VOLUME of *Vichy-Auschwitz*, about the events of 1942, appeared in the spring of 1983 in France. *Le Monde*, in a review under the headline "Holocaust-sur-Seine," commented: "What a shock!" The second volume, dealing with the years 1943 to 1944, was published in 1985. This volume provided the historical background to the cases of Barbie, Bousquet, Leguay, and Papon, which were all in the public eye at the same time.

ON JULY 18, 1986, at my suggestion, the mayor of Paris, Jacques Chirac, inaugurated the Place des Martyrs-Juifs-du-Vélodrome-d'Hiver. In his speech, Chirac quoted the concluding lines of *Vichy-Auschwitz*, a sentence I had spent a long time crafting: "The Jews of France will always remember that, while the Vichy regime ended in moral bankruptcy and dishonored itself with its efficient contribution to the loss of one-quarter of the Jewish population of this country, the remaining three-quarters effectively owe their survival to the compassion of the French people as a whole, and to their active solidarity from the moment they realized that the Jewish families who had fallen into German hands were doomed."

I felt, that day, as if the monumental work of ten years had been condensed into a few lines containing a truth that contradicted the narratives of numerous other historians—a truth that would, of necessity, prevail.

THE PAPON AFFAIR

IN THE MEANTIME, the Papon affair blew up. At that time, Maurice Papon was the French minister of the budget under Prime Minister Raymond Barre since 1978. Papon had been chief of the Paris police between 1958 and 1967, and many blamed him for the deaths of protesters in acts of police brutality in 1961 and 1962. Until now, however, few had been aware that some of the policemen who had carried out this repression had also taken part in the roundups of 1942, when Maurice Papon was already active in Bordeaux.

The Papon affair was begun by a young researcher, Michel Bergès, who recovered a mass of dossiers from Bordeaux's regional police headquarters that were headed for the garbage heap. Realizing that these dossiers included some from the Jewish Affairs Department and that the documents within incriminated Maurice Papon, Bergès sent them to Michel Slitinsky, a former Resistance fighter and the son of a murdered Jew who was calling for the truth concerning the fate of Bordeaux's Jews. Slitinsky passed the documents on to the satirical newspaper *Le Canard Enchaîné*, which, on May 7, 1981, revealed that Papon was implicated in the arrest and delivery of Jews to the Gestapo. Papon's response: "All this has little effect on me. *Le Canard Enchaîné* is nitpicking, but I have bigger things to worry about at the moment."

I demanded Papon's resignation in the pages of *Le Monde* the next day: "Papon played a role in these events; not a leading role, but his actions were real nonetheless. He probably did less than Jean Leguay, the only Frenchman to have been charged with crimes against humanity . . . But he did much more than the ordinary policeman who arrested Jews or the gendarme who escorted convoys of defenseless children to their deaths for the crime of being born Jewish."

My opinion on this case did not change between that 1981 article in *Le Monde* and my son Arno's momentous courtroom speech in 1998, when he was the only lawyer to ask not for life imprisonment but for a ten-year prison sentence for Papon, which is what the jury decided upon. In doing so, he probably saved the trial from an acquittal, which would have been the likely outcome if the jury had been forced to choose between acquittal and a life sentence. Arno concluded his speech with the words: "Why this unease? Because we are in the presence of an educated, civilized man who almost certainly would not have attacked a child on religious grounds. Because he is not a bloodthirsty monster, but simply a man who forgot the republican values of compassion and humanity in his desire for professional advancement. Maurice Papon hid behind instructions. For him, orders took precedence. He believed himself the spectator of a tragedy, in the shadow of his dossiers. And yet he was actively involved, becoming, without any internal conflict, an efficient instrument in the service of a crime against humanity. Maurice Papon is no Klaus Barbie or Paul Touvier. He did not assume the political role of a Leguay or of a Bousquet, either. To sentence him to life imprisonment would not correspond to the historical truth. But he is guilty because he never had the courage to say 'No!' just once, to his career or his chance for glory."

IN 1981, PAPON demanded—and was granted—a jury made up of former Resistance members. Among them were Father Michel Riquet, Marie-

Madeleine Fourcade, Daniel Mayer, Jean Pierre-Bloch, and Charles Verny, the rapporteur, who, on July 27, 1981, asked me for my opinion on the matter. I testified before the jury on September 29, 1981, but my testimony was met with hostility and incomprehension. My opinion—backed up by a detailed dossier containing a nine-page summary and forty-nine separate supporting documents—was that Maurice Papon should be tried for crimes against humanity.

On December 15, the jury gave its verdict in four points, presenting a highly ambiguous vision of Papon:

1. Papon is acknowledged as being a member of the Resistance from January 1, 1943.
2. He had to take part in acts apparently contrary to the jury's conception of honor and which, understandably, have shocked the French sensibility. But these acts must be seen in the context of the times. Moreover, several of them were not as significant as their revelation might make them appear . . . Maurice Papon should have resigned from his position as a policeman in July 1942 before the roundup.
3. The documents produced by *Le Canard Enchaîné* and by Serge Klarsfeld are authentic.
4. Of the sixteen witnesses, all—with the exception of Serge Klarsfeld—believed that there was no justification for legal proceedings against the leaders of the Bordeaux police.

I responded with a scathing press release: "As representatives of Jewish families, we can affirm that it was probably better to be saved by Vichy's anti-Semitic bureaucrats, who were sometimes loath to do the Gestapo's dirty work, than to be arrested and handed over to the Nazis by Resistance fighters or sympathizers like Mr. Papon and his kind. In delivering this verdict, the jury is, to my knowledge, the first mouthpiece of the Resistance to publicly declare that the Jews of France were sent to their deaths by a member of the French Resistance."

I worked very hard gathering complaints from witnesses about the deaths of young children delivered to the Gestapo in the summer of 1942 by the Jewish Affairs Department under Papon's authority, and I was in possession of original documents relating to these facts, signed by Papon.

So on May 10, 1982, I filed six new complaints that I was sure would not be rejected by the investigating judge—and I was proved right. On July 29, 1982, an investigation was opened, and on January 19, 1983, Papon was charged with crimes against humanity.

I went to Paris, Reims, Lens, and Versailles to offer support to our plaintiffs. This became a painful task in 1985, when Papon brought slander charges against them. These plaintiffs had lost mothers, brothers, and sisters, and now they were faced with an investigating judge who, in an attempt to uncover the truth, was treating them as the accused. None of them gave up their battle, in spite of the harassment they received in the form of threatening and insulting phone calls.

THE INVESTIGATION OF the Papon affair took a backseat once Klaus Barbie was brought back to Lyon in February 1983, as his trial became my overriding priority. Without the German occupation, there would have been no persecution of Jews by the French authorities; without Lischka, without Hagen, without Barbie, there would have been no Leguay, Papon, or Touvier.

CONFRONTING HOLOCAUST DENIAL

H OLOCAUST DENIAL WREAKED havoc in the early 1980s. Even from the beginning of this offensive, I found it painful but also useful in the sense that it provoked a more precise, rigorous form of historical research. There were not many works on the Holocaust at the time, and they were often written by amateur historians without the necessary time or documentary resources, not to mention a lack of objectivity: most of them were partisans who exaggerated events and numbers in one way or another. I campaigned passionately for the Holocaust to become a subject of rigorous study in universities, so that the facts—described, analyzed, discussed, accepted—would become undeniable.

In 1978, Beate and I began this process, creating an American foundation whose aim was to "publish indisputable, authenticated documents on the Holocaust." We published an English-language version of Joseph Billig's study of the Final Solution, and the works of Georges Wellers on the number of Jewish victims and the existence of the gas chambers. We even went to Germany to question Richard Korherr, the SS's inspector of statistics, tasked by Himmler with the secret mission of creating two reports on the liquidation of the Jews in Europe in late 1942 and in the spring of 1943. Korherr confirmed the contents of those reports, which we published in German and English in our book *The Holocaust and the Neo-Nazi Mythomania*.

We also set about publishing a crucial work on the gas chambers written by the onetime Holocaust denier Jean-Claude Pressac.

Pressac had doubted the existence of the gas chambers, but he was a scientist, so he went to Auschwitz to find out the truth for himself. There, after examining the ruins of the buildings where the gas chambers had been located, and inspecting the archived architectural plans, he became convinced that they really had existed. On his return, *Le Monde Juif* published the important study he presented to us on the gas chambers.

Beate and I paid for the dozen trips he took to Auschwitz, and we worked together on an immense project, written in French and translated into English, which we published in New York in 1989. We gave free copies of this book to about a hundred libraries and archives worldwide. Pressac published an abridged version of the book, which was very successful, and which forced the Holocaust deniers to retreat.

Another book we published, *The Auschwitz Album*, has an even more remarkable backstory. In the summer of 1979, we sent an eighteen-year-old student, Emmanuel Lulin, to Prague. His mission was to enter the Communist-run State Jewish Museum and to examine its contents. When he returned, Emmanuel handed over a mass of information and a cache of seventy photographs showing the arrival of a convoy at Auschwitz II–Birkenau. All the images seemed to have been taken by the same photographer. Some of the pictures were familiar to me: I had seen them in other works. But now, examining them all together, I had the sense that these photographs all came from the same source—and that there might be others still, never before seen. Emmanuel confirmed this, saying that there were about two hundred photographs in total. They had never been published in their entirety, even though they represented the sole detailed visual testimony of what had happened when a convoy arrived in Birkenau. For the Jewish people, these photographs were incalculably precious.

Emmanuel went back to Prague and obtained all of the photographs. According to the museum, they came from an album that had fallen into the hands of a former deportee. The Czech and Israeli historian Erich Kulka told us that, during the trial of Auschwitz guards in Frankfurt, it had been established that the photographs were taken either by Bernhard Walter, the head of the anthropometric authentication department at Auschwitz, or by his assistant Ernst Hoffman. The deportee's name was Lilli Zelmanovic. She had gone to Frankfurt in December 1964, from her home in Miami, to testify at the trial.

On July 25, 1980, having used a private detective to identify Lilli Zelmanovic, née Lilli Jacob, I met her in Miami. She entrusted me with her album, which a former *Life* photographer spent the night photographing for me, and the next day, I convinced her to donate it to the Yad Vashem memorial in Jerusalem. All she asked in return was that I pay for her and her husband to travel to Jerusalem and Auschwitz. Naturally, I agreed, and we published that extraordinary album for the first time in September 1980.

However, this great work of memory did not mean we had forgotten those who were attempting to destroy it.

AT THE TRIAL of the Holocaust denier Robert Faurisson, I declared:

The fact of having called into question the death of deportees has caused serious moral and personal damage to each and every member of our association; because, for us, it is not a question of defending general ideas, a theoretical question, an ideal or an ideology. It is a question of opposing the denial of the deaths of our parents, our brothers, our sisters, our grandparents, for whom we are not only representatives or spokespeople, but also the material and moral heirs. In affirming what you dared to affirm, you have attacked the dignity and honor of each member of our association. Good news—the gas chambers didn't exist! But in that case, where are our families? Where are our parents, whose memory has never left us and whom we dream about at night? Those parents who were not there to bring us up: Where are they, Mr. Faurisson? Are they billionaires in the United States, living under false names? Are they hiding somewhere in South America, like Nazi criminals? Or are they in Israel, where we go to visit them on a regular basis while pretending to mourn them between trips? Added to this moral damage is the fact that, by denying the existence of the gas chambers, you are deliberately fomenting anti-Semitic hate, because what you are saying is that the Jews lied. And, of course, our association would be the biggest liars of all. Such an accusation, if believed by some people, would inevitably lead them to hate and despise the Jews. It seems to me that this sly hatred toward the Jews—which can be detected in your writing—has something in common, albeit at a lower level, with the hatred that drove Hitler. Mr. Faurisson: you, who embody, in our eyes, a violent and incomprehensible hatred; you, who are, in our eyes, a sort of desecrator of graves; you should know that we are not prosecuting you out of hate, but for the faithful memories of our parents and all other victims of genocide.

Later, the Holocaust denier Robert Faurisson was convicted "of complicity in contesting the existence of a crime against humanity."

I SPENT SEVERAL weeks in Israel for the construction of our great Memorial of the Deportation, surrounded by the Forest of Remembrance, but it was not a happy time for me. My mother had died shortly before—on April 20, 1981, the anniversary of Hitler's birthday—and I was overcome with grief. Of course, death is in the nature of things. The loss of my mother did not outrage me or slow me down. I battled the sadness and depression I felt by trying not to think about it during the daytime and, little by little, I stayed in touch with her at night through my dreams, where she often appeared, as she does to this day.

Tracking Down Alois Brunner

THE DEATH THREATS kept coming. A Molotov cocktail was thrown at my sister's door. There was a hotel opposite our apartment on Avenue de Versailles, from where it would have been easy to shoot at us. We moved to Rue La Boétie, close to the Élysée Palace, where we had a permanent police guard for eighteen months, before moving back to our old building in the Porte de Saint-Cloud. This time, though, we were on the square itself, with no one overlooking us.

On June 23, 1982, I went to Damascus armed with another dossier, comparable to Barbie's: that of Alois Brunner. Between June 23, 1943, and August 18, 1944, Brunner deported twenty-four thousand Jews from France, many of them arrested by his Austrian SS Kommando, as were the Jews of Nice, my father among them. We'd had this dossier in our possession since 1977. In Vienna, Lisa and I monitored the homes of Anni, Brunner's estranged wife, and their daughter Irène. Anni's apartment was much too large for just one person. We deduced from this that her husband was helping her financially. As for Irène, Lisa managed to enter her apartment and to find her father's address and phone number in Damascus, where he lived under the name "Fischer." But this information could not be used for five years, because we were too busy with our other campaigns.

In 1982, we returned to the Brunner dossier. I went to Syria in June, just after Israeli planes had shot down dozens of their Syrian counterparts, at the height of the tension between the two countries. I had no visa, but I did have Brunner's dossier in my briefcase.

Before I went to Syria, we verified one last time that Georg Fischer and Alois Brunner were one and the same. Beate phoned him at his home in Damascus: "I'm calling on behalf of my manager, who is a judge; he's the son of someone who worked with you during the war. You should be aware that it's not a good idea to go to Switzerland to get your eyes treated, because there's an arrest warrant out for you there."

"I had no intention of going to Switzerland," "Fischer" replied, "but please thank your manager and tell him I will pray for him."

At the airport in Damascus, I explained my mission to the border police. I gave them the Brunner dossier so that it could be passed on to the relevant authorities. I had to spend the whole night sitting in a room at the airport. I used the time to work on my book about the Final Solution in France.

In the morning, the police told me that my dossier had been forwarded but that my request to enter Syria had been refused. I hardly expected any other outcome. But at least the Brunner case was now a live international issue, with press coverage all over the world.

Over the next five years, Beate and I did what we could to bring Brunner to justice, but with limited results. The West German government made a demand for extradition in 1984, but only verbally. We asked the East German government, so influential in Syria, to propose that the authorities in Damascus extradite Brunner to East Berlin, with the guarantee that the trial would not dwell on the question of Brunner's stay in Syria. In the United States, Beate rallied Jesse Jackson to the cause, and the reverend wrote to Hafiz al-Assad, from whom he had obtained the liberation of an American pilot, on the subject. All in vain.

In January 1987, I met Raymond Kendall, the secretary-general of Interpol, and persuaded him to issue an international arrest warrant for

Brunner, as well as a wanted notice to all its member nations, including Syria. This was a first for Interpol, which, before this, had not considered itself competent to deal with Nazi war criminals. But again, it made no difference: Brunner was a trusted henchman to the Assad clan, which showed its gratitude by protecting him.

On March 2, 1987, Beate was turned away at Damascus Airport, despite having received her visa in East Berlin.

But we would not give up.

The Barbie Trial

W E S P E N T M U C H of the four years prior to the Barbie trial in preparation for that event.

I got used to taking my lawyer's robes with me when I traveled to Lyon
for meetings with the excellent investigating judge Christian Riss. Along
with my colleagues Charles Libman and Richard Zelmati, I represented
more than a hundred plaintiffs. The judge met with all of them, and they
told him their stories.

At the same time, I started writing a book about the children of Izieu,
a crucial subject for the trial. To write it, I had to reconstruct the background of the family of each of those forty-four children. For the trial, I
had to find a plaintiff for each child. This seemed an impossible task, but
Beate and I managed it; we even got hold of a photograph of each child.
We found our plaintiffs not only in France, but in Germany, Austria, Belgium, Israel, the United States, Brazil, and Australia. So many trips, and so

many documents! Each plaintiff was heard by a judge and had to prove kinship with the child they wished to represent.

In *Le Monde*, we published articles about Barbie's collaboration with the American secret services. Judge Ryan, who was director of the Office of Special Investigations, responsible for the prosecution of Nazi war criminals, came to see us and left with a good haul of documents, which he used in compiling his famous report on Barbie. This report led to an official U.S. apology to France for having recruited, protected, and exfiltrated Barbie.

I was present for the confrontations between some of my plaintiffs and Barbie, an experience that made me realize just how traumatizing such face-to-face meetings could be for the victims.

Barbie expressed his desire to speak with me; I refused. No dialogue was possible between him and me. What struck me most during the investigation and the trial itself was the fact that some of the witnesses whom I knew to be the most credible were also the ones who were the least believed because they seemed fragile or unlikable, while others, who seemed less credible to me, convinced their listeners through their self-confidence and articulateness.

I remember one Holocaust survivor, a man who had lost his brother, saying that Barbie had set his dog on him, and the dog had bitten him in the thigh. Barbie responded sarcastically, "A dog! Mrs. Lagrange saw me with a cat in my arms; now it's a dog! Apparently, I had a whole pet store at my beck and call . . ." I sensed that the judge was dubious, that this story of the dog seemed too clichéd. We left the prison for the judge's office, and he showed me a dossier with an unopened seal; it had been sent from Lyon, and it concerned a woman, identified in an anonymous phone call to me, who was suspected of being Barbie's mistress. He opened it. In fact, the woman had been the mistress of another Gestapo agent, but in the dossier she told how, during a torture session that she had attended, she had told her lover to ask Barbie to call off his dog, which was biting the prisoner. That deposition had been made in 1946. For the judge and for me, this was an important reminder that, even if the criminal can sometimes appear more credible than the victim, we must always check the facts.

Barbie was trying to put a brave face on it, but it was clear that he considered his forced return to Lyon a defeat for Nazism, to which he remained loyal even if he didn't have the courage to proclaim that fact. As for his lawyer, Jacques Vergès, whom I knew slightly, I could foresee his strategy all too well: he was going to claim that Barbie had been abducted; he was going to denigrate the Resistance, threatening to reveal the truth about this or that Resistance member; and he was going to confuse the issue by claiming that the Izieu telex was a forgery.

Thankfully, this trial was conducted in exemplary fashion. It went exactly as we wanted, and not at all as Barbie and his lawyer would have wished. Members of our association of Sons and Daughters came to each hearing en masse to support us, and all the lawyers on our side, representing a vast number of plaintiffs, acted together with surprising coherence and efficiency.

FOR BEATE AND MYSELF, the trial in Lyon was less important than the one in Cologne, where Hagen and Lischka, two very high-ranking organizers of the Final Solution, had been tried. Moreover, the Cologne trial resolved a major legal issue between France and Germany. For the international media, however, the Lyon trial was more sensational, because Barbie corresponded to the stereotype of the criminal who flees to the ends of the earth but cannot escape punishment.

I spent three months in Lyon, staying in a small fourth-floor apartment in a building with no elevator. All the same, the place was so ideally located—directly opposite the front entrance of the courthouse—that, to me, it was better than Vergès's five-star hotel, even if my landlady's cat (which I had to look after) would dig its claws into my chest every night when I lay down in bed.

During the first hearing, Barbie once again blamed all his troubles on "that woman [Beate] coming to Bolivia." His lawyer played the kidnapping card and withdrew Barbie from the stand. The next day, most of the international media had disappeared. Only the French were left.

The other prosecution lawyers were furious that Barbie had given up on his own trial. But I wasn't. Because it was a lot easier dealing with Vergès than with Barbie. The lawyer had a poor grasp of the dossiers and objected to only a few witnesses; he let the others talk, and they impressed the jury with their dignity and their horrific accounts of physical and psychological torture. Without Barbie there to intimidate them, they were able to express themselves freely.

I prepared my closing speech in the Café des Négociants in Lyon, and it was my son, Arno, who, reading the draft, advised me to add, after mentioning the fate of each child, a phrase that repeated the child's first name: "Hans did not return"; "Monique did not return." An article in *Libération* described the effect of this speech:

> Serge Klarsfeld does not plead. He doesn't wave his arms about or use any vocal effects; he doesn't speak in a sad voice; he doesn't act like a lawyer at all. No, Klarsfeld reads. And what he reads . . . is devastating. Klarsfeld the historian, the campaigner, the Nazi hunter, the lawmaker haunted by the memory of Izieu's forty-four children. Klarsfeld, who simply reads out the names of those children, as if he is taking attendance at school. Forty-four names, recited in deathly silence. And their ages. And a few of the letters that they wrote to their parents prior to April 6, 1944. He reads their words. Brings them into the room. A shudder runs through us . . . Vergès looks tense; he takes these blows. We all do.

At the end of my speech, Vergès walked over to me and offered me his hand. I refused to shake it. He was our enemy, and I was not at the theater. I did not listen to his speech; I had no doubt that it would be so despicable that remaining silent, as I had to do out of respect for the court, would have been unbearable.

The night of the verdict, about 2:00 a.m., after Barbie had been sentenced to life imprisonment for crimes against humanity, I walked to Montluc Prison to gather my thoughts. At Montluc, I needed to be alone with the souls of those who had suffered there so much. I thanked the Almighty, the power of human will, and fate for having helped me get through that sixteen-year ordeal.

BEATE

Rauff in Chile

IN LATE 1983, I decided to go to Chile to try to obtain the extradition or expulsion of Walter Rauff. It was another opportunity to protest against a dictator—General Pinochet—and against the impunity of a vile Nazi war criminal.

Walter Rauff, aged seventy-seven, lived in Las Condes, a residential area of Santiago. His extradition had been demanded by West Germany but refused by Chile's supreme court in 1963, as war crimes had a fifteen-year statute of limitations in that country. How could we accept such a situation?

Since March 13, 1961, Rauff had been wanted by the Hanover prosecutor's office for the murder of at least ninety-seven thousand Jews in mobile gas chambers. In 1941 and 1942, Rauff had been head of the group II-D of the RSHA, the Reich Main Security Office. This group was responsible for preparing and equipping the Einsatzgruppen and for developing, running, and repairing the gas trucks, which were mostly used in the Soviet Union.

We had a photograph of Rauff, in uniform and a long leather coat, taken during his arrest by the Americans at his headquarters, the Hotel Regina in Milan, on April 30, 1945, and we made efforts to disseminate this image. Soon after this, Rauff had escaped from an American camp in southern Italy to Rome, where he took refuge for more than a year with various church organizations. He taught math and French in an orphanage. He moved to Damascus in 1949, but a coup d'état ousted the president, Husni al-Za'im, from power and left Rauff unprotected. So he fled to South America and, after traveling through Ecuador and Bolivia, he reached Chile, where he ran a fish cannery in the south of the country. No Chilean government had ever agreed to extradite Rauff.

I OBTAINED A one-month visa from the Chilean consulate in late November 1983. I arrived in Santiago on January 19, 1984, and issued a press release about the reasons for my visit. After listing Rauff's crimes, I added, "Tomorrow, in a country that is so desperate to rid itself of General Pinochet's dictatorial regime, I will try to mobilize public opinion to have Rauff expelled, as Barbie was from Bolivia upon the accession of a democratic government."

I took a room at the Hotel Cordillera and began by approaching Jewish youth movements with the help of a Bolivian Jewish student named Salomon.

On January 27, I led a protest group consisting of young Chilean Jews brave enough to ignore their parents' concerns about the dangers of breaking the law in a dictatorship. Our target was Rauff's home at Calle Los Pozos 7230. We covered his walls with graffiti; I held up a poster; my friends read out the names of extermination camps. The police came and asked me to desist; when I refused, they took me away. On January 31, I did it again. Pinochet's opponents got in touch with me; we arranged to meet on Constitution Plaza, outside the Moneda Palace, headquarters of the general's government. This was the first public protest to occur in this symbolic spot, under the dictator's windows. The police turned up in force, detaining the leaders of the protest and taking us in a bus to a police station. We were released soon afterward. These events made the headlines in the Chilean press the next day.

In Paris, Serge and the FFDJF organized a large protest outside the Chilean embassy on February 3; hundreds of our friends took part, mobilized by the images of my arrest outside Pinochet's headquarters. The Israeli minister of justice demanded Rauff's extradition, and the West German and British ambassadors attempted similar initiatives. None of it worked, however. As the Associated Press correspondent wrote, "Augusto Pinochet is not the man to authorize an expulsion."

I left Chile on February 9, 1984. Rauff was never expelled, but at least he heard those young Jews wearing yellow stars protesting outside his home before his death on May 14, 1984. Images of the funeral were broadcast all over the world, showing old Nazis raising their right arms in a salute over Rauff's grave.

The Hunt for Josef Mengele

WHEN I ARRIVED in Asunción, on February 9, 1984, the Mengele dossier, which I had brought with me, was several inches thick. We became interested in his case quite early, as it was unique for the degree of inhumanity shown in his so-called medical experiments on Jews and Romanies.

In 1973, our friend Lisa agreed to go to Paraguay to find out what she could about him. We knew that he was rich, that he had left Germany for Argentina a few years after the war ended, and that, just before Eichmann's abduction in 1960, he had been warned by the German embassy about the attempts to extradite him from Argentina, where he was living under his own name. Mengele had fled to Paraguay, where the dictator Alfredo Stroessner granted him Paraguayan nationality in 1959.

Lisa returned from Paraguay with these conclusions:

[. . .] The most interesting contact I made was a businessman, the owner of several nightclubs and two ranches. He was part of President Stroessner's entourage and accompanied him during his trip to Germany this summer. I spent a few days with him, but our meeting was too close to the end of my stay to be of any practical use. I am sure this man knows where Mengele is, but he is not going to divulge the information to anyone who asks. The key thing, if we want to get results, is to have plenty of time to earn these people's trust and to wait for the right opportunity to bring up the subject of Mengele. I also stayed in a hostel run by German colonists. The manager, a young woman from the Hohenau colony—which is in the south, near the Argentine border—told me that Mengele had lived in that colony after the war, but that he had left years before, probably for Brazil. I had confirmation of this. A Belgian, the owner of the luxury hotel El Tirol del Paraguay, told me that Mengele had lived in Hohenau under his real name, but that he also had Argentine papers. He used to come to the hotel quite often before Eichmann's abduction, but after that he disappeared. It is possible he is still in the region: it's easy to hide here, the man told me. (I found out later that he was a Nazi, sentenced to death in Belgium.) After discussing the matter with many other people from German colonies during my month in Paraguay, it seems possible to me that Mengele is hiding in the region of Alto Paraná, near the Argentine border, or even in Brazil.

Lisa had guessed right.

OUR OTHER CAMPAIGNS prevented us from going any further with this dossier, but we never forgot about it. In 1983, we met Hans-Eberhard Klein, the Frankfurt prosecutor in charge of the Mengele case. We believed that the Mengele family, which owned a large agricultural machinery business in Günzburg, was supporting him financially. Mengele's family situation was complex: he had divorced his first wife, Irène (with whom he had a son, Rolf, in 1944), and married his brother Karl Thaddeus's widow, Martha, in Uruguay in 1958. The son of Karl Thaddeus and Martha, Karl-Heinz

Mengele (also born in 1944), ran the firm with his cousin Dieter. After her wedding to Josef Mengele, Martha and her son lived in Argentina until 1961, then left for Europe, settling in Zurich.

A search of the firm's headquarters and the family members' homes would probably have uncovered Josef Mengele's whereabouts, but the prosecutor was afraid of making a blunder, and anyway, he could not follow Rolf, the son, on his travels beyond the borders of Germany. We did it for him, thanks to Lisa, who had just moved to Berlin.

Rolf was a lawyer, and he, too, lived in Berlin. Every morning, when the mail was delivered, Lisa would take his letters, open them, photocopy anything interesting—credit-card statements in particular—and put them back in his mailbox, before sending us the copies. One day, Lisa was bold enough to enter Rolf's apartment. She had seen Rolf leave, then his wife, Almut, and their children, so she knew the coast was clear, but not for how long. A quick search allowed her to find a passport in a drawer: it belonged to a young man, Wilfried Busse, born on July 26, 1947, five feet eleven (the same height and more or less the same age as Rolf), and inside it there was a customs stamp for Brazil: "arrival August 11, 1977—departure August 23, 1977." Lisa put the passport back in its drawer. This was valuable information. Rolf had gone to South America in 1977 to meet his father, using the identity of a far-right activist, Busse. Either he had gone to Brazil, or he had gone to Paraguay or another neighboring country via Brazil in order to cover his tracks. We communicated this information to the prosecutor's office in Frankfurt, but the prosecutor remained indifferent.

I HOPED THAT my protests in Paraguay would persuade the prosecutor to search the Mengeles' homes in Germany.

In Asunción, I met the minister of the interior, the minister of justice, and the president of the Supreme Court. All three assured me that they did not know Mengele's whereabouts and that he had probably left the country after losing his Paraguayan nationality on August 8, 1979. This was possible, but I felt sure that Stroessner and his secret services knew where Mengele was hiding, whether that was in Paraguay or elsewhere.

To maintain pressure on the government, I convinced my contacts in the liberal opposition party to follow me to the courthouse in Asunción. There, at 10:30 a.m. on February 17, 1984, I protested, along with about thirty brave activists who were clearly not used to protesting in front of the police. I held up a sign written in Spanish that translates as: GENERAL STROESSNER, YOU PROTECTED MENGELE; BRING HIM TO JUSTICE. The police watched me closely, as well as anyone who went near me.

I left Paraguay on February 19, and the next day I gave a press conference in New York for the American Jewish Committee. It was standing room only. The United States was involved in this case, as it turned out that Mengele had been arrested in 1947 in the American occupation zone in Germany and then freed. An official investigation was opened. I took advantage of this to return to Paraguay on November 22, 1984, this time in the company of the Brooklyn prosecutor Elizabeth Holtzman; the chairman of the Bergen-Belsen survivors, Menachem Rosensaft; and a Catholic priest, René Valero, from Brooklyn. From our headquarters in the Hotel Casino Ita Enramada, we met daily with Paraguayan politicians and judges whom I had already met in February. This was the necessary groundwork for any progress to be made in Paraguay. Stroessner had protected Mengele for twenty years, so it would take concerted pressure to make him change his stance.

IN ISRAEL THE next year, the twins on whom Mengele had experimented told their stories to an international jury. Mengele had often sent these children's parents to the gas chambers while keeping the children themselves for his nightmarish medical experiments.

All over the world, pressure was mounting on the German courts. I went to Asunción again on May 17, 1985, armed this time with a wanted notice and a substantial reward for anyone who could provide information. The wanted notice was published in two Paraguayan newspapers, and another one was published in Brazil. I traveled to Buenos Aires, where I received a warm welcome from the Madres de la Plaza de Mayo, the mothers of the disappeared victims of the junta, who had not forgotten my protests in Argentina eight years before, when the repression was at its worst.

Back in Asunción, El Diario published articles every day accusing me of leading a campaign against Paraguay. On May 24, I led a small protest, described as "peaceful" by the police, who nevertheless ordered the protesters to leave the courthouse and disperse. I remained alone with my poster, written in Spanish, which translated as: STROESSNER, YOU LIE WHEN YOU SAY YOU

DON'T KNOW WHERE MENGELE IS—DON'T GO TO GERMANY WITHOUT HIM. This was an attempt to prevent the dictator's official visit to Germany, set for July 3.

I was subject to further harassments prior to my departure, including being expelled from my hotel because the owner considered my behavior "offensive and disrespectful." By the time I returned to Europe, however, my main objectives had been met: (1) Stroessner had been forced to postpone his visit to Germany indefinitely (and he would never set foot there again). (2) The search that was finally carried out by the German police on May 31, 1985, in Günzburg led to the discovery of the truth about Mengele: he had died on February 7, 1979, while swimming off the coast of Brazil.

I RETURNED TO Argentina on December 21, 1987, to campaign for the extradition of Josef Schwammberger, who ran the Przemysl Ghetto in Poland. In 1982, Serge had published the memoir of a survivor of this ghetto, Markus Wolfshaut. When Schwammberger was spotted in Buenos Aires and his extradition demanded by West Germany, we put together a dossier based on the eyewitness accounts of Wolfshaut and Henri Gourarier. These two men became plaintiffs in Stuttgart, on behalf of their murdered parents.

Extradition was granted in 1988 and, on May 12, 1992, Schwammberger was sentenced to life imprisonment.

THE KURT WALDHEIM AFFAIR

A FTER LEARNING THAT Kurt Waldheim, the Austrian presidential candidate, had lied about his past, the World Jewish Congress that gathered in New York in 1986 had put together a thick dossier on him. For ten years secretary-general of the United Nations in New York, Waldheim also featured in the archives kept in the basement of that building as a Nazi war criminal classified in the same category as Klaus Barbie.

If Israel had failed to check Waldheim's past in 1972, it was probably because Simon Wiesenthal, another Austrian living in Vienna, did not object. Why was that? Either his investigation was a complete failure, or he never conducted an investigation out of sympathy for Waldheim or for the political party he supported.

Serge and I had revealed that, after the deportation of forty-two thousand Jews from German-occupied Thessaloníki, General Löhr and his general staff—which included Waldheim—had pressured the Italian army in Greece to deport the Jews from their zone of occupation, too.

In cooperation with the World Jewish Congress, we helped search for documents that would show Waldheim's involvement in the Yugoslavian repression and in the Greek deportations. But my main objective was to prevent him from getting elected.

I left for Vienna in May 1986 and organized several protests, aided by some young Austrians, in the capital and then in Graz and Amstetten. I was manhandled and insulted, but at least I was able to help the opposition to Waldheim be heard.

ON JUNE 25, 1987, while Serge was taking part in the thirtieth hearing of the Barbie trial, I tried to mobilize public opinion in Rome, raising awareness of the scandal represented by the Austrian president's visit to the Vatican, particularly given that the pope, who was Polish, was attempting to improve the Catholic Church's relationship with Jews. Waldheim was already blacklisted from visiting most Western countries. Four rabbis from New York traveled with me, and many young Jews from Rome joined us, expressing their disapproval not only of Waldheim but of a pope who would welcome him.

I arrived in Rome the day before Waldheim, armed with everything I needed to put my plan into action. Using the idea that the result of a papal election is marked by the release of white smoke, I decided to set off six black smoke bombs as Waldheim passed in front of the Vatican, symbolizing the six million Jews murdered by the Nazis. Unfortunately, I had no knowledge of how to handle a smoke bomb. When we decided to examine one of them, to work out how the pin came out, disaster struck. The smoke bomb went off in the hotel room, which filled with black smoke and caught fire. We set off the fire alarm and fled the room. But this disaster turned out to be a blessing in disguise: the fire brigade and police arrived on the scene, and they initially thought it was an act of terrorism; the media went into a panic, and the incident made headlines the next day.

Our protest of Waldheim's visit to the Vatican was effective, too, with photographs of the young Jews, dressed in concentration camp uniforms, surrounded by Italian police in front of Saint Peter's Basilica, printed in newspapers all over the world.

Waldheim's next official visit was planned for Jordan on July 4. Well, if he was going there, so was I.

King Hussein of Jordan called Waldheim "dear friend": as UN secretary-general, Waldheim had helped the Arab cause.

I took a room at the Intercontinental in Amman under my maiden name, and on July 2, I went to the Foreign Ministry with the Waldheim dossier. I was warmly received by the Jordanian official until he learned what the document contained. He refused to let me leave it there and escorted me to the exit. At the opportune moment—in other words, just as I was standing under gigantic photographs of Waldheim and King Hussein—I took off my jacket to reveal a black T-shirt bearing the words: WALDHEIM MUSS WEG (Waldheim must go), an image that again made the newspapers. Naturally, I was taken to the police station and questioned before being released and placed under surveillance in my hotel room. I was then invited to leave Jordan—a pressing invitation that I accepted without regret.

I WENT BACK to Vienna in December 1987 and March 1988, each time to protest Waldheim. For the second of these trips, the pope's visit to Austria, Serge, Arno, and I came up with the idea that one of us (it would be Arno) would wear the uniform that Waldheim had worn during the war and that someone else (it would be friends of ours, Benjamin Asenhejm and Willy Gruska) would wear papal robes. Our plan was to rent a room with a balcony in the hotel opposite Saint Stephen's Cathedral: that way, the spectators who had gathered to see Waldheim and the pope would see another pair just like them on our balcony. This part of the protest went off as planned.

The next day, our group went to the nunciature early in the morning. I walked at the front, followed by Arno in his Nazi uniform and Willy dressed as the pope, while the others held up signs. The police descended upon us, and Arno and Willy were arrested. We went to the police station where they had been taken, and I saw a policeman kicking Arno. I slapped his face. He did not dare respond. Arno's fingerprints were taken, and he wiped the ink onto a policeman's white shirt. The policeman yelled but did not hit him. We were kept behind bars for more than six hours before being released.

My last protest against Kurt Waldheim took place in Turkey. I flew to Istanbul with Rabbi Weiss, and we stood outside a school with our posters, waiting for the visit of Waldheim and the Turkish president. A group of policemen surrounded us, and then it was the usual routine: police station, interrogation, release. The next day, our protest was front-page news; it had completely overshadowed Waldheim's visit. Confronted with the loss of prestige that Waldheim's presidency had inflicted on Austria, the conservative party forced him to abandon his plans to seek reelection.

The Muslim Sector of Beirut

W HEN ISRAELI FORCES withdrew from Beirut in 2000, a few dozen Lebanese Jews ignored their warnings to evacuate the city, choosing to stay in the place they considered their home. They believed they were safe from the violence of the civil war due to their political neutrality. For ten of them, who were abducted and disappeared in 1984 and 1985, this decision would prove fatal. Haim Cohen and Isaac Tarrab were executed by the Organization of the Oppressed on Earth, which was demanding the liberation of all prisoners from the Khiam prison in southern Lebanon. We couldn't just accept these murders or those that threatened to follow, even if we knew our chances of success were slim.

I do not find it easy to leave my family behind, particularly when it means entering such a violent country, but how could we defend the memory of Jews murdered more than forty years before if we did not defend Jews whose lives were currently endangered?

I made my reasons for going to Beirut clear in a press release on January 17, 1986: "I am going to Beirut for two reasons. First, to denounce the murders of two Jewish hostages. The perpetrators of those crimes, committed against Lebanese Jews purely because they were Jews, are as low as Nazi war criminals. Second, as a German woman, I always feel a solidarity with Jews persecuted because they are Jews. That is why I am going, to try to save the lives of the five Jewish hostages who are still alive, and why I will propose to their kidnappers that they release those hostages and take me as a hostage in their place."

I had no visa, so I decided to enter Lebanon illegally by boat. When the ship docked in the port of Jounieh, I waited while all the other passengers disembarked, and then, when the customs officials had gone, I got off the boat with my suitcase. I was in the Christian sector of Beirut, and I needed to reach the Muslim sector, but when I took a taxi to the border between the two sectors, the guards checked my papers and sent me to a police station, where I spent the night. In the morning, the West German ambassador got me a two-month residence permit while advising me to leave because the city was too dangerous. I thanked him and went to the Muslim sector. There, I checked into the Hotel Cavalier, where foreign reporters stay.

The Lebanese press reported the reasons behind my visit. On February 3, Himat, a Shiite, drove me to the suburbs of Beirut. He stopped, and another car came to a halt beside us; a young man got out. We spoke to each other in English. He told me the hostages would not be freed unless all the prisoners in the Khiam prison were liberated first. "Why are you attacking innocents?" I asked. "All the Jews are brothers and all the Jews are responsible," he replied. He said he would be in touch with me if there was any news.

Serge went to Israel, where he was told that all the Lebanese Jews had been warned in plenty of time to leave the country and that there was no possibility of any prisoners being freed in an exchange.

On February 10, I went back to Paris, having achieved nothing. But at least I had done my best for three weeks in a city filled with gunshots and explosions. Two days later, Serge took over from me.

SERGE

IN THE LION'S DEN

I ARRIVED IN Beirut on February 20, 1986, on a tourist visa. Elie Hallak, a doctor famous for his work with the poor, had just been murdered. I read out a statement to the media assembled in the Muslim sector of the airport:

> I have come here to publicly protest the murders of Lebanese Jewish hostages and to appeal to the spiritual leaders of Islam, who have not spoken about this matter yet, to condemn these anti-Jewish crimes and to demand that the surviving hostages be freed . . . We must try to reason with the abductors by repeating to them: your conflict with Israel must not end in the Final Solution of the last Lebanese Jews, who chose to stay in this country because it is their home and who are innocent of any hostile act toward the various factions that are tearing Lebanon to pieces.

When I got out of the taxi outside my hotel, there was incredulity that I had made it that far. I knew there was a strong risk that I would be abducted between the airport and the Hotel Cavalier. Barely had I put my suitcase in my room than I left the hotel again and went to the offices of a Muslim newspaper: it was a strange sensation, walking through streets where I knew that anything might happen. The last time I had felt like this was in the streets of Nice, when we were trying to escape the Nazi roundups.

The telephone rang early that morning. It was the French ambassador, Christian Graeff: "If you remain in this sector, you won't make it through the day, after everything you've said about the Muslim killers or the Jewish hostages. Stay at the hotel, in the lobby. And be ready to leave." I followed these instructions. Soon afterward, two armored vehicles came to a halt in front of the hotel; heavily armed French gendarmes burst in and led me outside to one of the cars. We stopped in front of a convent and ran inside, crouching down low to avoid sniper fire. The gendarmes dropped some boxes of food; we ran back to the vehicles and sped across the green line out of the Muslim section. I gave my sincere thanks to the ambassador and the military attaché, a man I had eaten lunch with, and who was killed shortly afterward.

I took a ship to Cyprus and then a plane back to Paris.

None of the hostages survived.

WHAT LESSON CAN be drawn from this, except that, when a vast wave of anti-Semitism is approaching, the Jewish people can do only one thing: flee for their lives. How many patriotic German Jews, proud possessors of an Iron Cross, were killed by the Nazis? How many French Jews, awarded the Legion of Honor, were handed over to the Gestapo by the Vichy regime?

Raoul Mizrahi, Haim Cohen, Isaac Tarrab, Elie Hallak, Elie Srour, Henri Mann, Ibrahim Youssef, Yehouda Benesti, Isaac Sasson, Selim Jammous: these names are part of the long list of Jews put to death simply because they were Jews. Beate and I had patiently, doggedly, listed the eighty thousand names of France's Holocaust victims; the ten names of the executed Lebanese Jewish hostages, we wrote down in our own way, by throwing ourselves into the lion's den.

. . .

IN 1987, AFTER the far-right National Front leader Jean-Marie Le Pen described the gas chambers in an interview as "a minor detail" of the Second World War, we took him to court, as did many others.

Arno wanted to confront him personally, so he went to the congress of the National Front to protest. After his comrades slipped away, he decided to go in alone. We wanted to dissuade him, but we couldn't: we had shown him the way, after all. Arno, like Beate and I, knew perfectly well that there would be only one outcome: he would get beaten up. Under his jacket, he wore a T-shirt bearing the words LE PEN NAZI. When he jumped onto the stage as Le Pen was speaking and the crowd saw the message on his T-shirt, he was showered with blows by Le Pen's bodyguards. The police took him to the hospital; he lost some vision in his right eye.

But he had done what he set out to do. Never would he retreat in the face of danger; never would personal risk prevent him from fulfilling what he considered to be his mission.

Hunting Brunner in Damascus

IN JANUARY 1990, I went to the Syrian embassy in Paris and was granted a business visa. I wrote a letter to President Hafiz al-Assad, requesting his cooperation in helping us extradite Alois Brunner, and had it translated into Arabic. I made this letter public just before my departure on January 10.

At the French embassy in Damascus, I was told that I would meet the Syrian vice–foreign minister that morning. Then I was told that the meeting had been canceled. I went to the German embassy, where the ambassador told me there was nothing he could do about it.

All day long, I was followed by a plainclothes policeman. In desperation, I tried to get him on my side. Back at the hotel, I asked to hire a conference room for the next morning, where I would give a speech on the subject of Nazi war criminals, from Klaus Barbie in Bolivia to Alois Brunner in Syria. I was told that a small room had been reserved for me.

I took a taxi to the offices of Agence France-Presse. The policeman who was following me came over to talk to my taxi driver. I suggested he save time by simply riding in my taxi; he agreed. He spoke excellent French. When I returned to the hotel, I was told that the room I had booked was no longer available.

The next day, around 7:00 a.m., there was a knock at the door of my hotel room. A well-dressed man flanked by two soldiers in uniform politely informed me that I was being expelled from Syria. I barely had time to shave and dress before I was ushered into a car. The car broke down on the way to the airport. They fixed it. Instead of sending me back to Paris, I was put on a plane to Vienna. So, in the end, it was me, rather than the Austrian Brunner, who was expelled to Austria.

AN INVESTIGATION LAUNCHED in July 1991 eventually brought some important information: we learned from a Syrian living abroad whose family was neighbors with Brunner that the ex-Nazi had left his home on October 15, 1991. Hafiz al-Assad's chief bodyguard had taken it over. Brunner was removed by ambulance, supported by two nurses. We knew he was not long for this world.

Roland Dumas, the French foreign minister, announced that he would be making an official visit to Damascus on December 18, 1991. We decided to get there ahead of him.

BEATE

The End of the Brunner Affair

I T WAS MY turn to go to Damascus again. I needed a visa in someone else's name, so I decided to make myself look like a friend of mine, Trudy Baer, who is ten years my senior. Her father was executed by the Nazis; her mother and sister were deported. So she was Jewish and German. She had no difficulty obtaining a tourist visa, whereas I would certainly have been refused had I made the same request.

On December 5, 1991, a professional makeup artist helped me to look like Trudy. Even our friend, the American journalist Peter Hellman, who was in Damascus to cover the story for *New York Magazine*, did not recognize me at the airport, where he was waiting for me. I passed without incident through two police checkpoints on the road to Damascus and took a room at the Cham Palace, where Serge had stayed the previous year.

That night, I wrote the banner that I would carry with me the next day: PRESIDENT ASSAD, 99.98% OF THE VOTE IS NOT ENOUGH. EXTRADITE

THE NAZI CRIMINAL ALOIS BRUNNER AND FREE THE SYRIAN JEWS! I wanted to show my banner in a symbolic spot guarded by Syrian soldiers in uniform, a building with flags outside it. Unable to get near the presidential building, which was guarded by men carrying machine guns, I opted for the Ministry of the Interior, on Avenue Al Malek Farouk.

On Saturday, I walked directly toward the building's main entrance, ignoring the soldiers who signaled me to stop, and unfolded my banner. The soldiers rushed at me, tore the banner from my hands, and shoved me in a car. Inside my purse, they found my real passport, in the name of Beate Klarsfeld. They looked for a visa inside it and, naturally, did not find it. After my interrogation, I admitted that I was staying at the Cham Palace. They took me there and locked me in my room, with a policeman for company; this was the same man who had surveilled Serge a few months before. He complained that I was not as communicative as my husband.

On Monday, heavily guarded, I was taken to the airport and sent to Paris, where the press was waiting for me. The incident provoked headlines worldwide.

ON DECEMBER 10, Serge and I met with Roland Dumas—whose father was also shot by the Nazis—and the foreign minister reaffirmed his determination to have Brunner extradited, saying he would bring the subject up during his planned meeting with Assad. The result? His official visit to Damascus was postponed at the last minute, with the insulting excuse that President Assad was too busy to see him.

On January 14, 1992, we went to Strasbourg, where a two-hundred-million-dollar financial-aid package for Syria was due to be voted on. We had prepared a list of arguments for each European deputy, with a sixty-three-page dossier on Brunner. The next day, the parliament voted in a new resolution criticizing the fact that "this country shelters and protects the Nazi criminal Alois Brunner." When it came to the vote, Syria did not receive enough support to ratify the aid package.

As far as we knew, Brunner had died in 1992. The Syrian government became prisoners of their own lie: they could not prove that he was dead without exposing their dishonesty. So Brunner continued to live, and Syria to be criticized. In 1998, Hafiz al-Assad made an official visit to Paris, just as we were about to have Brunner tried in absentia. The dates of the visit—

July 16 and 17—were the anniversary of the Vél' d'Hiv roundup. I could not believe that Jacques Chirac, who had made the moving speech three years earlier accepting France's blame for the Vél' d'Hiv roundup, was now planning to welcome the dictator Assad, the protector of Alois Brunner. Our association held a highly visible protest during the visit.

On March 2, 2001, Brunner's trial in absentia began in Paris. This was notable for us as a family because it was the first and last time that Serge, Arno, and Lida all worked together on the same trial. Arno analyzed Brunner's personality, while Lida read out extracts from the deportees' witness statements.

That same year, Bashar al-Assad, son of Hafiz and the new Syrian president, was invited to Paris for an official visit. After Bashar's anti-Semitic declarations, we bought a quarter-page ad in *Le Monde*:

France, which has done so much in recent years to repair the harm done to French Jews by the Vichy government, will lose credibility by welcoming the Syrian president, Bashar al-Assad . . . who dared to say to the pope that Israel and the Jews wanted to "destroy all principles and all religions, in the same way that they betrayed Jesus and tried to kill the prophet Muhammad."

Nearly eighty thousand people gathered on the Esplanade des Martyrs Juifs du Vél' d'Hiv on June 25, 2001, to protest this visit. Two weeks before, I had placed another ad in *Le Monde*, directly addressed to the French president:

If Bashar's visit is not canceled or postponed . . . or if, on that day, you do not publicly denounce his opinion of Jews, your handshake with Bashar al-Assad will be seen as a little Montoire.*

It was hard for me to write those words, because I did not want to hurt someone I respected and who did not realize the true nature of the man he was about to meet.

Jacques Chirac did not hold those words against me for very long. In

---

*Montoire-sur-le-Loir was the site of the infamous handshake between Marshal Pétain and Adolf Hitler in 1940.

fact, he made me an Officer of the Legion of Honor in 2007. As for Bashar al-Assad, he made an official visit to Berlin on July 10 and, once again, was greeted by a passionate protest organized by our association.

Sadly, the future would show that we were right about both Bashar al-Assad and his father.

SERGE

Defending the Romanies
in Rostock

S UMMER 1992. THOUSANDS of Romanian and ex-Yugoslavian Romanies were at risk of being expelled by the Germans to Romania, where they were persecuted at the time, and to Serbia, which was ravaged by war. They were being unjustly denied their right to political asylum.

A conflict had arisen in the east of Germany, where the local government and the xenophobic public were readying themselves to strike at these people who, half a century earlier, had shared the fate of the Jewish people. If we, as the children of Jewish deportees, did not defend them, it would, we believed, be a desertion from the battlefield of memory.

Our association of Sons and Daughters made public its intention to protest in Rostock, where immigrants were being attacked in August and September 1992. Welcome centers were burned down, the police were reluctant to get involved, and most of the local population remained indifferent.

Together with a Romany delegation, we fixed a plaque to the façade of the city hall, commemorating the suffering of the Romanies and calling on Germany to put an end to its xenophobic brutality. Meanwhile, Arno led a group of young people inside the building and hung a banner from the Christian Democrats' window, reading: KEIN ANSWEISUNG DER ROMA AUS DEUTSCHLAND (No to the deportation of Romanies from Germany).

This was the first Jewish gathering in Rostock since Kristallnacht. Now we were not being marched toward the concentration camps; we were showing the German people the right path to take to avoid walking in the footsteps of Nazi boots.

IN A GYMNASIUM in Rostock, I witnessed a parody of judicial procedure. I saw an army of policemen bullying protesters. I saw identifications that were completely against the rules. Only the intervention of the French consul in Hamburg enabled some semblance of calm and reason, with the elderly and sick being allowed to leave that icy-cold sports hall, with its macabre echo of the Vélodrome d'Hiver.

The plaque that we put on Rostock's city hall was removed soon afterward. But twenty years later, in 2012, it was restored, officially this time. It bears these words (the original is in German):

> In this town, in August 1992, men again committed acts of racist violence against innocent families, children, women, and men.
>
> We remember the millions of children, women, and men who, because they were Jewish, Sinti, or Romany, were victims of the Nazi genocide.
>
> In one single night of unforgettable horror, on August 2, 1944, the last surviving three thousand Romanies in the Auschwitz-Birkenau camp were gassed.
>
> These experiences and these historical commitments must remain present in the memory of the German people in order to ensure that contempt for our fellow man and violence are never reproduced.

Dear Mr. President . . .

I LIKED FRANÇOIS MITTERRAND. When I first met him, I was seven years old. It was February 1943, and he had just made the life-changing decision to join the Resistance in Montmaur while my family was there in its brief role as cover for the printing of false papers. Years later, when I heard his speeches on the radio, I was impressed by his talents as an orator, his ability to cause controversy, and his sense of humor. We campaigned for his election as president in 1974 (when he lost) but not in 1981 (when he won) because he had been the only candidate not to rule out the transfer of Marshal Pétain's body to the Douaumont Ossuary, a symbolic act that would have signified the rehabilitation of the man who led the Vichy regime in its collaboration with the Nazis.

For Mitterrand, Vichy had been the starting point to a brilliant career. His family had idolized Marshal Pétain, and Mitterrand never lost his respect for the man.

And yet I was happy when Mitterrand was elected in 1981. Pragmatic as ever, he did not keep his promise to transfer Pétain's body, and he helped with the expulsion of Barbie from La Paz to Lyon. He also awarded Beate and myself the order of the Legion of Honor in 1984.

But every year from 1987 onward, on November 11—the day when France commemorates its war dead—President Mitterrand would place a wreath on Pétain's grave, and that disgusted me. For our association of Sons and Daughters, it was too much.

We had to pick our battles, however, and this was one we seemed almost certain to lose. So it was not until October 1990 that I finally decided I had to publicly oppose Mitterrand. It was clear by then that he was protecting Maurice Papon. But when René Bousquet's dossier, too, was effectively blocked, I decided to publish an article about Mitterrand's past, which—prior to his decision to join the Resistance—had included a spell working for the Vichy government.

The media reacted very discreetly to these revelations at the time, and it was only when Pierre Péan's book about the president's wartime years appeared in 1994 that people finally admitted I had been right four years earlier.

My most overt act of war against Mitterrand came in 1992, when I decided the time had come to shine a light on what I regarded as the "enormous scandal" of his annual wreath-laying on Marshal Pétain's grave. So Arno and I together came up with a plan. The solution, we decided, was to invent a believable lie that would trap Mitterrand in a no-win situation, similar to the one Beate and I had invented in the Continental Grain affair, back in 1971: I would publicly declare that someone close to the president had passed on a message to me from Mitterrand himself stating that he would no longer lay a wreath on Pétain's grave. If he then went ahead with the wreath-laying, it would be news—because he would have gone against what the media and public opinion expected of him. And so, on July 21, "with satisfaction," I made the announcement.

The journalist Georges-Marc Benamou was present when the president heard this news, and he wrote about it in a book entitled *Young Man, You Don't Know What You're Talking About*:

> The Agence France-Presse had just reported the president's announcement that he would no longer lay the wreath for Pétain. I was delighted. But Mitterrand immediately made clear that

the announcement was false, a lie completely invented by Serge Klarsfeld: "He's unbelievable, that Klarsfeld. He has some nerve. He must be a madman." His eyes lit up. "A madman . . . or a manipulator."

He paused, then began to think out loud: "That Klarsfeld, with whom I used to be on good terms, he's decided to lead me where he wants me to go. He has a plan, and he's willing to do anything to achieve it, even this kind of barefaced lie. I hadn't made any kind of decision about that wreath. And if I did have anything to announce, I would hardly have told him, this man who is openly at war with me . . ."

I saw a grimace of displeasure on his face. He was exasperated at the situation he had found himself in and was desperately seeking a way out of it. He had been trapped by Serge Klarsfeld's cunning trick.

On November 11, I went to the Île d'Yeu, where Pétain is buried, with three friends and a group of Jewish student activists. Unlike most of the rest of the French population, it seemed obvious to us that Mitterrand would lay a wreath on Pétain's grave—because he had not announced that he wouldn't.

We had to take a boat to the Île d'Yeu, and there was a terrible storm that made everyone on board—supporters of Pétain and protesters alike—violently seasick. There was only one boat back, and if we didn't take it, we would be stuck on the island, so we felt we had no choice. As the storm continued to rage, and as the boat took us away from Pétain's grave, we saw a helicopter descend on the island and the prefect of the Vendée place François Mitterrand's wreath next to the one left by the far-right National Front leader Jean-Marie Le Pen.

We organized a protest outside the Vélodrome d'Hiver, and I ordered a special wreath from the best florist in Paris: a very large bouquet in the shape of a francisque—the Vichy medal which Mitterrand received in 1943—and bearing the words "To François Mitterrand, with all my gratitude, from Philippe Pétain." It was insolent, but to the point. When the protest ended, three of our female activists went to the president's palace to present him with this wreath. Police intercepted them before they could get near the building and confiscated the controversial flower arrangement.

Mitterrand never laid another wreath on Pétain's grave.

Touvier Arrested,
Bousquet Charged

THE ARREST, IN May 1989, of Paul Touvier—the former leader of the Milice, the French militia created in 1943 to help fight the Resistance—put an end to a total of thirty-five years spent on the run from justice. There was a brief period, around 1972, when he came out of hiding after being officially pardoned; in June of that year, Beate and I took some young LICA activists (and Arno, who was six years old at the time) to protest this pardon—granted by President Pompidou—outside Touvier's house. Twenty-two years later, Arno would represent the Sons and Daughters at Touvier's trial.

In 1989, the FFDJF were plaintiffs against Touvier, and I helped the investigating judge, Jean-Pierre Getti, with documentary research. It was Getti and his predecessor Claude Grellier who were the driving forces behind Touvier's arrest. On May 23, the gendarmes searched the abbey in Saint-Michel-en-Brenne. They questioned the abbot after discovering some suitcases marked LACROIX, one of Touvier's aliases. The gendarmes told the abbot that Serge Klarsfeld and his organization were hunting Touvier and that it would be better for Touvier if it was the gendarmes who got their hands on him. He was arrested later that day.

ON SEPTEMBER 26, 1990, at the request of Pierre Arpaillange, the French minister of justice, the public prosecutor's office in Paris opened an investigation against René Bousquet for crimes against humanity.

Five days later, I was conducting a symposium in the Senate when an elderly, distinguished-looking gentleman appeared shyly at the entrance of the room. "I am the minister of justice," he told Beate, who led him to the stage.

Before the symposium, I had been talking with the Paris general prosecutor, Pierre Truche, who shared my opinion that the legal proceedings begun against Bousquet should lead to the criminal court, and not to the High Court, which had been inactive since 1954.

There was something strange about the speech given by Arpaillange that day: he mentioned his immediate aversion to Pétain and his politics, his membership in the Resistance, and his undying attachment to its values. Then he left and, that afternoon, resigned from the government. We realized that he had been pushed out when we discovered, on October 8, that the prosecutor general had changed his position and was now championing the High Court. Henri Nallet was named minister of justice, Georges Kiejman his deputy.

I angrily wrote a press release designed to make Kiejman lose his temper:

This U-turn can only be explained by the determination of those at the top of the political ladder not to let the anti-Jewish actions of the Vichy government, police, and administration go on trial. This attitude, which is unchanged since 1945, is against the interests of France. The prosecutor general's reversal of position can be explained by the change of the minister of justice on October 2. A deportee's son [Robert Badinter] was minister of justice when the chief of the Gestapo in Lyon was brought to France to be tried. A deportee's son [Georges Kiejman] was named deputy minister of justice to ensure the impunity of the head of the Vichy police. The FFDJF calls on Georges Kiejman to resign his position so that his name is not mixed up in the burial of the Bousquet dossier.

Kiejman's response was "My commitment within the government is a general commitment that goes well beyond my status as a deportee's son. And so I believe that, despite my respect for Serge Klarsfeld, I do not have to take moral lessons from him. On a more technical level, it seems preferable that it is the High Court or its equivalent that should try Bousquet." The closing sentences of his statement were extremely revealing about the nature of the instructions he had received: "Other than the technical problem, we must be aware that—beyond the necessary struggle for remembrance—it can seem important to preserve the civil peace. There are other ways to denounce the cowardice of the Vichy regime than through a trial."

On October 22, the corridors of the courthouse were taken over by the Sons and Daughters. In the meantime, I directly attacked the president of the Republic in the media by mentioning his work for Vichy in 1942.

In the end, the Bousquet dossier was not buried. On November 18, 1990, the grand jury courageously issued a decree in which it declared itself competent to investigate Bousquet's crimes against humanity.

Judge Getti, who was investigating both the Touvier and the Bousquet cases, was asked by the grand jury to provide a report answering a legal question: Did the evidence I had produced constitute new facts, ones that had not been considered during Bousquet's 1949 trial? The response, given in June 1991, was positive: Yes, this was new evidence. Bousquet was charged.

Subsequently, there were several hearings. The minutes of the meeting on July 2, 1942, involving Bousquet and the leaders of the SS were authenticated by Herbert Hagen, who wrote them and whom we had convicted in Cologne in 1980. But on June 8, 1993, just as the trial was about to begin, Bousquet was assassinated.

THE TOUVIER TRIAL

O N APRIL 13, 1992, the court of appeal in Paris exonerated Touvier, explaining that the only crimes against humanity without a statute of limitations were those committed on behalf of a state "pursuing a policy of ideological hegemony." According to the court of appeal, this was not the case for Vichy, "irrespective of its weaknesses, cowardices, and ignominies." And yet it was obvious that, when it came to the Jewish question, Vichy did pursue a policy of ideological hegemony. We put our faith in the court of cassation—the French equivalent of the U.S. Supreme Court—to put an end to this scandal.

On November 22, 1992, the court of cassation found in our favor, ruling that the Paris court of appeal had failed to take into account Touvier's complicity with the Gestapo in the case of the summary execution in Rillieux-la-Pape, where seven Jewish hostages were shot by Touvier's militia. And yet the court of cassation did not go far enough; it did not rule that Vichy was a state "pursuing a policy of ideological hegemony," and this enabled the Papon and Bousquet cases to be judged in terms of complicity, too.

When it came to the trial, we were in a difficult position: if the prosecutor and the plaintiffs stuck to this narrow definition of a crime against humanity, and if they based their accusation on complicity with the Sipo-SD, there was a major risk that Touvier would be given the benefit of mitigating circumstances, as his actions could then be explained in terms of him pressuring the Germans to reduce the number of hostages. This would also be dangerous from a historical standpoint, effectively absolving the entire Vichy regime on the same false lines.

Arno and I were determined to argue the historical truth rather than accommodating our arguments to the idea of complicity. Personally, I did not like the atmosphere of this trial nor the difficult relationships with the other prosecution lawyers, and I had no desire to read and try to memorize the very thick dossier on the Milice. So I left that to Arno, having every faith in his intelligence, memory, and firmness. In 1990, he had obtained his law degree after only eight months at New York University and passed the New York bar examination with the highest grade of any student. He also passed the state bar exam in California.

Touvier's defense was essentially that the Lyon Gestapo had demanded the execution of a hundred people in retaliation for the death of Philippe Henriot, the Vichy propagandist and part-time militiaman, and that the head of the Milice had succeeded in reducing this number to thirty, while Touvier, by choosing Jews, had managed to shoot only seven people. And yet nothing in the dossier or in the logic of events suggested that the Germans had demanded reprisals. We decided to argue the truth: that the French state of Vichy was complicit in the Third Reich's persecution of Jews; that the Milice collaborated closely with the Gestapo and that, as part of this collaboration, the Milice carried out its own reprisals for Henriot's death; and that Paul Touvier was the instigator of the massacre in Rillieux-la-Pape.

At our first meeting with the other prosecution lawyers, it became clear that there was a major division among us; they all feared that our argument would contradict the court of cassation's interpretation of a crime against humanity and that this would lead to Touvier's acquittal. If Arno capitulated to this legal logic, Touvier would only have been given an intermediate prison sentence, when what he deserved was life imprisonment.

I did not even enter the courthouse during this trial; my place was outside, protesting with the other Sons and Daughters. I also drove Arno to each hearing between March 17 and April 20, 1994. My son knew the dossier like the back of his hand, and his personality seemed better suited than mine to withstanding the pressure from his colleagues, who were already irritated by his stance and his youthful looks. They wanted and expected him to be lazy and superficial, but in fact he was brilliant and serious.

One of his most notable interventions came on April 1, when former high police official Jacques Delarue contradicted the damning investigation report that he himself had written in 1970, in which he claimed that there was no trace of any intervention by the Germans in this case. Delarue justified this U-turn by referring to a cross-examination of the Milice leader Joseph Darnand in 1945. But Arno presented the court with the minutes of Delarue's hearing, dated April 11, 1990, in which he stated that no credit be given to Darnand's lies in that cross-examination. Delarue tried to muddy the waters, so Arno asked him if he had been pressured, having been a policeman in the major roundup in Marseille in January 1943. There was an uproar in the courtroom, and the other prosecution lawyers distanced themselves from Arno. But Delarue's testimony collapsed.

Touvier's vile and unwavering anti-Semitism could be established simply by reading his notebooks; his role in the summary execution at Rillieux-la-Pape was backed up by witnesses, by the Resistance fighter who was not killed because he wasn't Jewish, by Touvier's secretary, by his chauffeur.

Arno gave his closing speech on April 14. His final words, addressed to the jury, forced them to face up to their responsibilities and demanded a life sentence: "It is through the severity of the sentence that you give Touvier that the world will judge whether the French people look more indulgently on crimes committed by a Frenchman in the Milice than on crimes committed by a German in the Gestapo."

The prosecutor, Hubert de Touzalin, pointed out that Touvier had been charged by the court of cassation and the Versailles grand jury with complicity with the Germans in crimes against humanity, whereas the entire investigation demonstrated the independence of his actions in the massacre at Rillieux. But the prosecutor then declared that the court of cassation's definition was sufficiently broad to encompass Touvier's crime: "I am convinced that there was no order, but only a German intervention." This nuance allowed the prosecutor to counter Touvier's arguments: "Seven Jews were murdered. That is a proven fact. It is the only one."

In *Le Monde*, the eminent essayist and novelist Bertrand Poirot-Delpech wrote: "Arno Klarsfeld chose fidelity to the evidence over that pragmatic U-turn. If the jury had not given Touvier a life sentence, Arno Klarsfeld would have taken the blame; thanks to him, and him alone, truth and justice went hand in hand, which is so rarely the case."

Trying to Reason with
War Criminals in Bosnia

I N FEBRUARY 1996, I asked the French Ministry of Defense if I could
  pay for a place on a military plane to Sarajevo, in order to avoid the long
journey by road from Belgrade. I intended to talk to the Serbs in Bosnia to
explain to them the advantages—not only to the international community,
but to themselves, too—of putting their political and military leaders on trial.

My request was accepted, and soon afterward I was spending the night
in a hotel near Sarajevo, whose façade had been destroyed by bombs. I
made a statement to local journalists explaining the reasons for my visit: to
try to convince Radovan Karadžić and Ratko Mladić to turn themselves
over to the international courts.

For the previous three days, the Serbs had been fleeing Sarajevo en masse
as the city fell into the hands of the Bosnian Muslims. Thousands of people
walked along a narrow dirt road, under heavy snowfall, to the city of Pale.

I spoke Russian with a Serbian civilian and managed to make him understand that I was looking for a car so I could follow this exodus to Pale. He had a dog with him; I showed him the photograph of my own dog, and we started chatting. He led me across town to a taxi, and the driver agreed to take the risk of driving me.

The mountain road was icy and filled with large numbers of cars, vans, and carts, all of them in a pitiful state. It took us six hours to drive the fifteen miles to Pale, which had become the headquarters of the Serbian forces in Bosnia.

There, I went to the press center run by Karadžić's daughter, Sonia, as that seemed the best way of ensuring that my message would reach its intended recipient. Sonia wasn't there, but her assistant read the message. His reaction was hostile; he violently disagreed with its contents and told me to wait at a motel two miles away.

It is not easy, being alone in a hostile environment, and wondering if it was really a good idea to attempt to reason with people who are beyond reason. I walked through the icy night to the Olympic Motel, which was more or less deserted, and drank tea in my room until around 8:00 p.m., when three plainclothes policemen entered my room, accompanied by a young woman, who acted as their interpreter.

I was told to follow them, and as I did they kept repeating, "You shouldn't be afraid," which only made me think that I probably should be. Sitting between two of the policemen in the backseat of the car, I started to wonder if we were going to an office or deep into the woods. Thankfully, we ended up in an office, where I was interrogated for two hours. They wanted to know if I'd had any contact with the Bosnians and on whose behalf I was acting. Then they tried to refute my arguments. Finally, they informed me that I had been ordered to return to Sarajevo the next day, and they accompanied me back to the motel.

In the morning, some English Reuters journalists, who had become worried when they hadn't seen me the previous evening, came to my room. Two policemen stayed with us, to monitor our conversation. The journalists drove me to Sarajevo on a more direct road, and I was eventually able to fly home.

ON FEBRUARY 27, I went to Zagreb to see the minister in charge of Croatian war criminals (six of them, including General Blaškić, had been charged by the International Criminal Tribunal in The Hague). I told him of my wish that General Blaškić—whose extradition, he explained, could only be granted if the Croatian parliament changed its laws—should be arrested. I also emphasized that the accused could go to The Hague himself (or be pressured into it).

Two weeks later, Blaškić was transferred to The Hague and arrested.

The Papon Case

IN 1993, THE Papon case was still under investigation, its focus limited to the year 1942, as only the charges filed by our plaintiffs had not been thrown out. I had chosen 1942 because that was the year when deportation was at its height (forty-three thousand people, including thirty-three thousand in eleven weeks) and when relations between the Sipo-SD, the police, and the French authorities had been at their most fluid, when the pressure that the Germans put on their French colleagues was least felt. Maurice Papon was the only one of the four French war criminals we had targeted (the others being the Bordeaux prefect Maurice Sabatier, Jean Leguay, and René Bousquet) who was still alive.

Unlike the other plaintiffs' lawyers, Arno and I were not perturbed by the relative slowness of the investigation. We had faith that it would end up in the office of the prosecutor general, and in August 1995, that is precisely what happened. Six months later, the case was directed, as we had hoped, to the criminal court in Bordeaux.

Incredulous at this outcome, Papon claimed he was the victim of a political plot and that I was working on behalf of a shadowy group of Jewish Americans of German origin with the aim of diminishing Germany's guilt in the Holocaust by making France share in it.

On February 9, 1997, *Le Monde* published an article by Laurent Greilsamer, who had been following my cases since 1978: "Serge Klarsfeld acts on behalf of the mission he has given himself, in accordance with the strategy he has chosen. First of all, he wanted to bring the German criminals to justice. Only then did he pursue their French counterparts . . . Sometimes, the work of one man can awaken or reawaken the memory of all."

WE KNEW THAT this trial would be difficult because there was, from the start, disagreement among the numerous other plaintiffs' lawyers and ourselves. Meanwhile, Arno digested all the volumes of the investigation and the historical archives that I had gathered. He would fight the case while I remained outside the courthouse with Beate and the Sons and Daughters.

We also knew that among the enemies we would face in this trial was the president of the criminal court. Unlike the United States or Germany, France is not a country where the presiding judge in the criminal court is chosen randomly. In France, the president of the criminal court is chosen by the first president of the court of appeal. Some friends of ours from Bordeaux told us that, during a dinner party for a few friends, the judge who would make that choice had expressed open hostility toward the idea of a trial of Papon, before it had even become a reality. Consequently, it seemed unlikely that he would choose someone who did not share his point of view. So we were well aware that there was a good chance that the president of the court would be in favor of acquittal.

From the start of the trial, our apprehensions were confirmed: the court president, Jean-Louis Castagnède, prevented Arno from speaking freely when it came to examining Papon's state of health. Arno was going to point out that the cardiologist who had been looking after Papon had refused to confirm that his health was in decline, which had led Papon to turn to another, more malleable cardiologist. The decision to free Papon, taken by the president, meant that, even if he were convicted, Papon would only go to prison the day before his appeal was heard at the court of cassation—and who knew when that would happen. If his appeal were accepted, he would spend only one night in prison; if it were rejected, he would stay there for the period of the sentence he would eventually receive. Papon was eighty-six years old.

Castagnède had effectively given Papon control of the trial: he could decide whether he attended it or not. If he believed that he was likely to be convicted, he would merely have to stay in bed, and the trial would be adjourned until a later session—in other words, never. On the other hand, if Papon believed that there was a chance he would be acquitted, he would continue making the effort to go to court, and he would only be convicted if he turned out to be mistaken about the probable outcome.

When the decision to free Papon was announced on October 10, Arno withdrew from "a trial that has lost its meaning." Outside the courtroom, where the Sons and Daughters were protesting, I declared, "The French courts took sixteen years to send Maurice Papon to prison; Judge Castagnède took three days to free him."

Meanwhile, the prosecutor general urged us to return to the trial. He also decided to go public with his opposition to President Castagnède by lodging an appeal—an unprecedented step! In those circumstances, we felt able to take our place in the courtroom once again.

On January 28, 1998, there was a dramatic turn of events, as we revealed that Jean-Louis Castagnède was the nephew of one of Papon's victims and that he could himself have been a plaintiff against Papon.

Micheline Castagnède was the daughter of the court president's only paternal uncle and his wife, Esterina Benaïm. She was the sole surviving member of her family, which was transported from Bordeaux to Auschwitz via Drancy in three separate convoys, all overseen by Papon.

We did not know about Micheline's existence until she got in touch with the regional office of the CRIF. She went there on January 26 and asked for information on the deportation of the Benaïm family. The secretary transmitted this request to me in Bordeaux on the morning of the twenty-seventh, and it was only the next day in Paris that I researched those convoys. On the afternoon of January 28, I called the CRIF office in Bordeaux and spoke to Micheline Castagnède, who explained to me that she had heard her cousin, the court president, as he examined the convoy of December 30, 1943, read out the names of her mother and her two sisters. She had told the CRIF secretary that she had regularly seen Jean-Louis until she was about sixteen or seventeen; that he knew who his aunt was; and that their distant relations now were due to the president's wife, who looked down on Micheline's branch of the family.

I did not ask Micheline to do anything; nor did Arno. But she spontaneously gave us information that we had every right to use. We had to do this for three reasons: first of all, because it was the truth; second, to prevent Papon's defense team from using this information—if they came into possession of it—either to recuse the president or as an argument in their defense or as a means of appeal; last, so that the president would take it upon himself to resign from his position. If we had asked Micheline Castagnède to become a plaintiff, which she would almost certainly have agreed to, we could have had the president recused immediately and without appeal. But we wanted him to make the decision himself. He did not.

President Castagnède claimed to be "flabbergasted" by this new information. We didn't believe him.

Our revelation of the truth was not the cause of the fuss that followed; there was nothing aggressive about Arno's press release. It concluded with the words: "To our knowledge, the president of the criminal court of Bordeaux, Jean-Louis Castagnède, avoided mentioning this kinship." In other words, he had hidden his direct relationship with a victim because otherwise he could not have served as president of the court and been allowed to be an associate plaintiff against Papon. The scandal blew up from the immediate, outraged solidarity toward the president shown by the other lawyers, both defense and prosecution, who issued a virulent press release of their own, calling for disciplinary and criminal proceedings to be brought against Arno and myself for slandering the court president.

But the practical result of our intervention was the formal agreement we got from Papon's lawyers not to use this information as the basis of an appeal.

We held firm, and very quickly the president, destabilized by this turn of events, altered his behavior, becoming much more severe toward Papon and his defense team.

IN HIS VIBRANT closing speech, Arno asked for a sentence of ten years. The other prosecution lawyers demanded life imprisonment. The prosecutor general sided with us, even if his demand for a twenty-year sentence was double what we were suggesting. The defense lawyers asked for an acquittal, and the other prosecution lawyers declared that they would prefer acquittal to an intermediate sentence. But to us, taking that risk was a betrayal of the victims' families, who wanted Papon to be convicted and who knew that acquittal would be a disaster. It would have meant that, from the prefect to the gendarme, no one active in the arrest of Jews was guilty except Pétain and Pierre Laval, respectively the head of the state and the head of the government.

On April 2, 1998, faced with these four possibilities—life, twenty years, ten years, or acquittal—the jury made its choice. Papon was convicted and, as we had asked, sentenced to ten years in prison. But Papon remained free until the day before his appeal to the court of cassation.

When that day came—October 20, 1998—Papon did not, as he was legally bound to, present himself at the door of the prison but fled with his granddaughter.

Some of the other lawyers were outraged by this, damning Papon as a "scoundrel." We, by contrast, saw him simply as a scared old man, overwhelmed by the prospect of this supreme humiliation.

And so he was forced to flee at the last minute, unprepared, at an advanced age. This in itself was a sort of poetic justice: he found himself in the same situation that a Jew of his age would have been in in 1942.

While Touvier was on the run for five decades, Papon's flight lasted only forty-eight hours. At 4:00 p.m. on October 21, the court rejected Papon's appeal. The next day, in Switzerland, Papon was arrested, and that very evening he was incarcerated in Fresnes.

Papon's imprisonment shows that, even for crimes going back nearly sixty years, a powerful man can be brought to justice. Despite all his efforts to evade prison, despite his lawyers, his appeals, all the protection offered to him—including that of President Mitterrand—this man was finally put behind bars.

HE DID NOT serve ten years in prison. In fact, he served only three before being released—thanks to a new French law—on grounds of ill health. On

September 4, 2002, Papon came out of prison, not on a stretcher, but on his own two feet.

He died on February 17, 2007, at the age of ninety-six.

THE PAPON CASE was difficult, unpleasant, and exemplary. We had to fight stubbornly against almost everyone, we were widely misunderstood, and our only solid support came from the collective will of the Sons and Daughters. But that was enough to sustain us.

BEATE

A Presidential Candidate

F OR MORE THAN thirty years, I have dealt with the secretarial duties of our Association of Sons and Daughters; I maintain the computer files on around fifteen hundred members, as well as the paper files, just in case. I wrap the books that we keep in our cellars (I was an apprentice at Woolworth's in Berlin in the 1950s, so I am good at wrapping) in brown paper and take them to the nearby post office in my shopping cart. I also send all our members the quarterly newsletter we produce. I must have written millions of addresses on envelopes over the years. I take care of all this between one in the afternoon and seven in the evening, and sometimes even later than that at home.

In the mornings, I look after the family and our animals, and I shop for groceries and do the housework. Every day, I go to see my daughter and my grandchildren. Our family life has always been simple: we hardly ever go out when we are in Paris, except for association meetings. We prefer to spend our evenings with our children or with the animals we have always had around us. Both Serge and I have an intense love of animals. It is impossible to feel low when we are with them.

ARNO AND LIDA had an unusual childhood. We were frequently absent, but Raïssa often looked after them, especially Arno; she spoke Russian to him, as she'd done with Serge. She took him to see her sisters in Bucharest and Saint Petersburg (or Leningrad, as it was at the time), and every year he would go to see his other grandmother, "Omi," in Berlin. He learned German in East Berlin. He went to see Auschwitz-Birkenau with Serge when he was twelve. He visited Italy, Australia, Japan, and particularly the United States, which always held a special appeal for him. Lida went to many of those places, too, but her favorite was Italy, and she speaks fluent Italian now. Both of them were brilliant students, and both became lawyers. As I write on paper, Lida is typing up this book on her computer.

Our friends in the Sons and Daughters generally have intense family lives, too: couples solidly bonded until death and a deep attachment between parents and children, strengthened by the tragic nature of the parents' childhoods.

Serge and I have always traveled a great deal, sometimes together and sometimes separately. We are both opera buffs and art lovers. My taste in opera is more eclectic than Serge's, but we are drawn to the same paintings and sculptures, perhaps because it was Serge who first introduced me to art. For both of us, the artist we admire more than any other is Michelangelo, that universal genius, so proud and yet so modest, who asked for his tomb in the Basilica di Santa Croce to be placed so that, each time the door was opened, he would be able to "admire Brunelleschi's dome."

I HAVE NEVER ceased to be active, and I still give speeches occasionally. In Berlin, I usually give the speech in commemoration of the bonfire of books organized by Nazi students on May 10, 1933.

In 2012, I took as my subject the story of the Stefan Zweig book *Amok*, plucked, slightly singed, from the fire and given to the Göttingen University French lecturer Mr. Larrose by his best student. A few years later, in 1940, Mr. Larrose, then working as an interpreter at the Ministry of the

Interior, saw that best student of his again: it was Helmut Knochen, who had in the meantime become the head of the Nazi police in occupied France, a man responsible for the deaths of seventy-five thousand deported Jews. Mr. Larrose gave me the book, and I passed it on to the Resistance Museum, La Citadelle, in Besançon.

In 2014, I spoke about Denise Bardet, a twenty-three-year-old French teacher and a lover of German literature, who was brave enough, in the middle of the war, to write in her private journal of her admiration for humanist German culture and her contempt for the National Socialists' barbarism. She worked as a teacher in Oradour-sur-Glane, where she was burned alive in the church with her students. As her beloved Heinrich Heine wrote, "Wherever they burn books, they will also, in the end, burn human beings."

THE ELECTION FOR the post of president of Germany in 2012 was almost uncontested: the conservative CDU (Christian Democratic Union), the social democratic SPD, the liberal FDP, and the Green Party all supported the same man, Joachim Gauck, a former Lutheran pastor who had come to prominence as a civil rights activist in Communist East Germany.

However, the left-wing party Die Linke wanted to present a symbolic candidate. Gesine Lötzsche, the party's copresident, told the press that if she could choose a candidate, it would be a woman like Beate Klarsfeld, whose personal courage and commitment she admired. A journalist from *Der Spiegel* asked me if I would accept in the event that Die Linke proposed me as a candidate. Spontaneously, instinctively, I said yes. Why? Because I remembered being sentenced to a year in prison and, in a flash, I saw the path that Germany—and I—had taken since 1968. And also because I represented the determination to purge Nazism and the Nazis' crimes from the Federal Republic of Germany, while Gauck personified the campaign for individual freedom in the German Democratic Republic. It would be the coming together of a man and a woman who each embodied an aspect of postwar German history.

On February 27, 2012, Die Linke nominated me as their candidate. And so it would be Beate Klarsfeld versus Joachim Gauck, though in truth Gauck's victory was never in doubt, and there was never any animosity between us; on the contrary, there was a great deal of mutual respect.

The night before the election, Serge, Arno, Lida, and I, accompanied by our group of friends from the Sons and Daughters, went to Berlin for a big party organized by Die Linke. The next morning, a limousine took Serge and myself, with a police escort, to the church in Friedrichstadt, where every major politician in Germany was gathered. We were the first people greeted by Angela Merkel. Later, in the Reichstag/Bundestag, where all the deputies and *Länder* delegates, or those from the individual West German states, came together, there was a room reserved for our group. We savored that moment, because each one of us had been arrested in Germany at least once during the course of our protests and illegal actions, and because—with the exception of me—each one of us had lost a father or mother in Auschwitz.

For the Sons and Daughters, my candidacy was a momentous occasion. Gauck was elected with more than 900 votes, while I got only 126, but a great deal had been achieved all the same. For me, this was a moment of personal fulfillment and official sanction—if I needed that—of the path I had chosen.

SERGE

COMPENSATING THE ORPHANS

THE ARYANIZATION AND despoliation of Jewish belongings took place on such a vast scale, and the concept of their restitution and compensation was so complicated and incomplete, that, in the late 1970s, it seemed impossible to me that any form of reparation would happen, however justified it would have been.

My viewpoint was clear: we would not be able to obtain anything until the French public's knowledge of the Jews' fate during the German occupation and under the Vichy regime had reached a higher level. That would take many years.

Those years passed . . . When I was told of what Jacques Chirac was going to say at the Vél' d'Hiv commemoration on July 16, 1995—that he would acknowledge the responsibility of France itself—I wanted our claims to be explained so clearly and forcefully that, the following day, the president of the Republic would legitimize them with the substance of his speech.

On July 15, 1995, a full-page article appeared in *Libération* under the headline "The Forgotten Theft of Jewish Deportees' Belongings." The journalist, Annette Lévy-Willard, wrote: "Serge Klarsfeld thought it was time to open another black chapter in the history of the French state."

That chapter concerned despoiled Jewish goods, and it would, later on, enable me to obtain a modest pension for all the orphans of Jewish deportees that would allow them to avoid falling into poverty.

ON FEBRUARY 5, 1997, the French prime minister Alain Juppé formed a committee, led by Jean Mattéoli—a former Resistance member and deportee—to study the circumstances in which the goods were despoiled, to assess the scale of the loss, to establish what happened to those goods, and to formulate proposals for what would happen to goods held by French public entities.

I served on that committee with six other people but soon found myself isolated. I was the only one who believed in the Jewish orphans' claims for compensation. Still, serving on the commission did allow me to obtain dossiers that had not yet been consulted concerning the arrests and transfer of Jews.

I set to work on my research with enthusiasm, as I was in a position to uncover and bring together documents that would enable me to construct something precious: in addition to the complete, precise identification of nearly eighty thousand victims, I could now provide the address where each arrest took place and the transit camps through which each deportee passed before being sent to a concentration camp.

The three years I spent on the committee were extremely demanding. Progress reports were published in December 1997 and February 1999, before a final report was published in the spring of 2000. Prior to the second progress report, I was worried that the issue of the orphans would not be addressed, so I presented the committee with the following statement, proposing that it should constitute one of the recommendations made to the government: "In these circumstances, the mission asks that the situation of the children of deportees from France be taken into account, irrespective of their nationality or place of residence, and that appropriate measures be taken, notably the payment of a compensatory life annuity for those who do not already receive compensation for the same purpose."

In early January, I met Jean Mattéoli and made clear to him that, if he did not support my proposal, I would resign from the committee and even begin a campaign against it. He assured me that I had his support. The fourth and final recommendation of the 1999 report concerned the orphans' situation. It differed from my proposal only in a few words.

I encouraged the members of our Sons and Daughters Association to write to the prime minister individually, telling their life stories as orphans of Jewish deportees, and explaining what the proposed life annuity would mean for them in their approaching old age. On September 23, 1999, Prime Minister Lionel Jospin wrote to me:

> With dignity and courage, each of those letters carries a fragment of the horror experienced by the children.
>
> You know that I am very attentive to the situation of orphans of deportation. I asked a special commission to examine the recommendations made by the Mattéoli committee in its second progress report. As soon as I have the results of that commission, I will make an announcement on the life annuity proposal. I know that time is pressing, and I want the issue to be resolved this autumn.

The commission's report was made public on October 25. It was very long and confused, but its final conclusion read: "We should, however, emphasize the practical difficulties raised by the Mattéoli report's recommendation . . ."

If the prime minister had followed the commission's advice, the life annuity would have been dead and buried. Thankfully, his sensitivity and strength of character allowed him to overcome the inspectors' objections and reservations. On November 13, 1999, he announced his decision:

> I have decided that the orphans of Jews deported from France should benefit—either in the form of a lump sum or a monthly pension—from a gesture expressing the duty we owe them. The necessary measures to implement this compensation will be prepared by the government in the coming weeks.

WEEKS PASSED. Months passed. By June 30 of the following year, I had still heard nothing. I was convinced that, if nothing was published by July 16, 2000—the anniversary of the Vél' d'Hiv roundup—the life annuity would never happen.

I sent letters to Jospin's advisers stating clearly that, if no official announcement had been made by July 13, I would publicly protest the prime minister's broken promise during the anniversary commemoration.

On July 13, the government's official journal published the announcement of a compensation to be paid to orphans of deportees, either a life annuity of 3,000 francs per month or a single payment of 180,000 francs.

My next battle was to have the amount of the life annuity indexed to inflation. This battle lasted years and only succeeded in the end thanks to Arno, who joined the cabinet of Prime Minister François Fillon in 2007. As a consequence, the monthly sum paid to each orphan now stands at 550 euros, and it will continue to rise in step with the cost of living.

This long campaign, so dear to our hearts, brought us the immense satisfaction and relief of knowing that none of the deportees' descendants would ever become destitute.

THE TRUTH ABOUT PÉTAIN

FOR THE FIFTIETH anniversary of the Jewish decree adopted by the Vichy government on October 3, 1940—which excluded Jews from various occupations—I organized a symposium at the French Senate. For the sixtieth anniversary, I made public a document that proved the decisive role played by Philippe Pétain in the writing of that decree and laid bare the marshal's deep-rooted anti-Semitism. The historian Robert Paxton wrote that it was "a very important discovery, a discovery that changes the way we look at that period."

There was now no doubt about the part played by Pétain in that infamous decree:

1. To the list of courts and jurisdictions from which Jews were excluded, Pétain added: "justices of the peace." To the positions forbidden to Jews, he handwrote: "all elected assemblies."

2. The original decree prohibited Jews from being superintendents, inspectors, principals, or directors of primary and secondary schools; Pétain widened this to "all members of the teaching staff."

3. Pétain removed an important exception made for Jews who were "descended from Jews born French or naturalized before 1860." Anyone who still believes Pétain wanted to protect French Jews has to take this removal into consideration and bear in mind that the Germans did not pressure the French into coming up with a decree on the Jews.

4. Pétain concluded this anti-Jewish decree with the demand— again in his own hand—that "the reasons to justify" it be published in the government's official journal. In other words, he was in complete agreement with the extremely anti-Semitic government note made public on October 17 and 18, 1940, making the Jews the scapegoats of the French defeat: "In its work to reconstruct the nation, the government has had to study the problem of the Jews and certain other foreigners who, abusing our hospitality, made a significant contribution to the defeat. Everywhere, but particularly in public service—however real the honorable exceptions that each of us will be aware of— the influence of the Jews has been felt in an insinuating and ultimately destructive way."

AFTER REVEALING PÉTAIN'S anti-Semitism in 2010, I had to react the following year to the intention of the high committee for the national celebrations to include the name of the French author and anti-Semite Louis-Ferdinand Céline in its celebrations on the occasion of the fiftieth anniversary of his death.

I appealed to the president, Nicolas Sarkozy, and within forty-eight hours the 2011 edition of the book published for the celebrations was pulped. Immediately, there was talk of the "Jewish lobby."

But Céline's literary genius does not alter the fact that his politics were despicable, just as Pétain's military glory does not change the reality that he led France into collaboration with the Nazis. If we are going to celebrate genius, shouldn't we also acknowledge Adolf Hitler's oratorical genius? Or Albert Speer's organizational genius? Acknowledge, yes, perhaps. But celebrate? No, never.

The French filmmaker Claude Lanzmann got it right when he wrote: "Celebrating Céline would be like killing the victims of the Holocaust for a second time. As Sartre wrote: 'Anti-Semitism is not an opinion. It is a crime.'"

IN THE FALL of 2014, a controversy was stirred up in France by the publication of a book by Eric Zemmour, *The French Suicide*, in which he claimed that Pétain was responsible for saving French Jews. With the aid of numerous documents, many of them previously unseen, I was able to explore this idea more deeply than it had ever been explored before.

The Vichy government was in charge of the survival of 190,000 French Jews and 130,000 foreign Jews living in French territory. On June 11, 1942, the Germans decided to implement the Final Solution in Western Europe.

On June 26, at a cabinet meeting, Laval brought up the Jewish question, emphasizing that it had been dealt with in an extremely severe way in Germany and that "French public opinion would have difficulty accepting identical measures being carried out in France, where this question has never had the same importance." He announced that he would take a census in order to discriminate between French and foreign Jews. On July 2, at a meeting between Oberg, Knochen, Lischka, Hagen, and Bousquet, the Frenchman explained that Laval, following a request from Pétain, wanted the Germans, not the French police, to conduct roundups in the occupied zone, and that the French police would only arrest foreign Jews in the free zone. But by the end of the discussion, Bousquet had agreed that the French police would conduct roundups all over France and deliver the contingent of Jews demanded by the Germans. This decision was ratified by Pétain and Laval at the next cabinet meeting.

In eleven weeks, between July 17 and September 30, thirty-three thousand Jews were arrested by French police and deported, and by the end of the year, more than forty-two thousand Jews had been deported, sixty-five hundred of them of French nationality.

What eventually slowed down the cooperation between the French and German authorities on the Jewish question was the pressure put on

Vichy by the Church and the French people, particularly following the deportation of families from the free zone.

Altogether, about twenty-five thousand French Jews were victims of the Holocaust: one-third of them French children with foreign parents; one-third naturalized French; and one-third French-born.

The French state committed a crime by collaborating with the Third Reich in the implementation of the Final Solution. The fact that, among the victims, the proportion of French Jews was smaller than that of foreign Jews is neither an excuse nor a justification.

THERE CAN BE NO COMPROMISE
WITH HISTORICAL TRUTH

I T IS ONE thing to discover a historical truth; it is quite another to impose it on historians and public opinion. This is illustrated by the case of the Jews shot at Mont-Valérien, which took more than twenty years to reach its conclusion. In 1987, after painstaking research, my friend Léon Tsevery and I were able to affirm that 1,007 people had been shot, rather than the 4,500 engraved in the granite slab in the middle of the clearing where the executions took place. On February 23, 2008, on that very spot, President Sarkozy declared, "Between February 1941 and August 1944, more than one thousand people fell here under the enemy's bullets." And on February 21, 2014, President Hollande repeated the same number.

The officials in charge of this memorial only admitted and corrected the false figure reluctantly and very gradually. The official declarations remained ambiguous, leaving enough room for doubt. One monument, unveiled in 2003, bears the words: AFTER THE WAR, THE NUMBER OF

VICTIMS WAS ESTIMATED AT 4,500. THE RESEARCH UNDERTAKEN IN FRANCE AND GERMANY HAS ENABLED JUST OVER 1,000 NAMES TO BE ENGRAVED IN THIS WORK BY PASCAL CONVERT. In other words: we haven't yet found the 3,500 other names.

As I pointed out in my 1979 work *The Book of Hostages*, the German military command, the head of the SS, and the German police in France all noted in turn the ineffectiveness of mass reprisals by executions in France and decided to deport Resistance members and other opposition to Germany rather than putting them to death in France.

I HAVE HAD to fight against this kind of falsehood on other fronts, too, notably regarding Switzerland (where numbers of Jews turned back from the border were grossly exaggerated) and Pope Pius XII, who has often been wrongly discredited for his actions during the war.

Goebbels noted in his journal: "The pope spoke at Christmas [1939]. A speech full of concealed but very strong attacks on us, the Reich and nationalism." Goebbels considered the pope an enemy, and generally in Nazi Germany he was known as the *Judenpapst*, the "Jews' pope."

But one example of what the pope actually did can be gleaned from the figures for Rome: while twelve hundred Jews were arrested in the sudden, brutal roundup of October 16, 1943, seven thousand others were able to find refuge in the city's churches. In other words, the pope helped to save a significant part of Rome's Jewish population.

ANOTHER CONTROVERSY CONCERNS the role of the French national railway company, the SNCF. Plaintiffs have been claiming compensation from the SNCF, both in France and in the United States. Those plaintiffs have never protested during any of our campaigns against the real culprits. The facts can always be interpreted in different ways, but if you modify the facts to achieve an end, you inevitably distort the past.

Charges were filed in December 2001 in the United States against the SNCF by assignees of the victims of the Final Solution, with the following argument: the SNCF "collaborated of its own free will" with the "German Nazi regime" by "providing trains for deportation with the aim of making a profit" and "transported the deportees to extermination camps"; its railroaders "dispossessed the deportees on the train platform" before "cramming the maximum number of Jewish families into cattle cars." In this way, the SNCF was "guilty of crimes against humanity."

These charges are at odds with the historical truth. They sully the memory of the 1,647 railroad workers who were shot or deported; they efface the role of the German authorities and that of the Vichy regime and dilute the responsibility of those who were in charge of the deportation of Jews from France.

The SNCF was a public company under the control of the French state and German authorities. It was requisitioned for each transport of Jewish detainees. None of the surviving deportees who have told the stories of their departures have accused the SNCF or its workers. It is also false to claim that it was railroad workers who searched and dispossessed the deportees, as is made clear by the note written by Röthke, head of the Gestapo's Jewish Affairs Department, on that subject: "All Jews must undergo a methodical body search by the French anti-Jewish police." In the survivors' testimonies, the railroad workers are mentioned as transmitting messages from the deportees to their families. Sometimes, they even managed to save people.

Furthermore, the SNCF was not paid by the Germans for its participation in deportation. Contrary to the plaintiffs' charges, the company could not have made any profit from its activities, because there were no payments.

Essentially, the question here is: What is a crime against humanity? If participation is enough, then the secretary who types lists, the gendarme who makes arrests, the railroad worker who shunts trains, are all guilty of crimes against humanity; they are links in a chain. But we must consider the degree of participation, the degree of autonomy, the knowledge of the victims' fate. As for the organizations that were declared criminal during the Nuremberg Trials—the Nazi Party, the SD, the Gestapo, the SS—their objective, made clear in many documents, was to definitively resolve the Jewish question. Their strength, their energy, and part of their raison d'être were devoted to this end.

IN FRANCE, THE Council of State put an end to claims against the SNCF. In the United States, the question was resolved only recently. In Washington,

D.C., on December 8, 2014, the United States and France signed an agreement that ended one injustice (by helping former French deportees who had since become American, and their families) and prevented another by shielding the SNCF from any future litigation in the United States. Arno and I were invited by the French government to attend the ceremony at the State Department.

Battling the New Anti-Semitism

I N MARCH 2014, I wrote in the Sons and Daughters' newsletter:

> We are now confronted with a new wave of French anti-Semitism
> that unites parts of the far right, the far left, anti-Israeli activists,
> and French youth of North African origin. The murder of Jewish
> children in Toulouse in 2012; the spread—in the streets and on the
> Internet—of anti-Jewish words and gestures; all this is creating a toxic
> atmosphere that reminds us, the Sons and Daughters of Jews Deported
> from France, of the dark years of our childhood, even if most of the
> French population is not affected by this infection and the public
> authorities are attempting to stamp it out. We have never been alarmist
> and we have always put our trust in the French Republic. Today,
> however, the new situation leaves us no choice but to sound the alarm.

Two months before this, we were forced into action by the Dieudonné controversy. Dieudonné is a popular French comedian who started out as an anti-racist political activist. Since the early part of this century, however, he has increasingly moved in far-right, anti-Semitic circles, and his shows and videos have made anti-Jewish sentiments popular and even chic among certain young people. On January 2, 2014, I learned that Dieudonné was starting a new tour in Nantes the following week, and this anti-Jewish revue was set to pass through the biggest cities in France. Instantly, I saw red: those performances would be held in the same cities where we had presented our exhibition on the 11,400 Jewish children deported from France. Dieudonné knew about us: Arno had denounced the menace that he represented as long ago as 2002.

On January 6, the minister of the interior, Manuel Valls, requested that the prefect in Nantes prohibit the show due to take place on January 9. The prefect in Nantes obliged, but Dieudonné immediately filed an appeal with the Nantes administrative court, which—at 2:30 p.m. on the day of the show—canceled the prefect's decree, as it did not see any anti-Semitic malice in the comedian's routine.

At 5:00 p.m., an emergency hearing at the Council of State overturned the verdict of the Nantes administrative court, and the show was—once again—prohibited. Other prefects and mayors would follow suit until Dieudonné finally surrendered and withdrew the incriminatory passages from his show.

During all of our protests against this anti-Semite, however, it has always been the same story: Jewish organizations have come out in force, and various politicians have spoken in support of us, but there has not been a word about it in the newspapers, not a single image on television.

France did not mobilize against this latest wave of anti-Semitism. In fact, in recent years, many French Jews have removed their children from public schools out of fear of seeing them beaten and humiliated for being Jewish. They no longer read the newspapers, whose biased views about Israel are a source of extreme irritation. They know that numerous websites are spreading anti-Jewish propaganda comparable to that of the 1930s, and they were shocked to discover that, during the Day of Anger protest on January 26, 2014, which brought together between fifteen thousand and twenty thousand marchers, the vilest anti-Jewish slogans were chanted. Hatred of Israel has become so commonplace that it has led to hatred of Jews becoming commonplace, too.

I am deeply concerned by the collusion of those on the right and the left who proclaim themselves anti-Zionist or anti-Jewish, and by the apathy of a population that has yet to truly accept the existence of this new wave of French anti-Semitism.

To combat it, we need support, not only from the French state but from the Jewish community, too. This is a long-term battle, and our central strategies are instruction, education, the training of teachers and other school staff, the surveillance and control of extremists and of so-called social networks that are, in reality, often antisocial.

The alternative is stark. Experience teaches us that, faced with a massive wave of anti-Semitism, there is no other outcome than mass exodus. If the people of France and Europe choose a future that is xenophobic and anti-Jewish, the Jews will continue to leave Europe. In 1939, there were six million Jews in the Americas, nine million in Europe, and two million in the rest of the world. Today, there are nearly six million Jews in Israel, seven million in the Americas, and only two million in Europe.

Lighthouses in an
Ocean of Forgetting

Militants regarding the memory of the Holocaust, we—the Sons and Daughters of Jews Deported from France—have fought battles on every front. In 1981, we organized the first group pilgrimage by plane to Auschwitz-Birkenau in a single day; in Israel, we raised the monument that bears the names of the eighty thousand Holocaust victims from France; we took thousands of young French Jews to Cologne for the famous trial; we led a thousand Sons and Daughters to Auschwitz-Birkenau in 1992 on the "memory train," following the same itinerary taken by the deportation trains; in 1993, we went from Tallinn to Kaunas, to Sobibor, to Majdanek, and to Auschwitz-Birkenau, to all the places where the Jews of France were transported or put to death; the thousands of photographs of Jewish children we have found are exhibited at the Mémorial de la Shoah in Paris, the Camp des Milles memorial, the United States Holocaust

Memorial Museum in Washington, D.C., the Holocaust Memorial in New York, the French pavilion at Auschwitz, and the memorial to the Vél' d'Hiv children in Orléans. We have provided countless original documents to the Mémorial de la Shoah, to Yad Vashem in Jerusalem, to the Museum of Jewish Heritage in New York. We have been responsible for the installation of plaques and other monuments at numerous sites of Jewish tragedies in France.

We have organized and presented major exhibitions about the Holocaust and, thanks to our friend Claude Bochurberg, have been able to make films, such as *The Last Survivor*, about Maurice Jablonski, who is today the sole survivor of his convoy, number 51, and *The Impossible Witness*, where the director and I were confronted with a 102-year-old Auschwitz survivor who stubbornly refused to answer our questions.

We have written or published so many reference works, including the *Memorial of Deportation*. I have also written more than a hundred prefaces and numerous articles published in *Combat*, *Le Monde*, *Libération*, *Le Quotidien de Paris*, and *Le Matin* and taken part in more radio and television programs than I can remember.

Our group has traveled by bus or train to so many German cities—Cologne, Hamburg, Düsseldorf, Munich, Berlin, Miltenberg, Bergen-Belsen, Rostock, Frankfurt, Stuttgart, Warstein, and others—to protest, as well as to Vienna, on several occasions, and even to New York, where we went to inaugurate the Museum of Jewish Heritage—A Living Memorial to the Holocaust, in 1997.

The FMS (Fondation pour la Mémoire de la Shoah, or Holocaust Remembrance Foundation) was founded in 2000 by the French government on the recommendation of the Mattéoli committee, on which I served. I am now a member of the FMS's board of directors and president of the Memory and Transmission Committee. I am on the board of directors for several memorials and a member of the committee for assisting victims of anti-Semitic despoliation in Monaco. I am a member of the Auschwitz-Birkenau Museum's International Committee, and the only French person appointed by the Polish government in the Auschwitz-Birkenau Foundation. I have to go to all these places and often work there.

This takes a great deal of time, probably too much, and I plan to reduce this activity, which deprives me of a few of life's simple pleasures.

IF THE HOLOCAUST had been concluded to the complete satisfaction of its initiators, all of Europe's nine million Jews would have perished. In reality, three million survived and they have testified to the suffering endured by the Jewish people of that period. Without all those people who have written, spoken, drawn, composed music—in other words, the survivors of deportation, of extermination camps, those who escaped the roundups; the orphans and the hidden children; the few who emerged from the ghettos and mass graves—we would know nothing, or almost nothing, about that immense tragedy that ranged over an entire continent. An authentic account of the Holocaust would need the testimonies of all six million who died, but their words can be heard only through their private journals or letters, documents buried in the bloodstained earth by certain Jewish Sonderkommando members from the crematoria of Auschwitz or hidden, like those of Emanuel Ringelblum in Warsaw. They can also testify through the voices of those who saw them die. Every account by a victim or a survivor is a stone in an edifice that will always remain unfinished, a fragment of an incomplete fresco expressing what the Holocaust was. That work is our legacy. It constitutes an immense memorial, a gigantic library where every page, every image, every object, represents those millions of Jews who are sounding the alarm for humanity.

The Holocaust historians, and the Holocaust documentation centers—the Center of Contemporary Jewish Documentation in Paris, Yad Vashem in Jerusalem, others in Auschwitz, Milan, Warsaw, Washington, D.C., Berlin, Mechelen, Amsterdam, Oslo, and elsewhere—are like lighthouses in an ocean of forgetting, there to rescue the memory of the victims.

Voices That Can Still Be Heard

M Y COMMITMENT TO the victims involves elucidating and explaining their fate by reconstructing the circumstances of their arrest and deportation, restoring their faces by finding photographs of them, and making their voices heard.

How is this achieved? By unearthing a deeply poignant letter written before or after they were arrested, revealing a personality or the power of a destiny. A facial expression in a photograph that cannot be forgotten. The name of a child in a list of deported adults; a child that was sent away, alone, without parents, whose memory you must keep in your mind because you cannot let that child be abandoned again. A drawing that expresses the hopes and betrays the fears of the person who drew it.

From my book *French Children of the Holocaust: A Memorial*, a powerful subterranean chorus rises from those thousands of too-brief lives, begging us not to let the horror be repeated, begging us not to forget them.

I think of **Louise Jacobson**, who died at seventeen. I think of the twenty-six letters she wrote from the prison in Fresnes and the six she wrote from the camp in Drancy. Reading the words of this adolescent girl who was so courageous and sensitive, happy and thoughtful, intelligent and curious, who—even in a prison cell—woke each morning determined not to give up, we are faced with all the charm and grace and generosity of youth. By murdering Louise, they murdered youth.

Louise Jacobson is France's Anne Frank. Her letters were adapted for a play that has been translated and performed in many countries, Germany most of all. In Italy, three hundred thousand copies of her letters were published. I remember poring over those cards that, because she had no paper, Louise covered with tiny handwriting in order to write as many things as possible. I read her words and was captivated by her effervescence. With the publication of those letters, Louise emerged from her forty-five-year sleep. While her contemporaries grow old, she remains forever young, a representative of all those children who were murdered.

I think of Georgy, **Georg Halpern**, that cheerful boy, the same age as me, whom I might have seen in 1941 at the OSE in La Creuse, at the Château du Masgelier; who was arrested by Barbie in 1944, while I had escaped arrest by Brunner in 1943; and whose story, drawings, and photographs I published.

I think of **Youri Riskine**, that fifteen-year-old genius, in whose memory I published a book of reminiscences written by one of his classmates at Lycée Louis-le-Grand. His friend Bertrand Poirot-Delpech has continued a dialogue with him throughout his life.

I think of **Noël (Nissim) Calef**, the author of *Drancy 1941*, a gripping book that, better than any other, explains what the first Drancy camp was like: the psychology of the detainees, the inhumanity of their gendarme guards, the creation of the camp's structures. In 1991, fifty years to the day after the roundup of August 20, 1941, I placed a copy of the just-published book at the foot of the Drancy monument.

I think of **Benjamin Schatzmann**, whose journal—written in the Compiègne camp—I published as part of the foundation's testimonies collection. Written on scraps of paper, it is an extraordinary text by a man of great intellect and moral stature, a man with a scientific background and a broad cultural knowledge, who described in painstaking detail the various stages of his descent into hell, tossed between hope and despair, while forcing his mind to think intensely, to analyze the reasons for the persecutions that he and his fellow prisoners were suffering: anti-Semitism, the pathology of Europe.

The unique life that created the personality of Benjamin Schatzmann—born in Romania, raised in Turkish Palestine, a student in France, an agronomist in New Zealand, a dentist in a chic part of Paris—ensures that this journal is his and only his. Through the depth of his self-knowledge amid this ordeal, his writing helps us to understand and defend human dignity.

On March 2, 1943, a convoy of 1,000 Jews left the camp in Drancy for Auschwitz. When it reached the extermination camp, 100 men and 19 women were chosen for forced labor; the other 881 deportees were immediately gassed. In 1945, only six survivors remained: four men and two women. One of those survivors was **David Olère**. He was assigned to the Sonderkommando, the Jewish special commando, in crematorium III, a building that combined a gas chamber and crematory ovens. Olère could have been killed soon afterward, as the vast majority of the Sonderkommando were. Another survivor, Dow Paisikovic, related after the war, "A Jew from Paris, named Olère, was in the Sonderkommando for a long time. He was an artist and, for the whole time I was there, his only task was to paint pictures for the SS."

David Olère is the only painter in the world to have entered the Birkenau crematoria and come out alive. He was born in 1902 in Warsaw. After stints in Danzig and Berlin, where he painted backdrops for Ernst Lubitsch's spectacular movie *The Loves of Pharaoh*, he moved to Paris in 1923. In Auschwitz, Olère was saved because he was an artist who spoke several languages: Polish, Russian, Yiddish, French, English, and German. It was his knowledge of this latter tongue and his gift as an illustrator that made him interesting to the SS. For them, he wrote beautifully handwritten letters, decorated with flowers, to their families. Sometimes, though, he had to "clean out" the gas chambers. Sometimes, too, he had to witness the paroxysms of horror that took place in the crematorium: the undressing in the changing rooms, the gassing, the collection of hair and fillings by barbers and dentists, the incineration of the bodies. And before the crematorium, the sexual services forced on young Jewish girls by the SS, the so-called medical experiments, the victims' terror, the Nazis' cruelty. When he told his wife what he had seen, she thought he was going insane. And so he drew *Memento*: more than fifty pictures that were key to his future work.

He died on August 21, 1985. His widow and his son asked me to dispose of his paintings and drawings in such a way that his work would, as he had wished, contribute to maintaining the memory of what happened to the Jews in Auschwitz. This was no easy task, because Olère's work is hard to look at. We also brought together all his works in a catalog, *The Eyes of a Witness*, published in 1989.

The documentary value of Olère's pictures is extremely high. No photographs were taken of what went on inside the crematoria. Only his eyes and his hand were able to reconstruct the terrible truth. He is often present in his own pictures, a ghostly figure, a horrified witness, observing those inhuman scenes that he could not remove from his virtually photographic memory.

I think of **Young Perez**, the boxer who fought with a Star of David on his shorts (even on November 11, 1938, in Berlin, the night before Kristallnacht) and who reached his peak of glory when he was crowned flyweight champion of the world in 1931, at the age of twenty. Thirteen years later, he found himself in the *anus mundi* of Auschwitz. He was forced to fight people for the amusement of the SS and had survived 140 bouts in fifteen months before collapsing on the death march that left the camp in January 1945. He was brought back to life in the excellent movie *Victor Young Perez*, released in 2013, played by a French Muslim boxer (and Olympic champion), Brahim Asloum.

I think of **Chana Morgenstern**. I edited the letters that her fiancé Isaac Schönberg exchanged with her while he was held at the Pithiviers camp. He was a painter who was deported and never returned. She was a laborer. Out of love for him, she married his best friend so that she would be able to remember Isaac every day; she became a painter, too, and found some fame. She donated the money she earned from her art to the Hadassah Hospital in Israel.

All these voices, these thousands of voices whispering in my memory . . . I continue to work so that they will be heard, long into the future, after I am gone.

Epilogue

So what message can we leave, Beate and I, to our readers and our descendants? What warnings can we offer based on what happened to us during our childhood and our experiences as adults engaged in political activism? First of all, that history is unpredictable: no one can imagine or foretell the political events of the future. They arise for impenetrable reasons that can only be analyzed afterward. We advance fitfully, as if through mist, even when there are prophets among us—like Theodor Herzl, who in 1900, fearing the destruction of European Jewry, began campaigning for the creation of a Jewish state.

Having entered a new millennium, some believe that history is behind us and there is no point in looking back at the vast black page of the twentieth century. That was certainly a cruel century, the cruelest of all. The First World War gave rise to genocide—of the Armenians. Had it been halted, as the international community wanted to do for some time, perhaps that first genocide would not have been followed by another during the Second World War.

The genocide of the Jews, however, can be distinguished from other twentieth-century catastrophes in several ways.

It was a tragedy of European civilization, carried out over the entire continent essentially by police rather than soldiers.

It was a tragedy of Christian civilization, a fact often forgotten. The contempt for Jews taught by Christianity over so many years made it easier for the organizers of the Final Solution, because few of those who did not take part in it actually opposed it; instead, they looked on indifferently.

It was a tragedy of Western civilization. The genocide was conceived and organized by a Western state, one of the most advanced in the world from an economic, social, technical, military, cultural, and intellectual standpoint.

The Allies are not free of blame, either, despite their courageous battle against the Axis nations: the United Kingdom, concerned about alienating the Arab world, prevented boatloads of Jews from entering Palestine, while the United States barely cracked open its own door and, in 1938, did nothing to help the Evian Conference find a solution to the vast numbers of Jewish refugees fleeing persecution by Nazi Germany. And neither nation took any real political or military initiative during the war to attempt to save the Jewish people.

It was a tragedy of modernity. Confronted with the technical difficulties of simultaneously putting to death thousands of human beings, the Nazis ended up designing an industrial-scale process for exterminating their victims in the most rational, rapid, cost-effective way. The gas chambers and the crematory ovens, the trains that always ran on time, the efficient organization of administrators, police, and diplomats, the use of cutting-edge communication—telexes, telegrams, dispatches, telephones—all of this modern technology was put in the service of a racist, murderous totalitarian regime.

It was a tragedy of human nature, revealing the infinite capacity of "civilized" man to do evil, an expression of the beast that crouches within. The concentration camps were the logical end of the National Socialists' racist ideology. The parallel existence of the Soviet gulags should serve to make those who defend human rights vigilant toward all extremists. Avoid political, economic, and social crises; educate the young to have absolute respect for human dignity: these should be the first duties of all democratic leaders.

It was a genocide of the Jewish people—the very people who brought monotheism to the world and gave birth to Christianity. The moral values spread by Judaism over millennia became the moral values of Western democracies. From the pharaoh to Hitler and Stalin, totalitarian regimes have always persecuted the Jews to some degree. Revolutions—in the United States and in France, for example—have liberated the Jews; democracies have given them the chance to flower. In their culture and in their memory of past sufferings, the Jews carry within them a love of freedom and respect for each human being.

It was an immense catastrophe, which the deniers want to erase from history and whose memory must be defended. Immediately after the war, this catastrophe still had no name: "Jewish genocide" was the term used at the Nuremberg Trials. In the United States and in Israel, the first countries to grasp the full significance of what had happened, the English word "Holocaust" and the Hebrew word "Shoah" emerged. In those two countries, dissertations were written, university courses devoted to the fate of the Jews in that period. From the 1980s on, other countries began to follow suit.

The Holocaust did not take center stage at Nuremberg during the trials of the Nazi criminals because there was still no Jewish state to speak on behalf of the victims. With the advent of the Cold War, a historical and judicial silence fell over the Shoah, and it was only when the Israeli government ordered the abduction of Adolf Eichmann, and the historic trial that followed this, that the truth about the Holocaust started to come to light. Since then, the light shone on those dark events has grown ever brighter. My generation, the children of deportees and survivors—volunteers such as Father Patrick Desbois and his team—have gathered and continue to gather documents and testimonies of every kind, fulfilling a scientific and moral mission on a scale equivalent to that of the tragedy: to write the name and the story of every single victim and every single episode of the Holocaust.

The memory of the Shoah has, paradoxically, been strengthened by the attempts of the Holocaust deniers to falsify history. Horrified by this vile questioning of the truth, the survivors and their descendants have responded in the best way possible: through documentation, through testimonies, and through memorials such as the United States Holocaust Memorial Museum in Washington, D.C., the Museum of Jewish Heritage—A Living Memorial to the Holocaust in New York, the Simon Wiesenthal Center in Los Angeles, the new wing devoted to the Holocaust at the Imperial War Museums in London, and the Holocaust Denkmal in Berlin, near the Reichstag. The words of Edmond Fleg, carved into the façade of the Mémorial de la Shoah, where I have been so often since 1956, promise that the memorial will "lead you to the highest peak of justice and truth."

FOR A LONG TIME, we did not want to write this autobiography. In 2012, we even wrote to our editor, asking to be released from the contract because of our "lack of need and desire to be known intimately by others, the conviction that it is better to be judged by posterity for what we have accomplished, rather than for what we were, our lack of interest in going back over our past, our lack of talent for storytelling, and so on." And yet, in spite of everything, we did finally write the book. We do not regret it. This way, our grandchildren and their descendants will know, if not who we were, at least what we did.

We learned through experience that we were capable of raising ourselves higher than we ever thought possible. Our readers will see this and will, we hope, realize that they would be just as capable as we were if circumstances demanded it.

EVEN AT THE advanced ages of eighty-two and seventy-nine respectively, Beate and I remain highly active, and we are constantly traveling. On July 16, 2015, we received an exceptional honor from Germany when the president of the Federal Republic, Joachim Gauck—my competitor in the 2012 election—bestowed upon us the Bundesverdienstkreuz 1 Klasse.

In October 2015, Irina Bokova, the Director-General of UNESCO, made both of us honorary UNESCO ambassadors for teaching the history of the Holocaust with the goal of preventing genocide. Swiftly, Beate launched into action: in Burundi—the poorest nation in Africa, with a population of 85 percent Hutus and 15 percent Tutsis—the situation was critical, with an increasing number of massacres occurring all over the country.

The only visa she could manage to obtain was a tourist visa. Armed with this, she took off for Bujumbura. As soon as she arrived in Burundi, she approached government officials as well as opposition leaders. And, while the government was far from happy about her visit, they did let her act as a UNESCO ambassador. Her public appeal was spread through all the local media:

> The political crisis that Burundi is going through could degenerate into a humanitarian catastrophe . . . The massacres that have been perpetrated in 2015 portend the worst . . . I appeal to the country's young people to choose peace and dialogue so that there is no repetition of the horrors of the past that Burundi has already suffered . . . I call for a resumption of peace talks to allow reconciliation in the interest of national unity. We must immediately put an end to blind killings, targeted assassinations, coups, and the multiplication of ethnically motivated crimes.

Beate's intervention was effective. The UN withdrew from Burundi and suspended its support for the country's government; the African Union ceased its military intervention; the negotiations in Entebbe, Uganda, between representatives of the government and the opposition had failed, but a few days after Beate left, a delegation of thirty-three members of the United Nations arrived in Bujumbura, followed on February 23 by the Secretary-General of the UN, Ban Ki-moon (whom Beate had met on January 27 in New York), and the situation does appear to have improved slightly, with the UN doing its best to restart negotiations, feed the starving population, and provide it with aid for sanitation.

On January 27, we were in New York, where Beate had been invited by the United Nations to give the keynote speech on Holocaust Remembrance Day in the General Assembly, in the presence of the organization's Secretary-General, Ban Ki-moon. Beate gave her speech in English and it perfectly encapsulates the meaning of her commitment. The speech was very well received, as is conveyed by this letter from Cristina Gallach, the UN's Under-Secretary-General for Communications and Public Information: "Thank you for your inspiring keynote speech, which helped us understand the considerable shifts Germany, and the German people, have made over the past 70 years. We admire the forceful and unique role you have played by building bridges between countries and cultures to help heal the wounds of the past, and your decades of dedication to justice and peace—

whether by bringing Nazi criminals to justice or protesting those that protected them."

AT THE BEGINNING of the year, the German Foreign Minister asked Beate to give a speech at the Goethe Institute in Beijing, which she was happy to do. In February, in Jerusalem, the Israeli Minister of the Interior awarded her Israeli nationality in recognition of her commitment to Jewish causes—the same honor that Arno and I had received fifteen years earlier. In May we were back in Jerusalem, invited on this occasion by the French Prime Minister Manuel Valls, who was there on an official visit.

As a member of several scientific committees and boards of directors for Holocaust museums in France and Poland, I must often travel to attend meetings, but that does not prevent me from assuming a role in French political life: the regional elections were about to take place, and I believed that if the National Front, the far-right party led by Marine Le Pen, were to control one or two regions, that could have a profound impact on the presidential election in spring 2017. I decided to throw myself into the battle. Two regions were particularly vulnerable: the North (Lille) and Provence-Côte d'Azur (Marseille and Nice). I publicly called for a Front Républicain, a union of left and right between all those who opposed the possibility of an electoral victory for the far right. On April 1, 2015, Beate and I appeared on the cover of the weekly French news magazine *Le Nouvel Observateur*, with the headline "The Klarsfelds' warning—If Marine Le Pen wins . . ." In the article, we declared that we would immediately leave France to continue our struggle in exile.

I wrote articles, gave speeches, and attended meetings, mostly in southeast France, since Nice was the city where I grew up. I did all I could to support Christian Estrosi, the mayor of Nice, and—in the north—Xavier Bertrand. To the surprise of many, my candidates won their electoral battles, and I felt certain that I had been useful to them—and that I could be useful again in 2017.

All the more so since our memoirs were, at that time, receiving a lot of positive attention and selling well in bookstores. We were often interviewed in newspapers and magazines, on radio and television programs, and this media exposure enabled us to get our message across to a large audience.

During the same period, I published the two-thousand-page second volume of *French Children of the Holocaust*, translated into English by two volunteers at the Museum of Jewish Heritage in New York, Nancy Fisher and Arlette Baker. I was able to gather and publish photographs of five thousand of the eleven thousand Jewish children deported from France. That book was the fruit of twenty years of research that came after the publication of the first volume, and it also led me to another project: creating a Garden for the Children of the Vélodrome d'Hiver Roundup on the very spot where the entrance to the velodrome had been located before its destruction in the 1960s. The renovation of the buildings that succeeded it allowed me to consider ideas for the seventy-fifth anniversary of the roundup—July 16, 2017—and I set to work on a monument that would bear the names of the four thousand children who were arrested on that day.

In Monaco, Prince Albert II awarded me the rank of Officer of the Order of Saint-Charles. After a decade's work, the five-man committee to which I belonged was able to shed light on the fate of the Principality's Jews between 1940 and 1944. Our detailed report was made public; the list of victims (forty-five in 1942, arrested by the Vichy police; thirty-one in 1944, arrested by the Gestapo) was also made public; the list of victims arrested by the Vichy police was drawn up with a high degree of accuracy; a beautiful monument was raised bearing the names of these deportees, and their heirs were entitled to very fair restitution.

At last, the great challenge arrived: the presidential election. Again, I called on the Front Républicain to resist the rising tide of nationalism and racism. In the end it came down to a direct confrontation between Marine Le Pen—daughter of Jean-Marie Le Pen and leader of the resurgent Front National—and the centrist leader Emmanuel Macron, who had, as if by some miracle, risen from nowhere to help avoid the catastrophic scenario of the far right battling the far left for the presidency. Beate and I fought hard to support Macron. We bought entire pages in the left-wing newspaper *Libération*, calling on its readers to unite against the threat of the National Front. Arno accompanied Macron to the Shoah Memorial and asked him, if he was elected, to attend the memorial at the Vélodrome d'Hiver on July 16. Macron promised that he would, and he wrote me a personal letter, thanking me for my "actions of a lifetime"; he would keep his promise. Macron gained ascendancy over Le Pen with a speech on France's responsibility for the Vél' d'Hiv Roundup and emerged victorious from a televised debate with the National Front leader. Thanks to him, our country escaped the nightmare scenario of a Le Pen presidency, and now France is governed by a brilliant young president who can, I hope and believe, bring the country the reforms it needs and continue the fight against the undying specter of anti-Semitism.

Before the July 16 ceremony I was able—as had been the case for the speeches by Jacques Chirac and François Hollande—to have a discussion with the advisor tasked with preparing the president's speech. It was a remarkable speech, in which Emmanuel Macron deepened the meaning given by Chirac and Hollande to the roundup: "That day France committed irreparable harm," and "this crime was committed in France, by France." President Macron gave even greater emphasis and clarity to this stance: "It was France that organized the roundup and then the deportation."

He explained in detail the perspective taken by himself, Chirac, and Hollande, and how it differed from that of General de Gaulle and François Mitterrand, for whom only one France existed—the France of the Resistance. This great and unanimously praised speech was preceded by the inauguration of the Garden for the Children of the Vélodrome d'Hiver Roundup, and I had the honor of guiding the President of the Republic during that visit.

In March and April 2017, Beate and I gave speeches at the University of Aix-en-Provence, in Paris, in Vienna, and at the Shoah Memorial. Beate spoke to middle-school children in Lyon, and also gave speeches in Osnabruck, Frankfurt, Kigali in Rwanda, and Roglit in Israel. For my part, I spoke in Clermont-Ferrand to high-school students and then at the university there, in a Paris synagogue, in Bucharest, Perpignan, Drancy, and Compiègne, to the students of two Parisian high schools, in Monaco, and at the Wannsee House in Berlin. This schedule—which does not take into account other meetings—gives an idea of the workload maintained by Beate and myself, even in our so-called dotage. It is true that I will be the first to weaken: my kidneys no longer function very well. Nevertheless, we continue to enjoy the delights of our little family: Lida, Carlo, and their children, Emma (8), Luigi (7), and Marco (1). Our son, Arno, is watching over us as he always has for the past twenty years.

Acknowledgments

Time, determination, persistence, painstaking work, a simple and reasonable line of thought, the precious support of our children and that extended family of Sons and Daughters of Jews Deported from France—that incomparable group of dear friends, those still living and those who have now left us but whose memory drives us on to remain intransigent when it comes to our essential task: defending and perpetuating the memory of the Holocaust—these are the things that sustain our commitments.

We are grateful to our American friends, who helped us to prepare and publish several of our reference books related to the Holocaust, including:

Cary and Sherry Koplin, for assistance with *The Holocaust and the Neo-Nazi Mythomania* (1978)

Philip Portugal, for assistance with *The Auschwitz Album* (1980)

Peter and Susan Hellman, for assistance with *The Memorial of the Jews Deported from France* (1983)

Richard and Carol Eisner, for assistance with *The Children of Izieu* (1985)

Peter S. Kalikow, for assistance with *Auschwitz: Technique and Operation of the Gas Chambers* (1989)

Felix Zandman, for assistance with *The Destruction of the Jews of Grodno*, 5 volumes (1989)

Peter Kovler, for assistance with *David Olère: The Eyes of a Witness* (1989)

Shelly Shapiro, for assistance with *Truth Prevails: Reply Against the Leuchter Report* (1990)

Ilan Kaufthal, for assistance with *The Fate of Romanian Jewry*, 12 volumes (1991)

Howard Epstein and Alida Scheuer-Brill, for assistance with *French Children of the Holocaust: Volume I* (1996)

George Klein, for assistance with *Nevek/Names: Hungarian Jews*, 11 volumes (2000)

Eugene and Emilie Grant, for assistance with *French Children of the Holocaust: Volume II* (2016)

Paul and Valerie Street, for assistance with *Memorial to the 3,500 Jewish Survivors Deported from France to Auschwitz* (2018)

We also thank many additional contributors whose support gave us the possibility to publish other reference works.

Index

A NOTE ABOUT THE AUTHORS

Beate and Serge Klarsfeld are renowned French activists whose work apprehending Nazi war criminals, seeking justice for victims and survivors of war crimes, and establishing the historical record of the Holocaust has brought them international recognition. Recipients of France's Legion of Honor and Germany's Federal Order of Merit, they were named UNESCO Ambassadors of Genocide Prevention by the United Nations in 2015 and were granted honorary Israeli citizenship by the Israeli government in recognition of their support of the Jewish cause. Beate is the recipient of the Jabotinski Prize, and both Beate and Serge have received the HIAS Liberty Award and the Raoul Wallenberg Prize.